LMS LOCOMOTIVE PROFILES

No. 3 – THE PARALLEL BOILER 2–6–4 TANK ENGINES

by

DAVID HUNT, BOB ESSERY and FRED JAMES

No. 2300 was photographed in BR days as it burst from Elstree New Tunnel with a northbound train. Since being built, the engine had received new buffers, outside steam pipes, snap-head rivets on the smokebox front and buffer beam, lifting holes in its front frames, oilbox lubrication of the upper slidebars rather than cups, altered tank vents, a Stanier chimney and washout doors on the firebox shoulders. Its exhaust steam injector had been moved outside the right-hand frame and the rear of the cab cut-outs had been filled in. It had also undergone many other alterations outlined in the text, but was still employed on the duty for which it had been designed thirty years before. To the end of their days, fast suburban passenger traffic was the bread and butter of the '2300s'.

BRITISH RAILWAYS (LMR D1083)

WILD SWAN PUBLICATIONS

One of the 'limousine cab' engines built after Stanier took charge of LMS locomotive affairs is seen leaving Birmingham New Street with a typical train on 7th May 1938. Built just 4½ years earlier, it was sent when new to Longsight but by the time this photograph was taken it had been transferred to Stafford. L. HANSON (1329)

Bogie and pony truck wheels were quite interchangeable on the '2300s' and swaps were not unusual following visits to the works. No. 2397, originally built with Stanier wheels, was photographed at Buxton in June 1936 with earlier-pattern ones on both bogie and pony truck and an oil cup on the upper slidebar. The power classification was still behind the cab doors and the 14in transfers were countershaded gold. W. POTTER

INTRODUCTION

The third in this series of monographs features the first really new Derby design to appear after the Grouping. Indeed, apart from the one-off Lickey Banker, it was the first since the introduction of the Somerset & Dorset 2–8–0s in 1914 and the only passenger engine since the '483' Class rebuilds of 1912. It was also, in some eyes, the best design to come out of the Derby Drawing Office since the Johnson Compound and the only one to feature what many saw almost as a prerequisite for a modem and effective steam locomotive – long lap, long travel valves. Altogether 125 of the type were built and they lasted nearly to the end of steam on British Railways. They were extremely successful machines and their basic design features were perpetuated in later series of taper-boiler engines so that the number of 2–6–4Ts built by the LMS eventually totalled 645. Together with the Horwich moguls and the 'Royal Scots', the early 2–6–4 tank engines established what E.S. Cox termed 'the definite LMS school (of locomotive design) with main features continuously traceable through the subsequent work of Stanier into the present (British Railways) era'. Thus, we consider them to be an important part of the LMS locomotive story as well as, according to the feedback we have received, a popular choice for inclusion in this series. In the future we hope to cover at least some of their taper-boiler successors.

As with our previous volumes, there may well be statements in this work at odds with what has been written before about these engines. If we are aware of it, we bring attention to the fact and give our sources or reasons for disagreement; otherwise we can only state that we have done our best to be accurate and if any reader knows better we would welcome the input. Differences in the locomotives as built as well as later modifications mean that there were many variations. Although we have tried to include sufficient detail to tell the '2300' Class story satisfactorily, we can't pretend to have given a description of every one of them at every stage in its life. Therefore, our previous advice to modellers and artists about using photographs of particular engines at specific times in order to 'get it right' is equally valid this time.

Our thanks, as usual, go to the staff of the National Railway Museum for their assistance in the preparation of this work. To a large extent, the availability to us of the drawings that we use makes these books possible and it is due to Dieter Hopkin that we have access to them. We are also indebted to Terry Essery for his engineman's appreciation of the locomotives and to a new member of our 'team', Phil Chopping, who has spent many hours transcribing, correlating and organising our notes as well as undertaking research at the Public Record Office on our behalf. As a result, we now have some structure to the semi-chaos from which we normally work and a valuable source of research effort, for which we are extremely grateful.

Previously we have asked for feedback from readers and are glad to be able to report that it is coming in. We have received some amplifications and corrections to points in our first two works in the series and have had to decide on the best vehicle for disseminating them. In October 2001 Wild Swan Publications launched a new occasional magazine called *LMS Journal* that is a spin-off from *Midland Record*. It seemed that an ideal way of supporting the books in this and our companion series, *Midland Engines*, would be to ally them with their 'natural' counterparts and so comments, corrections and amplifications concerning *LMS Locomotive Profiles* will appear in *LMS Journal* whilst those concerning *Midland Engines* will be covered in *Midland Record*. Issue 1 of *LMS Journal* should be available late Spring 2002. To contact the series editor, David Hunt, either write via Wild Swan Publications or visit our web site at *www.midlandrecord.com* where there are e-mail links.

Finally, we have to apologise to those readers who are collecting the series and have been waiting a long time for No.3 to appear. The hiatus has been caused by changes in personal circumstances for the editor that effectively precluded work on the books for over 12 months. However, all is now near normal so we hope that future publications will follow at reasonable intervals and trust that readers will forgive the interruption.

David Hunt, Bob Essery and Fred James

Delivered to traffic on 16th April 1929, No. 2341 is seen in this picture less than a year later at Nottingham Midland. The only visible differences between this engine and the first ones built were the taller side tank vents, wrought-iron bunker tank vents and the livery. In 2341's case it was black, lined vermilion with 14in Midland-style gold, shaded black numbers and matching letters. The engine was still in original condition with bogie and pony truck brakes.

COLLECTION R. J. ESSERY

ORIGINS

This photograph shows the first of the LMS 2–6–4 tank engines, No. 2300, as built in December 1927 and in lined crimson lake livery. Details of the livery stand out well and it can be seen that there was no lining on platform angle or footsteps. The engine number was applied in the original 10in characters and there was no shed code plate on the smokebox door. Although initially turned out wearing power classification 3, by the time this photograph was taken, it had been altered to 4. The locomotive ran in this condition until its first heavy repair and reboilering in May 1929. (More information on this picture is given on page 63.) COLLECTION R. J. ESSERY

The attractions of tank engines to steam locomotive designers were many. For a given size of engine, more adhesive weight could be concentrated on the coupled wheels if the coal and water supply was carried on it rather than in a tender. This, of course, was subject to the Civil Engineer's restrictions on the axle loading and weight per foot run and had a resultant limit. Providing that enough coal and water could be carried for the job in hand, a tank engine could be shorter overall than its tender-towing counterpart and if water replenishment was available at reasonable intervals, only the size of the coal bunker would limit the range. A shorter engine was easier to accommodate and to fit onto turntables, but in the absence of a turntable a tank engine was normally a better proposition for operating bunker-first at anything like passenger train speeds. There was less likelihood of the footplate crew getting blasted by cold air and coal dust if between them and the bunker was a cab back plate; at least, that was the theory and sometimes the practice if the engine was well designed. For short and medium distance passenger traffic, therefore, the tank engine was often the drawing office's preferred option. Indeed, in 1922 it was calculated that 40% of all British locomotives were tank engines and they hauled nearly 50% of this country's passenger train mileage.[2]

Most of the pre-Grouping companies made extensive use of tank engines for fast suburban and even, in some cases, what would now be called 'inter-city' services. At the Grouping the LMS had a wide selection of fast passenger tanks, some of which were quite large. The Western 'A' Division had the L&NWR 'Precursor Tank' 4–4–2Ts and 'Prince of Wales Tank' 4–6–2Ts, as well as the older and smaller Webb 2–4–2 and 0–6–2 tanks and ex-North Staffordshire 0–6–2Ts and 0–6–4Ts. The Western 'B', later Central, Division not only had the various 2–4–2Ts that were the mainstay of L&YR passenger services but the Pettigrew 4–4–2Ts and big Baltic tanks of the Furness Railway. North of the border, the Northern Division inherited the Caledonian's Lambie 4–4–0Ts, Pickersgill 4–6–2Ts and the G&SWR's massive Baltics as well as various 0–4–4 tanks from both. There was also a selection of 4–4–0Ts, 0–4–4Ts and 0–6–4Ts from the Highland. The Midland had used 0–4–4 passenger tanks since the 1870s, first Kirtley and then Johnson designs,[3] which had served it well. In 1907 it had followed them up with the '2000' Class 0–6–4T commonly referred to as 'Flatirons', that were basically large-wheeled tank engine versions of its H boiler class 3 goods 0–6–0s. The LT&SR section of the Midland Railway was predominantly a tank engine line and operated 0–6–2T, 4–4–2T and 4–6–4T versions, the latter being designed by R. H. Whitelegg, who was also responsible for the G&SWR Baltic tanks.[4] This list is not exhaustive but will give an idea of the range of passenger tank locomotives owned in 1923 by the newly amalgamated company.

By the time the LMS came into being though, train weights and timings were straining the capabilities of most of this inherited stock, which was small or medium sized, and none of the big tanks was really outstanding. From the outset, therefore, the LMS management realised that a large passenger tank engine was an urgent need for the combined system – but what should be the design? Each of the constituent companies was convinced that only its own designs were really suited to the particular conditions of its tracks but at least in the CME, George Hughes of the L&YR, the LMS had someone with a wealth of experience in inter-urban tank engine operation. Hughes had already identified the same need for the combined L&NWR/L&YR system before the Grouping and his answer was a 4–6–4T version of the Horwich 4–6–0 that appeared in 1924. It was not a particularly successful design, however, suffering as it did from the excessive weight penalty that was common to all the big inherited 4–6–2 and 4–6–4 tank engines as well as the poor cylinder and valve efficiency of the 4–6–0 from which it was developed. The next solution to be considered was a 2–6–4T version of the very successful Horwich mogul but before it could take shape, two events occurred that effectively stifled it. J. R. Billington, who had been Chief Draughtsman at Horwich and was Hughes' Technical Assistant responsible for scheming the mogul design, died suddenly in March 1925. In the July, Hughes resigned and, although he retained control of the 2–6–0 development, the 'Midlandisation' of LMS locomotive affairs took place.[5]

Much has been written about the politics that bedevilled the LMS in its early years and about the 'take over' by Derby of the combined system. Fortunately, they did not affect the 2–6–4T design to any marked or detrimental degree and so we can effectively ignore them. As it happened, Derby and Horwich had pretty similar ideas about what sort of engine was required and both were in favour of a 2–6–4T of about the same size.

Although the 2–6–4T was a relatively new layout on Britain's railways, the first ones being some goods engines designed by Robinson for the GCR in 1914 and the first passenger type Maunsell's SE&CR engines of 1917, the idea had been floating around the Derby Drawing Office for some time. Before Johnson left the Midland in 1903 he had realised that a larger passenger tank engine than the 0–4–4T was required and his staff had designed a 4–4–4T, five of which were authorised but cancelled almost as soon as he retired. Shortly afterwards, J. E. Anderson joined the Derby Drawing Office from Robert Stephenson & Co. and in the following couple of years schemed out several big passenger tanks including some 2–6–4Ts.[6] None came to fruition, however, and when Anderson became Chief Draughtsman in 1906 it fell to James Clayton to carry on scheming the big tank engines. Some of Clayton's proposals included outside-cylinder, superheated 2–6–4 tanks, one of the 1910 schemes being for an 81 ton machine with a Belpaire boiler. In the event, of course, none of them was ever built and the biggest Midland passenger tank was the 0–6–4T of 1907. We won't go into the arguments about their roadholding but would refer readers to Tom King's comments in *Midland Record No. 11* and, for a more detailed discussion of their evolution and Derby's many passenger tank engine schemes, to Phil Atkins' article in *Midland Record No. 9*. Clayton left Derby in 1914 and went as Chief Draughtsman to the SE&CR at Ashford from where, unsurprisingly, the first British 2–6–4 passenger tank engine appeared in 1917. The design, which gained some notoriety as the Southern Railway 'River' Class that was involved in the Sevenoaks disaster, had very similar features to the eventual LMS version.

Although Derby Drawing Office has been represented by some writers as retrenched and shortsighted in the 1920s, there were, in fact, some notably progressive personnel there who were quite ready, and had been for some time, to adopt modern design innovations. The fact that the wheelbase of the 2–6–4T was the 'hallowed' Derby 8ft + 8ft 6in has been cited by some as evidence of hidebound thinking, but that is arrant nonsense. The reason for the adoption of those measurements back in the 1860s was probably the construction of a set of gauges that enabled accurate machining and erection of frames and other components but by the 1920s there was a further cause for its retention. As James Clayton wrote after leaving Derby, the Civil Engineer's department of the Midland was an exceedingly conservative organisation that was reluctant to give any guidance to the Drawing Office on load curves (this trait wasn't peculiar to the Midland's Civil Engineer, as E. S. Cox confirmed). Designs had to be submitted by the Drawing Office and were then accepted or rejected out of hand without explanation, so designers usually had no more to go on than what had been accepted before.[7] Thus, the axle loading and weight distribution of an 8ft + 8ft 6in locomotive could be based on past practice in the knowledge that it would stand a chance of receiving the Civil Engineer's approval. That this was a ridiculous state of affairs is indisputable but it wasn't the Locomotive Drawing Office that perpetuated it.

The main point of contention in the design was the valve gear, concerning which there were two factions at Derby. In one camp were the 'traditionalists' led by followers of Anderson, in the persons of S. J. Symes, who was Locomotive Assistant to the CME, D. W. Sanford, head of the Experimental Section, and Jock Campbell who was one of the leading draughtsmen. This group believed that wear due to the movement of the valves as well as the die blocks and expansion link would economically outweigh any fuel consumption or performance advantage that long-travel valves had to offer. They were opposed by the 'progressives' who considered that enhanced performance and fuel economy made long-lap, long-travel valves the only option for a modern engine. The latter were led by the Deputy Chief Draughtsman, A. E. Owens, who had been brought in from the ex-North Staffordshire Railway headquarters at Stoke when Fowler and Herbert Chambers, by then CME and Technical Assistant/Chief Draughtsman, concentrated much of the LMS Drawing Office effort at their Derby headquarters. Owens was supported by Jock Henderson, the other leading draughtsman, and members of his section.

There is a widespread belief that the engine was designed initially with short-travel valves until Fowler attended a meeting of the Institution of Mechanical Engineers where a young ex-Derby apprentice called E. L. Diamond read a paper. In it he analysed the losses in cylinder efficiency of the Midland Compounds, concluding that they were caused in large part by the valve gear settings and that long-travel valves would greatly increase that efficiency. The story goes that Fowler was so impressed by these findings that he immediately ordered long-travel valves for the 2–6–4 tank. Whilst it is true that Fowler was present at the meeting, it seems apocryphal to suggest that he rushed back to Derby full of missionary zeal and changed things overnight. The actuality would appear to have been more protracted and prosaic than that.

Design of cylinders with long-lap, long-travel valves had been undertaken at Derby in 1918 when the Association of Railway Locomotive Engineers had started development of some engines intended to be standard classes that could be used by many railway companies in the aftermath of the First World War. Nothing had come of the exercise but the cylinders for a 2–6–0 based on Maunsell's SE&CR engines had been schemed at Derby. With the influence of such men as James Clayton, Maunsell and Churchward behind it, the design had been for cylinders with straight ports, large piston valves and long-travel Walschaerts valve gear. At Horwich, Hughes and Billington had been impressed by the performance of the Pennsylvania Railroad K2 Pacifics and the cylinder and valve design of their 2–6–0 was based on American practice, which was for long-lap, long-travel valves. Details of the mogul design and the American philosophy and engine performance behind it were, therefore, obviously well-known at Derby. So, when the 2–6–4 tank study was started in 1926, not only was there a faction at Derby in favour of 'modern' front-end design but drawings were extant showing what was wanted. There were also diagrams produced to support the ARLE 2–6–0 design showing the events and perceived advantages of such valves that had been sent from the Ashford Drawing Office. Added to all of that was the performance of the GWR 'Castle' that the LMS borrowed for comparative trials in the autumn of 1926 and, last but not least, Diamond's study. It seems more likely, therefore, that all the available evidence plus the influence of Owens and Henderson, whose section was entrusted with the design, persuaded Herbert Chambers that the engine should have long-travel valves, rather than a 'Road to Damascus' experience of a CME who, on his own admission, had little to do with locomotive design. The mechanical layout of the gear was based closely on the S&D 2–8–0, which had short-travel valves, but comparative valve diagrams were produced for both types before the final decision was taken late in 1926 that the new engine would have long-lap, long-travel ones.

The other departure from hitherto normal Derby practice was the use of multiple, thin piston valve rings. The Midland had been an early adopter of piston valves, the first use of them being on the '179' Class singles of 1893, which had Smith's patent valves with collapsible segments to relieve trapped water. They were followed by Schmidt valves with single, broad, stiff cast-iron rings – devices notable for their tendency to induce rapid wear in the liners, which led to steam leakage and increased coal consumption between repairs. Indeed, the 'Royal Scots' suffered so badly from this problem with Schmidt rings that their coal consumption increased by as much as 80% after a time in service. The tank engine was originally to have had Schmidt rings but at a late stage valves with four thin, flexible rings were substituted, although anecdotal and circumstantial evidence referred to later suggests that some were built initially with Schmidt rings.[8]

Apart from that, the design utilised components based on previous Derby experience and practice. One of Fowler's proposals when he tried to change the Horwich 2–6–0 design was to use an existing Derby boiler in the interests of standardisation so it was no surprise that the new engine had a G8AS in common with Midland 4–4–0s.[9] The adoption of a higher boiler pressure than the 180 psi that Hughes would tolerate meant that smaller cylinders than those on the Horwich moguls could be used. This, together with the relaxation of some loading gauge restrictions, meant that the cylinders did not need the steep inclination of the 2–6–0s. The pony truck was a Bissel swing-link type, copied from the American design used on the imported Schenectady 2–6–0 of 1899, that had also been incorporated into the S&D 2–8–0. Bogie, tanks, bunker and cab were adapted from the Midland 0–6–4 tank.

At a late stage in the design work, some derailments of the ex-SE&CR engines on the Southern Railway, culminating in the Sevenoaks disaster on 24th August 1927, caused the safety of the 2–6–4T layout to be questioned. According to E. A. Langridge, who was the draughtsman in charge of designing the valve gear, work on the project was 'soft pedalled' for a while pending a decision on its future. Because the Southern's problems had manifested themselves when the engines were hauling expresses and the LMS intended their 2–6–4 tanks for suburban duties, however, design work eventually proceeded. That the Southern's engines had significantly different bogies and pony trucks, were found to be quite stable on well-laid track, and the track where the accidents happened was not particularly good, also probably justified discounting their problems in the LMS context. In the event, the LMS engines ran at high speed over many of the company's routes without any stability problems.[10]

While design work was progressing on the 2–6–4 tank engine, that on the 'Royal Scots' and the Beyer, Peacock 2–6–0 + 0–6–2 Garratts was also under way. In order to avoid a lot of duplication of effort and to achieve some degree of standardisation, a number of features were common to two or more of them. In the case of the 'Scots' this was also due to the haste with which they were developed in order to enter traffic for the 1927 summer season. The 2–6–4T cylinders and bogie were used on the 'Scot' and some motion parts were common to all three designs.

So, the gestation of the new passenger tank engine passed with relatively little drama for the LMS of the late 1920s. Construction of an initial 25 engines was authorised in December 1926, an order for five of them placed in March 1927, and in December that year the first one entered traffic. For a short while at least, the first couple of engines were placed in power class 3 but after only a few months they were re-allocated to class 4 where they remained for the rest of their existence.

CONSTRUCTION AND MODIFICATIONS

All the '2300' Class locomotives were built at Derby. The initial order, O/6807, was issued on 3rd March 1927 and was for only five engines, but two weeks later this was increased to 25. On 24th October they were allocated numbers 2300–2324 and the first one appeared on 9th December. The long wheelbase, which resulted from adherence to the standard Derby 8ft + 8ft 6in coupled wheel spacing together with a boiler that was originally used for a shorter 4–4–0, resulted in a long expanse of platform in front of the smokebox and gave the engines a lean and purposeful look. Total wheelbase was 38ft 6in and the nominal weight in working order of 86 tons 5 cwt was distributed with 12 tons on the pony truck, 17 tons on the leading coupled wheels, 18 tons 3 cwt on driving and 16 tons 6 cwt on trailing ones. The bogie supported 22 tons 16 cwt. Tractive effort at 85% boiler pressure was 23,125 lb.

The estimated price for each of the first batch was £5,480, which was slightly less than they were later reckoned actually to have cost. Order details, costs and lot numbers for the engines were as follows:

Engine Nos.	*Order No.*	*Lot No.*	*Date Ordered*	*Cost*
2300–2304	6807	47	3 Mar 27	£5,654
2305–2324	6807	47	18 Jul 27	£5,654
2325–2334	7120	53	20 Apr 28	£5,245
2335–2354	7224	53	1 Oct 28	£5,185
2375–2384	8027	89	2 Dec 31	£4,878
2385–2394	8241	101	16 Nov 32	£4,816
2395–2401	8338	101	28 Jan 33	£4,917
2402–2414	8338	101	28 Jan 33	£5,007
2415–2423	8338	101	28 Jan 33	£4,917
2424	8338	101	28 Jan 33	£5,160

It is interesting to note the steady reduction in price up to 1933. Some of this was due to the re-use of patterns, etc. that had been charged against previous batches of engines, although the actual cost of construction also dropped. The £90 increase in the cost of Nos. 2402–2414 was due to the fitting of water pick-up gear, although there was no similar price difference recorded for other batches in which only some engines were fitted. No. 2424 was more expensive than the rest of the 'Stanier' engines because of some experimental features considered later. Full details of building dates are at Appendix A.

The locomotives were initially allocated to Engine Diagram 172. The change in overall length described later resulted in ED 172A being issued, 172B reflected the change in the number of small tubes, and the fitting of different superheater elements led to ED 172C.

D27-10684 – Boiler & firebox arrangement standard G8AS modified

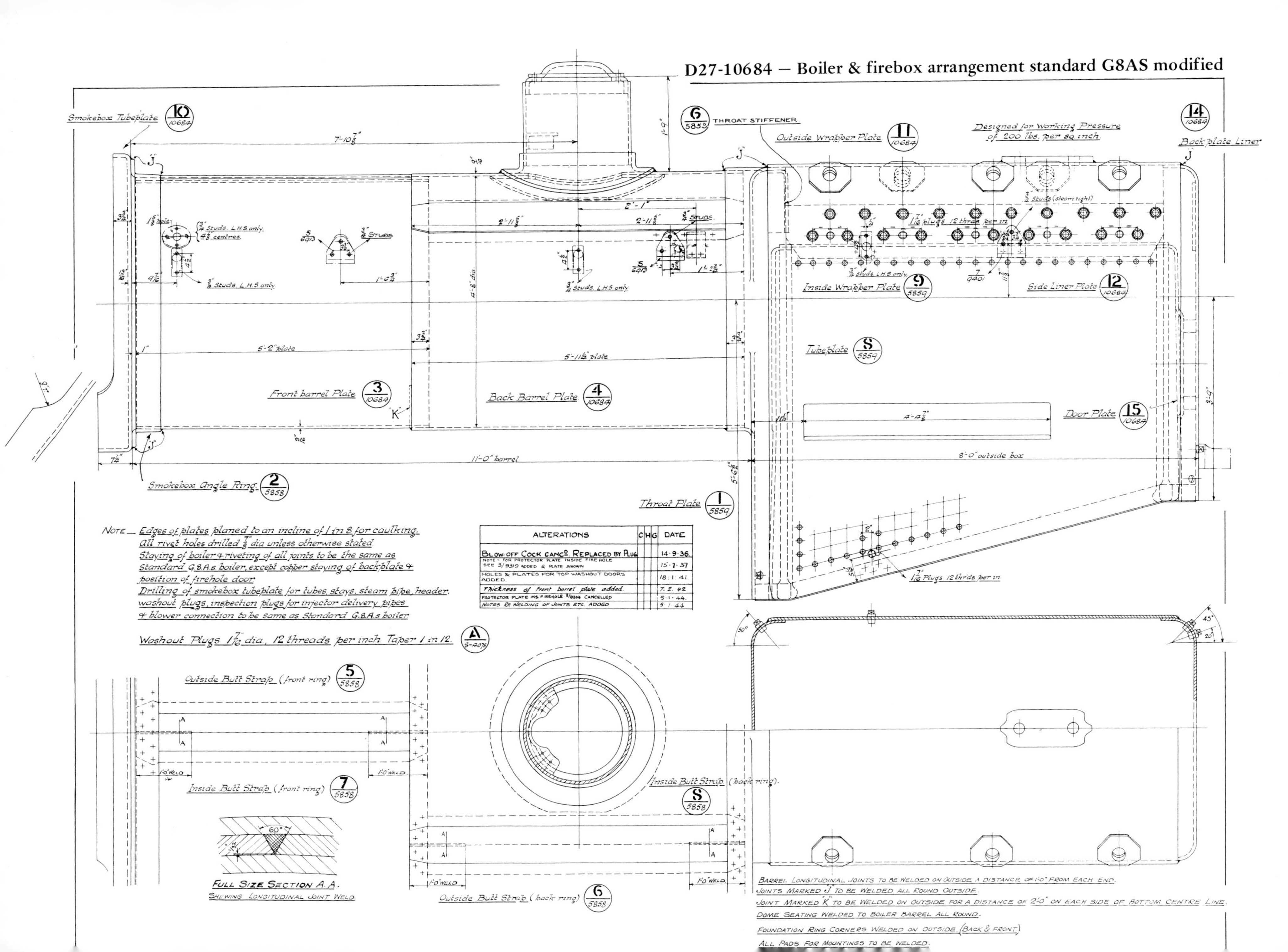

BOILER

Most of the boilers for the '2300s' were made at Derby but those for the last thirty engines were manufactured at Crewe. The boiler selected for the design was the standard Derby G8AS, pressed to 200 psi, with a circular front tubeplate and slight modifications to the positioning of the firedoor and stays. Known as G8AS (Modified), it was a development of the first Midland Belpaire boiler fitted to Johnson's 4–4–0s in 1902 and subsequently superheated.[11] The barrel was 4ft 8in diameter outside the front ring, 11ft 4¾ in between tubeplates and pitched 8ft 6in above rail level. In the mid-1930s the thickness of the copper firebox tubeplate was increased to one inch and, as a result, the distance between the tubeplates decreased by ⅛ in. The 146 small tubes were 1¾ in diameter and together with twenty-one 5⅛ in diameter superheater flues, gave 1,083 sq ft heating surface. The superheater elements added another 266¼ sq ft. The small tubes were actually wider for a few inches at the smokebox end and narrower at the rear, relevant diameters being 1⅞ in and 1½ in. This was a feature of Midland boilers from about 1912 and was adopted for two reasons. Firstly, it made extracting or refitting the tubes through the front tubeplate easier and secondly it enabled a wider bridge between tubes in the softer, copper firebox tubeplate. The front tubeplate, being steel, could have a narrower bridge. The superheater flues were steel with ¾ in narrower copper ends brazed on at the rear and a short steel ring inserted to reduce wear due to the abrasive action of the flue gases. Later boilers had only 138 tubes and in the mid-1930s a few had the number further reduced to 121. This was an experiment to provide more space for water to circulate between the tubes, which was initiated when it was observed that boilers with some blocked tubes still steamed satisfactorily. The trial does not seem to have been deemed successful, however, as the number of tubes was restored to 138. Most tubes were steel but a small number of boilers in the mid-1930s had a mixture of steel and copper, the number of copper tubes varying between 80 and 116. During the Second World War the LMS adopted standard superheater elements from the Superheater Company rather than having them specially made.

Steam was admitted via a conventional dome-mounted slide valve regulator through the main steam pipe in the top of the boiler to the saturated side of the superheater header. By the time the 2–6–4Ts were built, problems had been encountered with obtaining high-quality steel castings for the headers on Horwich moguls and so those on the tank engines were cast-iron. During the first few years it was found that steam was leaking from the joints in the regulator intake, so, starting in June 1935, the regulator rod tubes were expanded where they entered the collector.

The boiler was made from 9/16 in steel plates in two rings. Construction followed

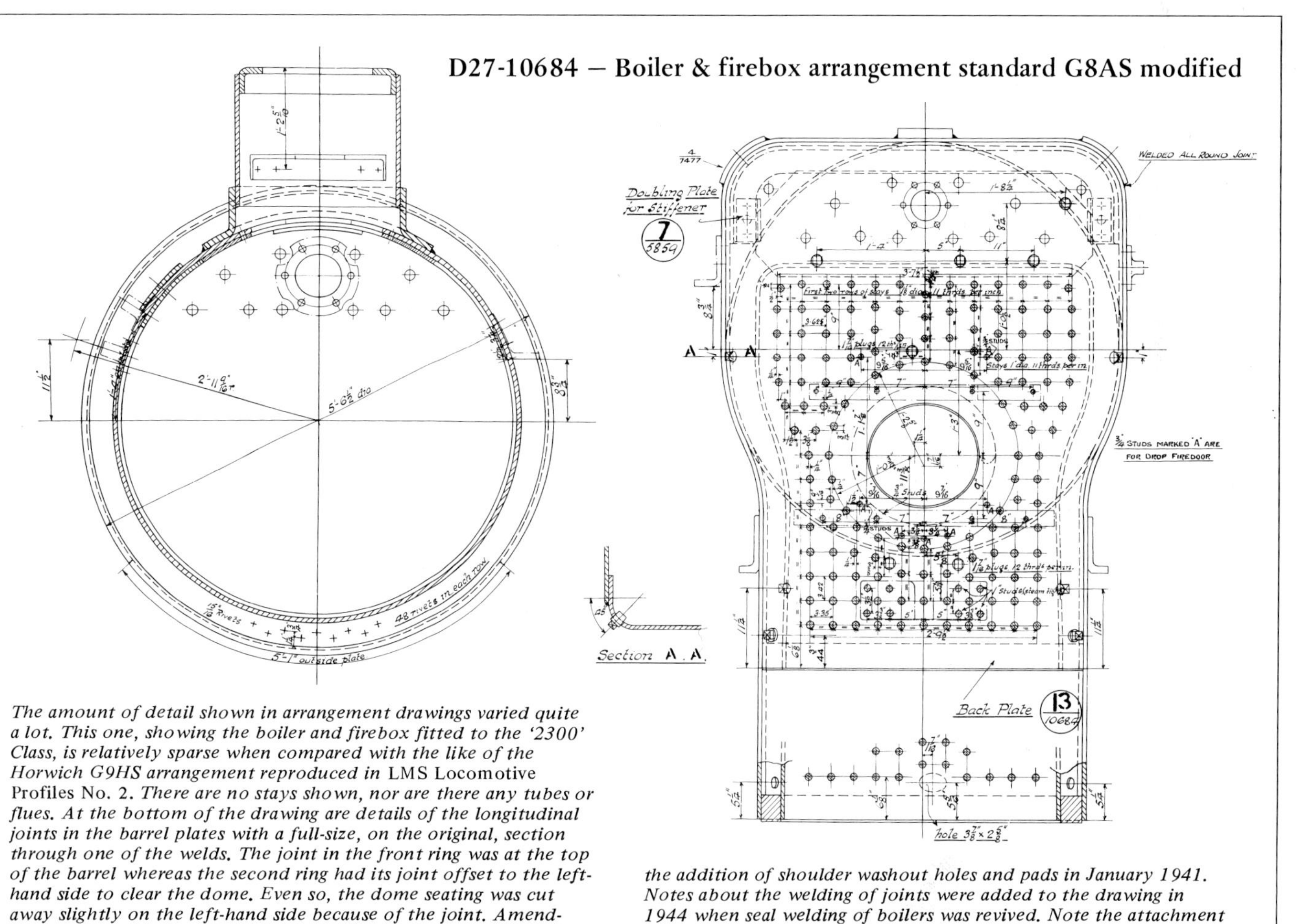

The amount of detail shown in arrangement drawings varied quite a lot. This one, showing the boiler and firebox fitted to the '2300' Class, is relatively sparse when compared with the like of the Horwich G9HS arrangement reproduced in LMS Locomotive Profiles No. 2. *There are no stays shown, nor are there any tubes or flues. At the bottom of the drawing are details of the longitudinal joints in the barrel plates with a full-size, on the original, section through one of the welds. The joint in the front ring was at the top of the barrel whereas the second ring had its joint offset to the left-hand side to clear the dome. Even so, the dome seating was cut away slightly on the left-hand side because of the joint. Amendments to the drawing were the deletion in September 1936 of the blow-down cock when continuous blowdown was introduced and the addition of shoulder washout holes and pads in January 1941. Notes about the welding of joints were added to the drawing in 1944 when seal welding of boilers was revived. Note the attachment brackets for the side tanks and the firebox expansion angles shown in the side and rear elevations.*

D27-10610 — Clothing arrangement

The clothing arrangement on Nos. 2300-2394 was a fairly standard Derby one, as shown in this drawing. Distance pieces, or 'stools', were carried on the boiler with bands, called 'crinolines', and longitudinal top and bottom bars attached to them by countersunk screws. Lagging was an asbestos blanket and the clothing was 14 iwg steel panels held in place by 2in wide bands of the same material over the transverse joints. A shaped copper fairing, held in place by the front band, covered the smokebox angle. At the top left of this page is a section through the boiler and clothing taken at the front tank stay with a side elevation below it. At the bottom right of the page are two full-size (on the original) sections at the bottom of the front (to the right) and rear (to the left) firebox clothing bands ana at the right-hand side a full-size section at the middle one. At the bottom left-hand corner of the page is a list of the seven detail drawings that went with the arrangement. On the following page is a split plan view. Above the centreline is an external view showing the clothing panels and bands, dome, safety valve base cover, etc, and below it an external view of the boiler with the clothing sectioned at the horizontal centreline. This shows the stools and crinolines as well as the stays by which the tanks were attached to the boiler. The upper half of the plan and the side elevation show the pockets in the clothing through which the stays projected. Below that are a view of the fairing round the front corners of the firebox (left), and a split section taken through the firebox to the left of the centreline and the boiler at the dome to the right. At the bottom right-hand corner is a rear view of the firebox backplate with a section taken through the corner halfway up the left-hand side at bottom left of it. This shows the pocket in the clothing for the reversing screw bracket. To the right of the plan is a full-size (on the original) section through the clothing to the side of the fire hole and to the right of the backplate view is a full-size section above it. The drawing was amended in 1941 to show the holes in the firebox panels, cover plates and alteration to the rear clothing band added when shoulder washout doors were fitted.

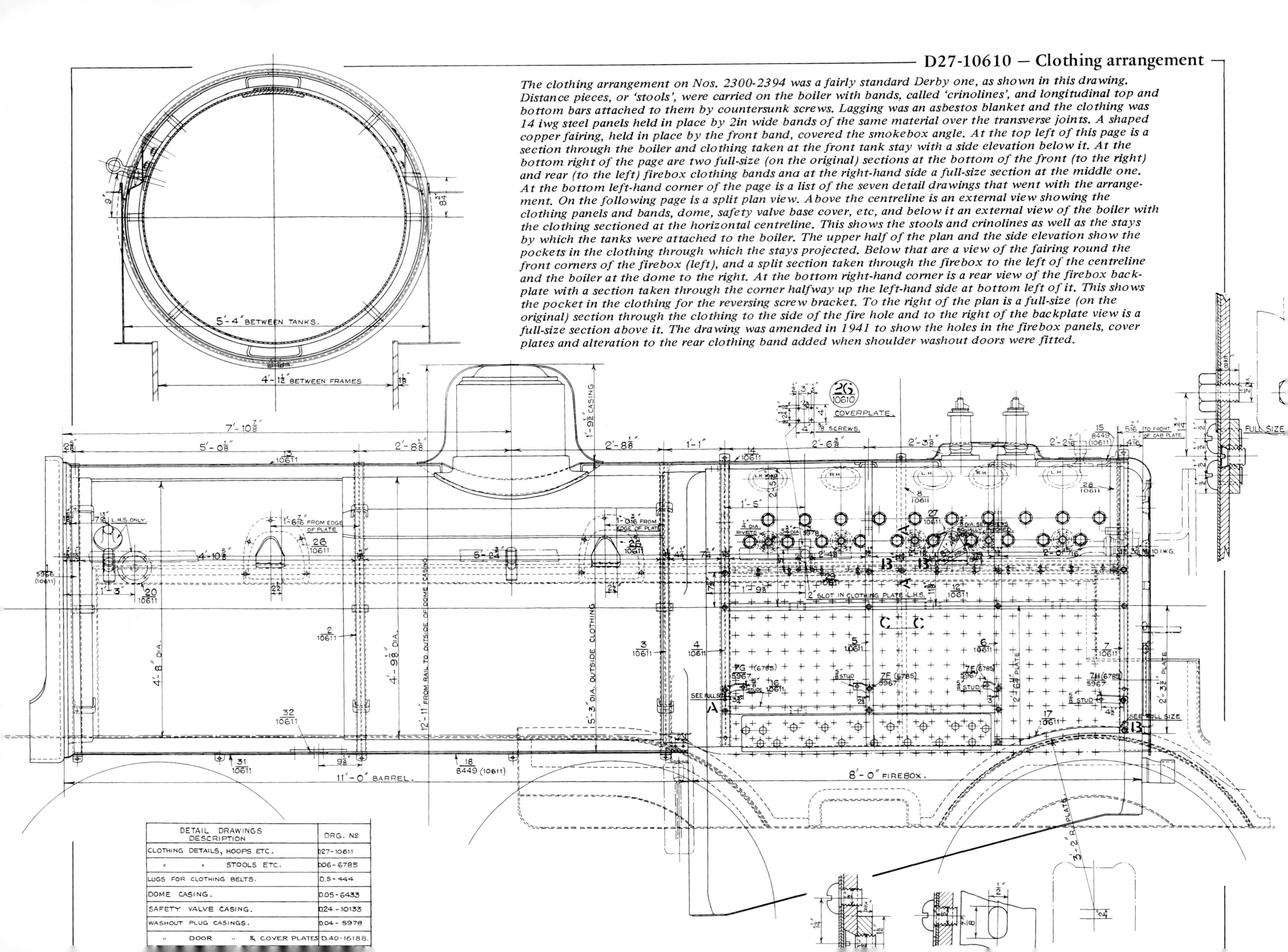

DETAIL DRAWINGS DESCRIPTION	DRG. Nº
CLOTHING DETAILS, HOOPS ETC.	D27-10611
" " STOOLS ETC.	D06-6785
LUGS FOR CLOTHING BELTS.	D.S-444
DOME CASING.	D05-6433
SAFETY VALVE CASING.	D24-10133
WASHOUT PLUG CASINGS.	D04-5978
" DOOR " & COVER PLATES	D.40-16188.

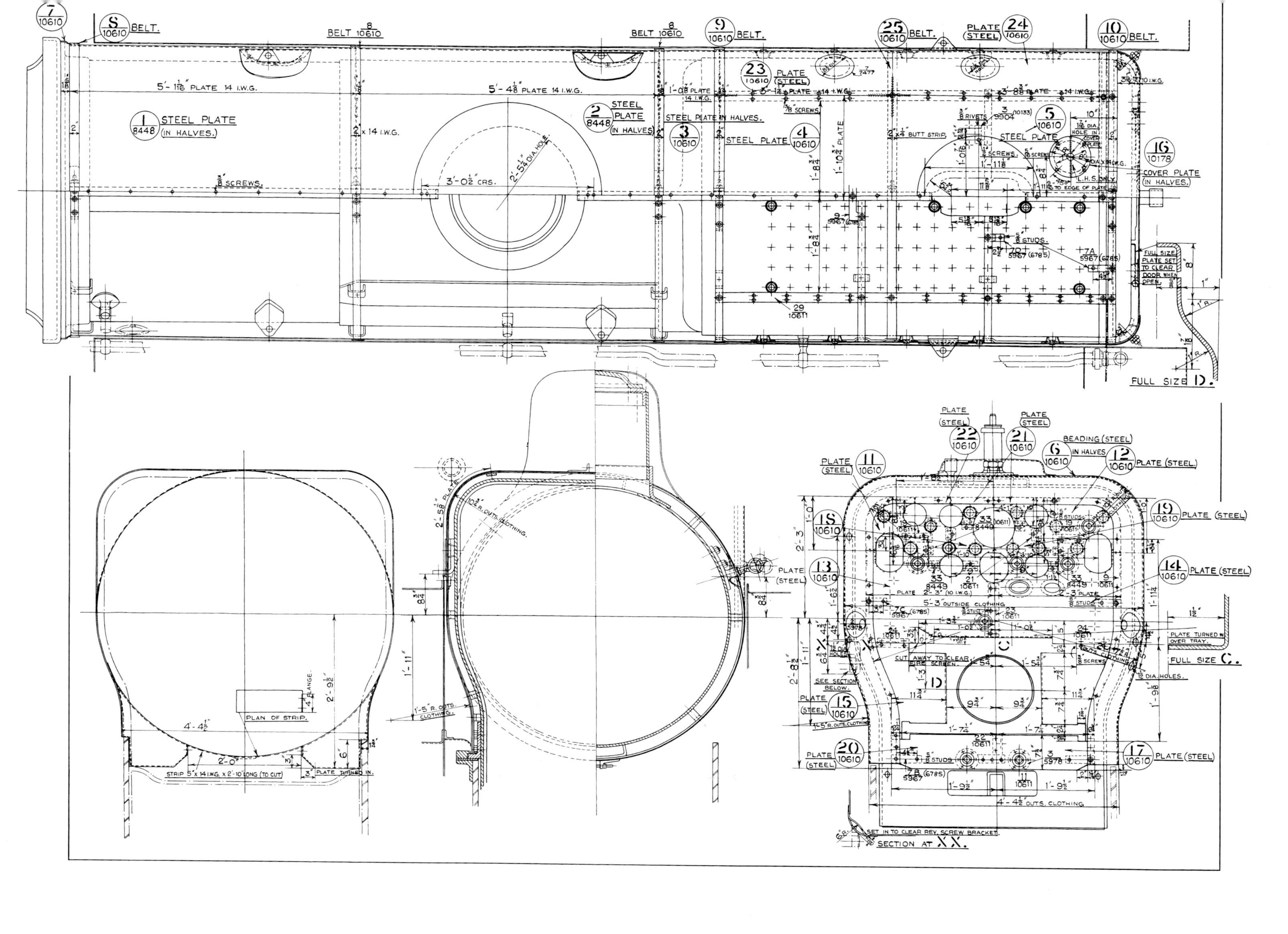

STEEL PLATE (IN HALVES.)
5'-1 1/16" PLATE 14 I.W.G.
5'-4 1/8" PLATE 14 I.W.G.
2'-5 1/4" DIA. HOLE
3'-0 1/2" CRS.
3/8" SCREWS.
STEEL PLATE (IN HALVES)
STEEL PLATE IN HALVES.
STEEL PLATE
3/8" RIVETS
3/8" SCREWS
2" x 1/4" BUTT STRIP.
COVER PLATE (IN HALVES.)
L.H.S. ONLY.
FULL SIZE PLATE SET TO CLEAR DOOR WHEN OPEN.
FULL SIZE D.
PLATE (STEEL)
BEADING (STEEL) IN HALVES
5'-3" OUTSIDE CLOTHING
CUT AWAY TO CLEAR FIRE SCREEN.
SEE SECTION BELOW.
PLATE TURNED IN OVER TRAY.
FULL SIZE C.
4'-4 1/2" OUTS. CLOTHING
SET IN TO CLEAR REV. SCREW BRACKET.
SECTION AT XX.
PLAN OF STRIP.
STRIP 5" x 14 I.W.G. x 2'-10" LONG (TO CUT)
PLATE TURNED IN.

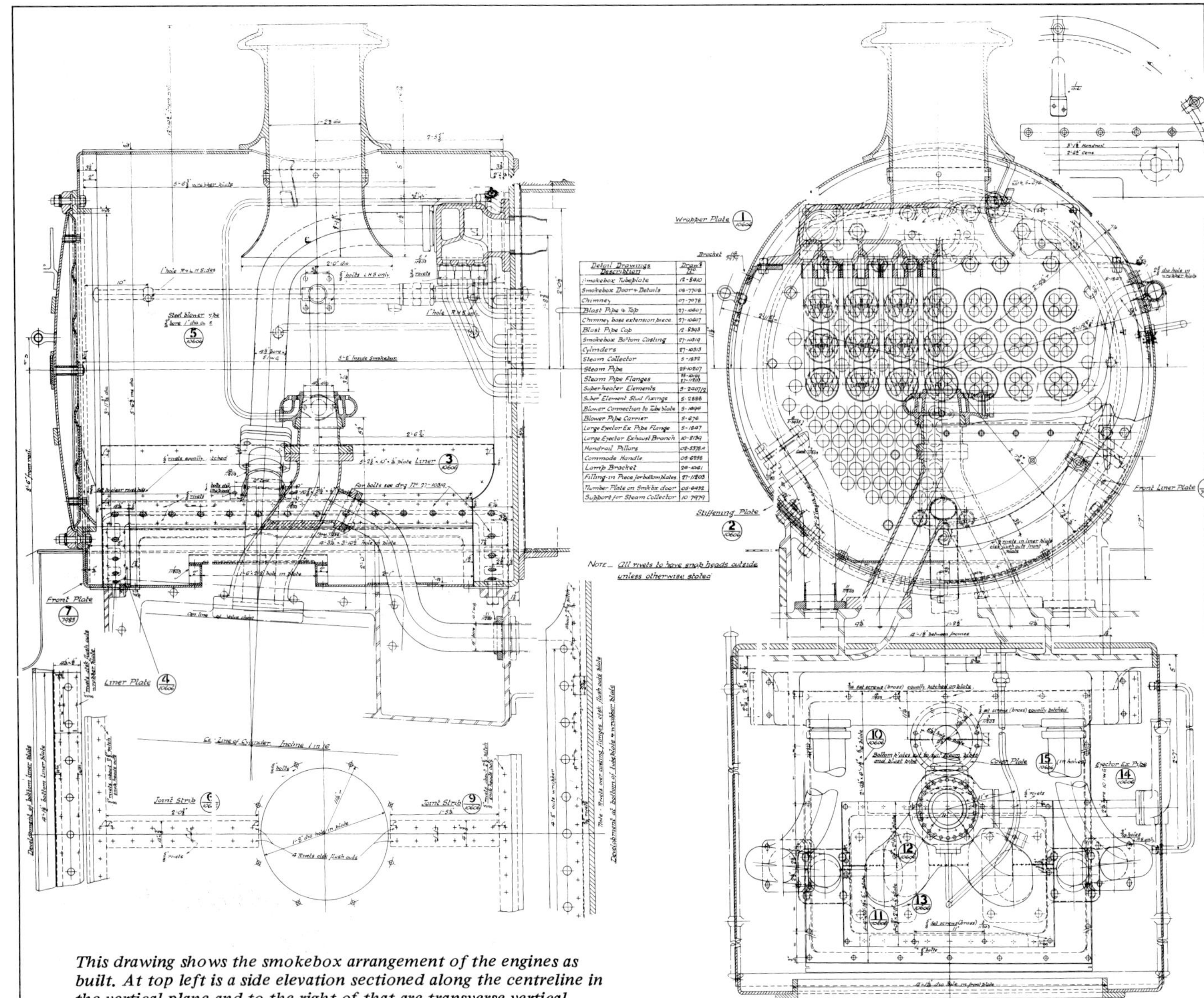

This drawing shows the smokebox arrangement of the engines as built. At top left is a side elevation sectioned along the centreline in the vertical plane and to the right of that are transverse vertical sections taken at various distances from the rear, all combined into a front elevation. To the right of that is a part outside front elevation and below it a horizontal section viewed from above with the front of the smokebox at the bottom. Bottom left is a part top view showing the hole for the chimney and top butt strips. Either side of that are developments in the flat of, to the left, the bottom liner plate at the front and, to the right, the bottom of the tubeplate and rear wrapper plate that joined smokebox and boiler. Saturated steam comes from the regulator via the main steam pipe, which can be seen passing through the tubeplate and into the rear of the superheater header at the top rear of the smokebox. It is then returned through the boiler in the superheater elements, which are the pipes coming from the bottom of the header, that run in the 21 superheater flues shown in three rows in the front elevation. After passing through the elements, the steam, now dry and superheated, passes through the dry side of the header and into the steam pipes that lead to the cylinders. They can be seen in the side elevation running forward from the header and then bending down just in front of the chimney centreline. In the front elevation they are shown curving round the periphery of the smokebox and down to the cylinder castings. The exhaust from the cylinders exits via the casting with the inverted Y-shaped front profile at the bottom of the smokebox and through the convergent opening at the top, which is called the blastpipe. The convergent shape of the blastpipe accelerates the steam and lowers its pressure as it passes through the smokebox and out of the chimney. Thus, the pressure in the smokebox is reduced and hot gases from the fire are drawn through the small tubes, seen below the superheater flues in the front elevation, as well as the flues themselves. The water in the boiler is heated by the walls of tubes and flues and the saturated steam in the superheater elements further heated by the flue gases. Around the top of the blastpipe can be seen the combined blower and large vacuum ejector exhaust ring. The small bore pipe entering the smokebox above the superheater header comes from the driver's blower valve and directs steam into the blower ring and out through the ring of small holes surrounding the blastpipe. This gives an annulus of high-speed steam up to the chimney, which has a similar effect to the blastpipe itself and pulls hot gases from the fire. It is used whenever there is a need for more draught, such as when the engine is being prepared for duty and the fire built up or to heat up the fire when more steam is needed. It is also used to keep the draught through the fire when the regulator is closed and the engine is coasting or when a back-pressure is likely through the chimney, such as when entering a tunnel. The ejector exhaust pipe is shown entering the smokebox at the right-hand side of the front and top elevations (which is actually the left-hand side of the locomotive) and joining onto another gallery around the top of the blastpipe outside the blower ring. The bell-mouth extension attached to the bottom of the chimney is the petticoat pipe, designed to gather the steam and gases issuing to atmosphere in another convergent duct. The pipe leading from the exhaust, just above the point where the branches from the two cylinders join, and exiting the smokebox at the bottom rear leads to the exhaust steam injector. The bit that gave trouble in the original 2–6–4 tank engine smokebox was the recessed rectangular hole in the bottom through which the exhaust pipes were routed. It was difficult to keep airtight and gave problems with corrosion, as described in the text. There were also problems where the steam pipes to the cylinders passed through the wrapper at a fairly acute angle.

the normal LMS practice of riveting all joints. After Stanier took charge, however, the practice was adopted of welding each longitudinal joint for one foot from each end and seal-welding the outsides of the circumference joints all the way round. The firebox plates, throatplate, front tubeplate, and fixings such as dome and safety valve mounting stay pads, tank brackets, and pads for firebox backplate fixings, were also welded. According to Arthur Cook, seal-welding of boilers was discontinued about 1937, reintroduced in 1944 and deleted again in about 1948.

The 8ft long Belpaire firebox had a 25 sq ft grate and provided 137¼ sq ft heating surface, so that total evaporative surface was 1,220¼ sq ft and total heating surface 1,486½ sq ft.[12] Staying followed normal Midland practice with Belpaire boilers. Between the front tubeplate and top of the outer firebox doorplate were through stays, longitudinal stays ran from the top of the doorplate to the top front corners of the outer firebox, and 'palm stays', so called because of their shape, fixed the bottom of the barrel to the front of the firebox. Barrel stays ran from brackets on the barrel plates to the front tubeplate. In the upper firebox water space were rows of transverse stays and the copper inner firebox was attached to the outer shell by direct stays. The front two rows of roof stays, however, were not connected directly to the outer firebox but were attached to links, or slings, pinned to brackets at the top. They were intended to give more flexibility to the structure at the place where maximum movement would occur when the inner firebox heated and cooled and were known as 'sling stays'. Mounted on top of the outer firebox were two 'pop' valves set to 205 psi. Either side of the firebox above the level of the side tanks were rows of washout plugs. In the 1940s some engines were fitted with fireboxes having additional shoulder-mounted washout doors, three on the left and two on the right, so that the top of the inner firebox could be cleaned of sludge and scale more efficiently.

At the beginning of 1942 it was decided that the arrangement of brick arches on all Standard and ex-Midland locomotives should be altered with a view to reducing the number of brick types in use and so effecting savings in stock holdings. For the '2300s' this meant altering the arrangement of carrying studs in the firebox before the standard bricks could be used. The alterations were carried out to job No. 5274 issued on 27th February 1942.

Although the smokebox was cylindrical and mounted on a saddle, thus avoiding some of the problems of flat-bottomed or 'built-up' smokeboxes, it had a weakness in its design that was to prove troublesome. It followed the layout of previous Derby smokeboxes in that the steam pipes from the dry side of the superheater header ran down the inside and a Y-shaped exhaust casting, mounted on the faces of the cylinders, was positioned between them. To accommodate the latter, there was a rectangular hole cut in the bottom plate and a flat section recessed into it through which the exhaust branches passed. Not only was it difficult to maintain this fabrication and the joints airtight, necessitating the use of cement to fill the gaps, but the accumulation of wet char in the corners and around the flanges led to corrosion. There were also problems where the steam pipes passed through the wrapper at an acute angle. As a result, in January 1937 it was decided to fit No. 2326 with an improved bottom plate and a year later an order was issued to modify the remainder of the class. The alteration consisted of removing the recessed section and filling in the hole with a curved plate so that the smokebox was cylindrical throughout. Flanges to accommodate the exhaust pipes were fitted and the shape of the steam pipes altered so that they passed through the wrapper more obliquely. These modifications only partly cured the problem, however, and corrosion still occurred around the steam and exhaust pipe flanges. When new, cast-steel cylinders were fitted in the 1940s, the opportunity was taken to redesign the smokebox, steam pipes and exhaust. The steam pipes were taken through the wrapper higher up and into the tops of the steam chests from outside. New blast pipe and exhaust castings were made with a separate blastpipe base welded directly to the smokebox saddle. Not only did this eliminate the leakage and corrosion problems of the original design, but it made life easier for the fitters who had to align the blast and petticoat pipes, and did away with the need to use cement to seal the smokebox.

The smokebox door was of the type introduced to the Midland by R. M. Deeley in 1904, which had six dogs on the seating ring. The dogs were tightened onto the rim of the door with nuts. The chimney was a one-piece iron casting with quite a sharply undercut, broad rim. In the 1930s Stanier's chimneys with smaller rims and larger radius undercuts began to replace them.

Water was fed to the boiler via a single No. 10 cone Gresham & Craven live-steam injector, of the type adopted as an LMS standard, on the left-hand side behind the cab footsteps and a Davies & Metcalfe No. 9 Class H exhaust steam injector on the right. Exhaust steam injectors were first tried on the Midland in 1911 when two '990' Class 4–4–0s were fitted with them and were achieving popularity in the 1920s. The idea was that on locomotives working for long periods with the regulator open continuously, the exhaust, which still had useful energy in it, could be used to inject water into the boiler. Thus, the diversion of 'live' steam directly from the boiler could be reduced and economies effected. Whether this was a good idea on engines designed for suburban passenger traffic, though, is another matter. At first it was positioned between the frames behind the ashpan where it gave problems due to overheating and the effects of detritus being deposited onto it, not to mention the difficulty of attending to it for maintenance or rectification. This was quickly recognised, however, and on 2nd January 1928 it was ordered that from No. 2306 the exhaust injector be moved outside the right-hand frame just ahead of the footsteps. From No. 2325 onwards its position was lowered and eventually all the earlier engines were altered to the same layout.[13] The steam pipe to the exhaust injector came out of the back of the smokebox below the boiler to a grease separator between the frames, then out through the right-hand frame just in front of the driving wheel and along the underside of the platform to the injector. The grease separator was necessary to prevent oil, which was picked up from the cylinders by the steam and held in suspension, from getting into the injector cones or back into the boiler. If it got into the cones it could form a coating and cause the injector to stop; in the boiler it would lead to the formation of sludge. Inside the inlet to the separator was a fixed vane that imparted a swirling motion to the steam. The suspended oil was flung against the side of the casing and the steam continued via a more restricted exit. The oil then collected in the bottom of the casing where an automatic drip valve allowed it to escape. At the bottom of the body of the injector was a water strainer. In 1940 there was an exceptionally severe

D36-14773 — Smokebox arrangement

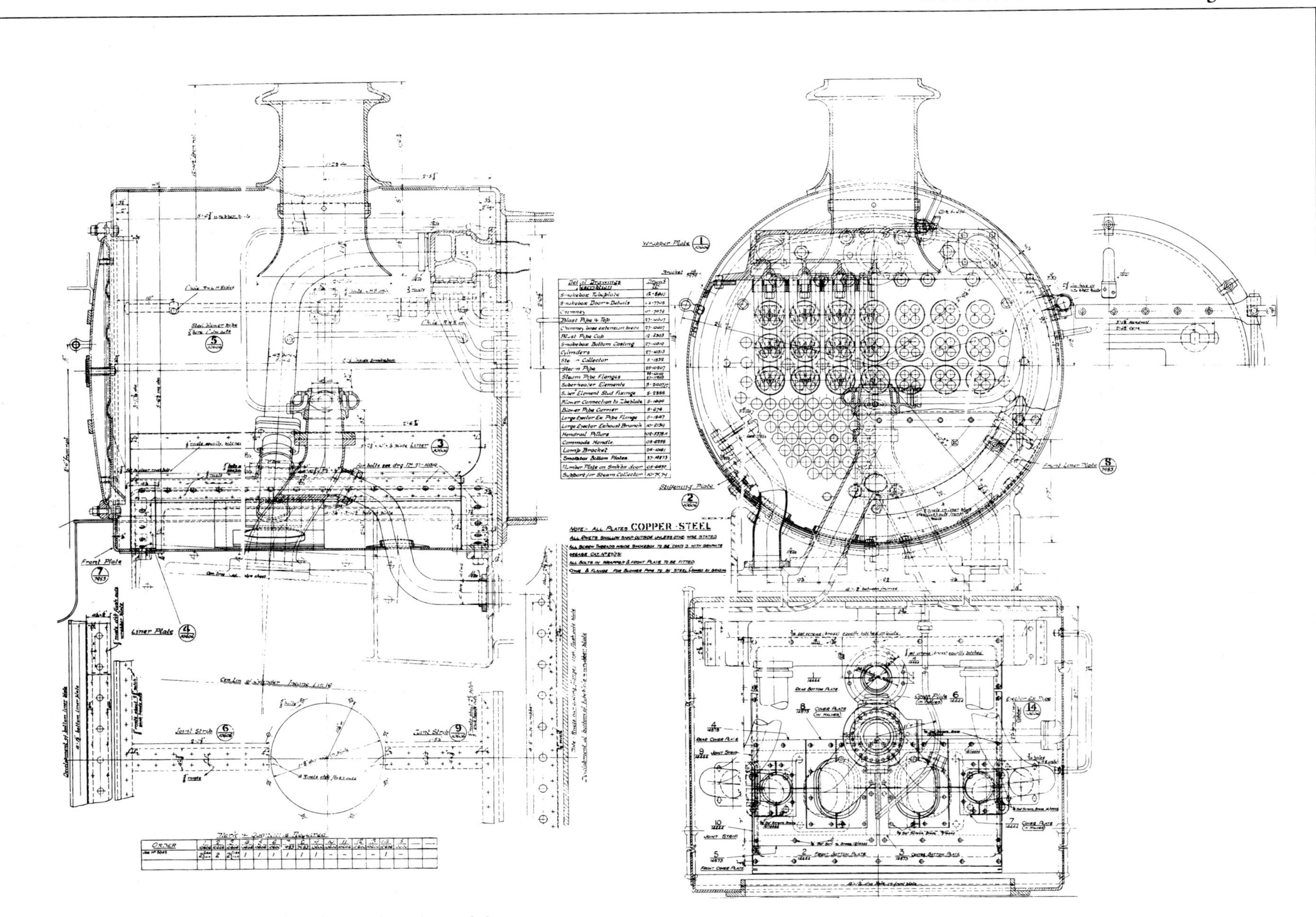

This drawing illustrates the alterations made to the smokebox in 1937. The modifications to the bottom plate and the steam pipes are evident when compared with D27-10606.

winter and trouble was experienced with the injectors freezing up, so drain cocks were manufactured at Derby and fitted to the water strainers between 1940 and 1947.

Boiler and firebox were lagged with an asbestos mattress under thin steel sheet clothing panels. The first Derby trial of asbestos lagging had been in 1924 when two '700' Class 4–4–0s were fitted with one white and one blue asbestos mattresses to O/6103 (the reaction of a modern-day health and safety inspector can only be imagined). The clothing panels were attached to hoops and longitudinal bars, or 'crinolines', fixed to the boiler structure, bringing the outside diameter to 5ft 3in. On engines with the later boilers that had washout doors in the firebox shoulders, holes were cut in the clothing panels to accommodate them. Because the clothing panels stayed with the locomotive rather than the boiler, once an engine had received washout doors the holes in its clothing were always present. Therefore, if a subsequent boiler change meant that it no longer had the doors, blanking plates had to be fitted to the clothing. These alterations were detailed in 1941 but we know of only one engine, No. 2390, that definitely had shoulder washout doors before 1948. It may have had them as early as January 1943 but it could have been November 1947 before it got them. Nos. 2319, 2320, 2322 and 2328 possibly had them in 1944 or it could have been as late as January, May and August 1948 respectively. Since our only evidence comes from photographs cross-referred to history cards, however, we can't be sure; neither can we state when the first ones appeared. Those we know to have had them at some time in BR days were 42300, 42305, 42307, 42311, 42314, 42319, 42320, 42322, 42328, 42333, 42340, 42353, 42359, 42366–42368, 42371, 42372, 42379, 42381, 42390, 42394, 42395, 42402, 42403, 42405–42407, 42410, 42412, 42415, 42417, 42420, 42421 and 42424. The extremities of the flat-topped dome casing and chimney were notionally

D40-16175 – Smokebox arrangement

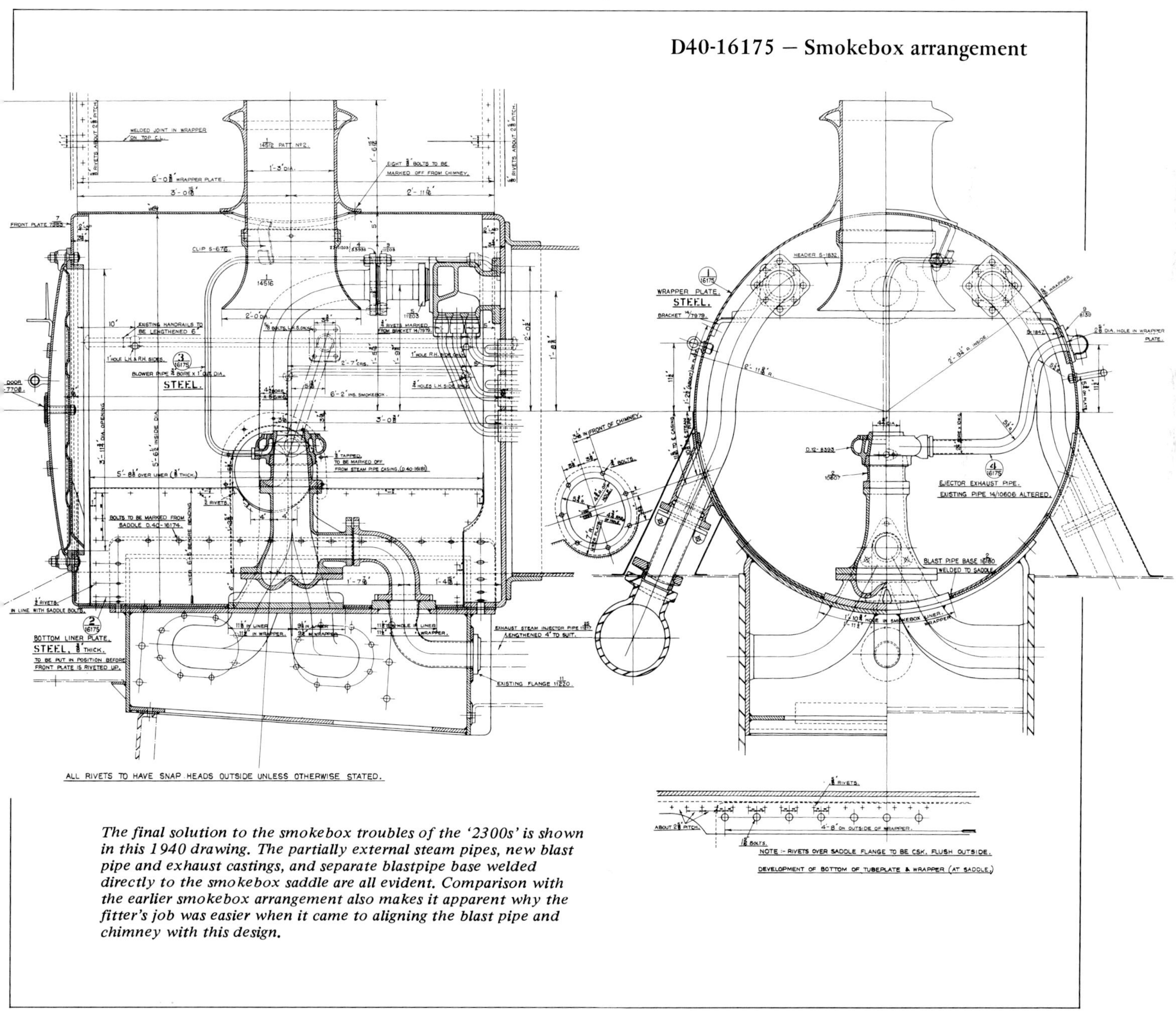

The final solution to the smokebox troubles of the '2300s' is shown in this 1940 drawing. The partially external steam pipes, new blast pipe and exhaust castings, and separate blastpipe base welded directly to the smokebox saddle are all evident. Comparison with the earlier smokebox arrangement also makes it apparent why the fitter's job was easier when it came to aligning the blast pipe and chimney with this design.

D27-10626 – Motion arrangement

This drawing illustrates the motion arrangement of the 'pre-Stanier' engines Nos. 2300-2394. Comparison with the motion arrangement of the Horwich moguls in LMS Locomotive Profiles No. 2 *will show the difference in the positioning of the reversing shaft and lifting link between the '2300s' and what E. A. Langridge called 'the usual LMS method' used on the 2–6–0s. Rather than the radius rod being lifted by a vertical link in front of the expansion link, it was slotted at the back and lifted from the rear by die block, thus avoiding the need for a pocket in the side tank in which the lifting link would be hidden. The long expansion link with relatively small swing can readily be seen, the extent of the swing being indicated on the drawing. As with most motion arrangements, very little detail of any other part of the locomotive is shown. The drawing has been altered to show the single oil cup on the upper slidebar as used on engines after 1933 but still shows Schmidt valve rings – drawing 30-11733 being referred to for details of narrow ring valves. As well as side elevation and plan of the motion, at top right there is a section through the left-hand motion bracket and leading wheel looking to the rear and, below that, a section through the left-hand part of the reversing shaft, bearings and bracket. Clearances of connecting and coupling rods are indicated on each section. To the left of the plan is a section of the left-hand pendulum link, valve spindle crosshead and bracket looking forwards.*

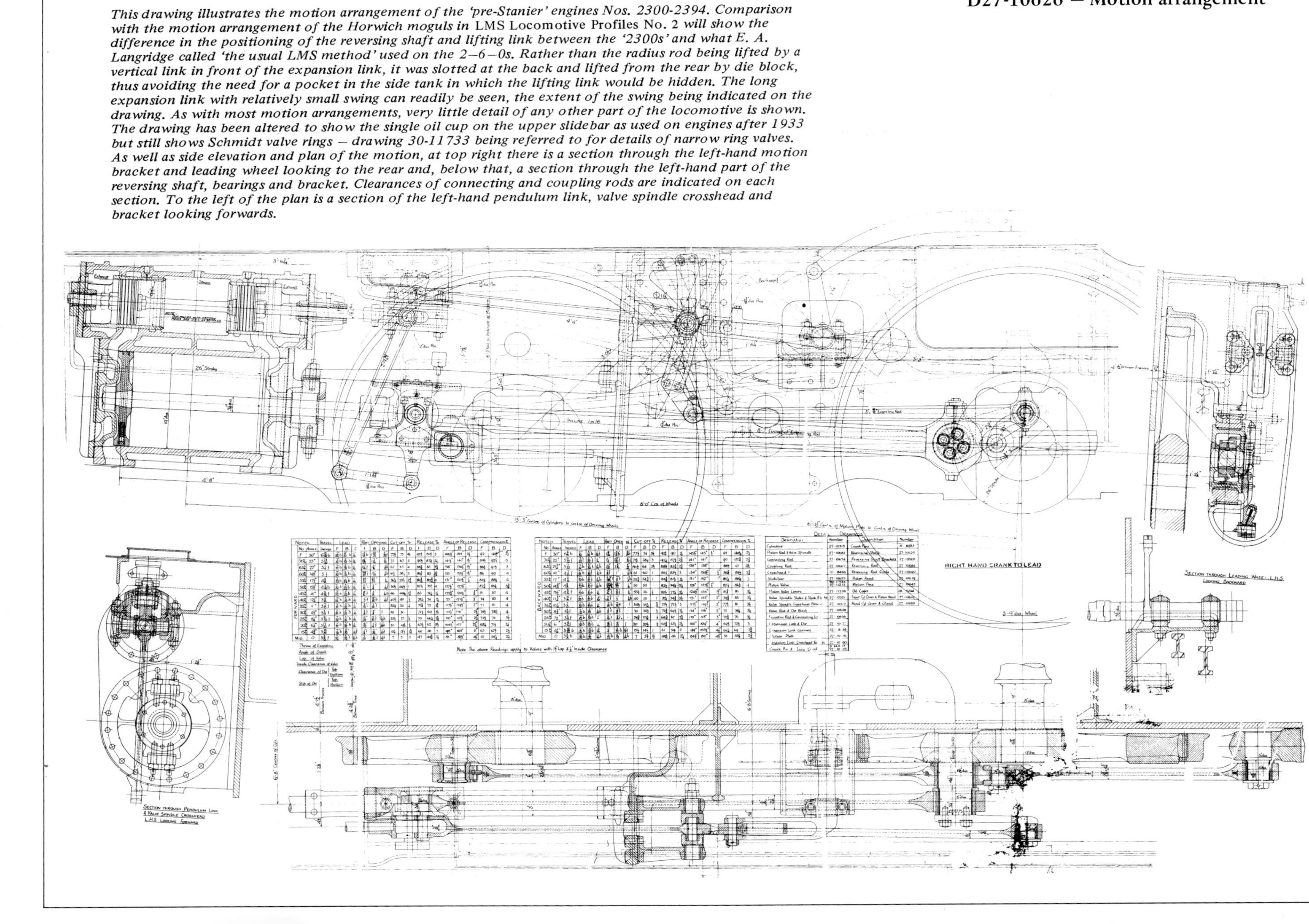

This photograph shows a wealth of detail of the 1929 engines as running in about 1933 or 1934. Note the two oil cups on the upper slidebar, buffers with altered 2½in thick packing blocks, extended vacuum stand pipe and bracket, lifting holes in the front frames, bogie and pony truck brakes, flat footsteps, and full-length cab cut-out, all of which help to date the picture. The oil box on the rear of the frame for the bogie slide shows up quite clearly.
A. G. ELLIS (15680)

12ft 10½ in above the rails to ensure maximum route availability.

In order to minimise the accumulation of harmful salts in the boiler, a system known as continuous blowdown was developed whereby a constant slight drain of water was allowed from the boiler into the ashpan whenever the regulator was open. The order to fit continuous blowdown to the '2300s' was first issued in April 1936 but we can't state when it was completed. Coincident with the fitting of continuous blowdown was removal of the blowdown cocks and replacement by plugs. Because cold water was used for washing out the boilers on the vast majority of LMS engines, it was necessary to restrict the rate at which the boiler was cooled to avoid unacceptable thermal stresses. To ensure that the required cooling rate was not exceeded, from late 1938 flow restrictors were fitted to the injector overflow pipes through which cold water was fed into the boiler.

CYLINDERS AND MOTION

As previously mentioned, the 19in diameter, 26in stroke cylinders were virtually the same as those used on the 'Royal Scots' with straight ports and 9in diameter piston valves. E. A. Langridge, who designed the cylinders and valve gear, stated 40 years later that the first engines built had Schmidt rings, and the multiple ring arrangement was only adopted later from a Doncaster drawing. Apart from this statement, however, we can find no other evidence of exactly which engines first had Schmidt rings or when they were changed. The 1927 motion arrangement shows Schmidt rings on the valves and has a note referring to two valve drawings produced in 1927 and 1930 with the later one being annotated 'for valves with narrow rings'. However, there is no reference in the history cards or any other documentation we have seen to any of the engines having its valves altered, so we are unable to resolve the issue. The cylinders were copied from the design that had been developed for the ARLE 2–6–0 referred to earlier with only minor adjustments. Steam pipes were inside the smokebox and the valves were inside admission.

The cylinders and valve chests were cast-iron on all but No. 2424, the last engine built, which had them fabricated from steel with cast-iron liners. This was the result of an order issued on 5th April 1933 that called for an experimental set of cylinders to be produced by electric welding. Although it was reported that the cylinders were much lighter than the norm, they were more expensive to make and so no more were produced. When the LMS started using cast-steel cylinders in the 1940s, however, those on 2424 were partially used as patterns for the new castings that were adopted for the '2300s'. From about 1948, inspection holes with cover plates were provided in the cylinder clothing for access to the atomiser oil feed pipes.

The solid pistons each had two rings and initially the rods had the LMS standard whitemetal and gunmetal packing rings, the whitemetal being protected from high temperature superheated steam damage by further spring-loaded bronze rings. The latter, known as MacNamee rings, were complex and costly and Stanier's designs used the simpler system of two sprung cast-iron rings. In December 1934 Job No. 4933 was issued for replacement of the earlier arrangement by Stanier rings but many engines weren't modified until they received new cylinders in the 1940s and 1950s.

So that the driving pistons on piston valve engines did not act as pumps when the regulator was closed, thus drawing smokebox gases and debris into the cylinders, some form of air relief or 'snifting' valve was normally provided. Snifting valves were generally fitted to the saturated side of the superheater header, but the Midland, and then the LMS, favoured air relief valves connected directly to the cylinders. On the '2300s' they were fixed to the frames just forward of the valve chests. Although they worked well, the valves tended to chatter at low speed and wore rapidly, so in 1934 the design was changed. The new type had a cast-steel valve with a dashpot, or damper, below it to reduce the chatter. Problems were then encountered with corrosion of the sheet metal casing and in 1940 a new type having a cast-iron casing was introduced. On Nos. 2300–2394 the 1934 pattern valves were fitted at the same time as the bye-pass valves were removed. The 1940 type was fitted on an *ad hoc* basis until 1943 when it was decided that any locomotive requiring the valves replacing or repairing would receive the later pattern ones.

In addition to the air relief valves, Fowler/Anderson bye-pass valves were fitted to the inside faces of the cylinder castings between the frames of Nos. 2300–2394 when built. They allowed communication between the two ends of the cylinders when steam pressure fell, thus providing another guard against cylinder damage when the regulator was closed. They were later seen as an unnecessary complication and source of trouble, since a failed valve would effectively stop a locomotive. Therefore, Nos. 2395–2424 were built without the bye-pass valves and, starting in 1934, they were removed from the earlier engines. Reliance was then placed on the air relief valves but they weren't as effective at counteracting the pumping action of the pistons and so it was necessary to have the regulator open a fraction when coasting. Many drivers disliked this and didn't consider the engines to be as good without the bye-pass valves. The cylinder drain pipes were extended forwards and clipped to the rear of the front footstep supports. Beginning in 1942 those on some, but by no means all, the engines were cut short and projected only a few inches forward of the relief valves.

Lap of the valves was 1½ in, lead 7/32 in, and travel varied between 3⅜ in at mid gear and 6 13/32 in the full forward position. Travel in full reverse gear was slightly less at 6 5/16 in. Apart from agreeing to the use of long-lap valves, Chambers instructed that the motion design should 'follow the 2–8–0', which was the S&DJR heavy freight engine built at Derby and one of only three other Derby designs to have Walschaerts' valve gear.[14] He also insisted on 1/16 in exhaust clearance being incorporated as it had always been found necessary on Midland engines, although it was absent on the ARLE design and many other long-travel valve gears.[15] Consideration was given to using parts from the Horwich mogul gear but in the event none was adopted. Mounting the lifting link and reversing shaft above the gear would have required a pocket in the tank, which would have made access difficult, so the Gresley arrangement of lifting the die block by a horizontal reversing crank was used. This was considered to be the ideal arrangement for tank engines as the die block slip is the same whether running forwards or backwards. Before incorporating this feature in the design, Langridge went to King's Cross and measured the relevant bits on a Gresley 2–6–0. The long expansion link with relatively limited swing was similar to that on the Horwich mogul, which was derived from American practice, and countered some of the 'traditionalist' concerns of die block wear.

Lubrication of cylinders, piston rods, valves and valve spindles was by a Silvertown mechanical lubricator mounted on the left-hand platform in front of the side tank and driven via a linkage by an operating rod from the expansion link. A handle was provided on the inside of the lubricator housing so that it could be operated by hand when the engine was stationary. Beginning in March 1938, additional handles were fitted to the outsides of the lubricators under Job No. 4980 so that hand operation would be easier. All engines were reported as being altered by the end of 1947.

Crossheads and slidebars were Midland types. Langridge stated that consideration was given to using the Horwich mogul versions but that trouble had been experienced with them until the working clearances and lubrication were sorted out (we forgot to include this in *LMS Locomotive Profile No. 2*).[16] The LMS Garratt connecting rod was found to be just right for the tank engine and so was utilised. Unfortunately, the Beyer, Peacock draughtsman who had drawn the Garratt valve gear had omitted the piston packing box from the drawings and the 8ft 9in rod would have been foul of it by 1½ in, so it had to be shortened to 8ft 7in on both engines. Lubrication of the lower slidebar was from an oil box on the crosshead and the upper one initially had two oil cups on top of it. From, we think, No. 2385 (it was certainly between 2379 and 2387) the rear cup was omitted from new engines and after 1933 earlier ones had them removed as they passed through the shops. Later, in May 1935, oil boxes with lids began to replace the cups and by nationalisation all engines seem to have had them. For a while in the mid-1930s, however, all three types of upper slidebar lubrication could be seen.

Coupling rods were fluted on Nos. 2300–2384 with solid bushes on middle and trailing crankpins but rectangular ends with half brasses and cotters on the leading ones. They were made from nickel-chrome-steel alloy. Those on Nos. 2385–2424 were Stanier pattern flat-section, manganese-molybdenum steel rods with rounded leading ends and solid crankpin bushes. These rods were supposed to be more flexible and better able to resist permanent deformation should the engine slip.[17] After 1933 replacement rods on earlier engines were also of this type.

FRAMES, WHEELS AND RUNNING GEAR

The main frames were made from 1⅛ in thick steel plates spaced 4ft 1½ in apart. They were common to the whole class with some modifications being made to the bogie centres and pony truck mounts for the last batch of 'Stanier' engines, Nos. 2395–2424, built in the second half of 1933 and January 1934. The rear portions between the bogie wheels were also shallower on these engines. No. 2424 was somewhat different from the rest as several of its stretchers were welded to the frames as an experiment, although the riveting was retained. The affected stretchers were the hind buffer beam, under the footplate, in front of the coal bunker, behind the firebox, above the driving wheels, between the motion plates, behind the smokebox, the pony truck swivel mounting and between the cylinders. A number of other small components were welded to the frames. We have been unable to find any reports on the results of the trial. The engines built in the 1930s, No. 2375 onwards, had 3⅛ in diameter lifting holes in the frames above the front platforms with 1in thick annular reinforcing plates riveted to the inside faces. Earlier locomotives, built with plain frames, had the holes cut and plates fitted as they passed through the shops in the mid- to late-1930s. The earliest modification of which we are aware was to No. 2347, which was photographed in April 1933 in altered condition.

Like the frames of the Horwich moguls, those of the '2300s' were deep, well stayed and gave little trouble with cracks. The main problem associated with them was corrosion around the cut-outs for the exhaust passages, which was finally cured when cast-steel cylinders were fitted. The first engines to receive new cylinders in December 1943 and early 1944 had the cut-outs filled by welding in a piece of frame plate This was then dressed to get as tight a joint as possible between the cylinders, frames and smokebox saddle. The difficulty of the process depended on how bad the corrosion was and on some engines it was very bad indeed, as one of us can testify. Thus, it often took a long time for the repairs to be effected and, due to wartime demands, a quicker method had to be found. That eventually used was to make two 'washers' of frame plate, sur-

This photograph was taken inside Derby Works on 13th October 1933 and shows one of the last 30 engines under construction. The actual locomotive, as the plaques on the buffer beam reveal, was No. 2410 (engine 16 of O/8338). Of interest are the mounting at the front of the cylinder casting for the air relief valve and the pocket in the boiler clothing through which the tank stay bracket can be seen. The bracket for the rear tank stay can also be seen on the side of the firebox. Fillers for the front and middle sand boxes are evident, the front one just above the cylinder and the middle one protruding through the frame between the rears of the slidebars. A support bracket for the raised platform is apparent projecting between the two ladders with ones for the rear platform behind, whilst a forward stay can be seen between the platform angle and frame in front of the cylinder. Twelve days after this picture was taken, the engine was recorded as complete.
NRM (DY 4389)

face ground on each side, which were then drilled to fit onto the studs that attached the cylinder exhaust ways to the smokebox saddle. Both surfaces had jointing compound applied, which made the joint steam tight. The cut-outs in the frames were de-scaled and cleaned up to prevent further corrosion. This method was used on the majority of locomotives.

Buffer beams were also 1⅛ in thick steel and originally were flush riveted but later repairs often used snap-head rivets. Originally, buffer casings were mounted on one inch thick spacing blocks and the oval heads were forged onto the buffer shanks. In this condition the engines measured 46ft 11¾ in over the buffers and were allocated to ED 172. From, we think, 2375 onwards, however, 2½ in thick spacing blocks were used to alter the relationship between buffers and couplings, which increased the overall length by 3in and resulted in the engines being allocated to ED 172A. Earlier engines were altered in the same way. The last thirty locomotives had longer casings with diamond-pattern steps on top of them and deeper, separate, oval plates riveted onto standard shanks with circular heads. Replacement buffers tended to be the later pattern, although not invariably so, and some engines afterwards reverted to the earlier type. At the same time as the buffer length was increased, the vacuum standpipes were moved away from the beams by 1½ in and the support brackets extended on most engines. There were some instances, however, of locomotives that had longer buffers but unmodified standpipes for a time. Because of the long overhang at either end, the draw hooks were pivoted between the frames and slid laterally in slots cut in the buffer beams. Problems were encountered with wear and so in 1931 steel rubbing blocks were added.

Coupled wheelbase was 8ft + 8ft 6in and the cast-steel wheels of Nos. 2300–2394 had 5ft 9in tyres riveted on. Balance weights on these engines were cast integrally with the wheels and crescent shaped, covering 4½ spaces on leading and trailing wheels and 6½ spaces on driving wheels to balance ⅔ of the mass of the rods and motion respectively. The Stanier pattern wheels fitted to Nos. 2395–2424 had triangular section rims, Gibson ring tyre fixing and built-up balance weights shaped as segments of crescents. Unlike some other pre-Stanier LMS locomotives, we can find no evidence of Nos. 2300–2394 ever receiving replacement Stanier pattern coupled wheels.

In 1940 it was decided to increase the side play on the leading and trailing coupled wheels of many LMS 6-coupled engines including the 2–6–4 tanks. This involved machining ⅛ in from the inside faces of the wheels and was intended to case the flange stresses when traversing sharp radius curves. Although there are records showing that many of the engines were so treated, we do not know whether the modification was applied to all of them. Note that it did not allow the engines to traverse tighter curves but merely relieved some of the stresses. The minimum radius over which the engines were allowed was 6 chains or 4½ chains dead slow.

One locomotive, No. 2408, was made without any balance for the reciprocating parts as an experiment to eliminate hammer-blow. In 1941 it was reported that horizontal oscillations were within acceptable limits at all speeds and that axlebox wear, although greater than normal, was by no means excessive for the mileage run. It was certainly not sufficient to cause the engine to be stopped early for repairs and no adverse reports had been made on its running. Unfortunately, we have been unable to locate any other reports on this experiment or assessments of its effectiveness.

The coupled axleboxes, Midland type on Nos. 2300–2394 and Stanier pattern with pressed-in brasses on the rest, had generous bearing surfaces, although the Stanier ones were less likely to run hot. In order to reduce the effects of dirt getting into the Midland boxes, they were fitted with dust shields from October 1936. Both types were lubricated by a Silvertown mechanical lubricator mounted on the right-hand side of the platform in front of the side tank and driven via a linkage by an operating rod from the expansion link. Oil pipes to the axleboxes were generally rubber but Nos. 2327–2335 were built with pipes made from a material called 'Midflex'. Whilst we don't know what this substance was, O/7366 issued on 26th March 1929

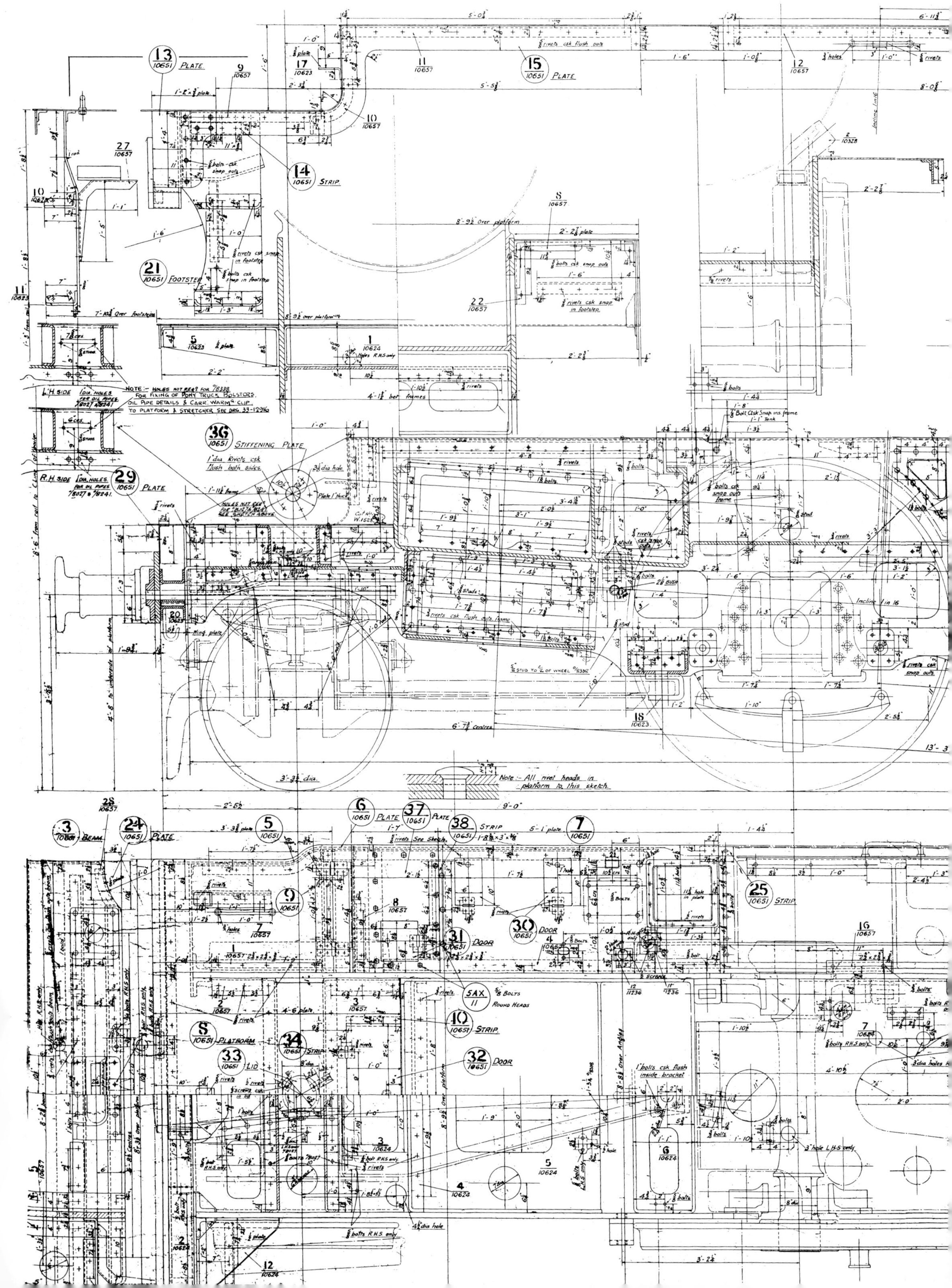

13 10651 PLATE
15 10651 PLATE
14 10651 STRIP
21 10651 FOOTSTEP
rivets csk flush outs
rivets csk snap in footstep
bolts csk snap outs
7'-10½" Over footsteps
8'-9½" Over platform
4'-1½" bet. frames
L.H. SIDE
R.H. SIDE
NOTE:- HOLES NOT REQ'D FOR 7/8338 FOR FIXING OF PONY TRUCK BOLSTERS. OIL PIPE DETAILS & CARR. WARM'G CLIP TO PLATFORM & STRETCHER SEE DRG. 33-12916
36 10651 STIFFENING PLATE
1" dia. Rivets csk flush both sides
29 10651 PLATE
Plate 1" thick
Incline 1 in 16
Ring plate
6'-7½" Centres
3'-3½" dia.
Note:- All rivet heads in platform to this sketch.
8'-6" from rail to Line of platform
4'-8" to underside of platform
9'-0"
3 10651 BEAM
24 10651 PLATE
5 10651
6 10651 PLATE
37 10651 PLATE
38 10651 STRIP
7 10651
9 10651
25 10651 STRIP
31 10651 DOOR
30 10651 DOOR
5AX 11 5/8 BOLTS ROUND HEADS
10 10651 STRIP
8 10651 PLATFORM
34 10651 STRIP
33 10651 LID
32 10651 DOOR
8'-8½" Over Angles
1" bolts csk flush inside bracket
3" hole L.H.S. only
4½" dia hole
bolts R.H.S. only

D27-10651 – Frame arrangement

Caption on page 63

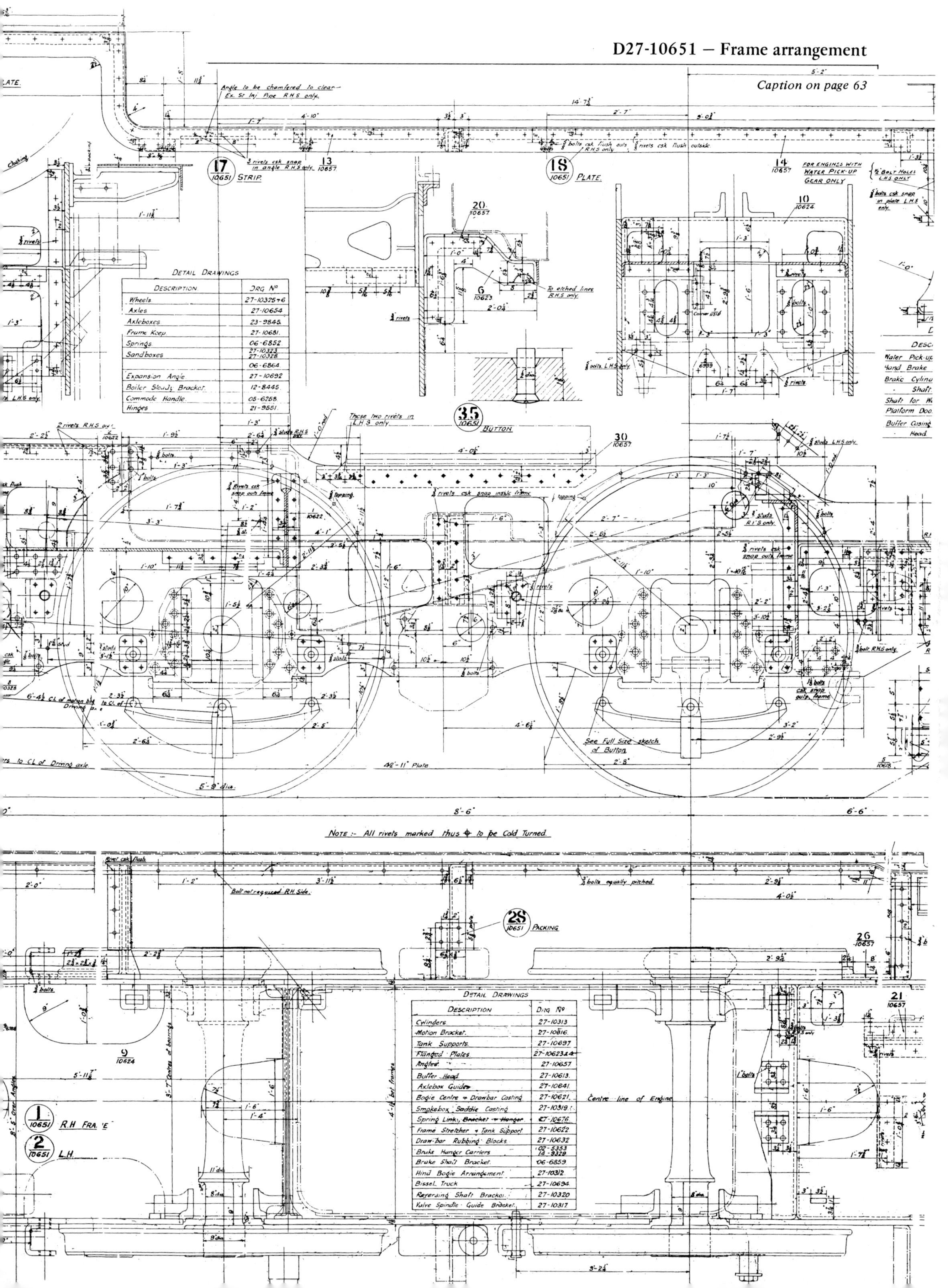

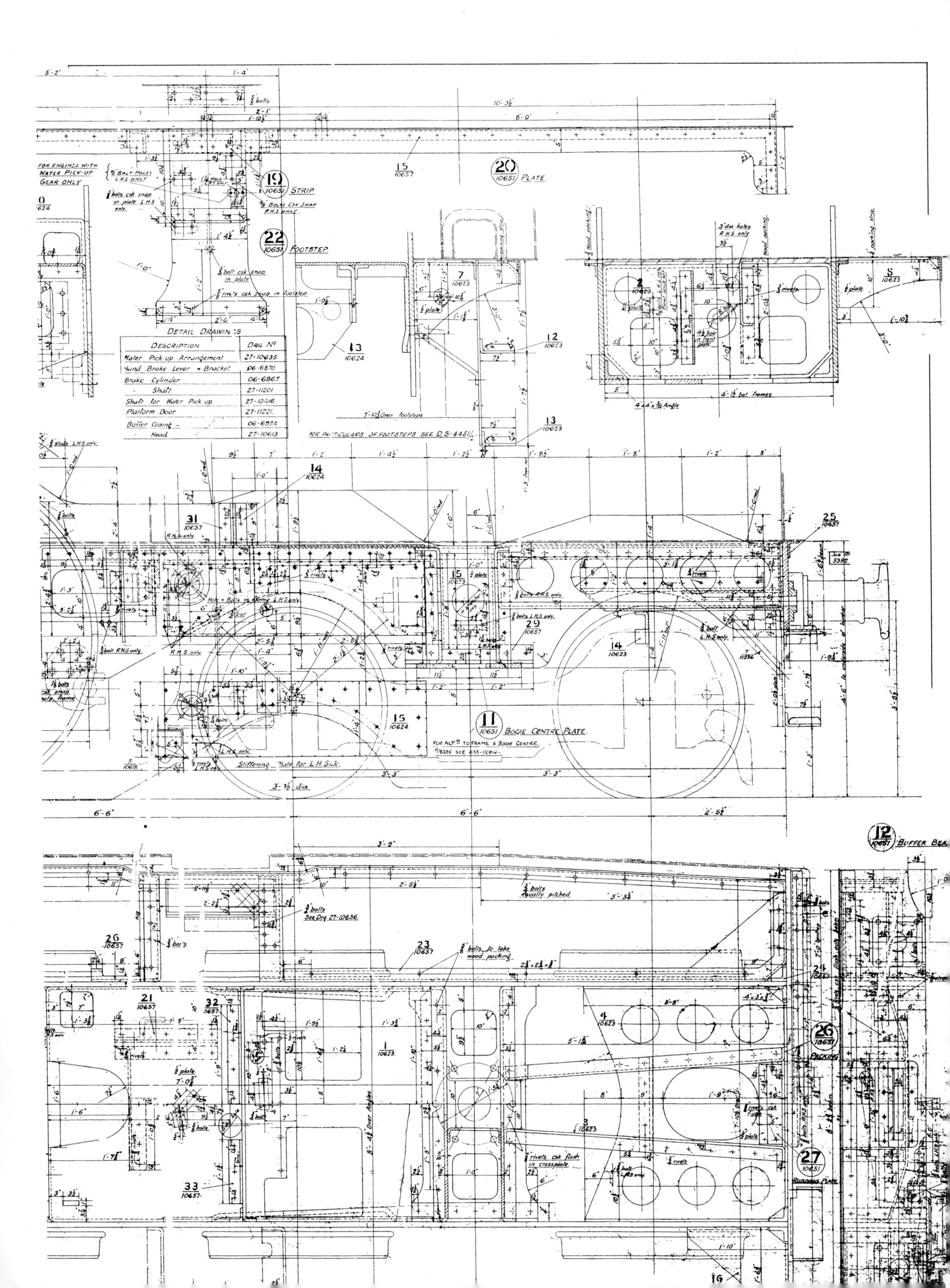

DESCRIPTION	DRG No
Water Pick-up Arrangement	27-10635
Hand Brake Lever & Bracket	06-6870
Brake Cylinder	06-6867
" Shaft	27-11201
Shaft for Water Pick-up	27-10616
Platform Door	27-11221
Buffer Casing	06-6974
" Head	27-10613

ordered its replacement with rubber pipes as the Midflex ones 'have not given satisfactory service'. The Midland axleboxes had gunmetal pads screwed to the outside faces where they came into contact with the wheel bosses and these pads had a tendency to work loose. In 1939 it was decided to do away with them and to face the axleboxes with whitemetal instead. If the wear on axleboxes and wheel bosses was excessive, however, the pads were retained and whitemetal applied over them. Leaf springs, each having 14 plates, were used for all three coupled axles and were attached to the frames by non-adjustable solid spring links. Those originally fitted to the first 75 engines were found to be too weak and in 1931 an experimental order D/LD/482 was issued for the trial on five locomotives of stronger ones with ½ in thick plates. Following a successful outcome, the remaining 70 engines were altered to O/8009 issued on 7th November 1931. Nos. 2375 onwards had the stronger springs when built. In the mid-1930s it was recorded that 'standard radius' springs were fitted to at least some of the '2300s' but, as with the Horwich moguls, we have no further information on them. In April 1946 Nos. 2355 and 2377 were fitted with Horwich type hornstays but we don't know why this was done and have no record of any other engines so treated.

Midland-style brake hangers were fitted ahead of each coupled wheel, activated by steam cylinders underneath the front of the cab and a handbrake standard at the front of the bunker on the fireman's side. In the 1950s, locking clips were added to the brake hangers to prevent them working loose. Steam sanding was provided to the leading and middle coupled wheels in the forward direction but only to the middle wheels when running bunker first. The sandboxes for the leading wheels were inside the frames with the fillers above the platform just in front of the side tanks. Those ahead of the middle wheels were also inside the frames with the fillers on top of the boxes and accessed through holes in the frames. Boxes behind the middle wheels were mounted outside the frames with the fillers on top.

This detail shot of 42374's bogie was taken at Longsight in July 1964. Note that, as with 42406, the original snap-head riveted footsteps had been replaced by flush-riveted ones.
R. J. ESSERY (232A)

BOGIE AND PONY TRUCK

The bogie used on the first 95 engines was the same as that on the 'Royal Scots' with slightly more sideplay. It had 1⅛ in thick steel frames spaced 2ft 7¾ in apart and the 4⅜ in lateral movement each way was controlled by volute springs in front of and behind the pivot. Lubrication of the slide-bars was originally intended to be from oil cups but they were replaced by an oil box on the left-hand locomotive frame with a pipe running to the bogie centre. Suspension was by an 11-plate inverted leaf spring outside each bogie frame that was linked to a longitudinal beam bearing on the tops of the axleboxes. The cast-steel 10-spoke wheels had 3ft 3½ in diameter tyres. As built the bogies on the first 85 locomotives were fitted with brakes to all four wheels, a steam cylinder being mounted outside each frame with opposed pistons pushing the brake shoes onto the tyres.[18] Stanier was against the use of bogie brakes so the engines built after 1932 did not have them and, commencing in March 1933, Nos. 2300–2384 had them removed.

Nos. 2395–2424 had Stanier pattern bogies in which the weight was borne by spherical bolsters with sliding pads. Their wheels were Stanier pattern with distinctive triangular section rims. It would seem, however, that the type of bogie wheels fitted to locomotives following repairs was variable and some early engines would re-emerge from the shops with Stanier wheels and vice versa. Stanier bogies fitted to some other locomotives had their rate of side movement controlled by spring-loaded pads covered with 'Ferobestos' (similar to car brake linings) but the parallel boiler 2–6–4Ts weren't among them.

The pony truck on Nos. 2300–2394 was the swing-link or Bissell type and was a direct descendant of the two-wheeled truck first seen on the Midland when some American-built 2–6–0s were imported in 1899.[19] It was developed from the truck on the S&DJR 2–8–0s and was virtually identical to that used on the '15500' Class (later Nos. 1–70) 2–6–2s. It had 4in lateral movement each way and on the first 85 engines was fitted with clasp brakes to the wheels, which were the same as those fitted to the bogie. The brakes were operated via a system of linkages by a steam cylinder behind the truck pivot. Nos. 2385–2394 were built without the brakes and, as with the bogies, they were removed from the earlier engines starting in March 1933. Lubrication was from oil boxes mounted on the frames and suspension was by 9-plate leaf springs, each plate being ½ in thick. The rearward extension of the truck frames was pivoted between the locomotive frames 6ft 7¾ in behind the centre of the truck axle.

One of the advantages claimed for swing-link trucks was a lack of friction in their sideways movement but it actually led to some problems in the early 1930s. There were several derailments of locomotives from different classes fitted with swing-link trucks when traversing 1 in 8 diamond crossings on curves at slow speeds. It was found that the centring force at the point where there was no inside check rail was moving the truck sideways when it reached the gap in the crossing, causing the wheels to take the wrong road. At high speeds there was insufficient time for the truck to move enough and there was no problem on straight crossings. The solution was to fit Ferobestos pads that bore on the truck frames under spring pressure. The friction produced by these pads slowed down the sideways movement enough to prevent the outer wheel from entering the gap as it was traversing it. The modification was authorised in June 1936 and O/9679

D27-10312 – Bogie arrangement

This drawing illustrates the spring centre bogie with brakes as fitted to the first 85 engines before Stanier took office. The side elevation is split about the centreline with the left-hand side showing the bogie cut in half and viewed from the inside. To the right of the centreline is an outside view of the main bogie structure with sections through the brake cylinder and axlebox bearing pin. The end elevation shows a lateral section to the left and an external view of the leading end to the right. Above the plan centreline are horizontal sections taken at different planes through various components whilst below it is an external view from above. Although the drawing has been updated to 1948, it still shows the bogie brakes as to remove them would have required a new drawing, which was obviously not considered worthwhile.

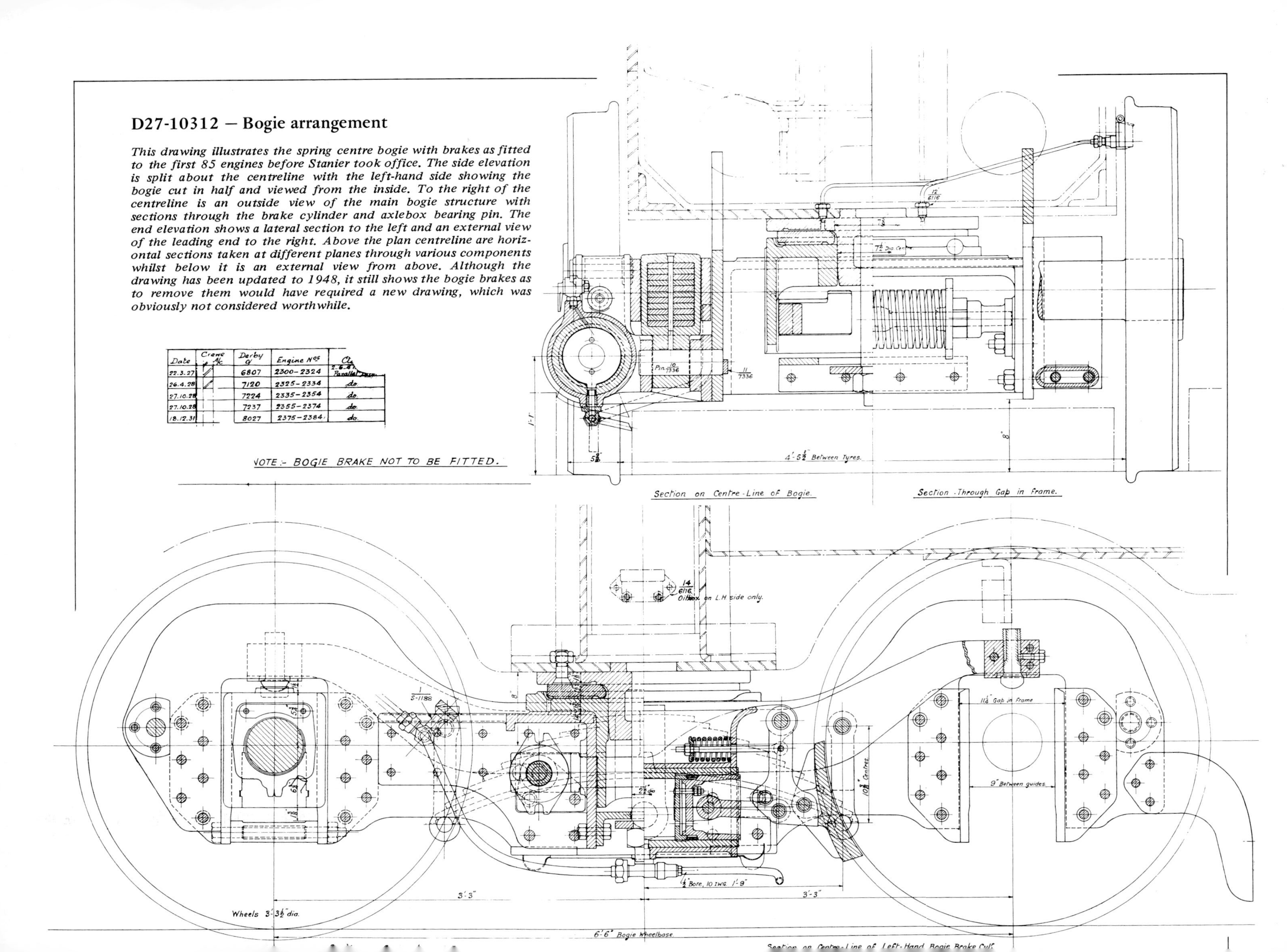

Date	Crewe A/c	Derby O	Engine Nos	Cl...
22.3.27		6807	2300–2324	2-6-0 Parallel Draw...
26.4.28		7120	2325–2334	do.
27.10.28		7224	2335–2354	do.
27.10.28		7237	2355–2374	do.
18.12.31		8027	2375–2384	do.

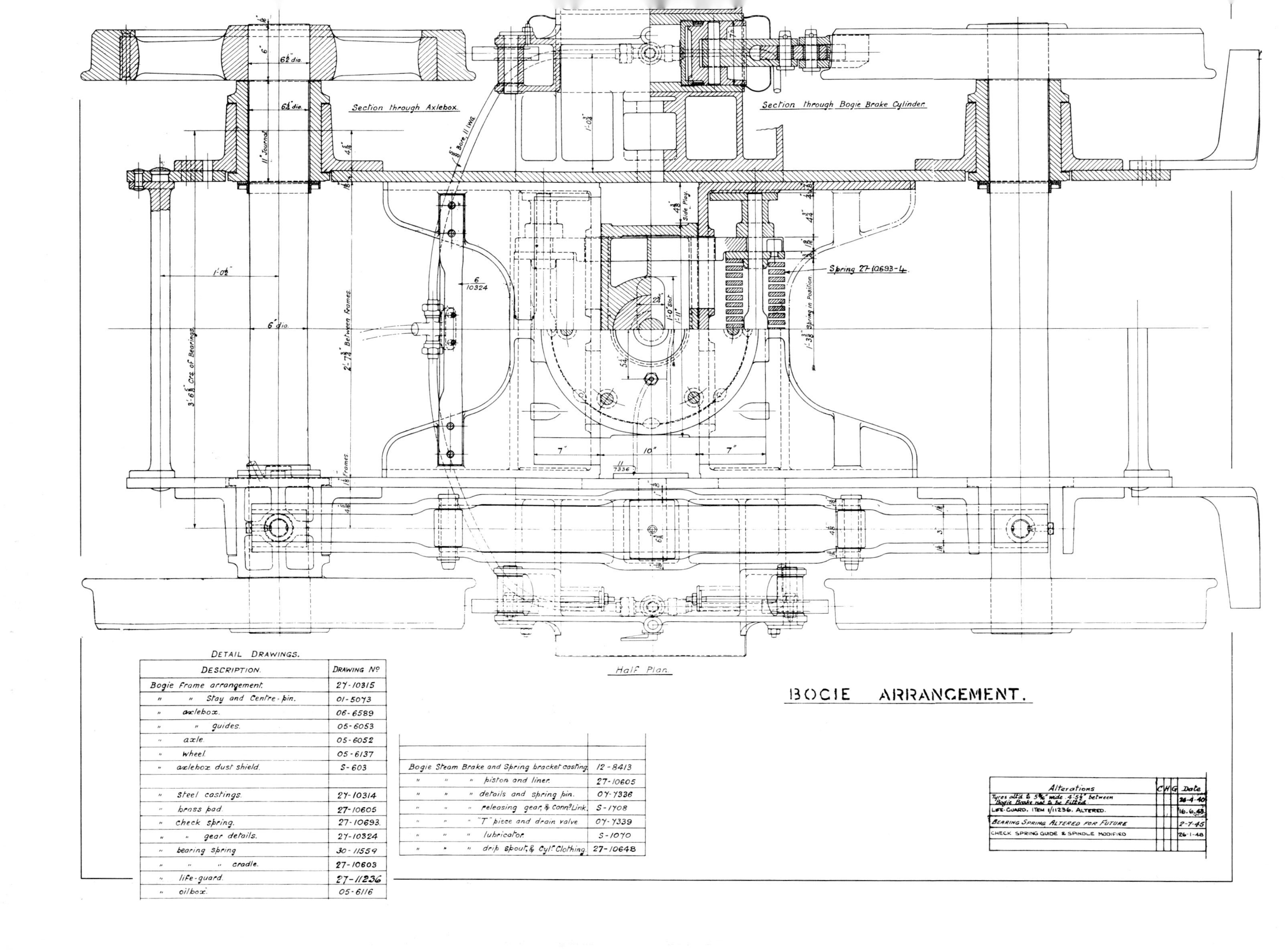

DETAIL DRAWINGS.

DESCRIPTION.	DRAWING No
Bogie Frame arrangement.	27-10315
" " Stay and Centre-pin.	01-5073
" axlebox.	06-6589
" " guides.	05-6053
" axle.	05-6052
" wheel.	05-6137
" axlebox dust shield.	S-603
" Steel castings.	27-10314
" brass pad.	27-10605
" check spring.	27-10693.
" " gear details.	27-10324
" bearing spring	30-11559
" " " cradle.	27-10603
" life-guard.	27-11236
" oilbox.	05-6116

Bogie Steam Brake and Spring bracket casting.	12-8413
" " " piston and liner.	27-10605
" " " details and spring pin.	07-7336
" " " releasing gear, & Conn.g Link.	S-1708
" " " "T" piece and drain valve	07-7339
" " " lubricator.	S-1070
" " " drip spout, & Cyl.r Clothing.	27-10648

Alterations	C	H	G	Date
Tyres alt'd. to 5 5/16" wide. 4'-5½" between Bogie Brake not to be Fitted.				28-4-40
LIFE-GUARD. ITEM 1/11236. ALTERED.				16.6.43
BEARING SPRING ALTERED FOR FUTURE				2-7-45
CHECK SPRING GUIDE & SPINDLE MODIFIED				26-1-48

D27-10694 – Bogie arrangement

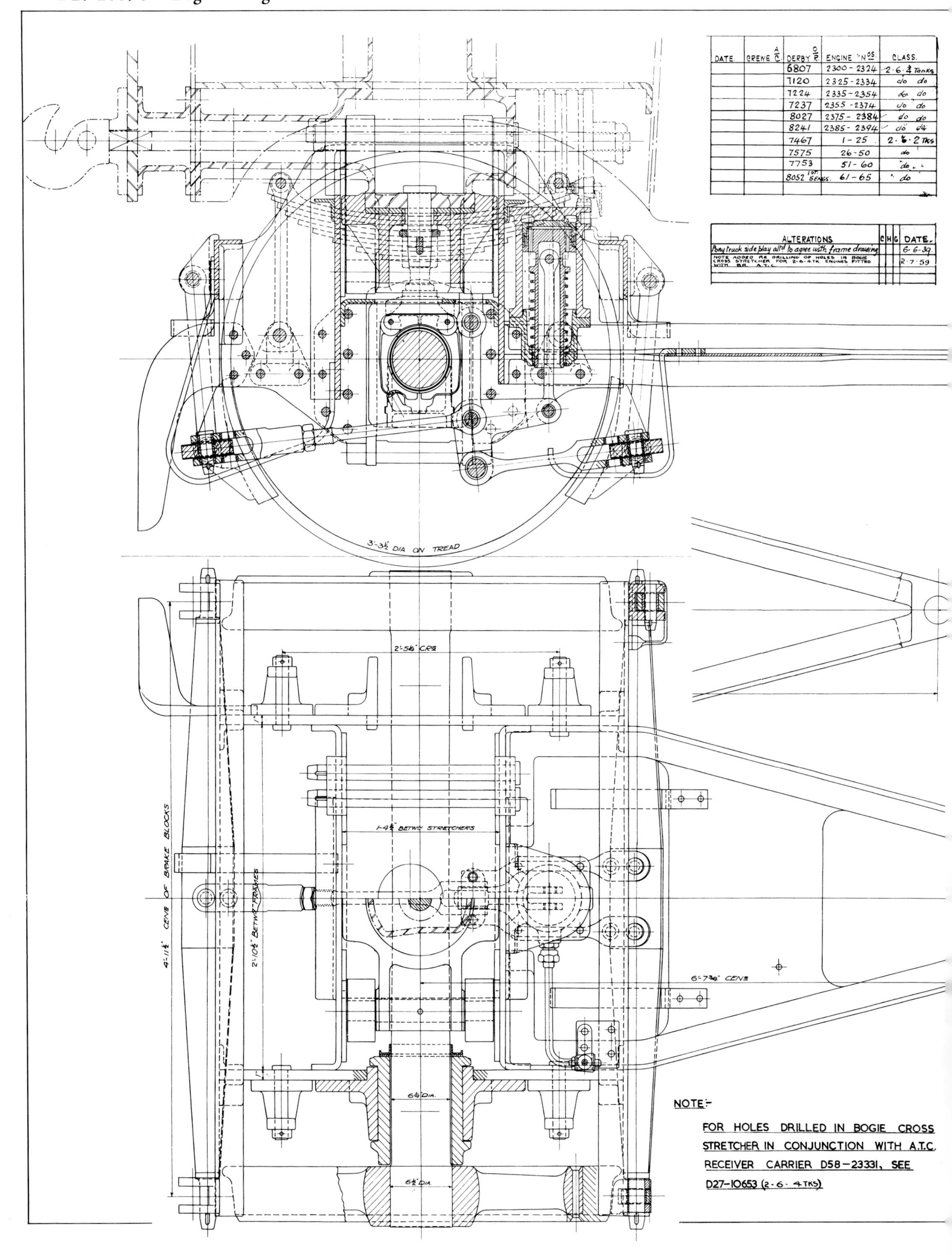

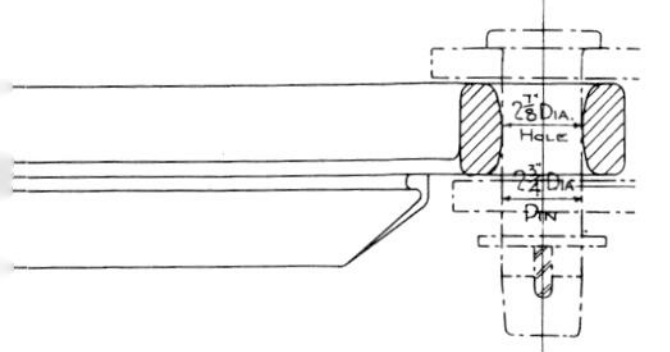

The title of this drawing is a little confusing as it actually refers to the swing-link pony truck fitted to the first 95 locomotives. It shows the truck with brakes, as provided on Nos. 2300-2384 when built, and despite having been updated as late as 1959, has no reference either to the removal of the brakes or the addition of the spring-loaded pads to slow down the rate of sideways movement. The truck was identical to that fitted at both ends of the parallel-boiler 2–6–2 tank engines except for the amount of lateral movement allowed and the drawing was, in fact, used for all of them. The action of the truck was as follows: the inverted, truncated V-shaped casting seen in the centre of the front view was free to swivel on the pin projecting down from the centre socket. Longitudinal pins passed through the ends of this casting and also through the bottom ends of the links so that they were free to rotate. The longitudinal parallel bars were fixed to the truck frames and fitted in to the tops of the kidney-shaped holes in the tops of the links. Thus the truck was attached to the locomotive by the links and the wheels forced down onto the rails by its weight. When the locomotive entered a curve, the wheels moved sideways and the links swung on the bars, as seen in the displaced position in the front elevation. The effect was for the lower ends of the links to rise, thus shortening their effective length in the vertical and compressing the springs. This was translated into a lateral force opposing the sideways movement of the truck, which tended to pull the front of the locomotive into the curve. To prevent the truck swivelling around the centre pin and derailing, the frames were extended rearwards in a vee to another pin fixed to a stretcher between the locomotive frames.

CLASS.	X
2-6-4	4"
2-6-2	3½" FRONT. 3⅝" HIND.

detailed the work for the first fifty of the '2300s' on 28th July. The remaining forty-four engines were altered to NWO 230 of 10th September 1937 and all were reported as being completed by March 1949.

The design of the last thirty engines was altered to have a Stanier pattern side bolster truck and wheels with triangular section rims. As with the bogies, however, engines could later be seen with either type of wheels on their trucks. In 1935 it was decided that an increase in friction between the sliding surfaces of the bolster would be beneficial for the same reason that the Ferobestos pads were added to swing-link trucks. The implementation of this decision was simpler than the equivalent modification to swing-link trucks, merely consisting of Ferobestos lining on the slides, and was ordered in October 1935. Once again, it was 1949 before all locomotives were reported as being fitted.[20]

A potential problem with the use of side bolster bogies and pony trucks was that the weight of the locomotive was transmitted to them directly via the sliding pads. Thus, any unequal wear on the tyres of the carrying wheels compared with the coupled wheels would lead to an alteration in the weight distribution of the engine, more coupled wheel tyre wear transferring weight to the carrying wheels and vice versa. Starting in 1940, therefore, a range of pads having different thicknesses to compensate for uneven wear was produced and fitted as required when the engines passed through the shops. There was, of course, a limit to the difference that could be accommodated and carrying wheel tyres could be no more than ¼ in thicker or ¾ in thinner than those on the coupled wheels.

PLATFORM, CAB AND TANKS

The ¼ in thick steel plate platform was 8ft 9½ in wide over most of its length but tapered from just behind the cab to 8ft 3in at the hind end. The front platform was stepped in just ahead of the front fall plates to 8ft 3½in. Throughout its length it was stiffened at the edge by 5in deep, ⅜ in thick angle. Between the frames in front of the smokebox were two fall plates for access to lubricators, train pipe, etc. Footsteps below the platform were provided on each side immediately behind the front buffer beam and at the cab as well as a single set just inboard of the left-hand rear buffer. At first the steps were flat with flush rivets attaching them to their support plates.

D33-12958 – Cab, side tank & bunker arrangement end views

Caption on page 63

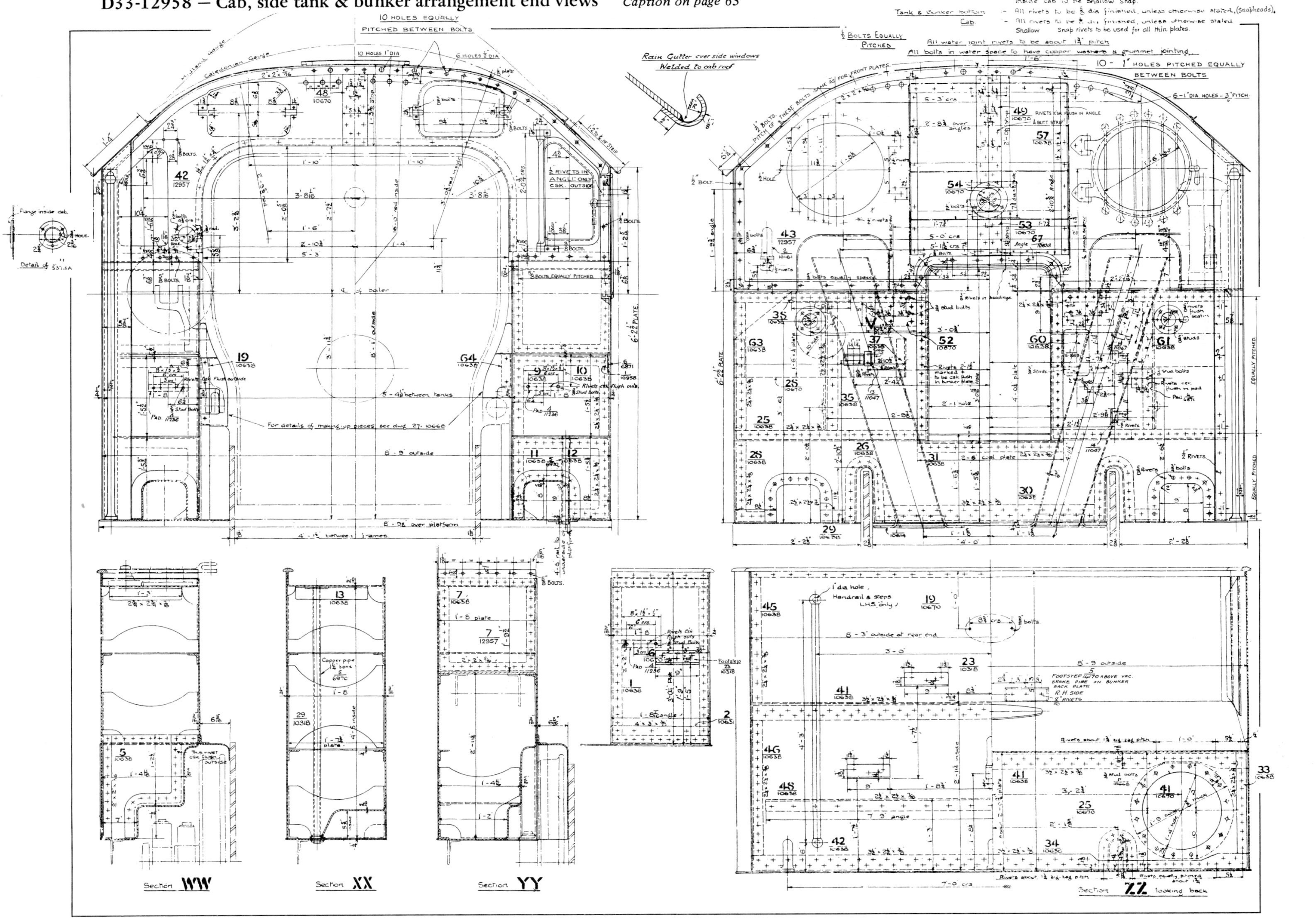

Riveting
Tank & Bunker sides & top :- All rivets to be ¾" dia finished, unless otherwise stated. All tank & bunker rivets inside cab to be shallow snap.
Tank & Bunker bottom :- All rivets to be ⅞" dia finished, unless otherwise stated, (Snapheads).
Cab :- All rivets to be ⅝" dia finished, unless otherwise stated. Shallow Snap rivets to be used for all thin plates.
All water joint rivets to be about 1¾" pitch.
All bolts in water space to have copper washers & grommet jointing.

Rain Gutter over side windows
Welded to cab roof

Section WW

Section XX

Section YY

Section ZZ looking back

Another of the 0/8241 engines, this time 2391, is seen in this study at a more advanced stage of construction than 2387. The turned-up ends of the footsteps fitted to Nos. 2375 onwards are evident, as is the asbestos mattress wrapped around the dome prior to fitting the dome cover. Note that although snap-head rivets were used on footsteps, tank, cab and bunker, those on the buffer beam were still flush. The steam cock and mounting for the carriage-warming hose can clearly be seen under the right-hand side of the buffer beam.
C. L. TURNER

From No. 2325 onwards, however, snap-head rivets were generally used both for new engines and repairs to earlier ones, and on engines built in the 1930s, i.e., 2375 *et seq*, the ends of the steps were turned up to give more secure footing. The earlier engines subsequently had just the corners of their steps bent up to similar effect, although it took a long time for them to be dealt with and not necessarily all the steps would be altered in one go. It would also seem that when steps needed replacing the later pattern ones with turned-up ends were commonly used. Thus, locomotives in the 2300–2374 series could be seen after the mid-1930s with a mixture of flat, bent-up corner and turned-up end steps. In BR days, however, there were instances of bent-up corner steps replacing later pattern ones as well as engines that had been built with snap-head rivets on the steps acquiring ones that were flush-riveted. At the same time as snap-head rivets were being used on footsteps for new construction, they were also replacing flush rivets on top of the platform and were often used for later repairs.

Tanks, bunker and cab were designed by E. S. Cox using the Midland 2000 series 0–6–4 tank engine as the basis. Except for a few places, such as the butt strips joining the cab roof to the sides, externally they were flush-riveted on Nos. 2300–2374. Once Stanier took charge, however, Nos. 2375 on were built using snap-head rivets throughout. The side tanks were stayed to the boiler and attached to the platform by

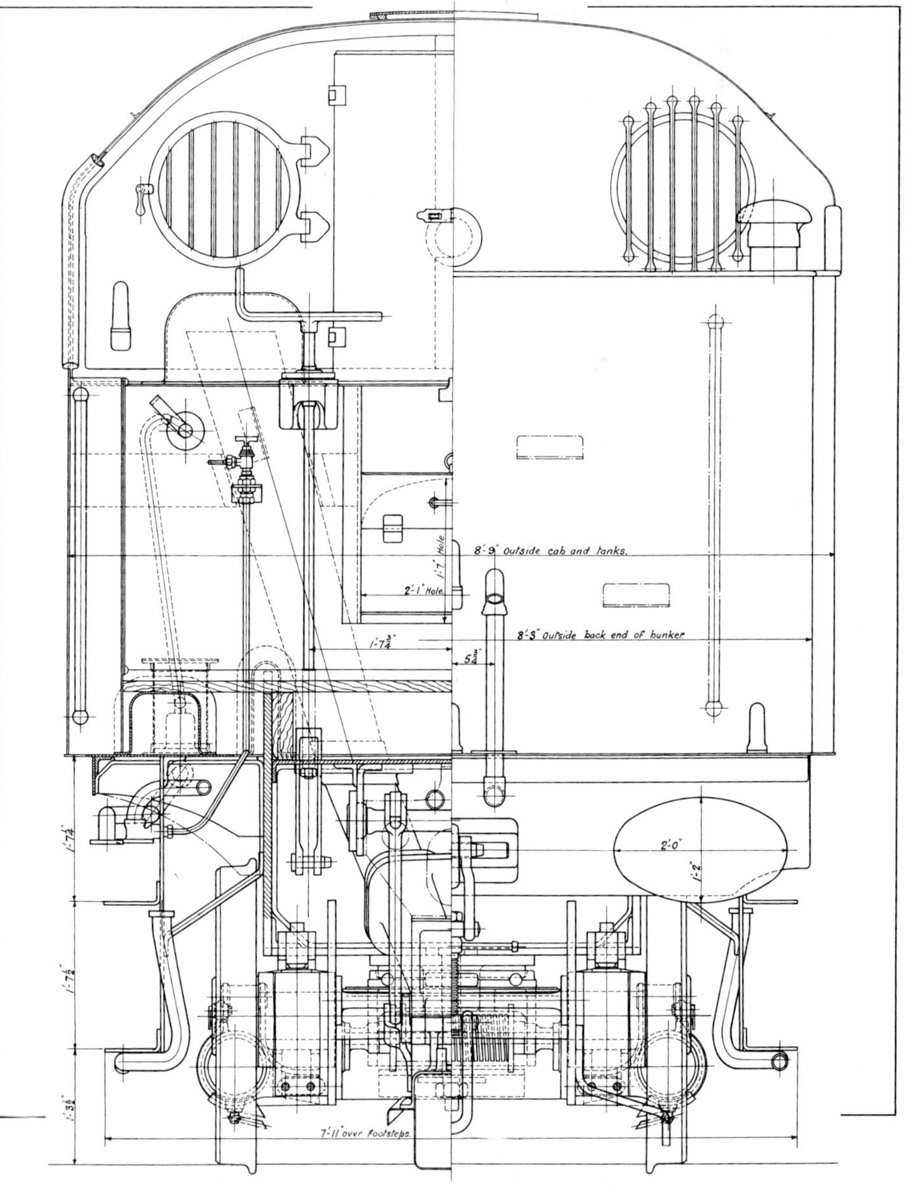

D28-10986 — End views and cross-sections 2–6–4 tank engine

This drawing is of value to the modeller, showing as it does front and rear external elevations, half of the firebox backplate and cab interior, and three other cross-sections. It is the companion drawing to D28-10985 and shows one of the 2300-2324 series before most of the modifications described in the text were made. Some of the views are extremely valuable as they represent the only drawings we have located of some aspects of the engines, e.g. the firebox backplate and cab fixings, tank stays and fire iron holder. The smokebox and firebox cross-sections should be read in conjunction with the boiler arrangement for added detail of the tubes, superheater flues and elements, and firebox stays.

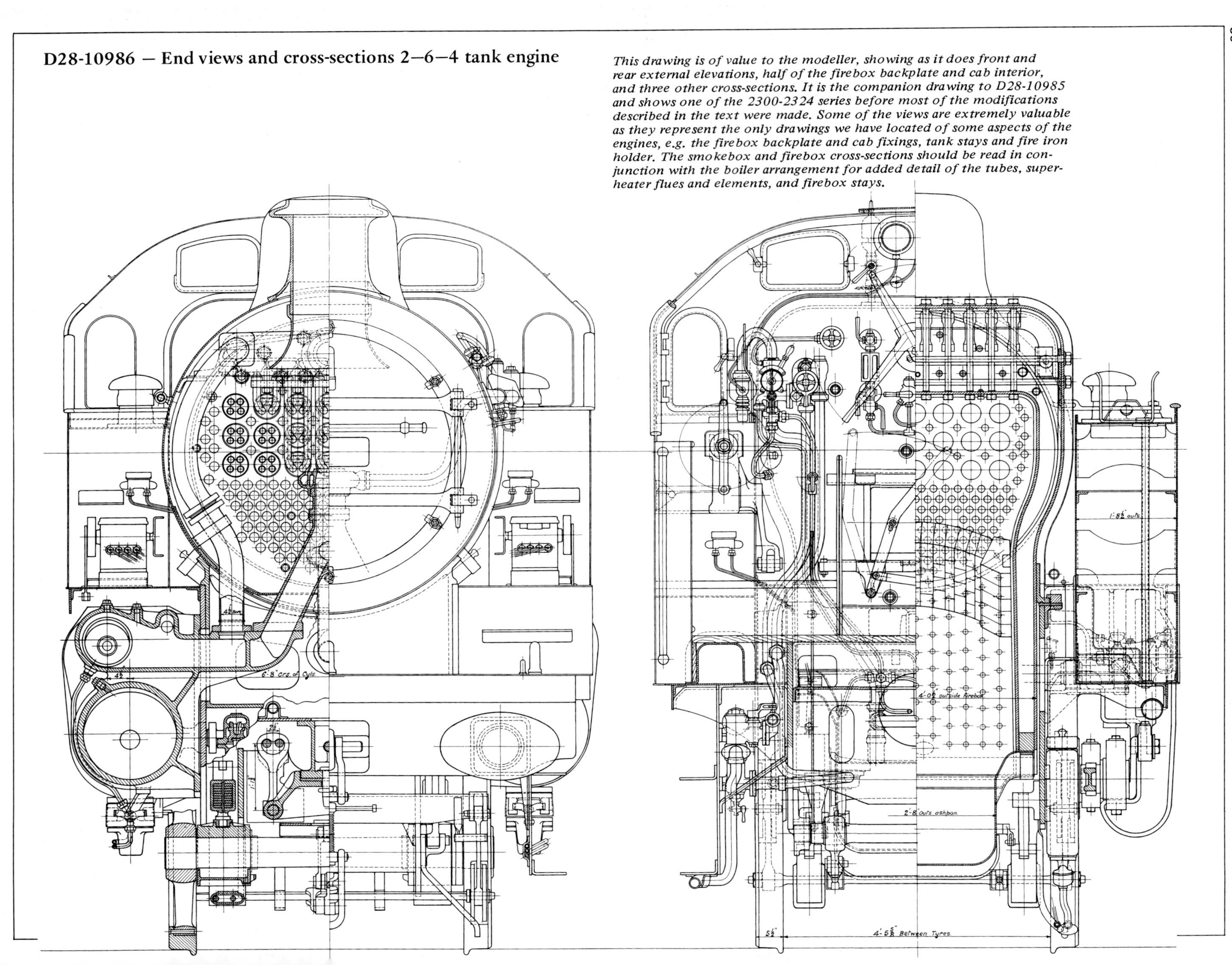

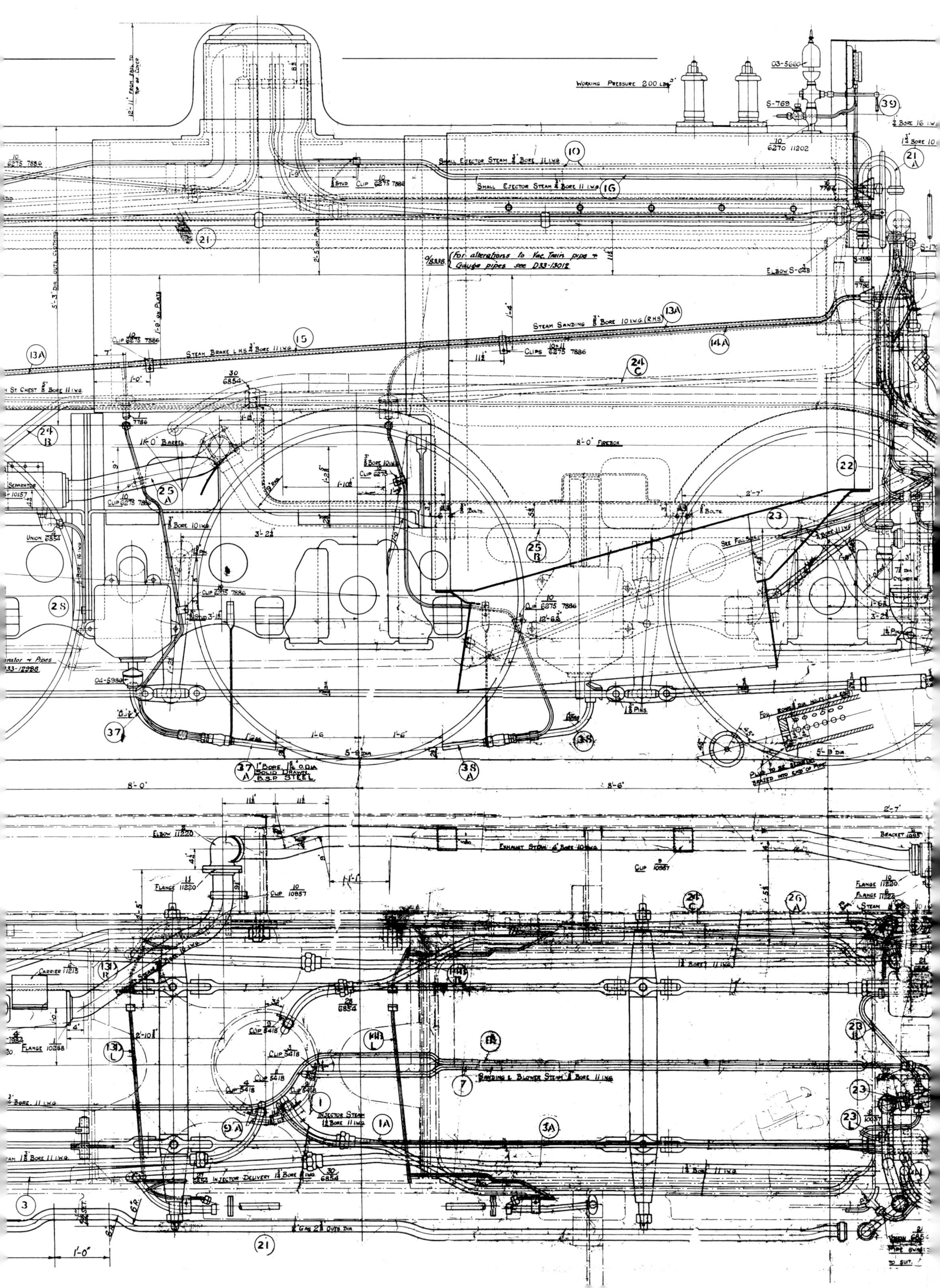

Working Pressure 200 lbs
Small Ejector Steam ¾" Bore 11 I.W.G.
Small Ejector Steam ¾" Bore 11 I.W.G.
For alterations to Vac. Train pipe & Gauge pipes see D33-13012
Steam Sanding ⅜" Bore 10 I.W.G. (R.H.S.)
Steam Brake L.H.S. ¾" Bore 11 I.W.G.
Clips 6275 7886
8'-0" Firebox
1'-0" Barrel
Separator
Union 6854
5'-8" Dia
5'-8" Dia
37 A 1" Bore, 1¼" O.Dia Solid Drawn B.S.P. Steel
8'-0"
8'-6"
Elbow 11220
Flange 11220
Exhaust Steam 4" Bore 10 I.W.G.
Clip 10857
Carrier 11215
Flange 10288
Sanding & Blower Steam ⅝" Bore 11 I.W.G.
Injector Steam 1⅜" Bore 11 I.W.G.
Injector Delivery 1⅜" Bore 11 I.W.G.
Bracket 11093
Flange 11220
Working Pressure

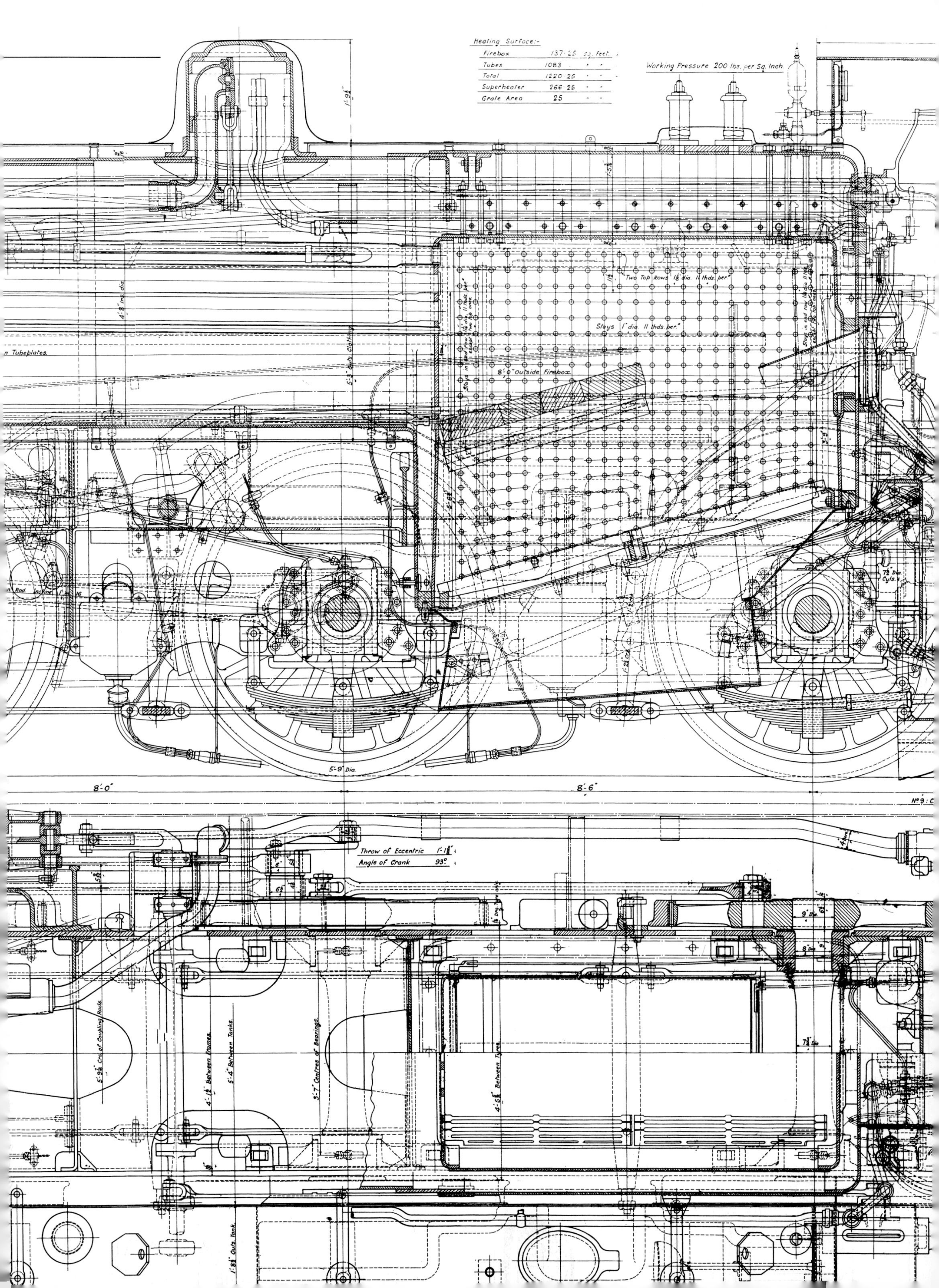

Heating Surface:-
Firebox 137·25 Sq. Feet.
Tubes 1083
Total 1220·25
Superheater 266·25
Grate Area 25
Working Pressure 200 lbs. per Sq. Inch.
Two Top Rows 1⅛" dia. 11 thds. per"
Stays 1" dia. 11 thds. per"
8'-0" Outside Firebox
n Tubeplates.
5'-9" Dia.
8'-0"
8'-6"
Throw of Eccentric 1'-1⅛"
Angle of Crank 93°
5'-9½" Crs. of Coupling Rods.
4'-1⅛" Between Frames.
5'-4" Between Tanks.
3'-7" Centres of Bearings.
4'-5⅜" Between Tyres.
9" Dia.
8" Dia.
7⅞" Dia.
7⅞" Dia. Cyls.

D28-10985 – General arrangement 2–6–4 tank engine

Caption on page 63

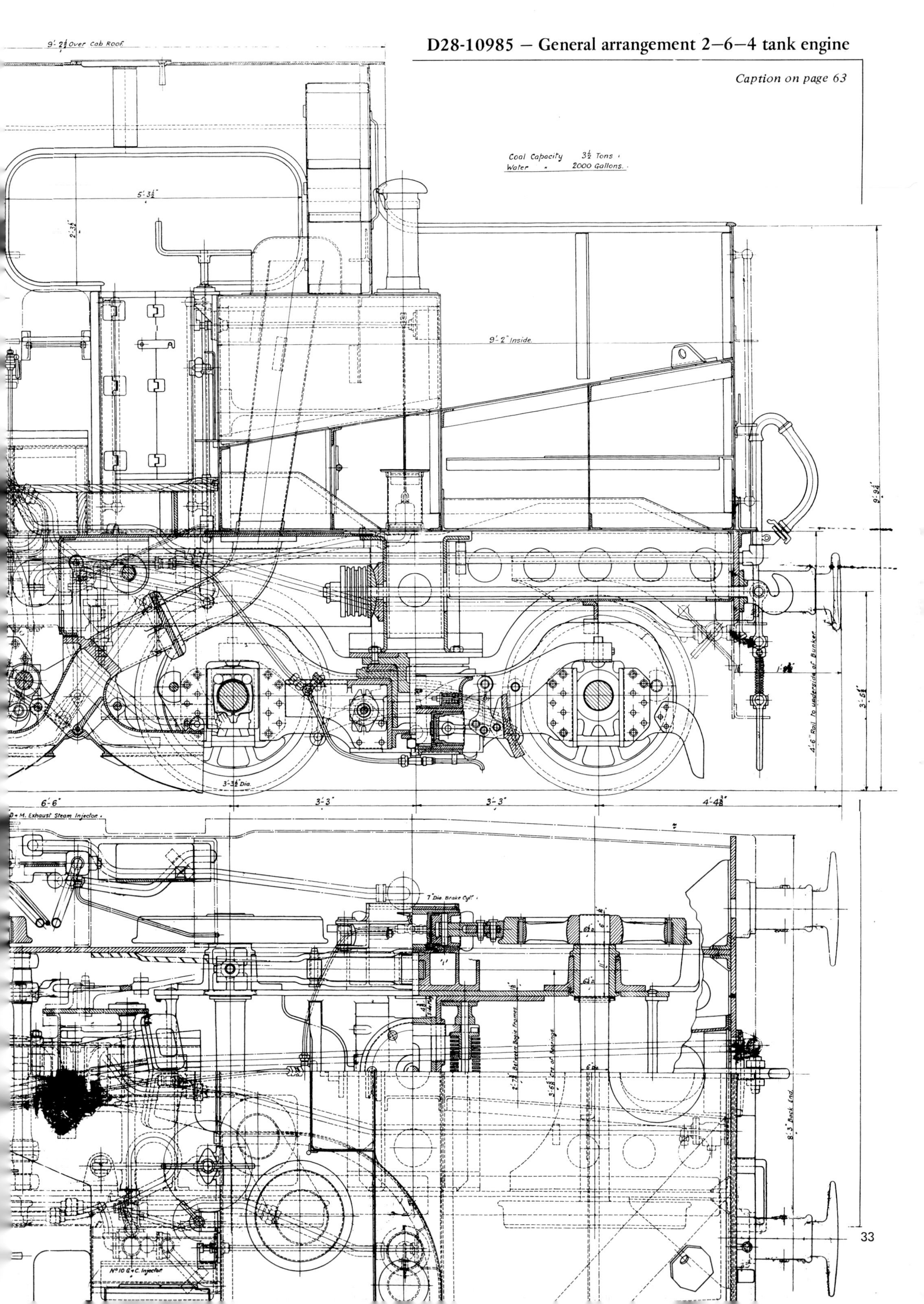

D27-1127 – Pipe and rod arrangement

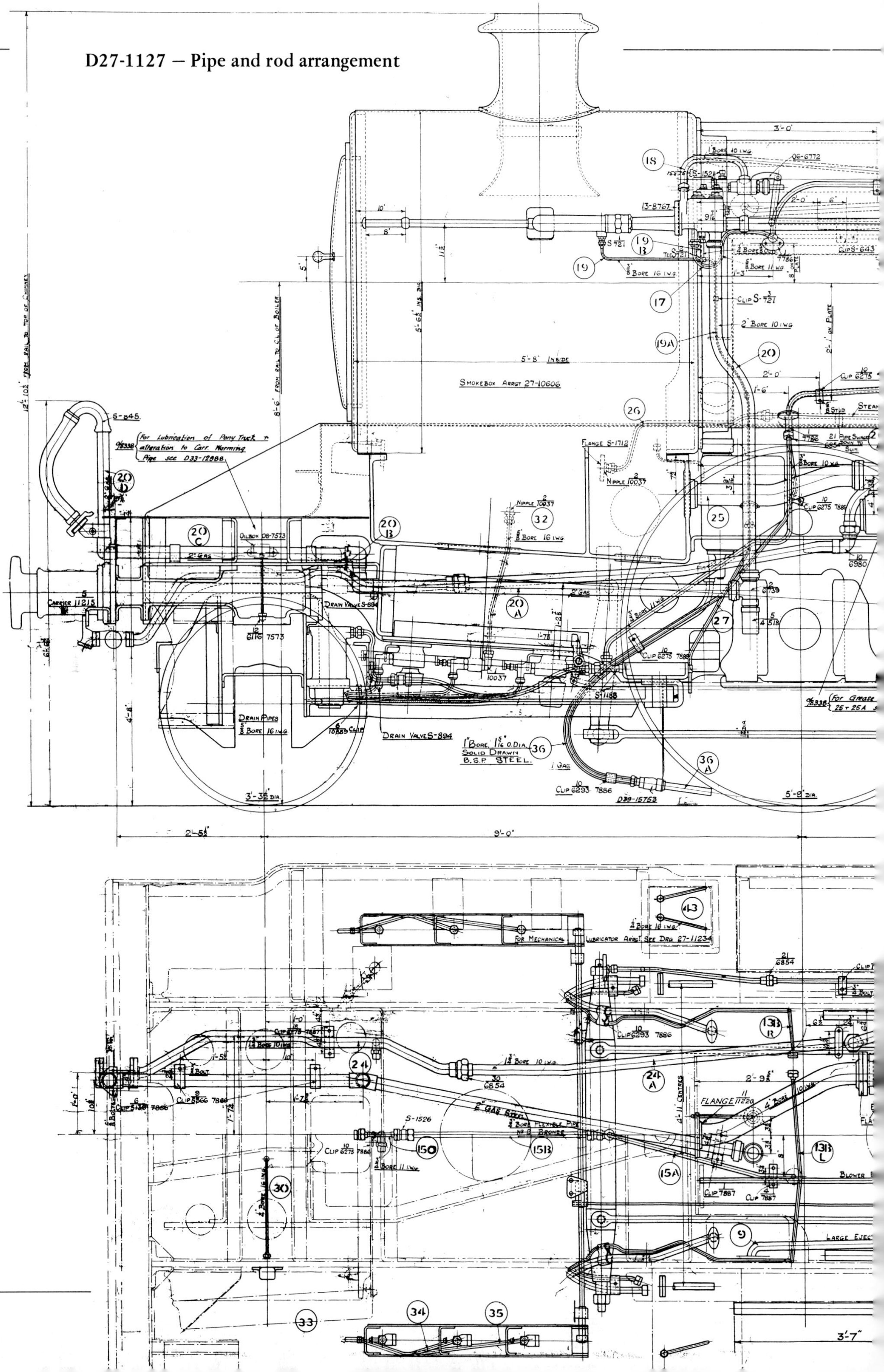

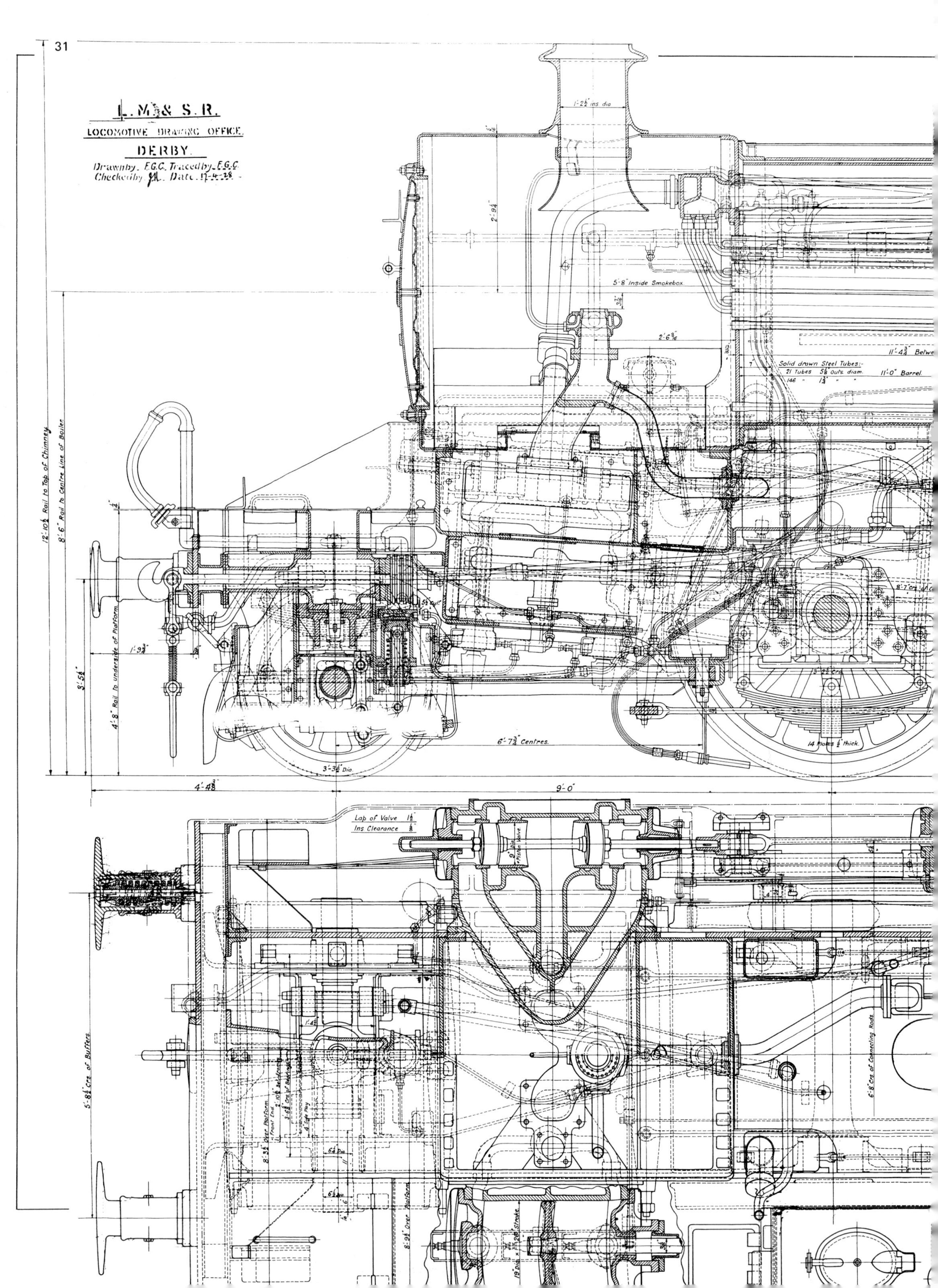
L.M.& S.R.
LOCOMOTIVE DRAWING OFFICE.
DERBY.
Drawn by. F.G.C. Traced by. F.G.C.
Date. 17-4-28
1'-2½" ins dia
2'-9¼"
5'-8" Inside Smokebox
3½"
2'-6¾"
Solid drawn Steel Tubes:-
21 Tubes 5⅛" Outs. diam.
146 " 1¾" " "
11'-0" Barrel
12'-10½" Rail to Top of Chimney
8'-6" Rail to Centre Line of Boiler
4'-8" Rail to underside of Platform
3'-5½"
1'-9¾"
6'-7½" Centres.
3'-3½" Dia.
14 Plates ½" thick.
4'-4⅜"
9'-0"
Lap of Valve 1½"
Ins Clearance ⅛"
9" Dia Piston Valve
5'-8½" Crs. of Buffers
6'-8" Crs. of Connecting Rods
8'-3⅛" Over Platform
19" Dia. 26" Stroke

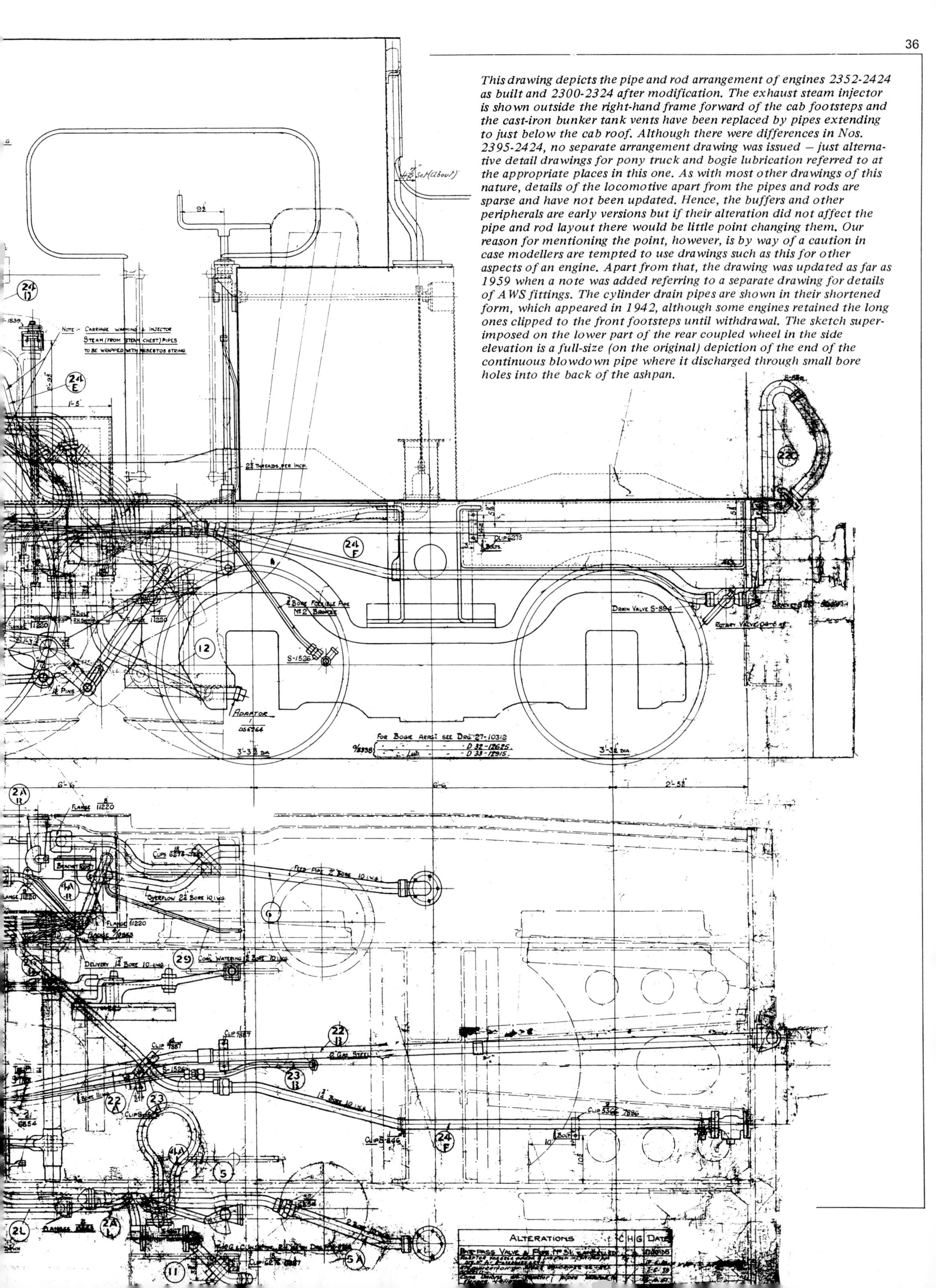

This drawing depicts the pipe and rod arrangement of engines 2352-2424 as built and 2300-2324 after modification. The exhaust steam injector is shown outside the right-hand frame forward of the cab footsteps and the cast-iron bunker tank vents have been replaced by pipes extending to just below the cab roof. Although there were differences in Nos. 2395-2424, no separate arrangement drawing was issued – just alternative detail drawings for pony truck and bogie lubrication referred to at the appropriate places in this one. As with most other drawings of this nature, details of the locomotive apart from the pipes and rods are sparse and have not been updated. Hence, the buffers and other peripherals are early versions but if their alteration did not affect the pipe and rod layout there would be little point changing them. Our reason for mentioning the point, however, is by way of a caution in case modellers are tempted to use drawings such as this for other aspects of an engine. Apart from that, the drawing was updated as far as 1959 when a note was added referring to a separate drawing for details of AWS fittings. The cylinder drain pipes are shown in their shortened form, which appeared in 1942, although some engines retained the long ones clipped to the front footsteps until withdrawal. The sketch superimposed on the lower part of the rear coupled wheel in the side elevation is a full-size (on the original) depiction of the end of the continuous blowdown pipe where it discharged through small bore holes into the back of the ashpan.

brackets, which allowed quite a lot of movement and so they tended to leak rather badly. Inside the left-hand side tank was a float that operated a water level indicator in front of the driver's spectacle glass. The tanks had fillers right at the front, so when the engine came to a halt, the water surging forward in them could put quite a bit of pressure on the underside of the lids. Even if the lids were properly secured, water would often squirt out, but if they were not fully tightened down, a deluge could erupt to the detriment of anyone nearby. Reportedly there were cases of lids bursting open even after being properly fastened. Since most of the stops were at passenger stations this was seen as a bad thing. As a result, O/8597 was issued in December 1933 for the fitting of anti-splash devices inside the tanks. These were basically V-shaped baffles in the upper parts of the tanks just behind the fillers, designed to stop the surge before it could do a great deal of damage. In November 1934 another order, 8927, was issued to complete modification of the class. The first 25 engines were built with air vent pipes projecting only a few inches above the side tanks but they were found to be too short and were lengthened to 1ft 2in from No. 2325 onwards. Earlier engines were then retro-fitted with the longer pipes. There were complaints from footplate crews, however, that the increased height vents obstructed the view from the cab, so O/4583 was issued in 1942 to fit replacements that were bent inwards out of the required line of vision. As there was no provision for draining away any water that collected on top of the tanks, a fair amount could end up sloshing around up there to the potential discomfort of enginemen and bystanders. It took until 1948 for someone to realise that cutting a one inch wide slot in the lip of the inner tank side would enable the water to drain away and until 1956 for it to be done to all the engines.

The first batch of locomotives was built with cast-iron mushroom vents to the bunker tank, the tops being immediately behind the cab and level with the spectacles. As on many other locomotives and tenders having this type of vent in the coal space, however, they were a source of trouble because of breakages as well as coal dust and grit finding its way into the tank and clogging filters and pipes. As a result, the design was altered and from No. 2324 the engines had 2in internal diameter wrought-iron pipes routed up the front corners of the bunker, round the outsides of the spectacles and under the roof overhang. Their open tops were right up against the roof line and so avoided much of the contamination problem. Earlier engines were soon modified to O/7402 issued on 6th June 1929. Total water capacity was 2,000 gallons, the side and bunker tanks being connected by tunnels under the cab. The rear of the bunker had a commode style vertical handrail above the left-hand buffer and two footsteps to the left of the centreline. Following trouble with vacuum standpipes being damaged by falling coal, O/9924 was issued on 4th January 1937 to fit protectors on the bunker rears.

The cab was pretty much the same as the 0–6–4 tank engine from which it was derived. On the first 24 locomotives built there were no access doors from the cab into the bunker. Thus, to clear a coal jam or to bring coal forward in the bunker, the fireman either had to poke around with the fire irons and shovel through the shovelling hole or he had to go outside and climb up onto the bunker. This was also a

One of the crimson engines was No. 2315, seen here with its original 10in high numbers. Note the cast-iron mushroom tank vents in the bunker, which were only fitted to the first batch of locomotives and removed from June 1929 onwards. V. R. ANDERSON (1381/20)

We cannot state with certainty which of the '2300s' wore yellow, shaded vermilion numbers and letters in the late 1930s, but 2377 seems almost certainly to have had them in this June 1939 picture. Transfers apart, its general appearance was typical of a 2375-2384 series engine at that time. Since being built, it had been fitted with later-type rear buffers and casings with diamond-pattern steps on top. As a result, it had reverted to thin spacing blocks. The cab cut-out had been shortened and a protector to prevent falling coal damaging the vacuum stand pipe had been fitted to the rear of the bunker. Note the turned-up ends to the footsteps, which were fitted from No. 2375 et seq. COLLECTION R. J. ESSERY

No. 2409 was built with a 'limousine cab' and other Stanier design alterations in October 1933. It was sent to Wigan where it was photographed in 1934 in lined black livery with what appear to be glazed lake and vermilion countershaded transfers. Note the white enamelled Central Division C16 shed code plate on the smokebox door. COLLECTION R. J. ESSERY

The last locomotive built using flush rivets in the construction of its tanks was No. 2374 in October 1929. Originally stationed at Manchester, it was photographed at St. Albans in May 1934, by which time it had lost its bogie and pony truck brakes and had the rear of its cab cut-out shortened. The original profile can just be seen by close examination. It was also the last engine to be built with flat footsteps although, by the time this picture was taken, the corners of its steps had been turned up. A. G. ELLIS (0886)

problem on the Midland 0–6–4Ts but nothing was changed until access doors were built into Nos. 2324 *et seq.* As they passed through the shops for heavy repairs, Nos. 2300–2323 were also fitted with doors to O/7402 issued in 1928. Other early modifications in the cab were to the firehole deflector plate, so that better light shielding was achieved for the driver, and improved handles and slides for the fire doors. In 1936 the fixings of the drivers' leg guards were made more secure and the slaking pipes were attached to the cab sides with Jubilee clips. Starting in about May 1937, extra angle-iron was fitted inside the joints between the roof and front and back plates.

Alterations to the rear frames and the different arrangement of the Stanier side bolster bogie on the last batch of engines can clearly be seen in this photograph of 'limousine cab' No. 2414. Note also the Stanier pattern wheels with triangular section rims, flat-section coupling rods, turned-up ends to the footsteps and full-height door in the cab. The coal bunker gives ample illustration of why the original short, cast-iron tank vents were prone to blockages and damage. AUTHORS' COLLECTION

At first the cabs had equal-sized cut-outs either side of the gangway. Whilst the design was quite acceptable when running chimney first, operating the other way round at any speed led to extremely uncomfortable blasts of coaldust-laden air assaulting the crew from round the sides of the cab and in through the cut-outs. At times it could be so bad that drivers had problems seeing the road ahead when running bunker first and firing was made extremely difficult. Under experiment D/LD/676, conducted in late 1932 and early 1933, Nos. 2339, 2370 and 2371 had the length of the rear cut-outs considerably reduced, which partially cured the problem. At least drivers could see to the rear at speed, although it could still be what Terry Essery described as 'an eye-watering experience'. Following positive reports on the experimental engines, the design of Nos. 2385–2394 was altered to have the shorter rear cutouts and, after vice-presidential authority was granted on 11th April, a start was made modifying twenty earlier locomotives to O/8382 issued on 3rd May 1933. Orders for altering the remainder were issued on 13th December 1933 and 22nd February 1935.

A more comprehensive solution to the draught problem was arrived at with the last thirty engines built between August 1933 and January 1934. Nos. 2395–2424 were fitted with what became known as 'limousine cabs', which had side windows and full-height doors with drop lights in the upper parts. The rear of the two side windows could be slid open and was originally secured with a spring-loaded catch. The catch, however, tended to work loose and in March 1933 O/9575 was issued for their replacement with unsprung handles and catches. From about August 1935 extra rain gutters were welded to the edges of the forward part of the roof above the side windows. Midland, Western and Central Division engines all seem to have been altered by the end of 1938 but the Northern Division was slower to modify its locomotives and some remained to be fitted at nationalisation. At least two of them, 42417 and 42421, were never fitted with the gutters and were withdrawn still with plain edges to their roofs. Alterations to driver's leg guards, Jubilee clips on slaking pipes, and extra roof angles were fitted as for the earlier 'open cab' engines. In 1941 a modification was ordered to the front windows so that they could be opened about 2in and secured in that position for extra ventilation when black-out screens were fitted (the earlier engines,

D27-10670 – Cab, side tank & bunker arrangement *Caption on page 63*

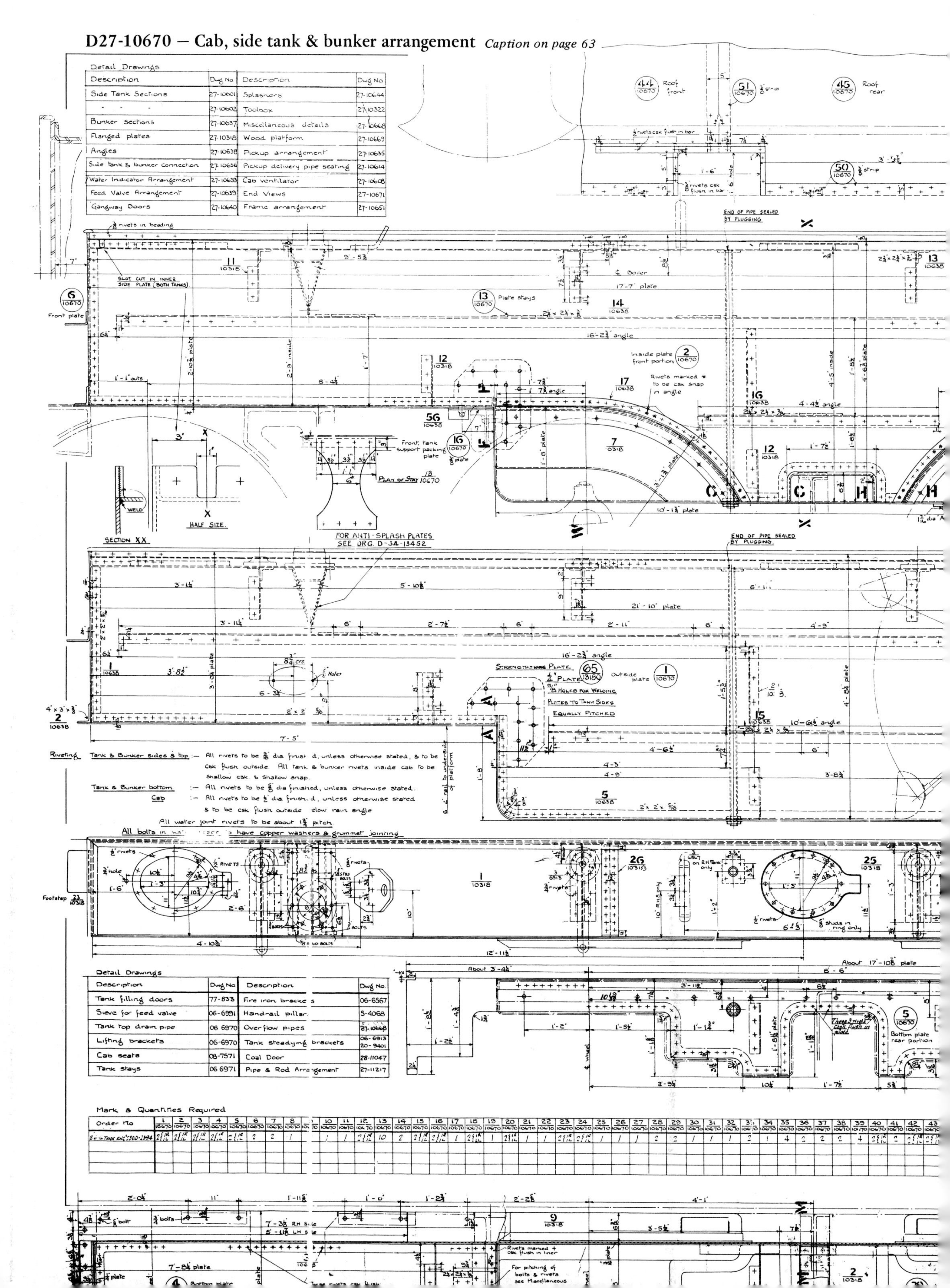

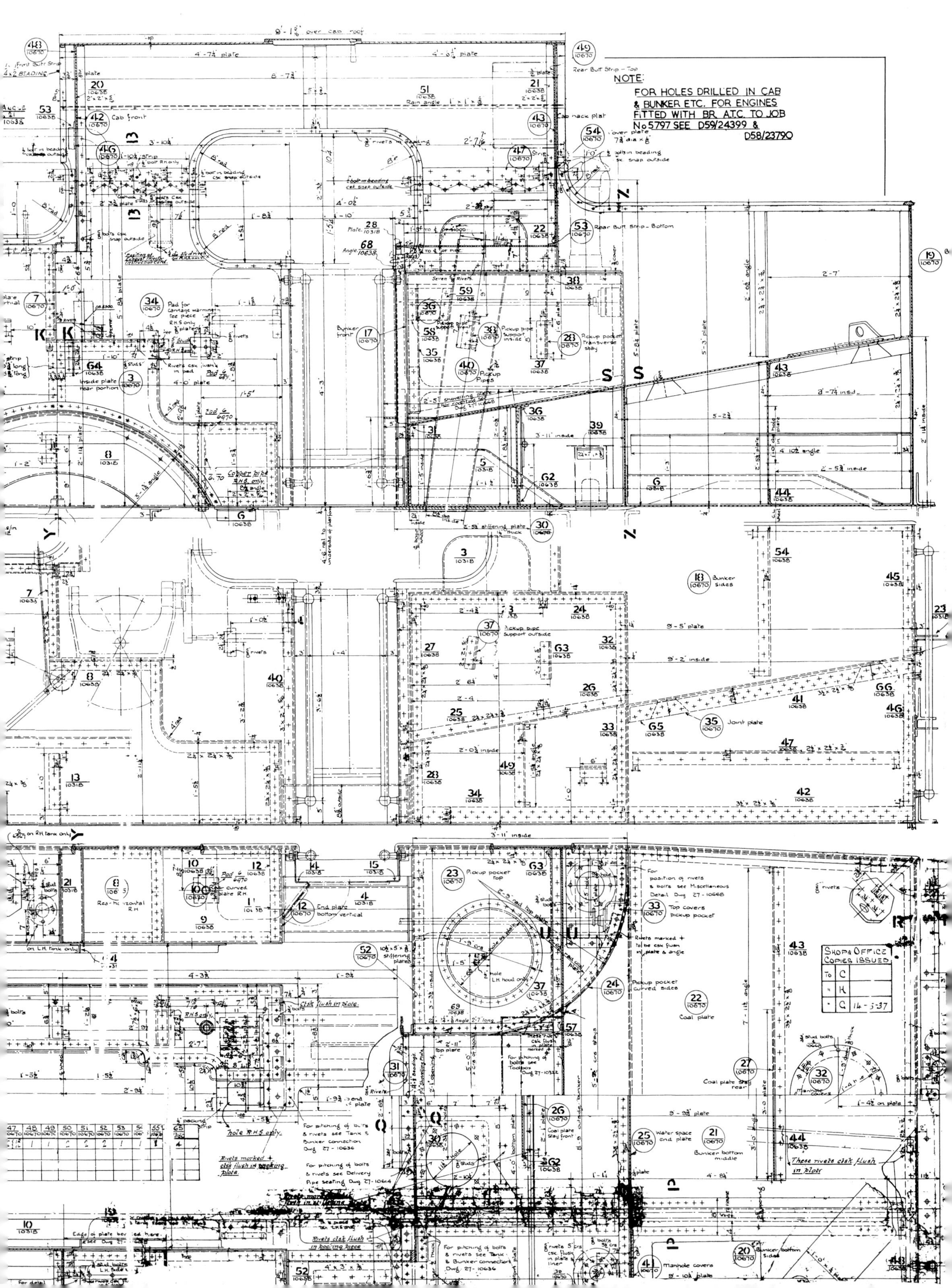

9'-1 5/8" over cab roof
NOTE:
FOR HOLES DRILLED IN CAB & BUNKER ETC. FOR ENGINES FITTED WITH BR. A.T.C. TO JOB No 5797 SEE D59/24399 & D58/23790
Rear Butt Strip - Top
Rear Butt Strip - Bottom
Cab front
Cab back plate
Rain angle
Bunker front
Pickup pipe support inside
Pickup pocket transverse stay
Pickup pipes
Pad for carriage warming tee piece R.H.S. only
Inside plate rear portion
Copper pipe R.H.S. only
stiffening plate
Bunker sides
Pickup pipe support outside
Joint plate
Rear horizontal R.H
End plate bottom vertical
Pickup pocket top
Top covers pickup pocket
Pickup pocket curved sides
Coal plate
Coal plate stay rear
Manhole covers
Water space end plate
Bunker bottom middle
Bunker bottom sides
Coal plate stay front
For position of rivets & bolts see Miscellaneous Detail Dwg 27-10668
For pitching of bolts & rivets see Tank & Bunker connection Dwg 27-10636
For pitching of bolts & rivets see Delivery Pipe seating Dwg 27-10614
For pitching of bolts & rivets see Toolbox Dwg 27-10322
These rivets csk flush in plate
Rivets marked + to be csk flush
Hole R.H.S. only
SHOP & OFFICE COPIES ISSUED
14-5-37

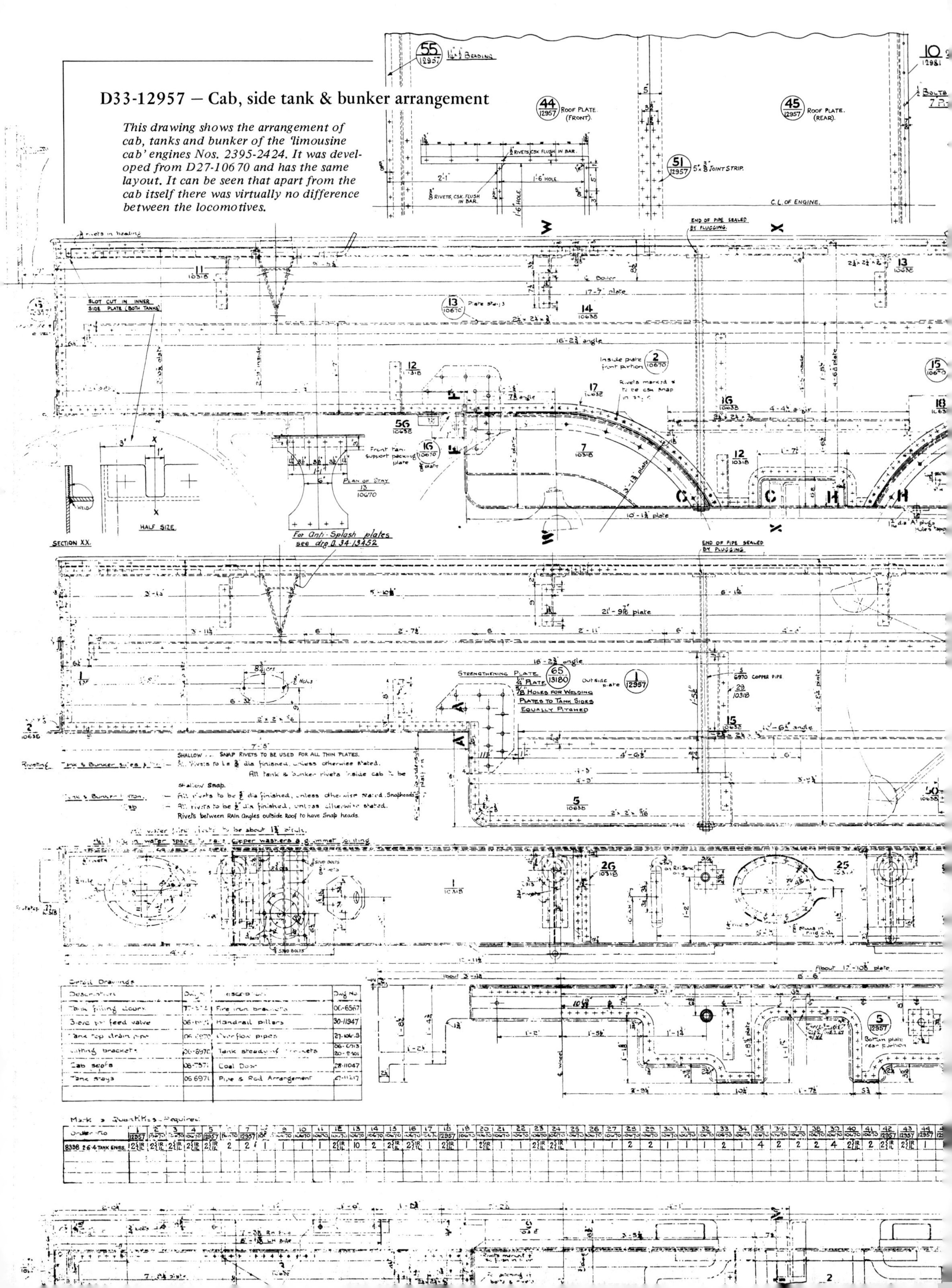

D33-12957 – Cab, side tank & bunker arrangement

This drawing shows the arrangement of cab, tanks and bunker of the 'limousine cab' engines Nos. 2395-2424. It was developed from D27-10670 and has the same layout. It can be seen that apart from the cab itself there was virtually no difference between the locomotives.

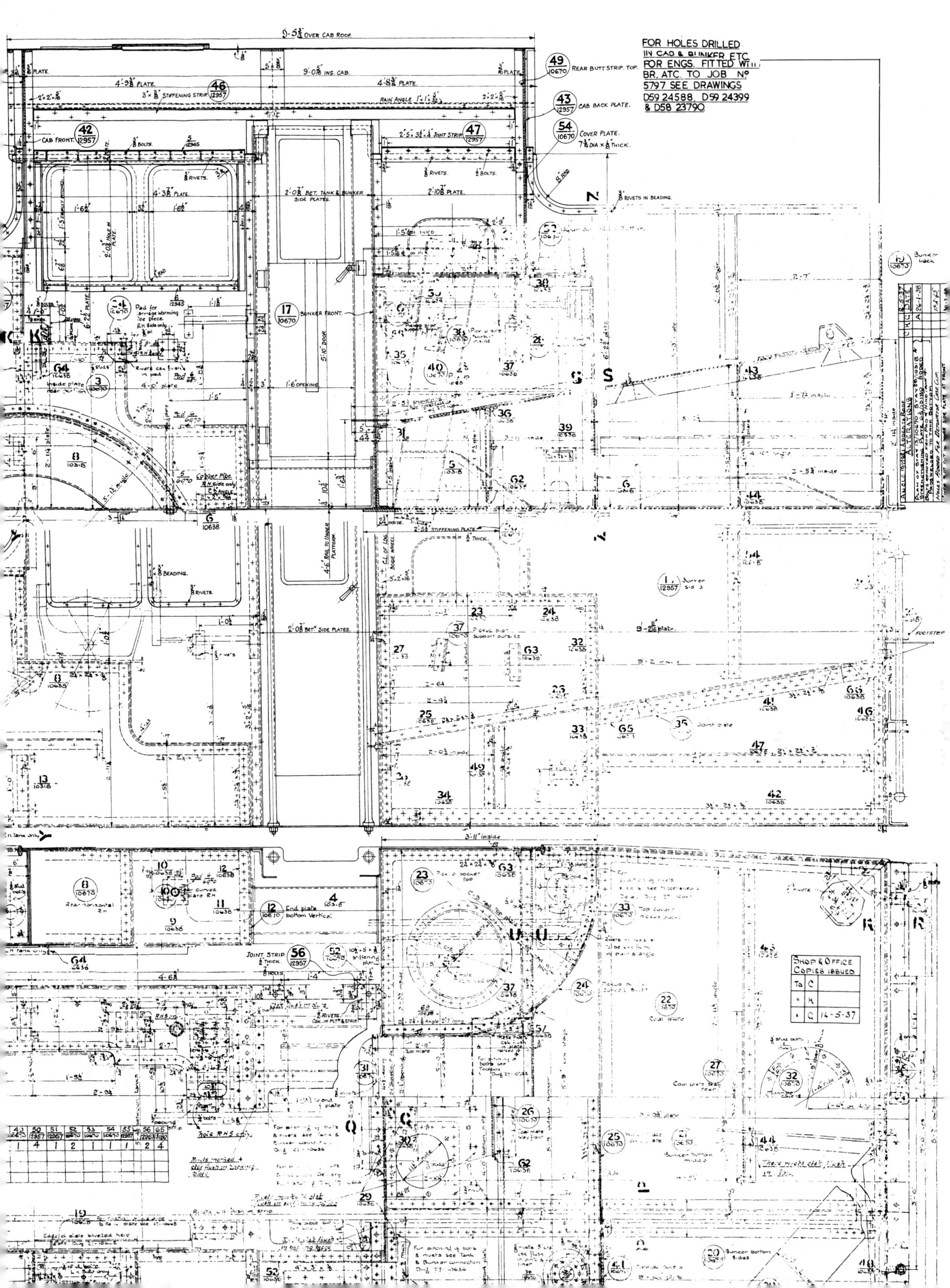

OVER CAB ROOF
FOR HOLES DRILLED
IN CAB & BUNKER ETC.
FOR ENGS. FITTED WI
BR. ATC. TO JOB No
5797 SEE DRAWINGS
D59 24588, D59 24399
& D58 23790.
PLATE.
INS. CAB.
STIFFENING STRIP.
RAIN ANGLE
REAR BUTT STRIP. TOP.
CAB BACK PLATE.
COVER PLATE.
THICK.
CAB FRONT.
BOLTS.
RIVETS.
JOINT STRIP
BET. TANK & BUNKER SIDE PLATES.
RIVETS IN BEADING.
BUNKER FRONT.
DOOR
OPENING
Inside plate rear portion
Copper Pipe
STIFFENING PLATE
RAIL TO UNDER PLATFORM.
BEADING.
BET. SIDE PLATES.
FOOTSTEP
Joint plate
Rear horizontal
End plate bottom Vertical
JOINT STRIP
HOLES.
Coal plate
SHOP & OFFICE
COPIES ISSUED
14-5-37
Bunker bottom sides

having swivelling front windows, did not require modification). Between December 1945 and May 1946 some 'side window' engines had the full-height doors removed and half-height gangway doors fitted instead to NWO 5494. Locomotives we know to have been altered were 2395, 2397, 2401, 2404, 2405, 2410, 2411, 2413 and 2421 but we can find no record of why it was done.

Not all the '2300s' had full water pickup apparatus fitted. One that did was No. 2349, seen here with a train of very mixed stock at the start of Brock water troughs. From the condition of the engine, without lifting holes in the frames and still having full-width cabside cut-outs and flat footsteps, we would hazard a guess that the photograph was taken between 1930 and 1935.
A. G. ELLIS (28221)

WATER PICK-UP APPARATUS

The '2300s' were designed to have water scoops between the hind coupled wheels and leading bogie wheels that could pick up in either direction. The equipment was, however, quite costly to manufacture and maintain and in January 1930 No. 2309 had the external apparatus removed. In July 1931 a decision was taken that engines not regularly needing to use them weren't to be fitted with the scoops or operating gear and an order was issued for another twelve engines to have the equipment removed. There was much confusion over which engines did and did not have scoops fitted and a decision was made that nine of the locomotives in the 1932 building programme would have them omitted instead of removal from earlier ones. This did not happen as planned, though, and from the information we have it would appear that Nos. 2300, 2302–2307, 2318, 2319 and 2322 had the external apparatus removed and only two of the 2375–2384 batch were built with full equipment. One of them was 2375 but we haven't been able to identify the other. Nos. 2385–2394 all had complete pick-up apparatus fitted from new but of the last thirty engines built, only 2402–2414 were fully equipped, the others having just the internal portions fitted and the frames drilled for the scoops and operating gear. In 1934 full equipment was refitted to Nos. 2300 and 2302–2307.

AWS

The idea of repeating signal aspects in locomotive cabs was one with which Stanier had been involved for many years before joining the LMS. In December 1914 he was one of five engineers to present papers on the subject at a symposium held by the Institution of Mechanical Engineers. There he outlined what was to become the Great Western system in which a shoe on the locomotive made mechanical and electrical contact with a ramp between the rails, but by the time he joined the LMS, that system had been bettered. The installation on the ex-LT&S section of the Midland Division was known as the Hudd system and it had the advantage that no contact was required between locomotive and ramp. Thus, there was no potential problem either of poor electrical contact, because of frost or foreign objects, or mechanical failure due to shoe movement being outside operating limits. The system worked as follows. Two magnets, or inductors, were placed several yards apart approximately 200 yards on the approach side of a distant signal, the first being a permanent magnet and the second an electromagnet energised only when the aspect was clear. A receiver assembly on the locomotive, set about 5in above rail level, would pass over the first magnet, which would rotate an armature and open a valve. This allowed air to enter an evacuated pipe and operate a warning horn at the same time as reducing the vacuum. If the aspect was at caution, the valve would remain open and, when the degree of vacuum had decayed sufficiently, the brake valve would operate and gradually apply the train brakes. If the aspect was clear, however, the second magnet would be energised and would return the valve to the closed position, cancelling the warning horn and closing the air valve so that the vacuum was quickly restored. The horn and brake application could also be cancelled by the driver pulling a small lever that caused a permanent magnet to be drawn through a coil and so induce an electric current. This current would energise a resetting coil in the receiver, which would have the same effect as the second track magnet being energised. However, cancellation by the driver also caused an indicator disc to rotate and show a black and yellow aspect as a reminder that the last distant signal had been passed at caution. Thus, the system was not entirely foolproof and, although sometimes referred to as Automatic Train Control, should really be called an Automatic Warning System or AWS. On 28th June 1935 O/9156 was issued for the fitting of '2300' Class engines Nos. 2325–2327 of St. Albans shed with the Hudd apparatus. In October 1948 No. 42328, also of St. Albans, was fitted with the same system.

Because of its advantages over the GWR version, it was the Hudd type that was developed into the British Railways AWS system after nationalisation. Some of the '2300s' were equipped in 1960–1961 at a cost of around £390 and could be identified by the receiver mounted behind a protector plate under the front buffer beam and an electrical conduit clipped to the bottom edge of the footplate angle from buffer beam to cab. Unfortunately we have been unable to locate an installation drawing.[21] Locomotives we know to have been fitted with AWS were 42306, 42315, 42316, 42351, 42353, 42359, 42366, 42367, 42368, 42374, 42406, 42407, 42409, 42411 and 42422.

THE ENGINES IN SERVICE

Another of the early lined crimson lake engines was 2308, photographed in charge of a selection of coaching stock shortly after entering traffic in January 1928. No. 2308 was the third engine to be built with the exhaust steam injector outside the right-hand frame and in this picture it is located in its final position.
AUTHORS' COLLECTION

When new, the engines were sent to districts that provided motive power for intensive suburban operation, the 1927–1929 production being distributed as follows:

2300–2302 and 2325–2329	Cricklewood
2303–2306 and 2342	Bradford
2307–2309	Nottingham
2310–2315, 2355–2358, 2372–2374	Manchester
2316–2322	Swansea (these engines actually went to other districts initially but ended up at Swansea within a few months)
2323–2324 and 2365–2371	Buxton
2330–2335	Leicester
2336–2341	Nottingham
2343–2348 and 2354	Stoke
2349–2353	Shrewsbury
2359–2361	Carnforth
2362–2364	Lancaster

Engines built in the 1930s were sent initially to the following districts:

2375–2382, 2385, 2386, 2388 and 2389	Willesden (2385 and 2386 went to Crewe for a short time at first)
2383, 2384, 2405, 2406 and 2408	Newton Heath
2387	Stafford
2390	Bangor (Crewe for a short time initially)
2391–2394	Crewe
2395–2399, 2403 and 2404	Longsight (2396 and 2398 to Stoke for a short time at first and 2404 to Swansea for 1 month)
2400	Stockport
2401 and 2402	Carnforth (2401 initially to Shrewsbury for 2 months)
2407 and 2411–2414	Accrington
2409 and 2410	Wigan
2415–2417	Polmadie
2418–2424	Greenock

On 11th March 1929 the Chief General Superintendent's Department issued a circular on route availability for the '2300' Class. Excluding joint lines, they were allowed over all routes ***(except those shown in the table on page 46).***

An additional note pointed out that there would be some restrictions as to certain other sidings, crossover roads, bridges carrying coal drops, landings in goods yards, etc on curves and that if there was any doubt, the matter should be put forward to Headquarters. We have been unable to locate details of the restrictions pertaining to the Northern Division. In later years, alterations to alignments, bridges, installations, etc. meant that many of the above restrictions were lifted and the 2–6–4 tanks could be seen on previously banned routes.

The performance of the '2300s' was all that could have been hoped for with sharp acceleration and a top speed well into the 80s when hauling the suburban trains that were their bread and butter. In the 1930s they were frequently recorded reaching 80 mph with 190 tons loaded weight trains between Watford and Euston and improving on the booked 21 minutes for the 17½ mile run. They often worked the 'Mancunian' between Manchester and Wilmslow and on many occasions the 270 ton train was recorded passing through East Didsbury at over 70 mph. There were many other instances of sparkling performances by the engines on different parts of the LMS system and it is true to say that they were masters of the tasks set them. Even in post-nationalisation days, generally they remained on the workings for which they were designed and escaped the fate of slipping into gentle obscurity that befell many of their contemporaries.

The '2300s' were popular with footplate crews but, as Terry Essery put it, just about at the bottom of the ratings list for shed crews when it came to disposal. Preparation was straightforward and access to all parts of the engine good. Filling the sandboxes was easy compared with some other locomotives, but wielding fire irons in the enclosed cab could be tricky. The fireman's choice of shovel was also problematic as the long one, which was better suited to the bunker and firebox, could result in grazed knuckles but the short version wouldn't reach far enough into the bunker and required an awkward stance. The large grate and deep firebox made maintenance of the fire reasonably straightforward and the draughting was good. Room in the cab was a bit restricted and floor space limited due to the platforms at

Vermilion and glazed lake shaded, or 'countershaded', transfers were used on engines from, we think, 2350 onwards, albeit possibly not exclusively. No. 2364 was typical of locomotives in the 2350-2374 series as running in the mid to late 1930s in that it had countershaded letters and numbers but its footsteps did not have turned-up ends, merely bent-up corners, and its tank sides were flush-riveted. By the time it was photographed at Crewe South on 19th April 1936, it had lost the rear oil cup from the upper slidebars but had not had the front one replaced by an oil box. Bogie and pony truck brakes had been removed and the cab cut-outs had been shortened. Its original buffer casings were mounted on thick spacers, the vacuum stand pipe had been extended, and the engine still had its original chimney. L. HANSON (838)

ROUTES OVER WHICH THE '2300' CLASS WERE NOT INITIALLY PERMITTED TO WORK

Midland Division

Routes:

Petteril Bridge Goods; Hawes Junction to Hawes; Keighley to Oxenhope; Middlestown Junction to Dewsbury (Goods); Barnsley to Cudworth (North and South); Barnsley West to Monk Spring Junction; Barrow Hill and Staveley to Mansfield via Glapwell or Clowne; Westhouses to Mansfield via Teversall; Pye Bridge or Codnor Park to Ambergate or Little Eaton Junction; Langley Mill to Ripley; Basford Junction to Kimberley; Sutton Junction to Sutton; Kimbolton to Huntingdon; Cricklewood to Acton Wells Junction; Hornsey Road to Barking; Woodgrange Park to East Ham; Fenchurch Street to Plaistow; Upminster to Romford and Grays; Barking to Grays and Pitsea; Ancoats to Ashburys; Chinley South Junction to Chinley East Junction; Miller's Dale to Buxton; Stenson Junction to Chellaston; Chellaston East Junction to Ashby; Evesham to Ashchurch; Stratford on Avon lines; Stonehouse to Stroud and Nailsworth; Bristol to Mangotsfield and Bath.

Branches:

Barnoldswick; Grassington; Otley; Snydale; Rotherham Westgate; Sheffield Nunnery; Wicker Goods Station; Unstone; Killamarsh; Sheepbridge Goods; Brampton Goods; Grassmoor; Pilsley; Blackwell; Holwell; Cottesmore; Loddington; Hitchin; Hemel Hempstead; Thames Haven; Hayfield; Wirksworth; Netherseal; Stockingford; West Bridge; Burton Brewery Sidings; Brownhills; Halesowen; Dursley; Tewkesbury.

Colliery branches:

Featherstone; Wharncliffe; Aston; Mapperley; Mansfield; Rufford.

Western Division

Routes:

Bullgill to Brigham; Workington to Cockermouth; Whitehaven, Cleator and Egremont line between Birks Bridge and Marron Junction, Cockermouth, Keswick and Penrith, Carlisle goods lines to London Road Junction, Crown Street Warehouse and Rome Street Junction; Tebay – South Durham Junction Down Line; Carnforth – Junction from Furness Bay platforms to Furness Down Line; Knott End Line; Bridges over Lancaster Canal at Preston Coal Yards; Standish Junction and Red Rock to Hindley and Bamfurlong via Whelley; Pennington, Leigh and Tyldesley, Pennington, West Leigh, Atherton and Bolton; Siding Bridge 37A at Latchford; Liverpool – Gulf Structure at North Docks, No.5 Hydraulic Drawbridge at Garston Docks; Birkenhead – Portion of No. 2 Bridge leading to Abbey Street coal yard, No. 59 Bridge to Coal Yard; Manchester – Bridge No. 62A at Gloucester Street, Slow Lines between Ordsall Lane and Exchange Station; Guide Bridge to Crowthorne Junction and Guide Bridge Goods; Park, Miles Platting and Manchester London Road; Holyhead Mail Pier Jetty; Anglesey Central Line – Holland Arms to Amlwych; Hereford, Hay and Brecon Line – Hereford to Three Cocks Junction; Swansea Vale Line and branches; Hindlow and Ladmanlow; Parsley Hay and Cromford (High Peak Junction); Haydon Square Depot; Poplar (High Street Bridge) to Poplar Dock, Crossover road between Nos. 3 & 4 bay platforms in Shrewsbury Joint Station.

Branches:

Coniston; Lakeside; Little Hulton; Runcorn Docks; Newfields; Chesterton; Grange; Adderley Green; Harborne; Leighswood; Victoria (or Wyken); Newport Pagnell; Haydon Square Depot; not to exceed 20 mph on the Hincaster Branch.

Colliery Branches:

Haydock; Havannah; Pemberton – Norley.

Central Division

Routes:

East Lancashire Lines between Ribble Viaduct and Preston Station; Blackburn to Hellifield (until bridge at Clitheroe is propped); Wyre Dock Sidings; Hindley to Pemberton; Hesketh Bank to Tarleton; Bradley Wood Junction to Wyke and Norwood Green; Mirfield to Huddersfield.

Branches:

Deepdale Goods; Hoddlesden Goods; Kearsley Goods; Silkstone Colliery.

A highly unusual, if not unique, modification was the addition of coal rails to the bunker of this unidentified '2300' photographed at Coniston on 13th August 1934. We have never seen any reference to this alteration and cannot shed any further light on when it was carried out or to which engine(s).
S. V. BLENCOWE

No. 2341 was stationed at Nottingham when this photograph was taken there in 1936. Since being built in April 1929, the engine had been altered to have lifting holes in its front frames, 2½in blocks behind the buffer housings, a Stanier chimney, turned-up corners to its footsteps and shortened cab cut-outs.
V. R. ANDERSON (1383/36)

either side. The roof ventilator of the early engines was not very efficient and it could get rather warm in the cab, especially for the fireman, when running chimney first, so the front windows were normally opened to provide some cooling air. When running bunker first, however, the disturbed air stream around and through the bunker caused severe draughts to enter the cabs of the pre-Stanier engines, even after modifications to the cut-outs, and in winter the fireman was often glad of the physical exertions of firing. Geoff Holt, who knew a number of Stockport drivers in the 1940s and 1950s, says that they were known as 'pneumonia engines' as a result. Nos. 2329 and 2374 received the same epithet when they were sent to work on the Tilbury line. The Stanier side window 'limousine' cabs were much more comfortable. According to Terry Essery, 'You could stay reasonably cool in the summer with the windows and ventilator open without being blasted to pieces bunker first and they were more snug in winter.' One thing that all footplatemen with whom we have spoken were unanimous about was the quality of the ride. At all speeds and in both directions they were smooth and fairly quiet, in stark contrast to many contemporary locomotives. Terry Essery described the riding qualities at 80 mph as 'truly superb – quiet, stable and with no fuss'. He also said that they never seemed short of steam no matter how hard they were thrashed.

For disposal crews, however, the '2300s' were far less popular. When the engine was stationary, the cab could get very hot, especially in summer, which wasn't so bad for a train crew but for disposal men who had to labour in those conditions it could be almost untenable. There were just two large sets of firebars, which couldn't be manipulated to drop the clinker into the ashpan so it had to be dragged out through the firehole. Unfortunately, the restricted space in the cab meant that only a short clinker shovel could be used, which wouldn't reach to the front of the firebox. Additionally, the shovel would often catch on parts of the cab and its fittings when trying to manoeuvre it out full of red-hot ash and clinker. Since the floorboards were invariably oil-soaked this frequently resulted in small fires in the cab, so the floorboards of 2–6–4 tank engines were generally well charred. Fortunately, the provision of passenger grade coal and the relatively short runs on which they were employed, meant that smokebox and ashpan cleaning was relatively easy. None of the '2300s', however, benefited from such labour-saving devices as self-cleaning smokeboxes or rocking grates.

With regard to maintenance, their Achilles heel was the smokebox before the final solution was arrived at when cast-steel cylinders were fitted. The side tanks also leaked badly but, that apart, they were reliable engines and even the exhaust steam injectors, once they were moved out from their original location, didn't give nearly as much trouble as they did on some other LMS locomotives. One annoyance for fitters was that the spring links were fixed and solid. If adjustment was needed, the only way to do it was to remove them and have the smiths alter the length on a trial and error basis until the required change had been effected.

In the early 1930s there were several trials of speed indicators and recorders on the LMS in connection with accelerated services. One such, to do with acceleration of the Broad St., Euston and Bletchley trains, was the fitting of a Flaman speed indicator to No. 2424 to O/8569 issued on 30th November 1933. By November 1934 it had been removed and was fitted to No. 2517. In March 1936 Nos. 2321 and 2343 were fitted with modified baffle plates for the sliding firedoors as an experiment.

This photograph illustrates the difficulties of deciding whether an engine had gold, countershaded vermilion and glazed lake or chrome yellow, shaded vermilion transfers. A few days after instructions were issued to use vermilion and glazed lake countershaded transfers, No. 2354 was turned out from Derby Works paint shop on 20th June 1929. By the time the picture was taken at Bourne End on 1st May 1938, it had been repainted twice, but which transfers were used is uncertain. Try as we may, we cannot say for certain although countershaded gold looks likely.
COLLECTION R. J. ESSERY

One of the duties, apart from hauling fast suburban passenger trains for which the '2300s' were well known was as 'Tebay bankers' on the climb up to Shap. This photograph shows 'limousine cab' Nos. 2404 and 2424 waiting at Shap summit to return to Tebay after assisting a train up the bank sometime between 20th April 1946, when 2404 was rebuilt with new cylinders and outside steam pipes, and 18th September 1948 when it was renumbered 42404. Both locomotives were quite smartly turned out in plain black with chrome yellow, shaded vermilion transfers and had been fitted with protectors on the bunker rears to prevent damage to the vacuum stand pipes from falling coal. AUTHORS' COLLECTION

The down 2.0 p.m. ex-Manchester Victoria and 2.15 p.m. ex-Liverpool Exchange to Glasgow and Edinburgh train was photographed near Scout Green on 9th June 1950. It was headed by Class 5 No. 44708 and piloted from Oxenholme to Shap summit by '2300' Class No. 42314 with operating number 82. Both engines were in unlined black with 'BRITISH RAILWAYS' in cream Gill Sans 10in letters on the tank and tender sides. No. 42314 had its number applied to the bunker sides in 12in 1946-style numerals and on its smokebox in a Derby/Bow Works-style plate.
E. D. BRUTON (P5384)

Twelve months later 2321 was reboilered, followed by 2343 in June 1937, and we can find no more record of the trial. Another experiment about which we have no information other than the Works Order was the fitting of an overflow pipe to the coal bunker of one engine for testing on Loughborough water troughs to O/9575 on 13 May 1936.

Between 1933 and 1935 the LMS compared the costs of operating individual locomotives and the '2300s' came out very well. Their average annual mileage was 40,460, which was bettered only by the 3-cylinder Stanier 2–6–4 tank engines at 40,492. In comparison, the various Baltic tanks did around 32,000, the L&NWR 4–6–2Ts 26,000, CR 4–6–2Ts 20,000, LT&S 4–4–2 tank engines 35,674, Standard 2–6–2Ts 32,879, L&YR superheated 2–4–2Ts 27,620 and saturated engines 24,294, MR 0–4–4Ts 31,051 and 64XX tank engines 32,209. Their average 121,160 miles between general repairs was bettered only by the North Staffordshire locomotives and no engine of comparable size could equal their coal issue per engine mile of 49.01 lb. Total cost per engine mile, including repairs, renewals, interest and coal, was 10.25 (old) pence, which was only beaten by the smaller 2–4–2Ts and 0–4–4Ts. Weekdays in service were 251 on average, only the 3-cylinder tank engines' 256 being higher, and average number of days under repair was 55. Whilst this was not the best, the reasons were complex and it was still a respectable figure.

The Bradford area was common ground for the 2–6–4 tanks and a regular sight was No. 42411, photographed leaving Exchange station with a Mirfield train in January 1956. The picture provides a graphic illustration of why the tall side tank vents were altered in the 1940s to be out of the driver's line of sight from the spectacle.
R. S. CARPENTER

LIVERY

There were four distinct livery styles generally applied to the '2300s'. Within those styles, however, there were many variations and some exceptions. Fifteen of the first 25 engines were turned out in fully-lined LMS crimson lake and the remainder in lined black. Eventually the early engines, too, became black, but photographic evidence suggests that it wasn't until at least 1933 that the last example of the crimson livery disappeared. During the war they were painted plain black and after nationalisation BR lined black livery was applied. We also have evidence that one engine was painted in a fifth style, which was unlined BR green.

Eighteen months after being built, No. 2300 went back to Derby Works for a heavy repair. By that time an order had been issued for the original 25 engines to be modified as they passed through the shops in line with the later ones then being built. In June 1929 No. 2300 reappeared in the condition shown with extended vents on its side tanks and other internal alterations described in the text. Its livery had also been slightly altered with 14in numerals on the bunker and the addition of a 'P' to the power classification. It had also received a cast shed code plate. When this photograph was taken on 22nd June, the engine was awaiting its return to traffic with the smokebox door numbers still painted black and 3-link couplings on the front hook. The fitting at the rear of the smokebox above the tank was the combined large and small ejector for evacuating the automatic vacuum brake equipment. H. C. CASSERLEY (6009)

LMS LINED CRIMSON LAKE

When construction began in late 1927, LMS passenger locomotives were painted in lined crimson lake and so that was the scheme in which the first '2300s' appeared. On 7th February 1928, however, instructions were issued that henceforth only five classes were to be painted crimson lake – the 'Royal Scots', 'Claughtons', L&Y Class 8 engines, 'Prince of Wales' Class and the standard Compounds. This was cancelled on 25th February but then reinstated on 24th March. Whilst this change and counter-change was going on, Nos. 2312 to 2317 were going through the Derby paintshop with the result that Nos. 2300–2311 and 2314–2316 were initially crimson whereas 2312, 2313 and 2317 onwards were black.

The crimson was reputedly the same as Midland Lake and lining the same straw shade as used by the Midland, i.e., paler than the middle chrome yellow used in post- 1935 LMS paint schemes.[22] Details of the crimson lake livery were as follows:

Ownership was indicated by 14in high gold, shaded black 'LMS' serif transfers spaced 40in apart on the tank sides, although it is possible that at least the first few engines had the characters handpainted before transfers became available. Locomotive stock numbers were in 10in high gold, shaded black scroll and serif transfers but possibly hand-painted initially. The power classification, for a while 3 on at least Nos.

Frames	Inside faces vermilion. Outside faces, motion brackets, valve spindle guides and brackets, life guards, injectors, pipework, brake and sanding gear black.
Axles	Vermilion, ends black.
Wheels	Black, ½ in straw line on inside edges of rims.
Cylinders and motion	Cylinder clothing crimson lake. End covers black. Clothing edged 1½ in black, lined ½ in straw on inside. Anti-vacuum valve casings black. Cylinder relief valves and drain cocks black, drain pipes copper. Motion bare metal.
Platform	Black. Platform angles crimson lake. Footsteps black; supports crimson lake. Grab handles polished metal. Mechanical lubricators black. Sandbox fillers black. Oil boxes brass.
Buffer beams	Vermilion, edges black and face edged ½ in black, lined ½ in straw inside. Top of beam between black edging and platform crimson lake. Vacuum stand pipe black. Buffer casings vermilion; casting beads black, lined ⅜ in straw on inside. Buffers and coupling hooks bare metal.
Boiler, firebox & smokebox	Boiler and firebox clothing, dome cover and safety valve base cover crimson lake. Clothing band next to smokebox black, lined ½ in straw at rear. Other clothing bands plain crimson lake. Angle between cab front and firebox clothing black, lined ½ in straw on front edge. Smokebox and chimney black. Smokebox number and shed code* plates black with polished characters. Handrails and ejector pipework crimson lake or black to match adjacent colour. Safety valves and whistle brass.
Side tanks, bunker and cab, outside	Fronts and sides of tanks, cab front, rear, and sides up to rainstrip, and sides and rear of bunker crimson lake. Tank fronts edged 2¼ in black, lined ½ in straw inside. Sides of tanks, cab and bunker edged 2¼ in black, lined ½ in straw inside as one panel but no edging or lining adjacent to cab roof rainstrip. Bunker rear edged 2¼ in black, lined ½ in straw inside. Tank tops, cab roof inside of bunker, tank vents, fillers and stays black. Cab handrails black, bunker handrail crimson. Oil boxes on tank fronts brass. Makers plates and bunker water capacity plate black with polished borders and characters. For lettering and numbering details see text.
Cab, inside	Below waist level crimson lake edged 2¼ in black, lined ½ in straw inside. Above waist level grained oak finish. Firebox backplate black, roof white (rapidly becoming cream).

*Not all locomotives carried shed code plates at this time.

2300 and 2301 but then 4, was placed just in front of the cab-side cut-out in 2in high gold, shaded black characters. Note that all quoted character sizes are without shading.

A letter was issued on 18 April 1928 stating, 'It has now been decided that three sizes of figures shall be used – 10in, 12in and 14in (14in are similar to those that have been stocked for a considerable time).' The 14in ones were, in fact, the old Midland face whereas 10in and 12in examples were a similar but less attractive LMS version. The same letter gave instructions that the letters P and F be added to passenger and freight engine power classifications. The policy was to use the largest numbers that would fit comfortably on the cab or bunker side which, on the '2300s', meant 14in ones. By this time all the crimson examples were in traffic and should have become black at their first repaints, but at least two of them, 2300 and 2302, were photographed in 1929 after undergoing heavy repairs at Derby and freshly turned out in lined crimson with 14in numerals. They were the second and third '2300s' to have heavy repairs in April/May and May/June 1929 respectively, the only one prior to that being 2311 which was at Derby for some reason between June and August 1928 only a few months and 5,830 miles after being built. It would seem, therefore, that someone at Derby Works decided to return the engines to traffic in their original colour scheme with the new numeral size but whether the same thing was done for any of the other 13 crimson '2300s' we can't say.

LMS LINED BLACK

When freshly applied, the lined black LMS paint scheme with 14in gold, shaded black transfers looked quite smart. No. 2314 was originally painted in lined crimson lake and by the time it was repainted black, glazed lake and vermilion transfers had been specified for engines with vermilion lining. Some locomotives, however, still received gold, shaded black ones, No. 2314 amongst them. A. G. ELLIS (15676)

Except for the fifteen crimson lake examples, the rest of the class was turned out in lined black livery. The entire locomotive was black except for the following:

Inside faces of the frames – vermilion.
Axles – vermilion.
Buffer beams and casings – vermilion, beam edges black and faces edged one inch black.
Inside of the cab roof – white, rapidly darkening to cream.
Motion – bare metal.
Buffers – bare metal.
Couplings and hooks – bare metal.
Cylinder drain pipes – bare metal.
Safety valves and whistle – bare metal.
Smokebox numberplate, makers' plates and capacity plate – polished metal borders and characters.

All the handrails and grab rails appear to have been painted, although some of the latter seem later to have been bare metal – possibly as a result of wear. Tank fronts and sides, cab front, sides and rear, bunker sides and rear, boiler and firebox clothing, dome cover and safety valve base cover were varnished.

The boiler clothing band next to the smokebox had a ½ in vermilion line around the rear edge and the angle between firebox clothing and cab front had the same around the front edge. On the original 'open' cab engines, vermilion lining ⅜ in wide was applied to the tank, cab and bunker sides as a single panel on each side, probably inset 2½ in from the edges. There was no vermilion line adjacent to the cab rainstrip. On engines with snap-head rivets on the tanks, cab and bunker, the lining was just inside the rows of rivets at the edges. In both cases the lining had rounded corners. At first letters were 14in serif gold, shaded black, which usually appeared to be unshaded against the black paint. In some conditions, however, it could stand out in photographs and give the erroneous impression of being a different colour. Numbers on at least 2312, 2313 and 2317 were 10in LMS style scroll and serif whereas from 2320 onwards 14in Midland pattern numerals were used, both being gold, shaded black. We don't know which size Nos. 2318 and 2319 had originally. On 17th June 1929 it was announced that letters and numerals would in future be supplied shaded vermilion on the right-hand side and glazed lake below (a style sometimes referred to as 'countershading') but that existing stocks of black shaded transfers were to be used up. Twelve months and a day later it was ordered that the new-style transfers would be exclusively for use on lined black engines. However, from photographs taken on orthochromatic film, the difference between black and red is difficult to assess at the best of times; with light reflections or a layer of grime covering the characters it can be virtually impossible. Thus, we cannot say with any certainty when the change-over happened on the '2300s', although we are fairly sure that up to and including 2341 had black shaded characters and it would seem that from 2350 onwards vermilion and glazed lake shaded ones were used. There were some engines after 2350, though, that appear in photographs to have had no shading but whether that is because of the film used we can't say.

One of the 1928 locomotives, 2313, was named *The Prince* following a visit to Derby Works by the then Prince of Wales

We know of very few photographs showing the original cast-iron bunker tank vents fitted to the '2300s'. This one, of the engine named in honour of a visit to Derby Works by the Prince of Wales when it was being built, shows how low they were and, as a consequence, how prone to damage and coal dust ingestion. By the time this picture was taken the exhaust steam injector had been moved from its original position to the much more sensible and accessible one in front of the right-hand cab footsteps. However, the engine still had short side tank vents and thin buffer spacing blocks. Also apparent are the fluted coupling rods with half brasses and cotters to the leading crankpins as fitted to Nos. 2300-2384 when built. At first glance the engine appears to be in plain black but a close examination shows that it did, in fact, have vermilion lining.
NATIONAL RAILWAY MUSEUM/REAL PHOTOGRAPHS

Although it has been written in the past that The Prince *lost its name when it received 14in numbers, this photograph taken at Stafford on 1st March 1930, proves that not to have been the case. The engine was still in original external condition, except that it had been fitted with 2½in buffer spacing blocks, but shortly afterwards it went to Derby for a heavy repair and was altered in line with the 1929 production locomotives. Note the cast-in crescent-shaped balance weights on the coupled wheels and the oil box on the hind end of the frame for lubricating the bogie slide, both features peculiar to locomotives up to No. 2394. The two oil cups originally fitted to the upper slidebars are also apparent, as is the enamelled shed code plate.*
W. L. GOOD (2592)

The 2385-2394 series of locomotives was built with reduced-length cut-outs to the rear of the gangways, as shown in this study of No. 2387 taken at Derby before it entered traffic in May 1933. This and subsequent batches of engines were turned out with flat-section coupling rods having solid front bushes and rounded ends as well as bright metal motion parts, cylinder and valve chest covers, tyres and wheel bosses. Bogie and pony truck brakes were omitted, as were the rear oil cups from the upper slidebars. Note the inverted leaf spring behind the equalising beam of the bogie, the depth of the main locomotive frame at that point, and the oil box on the outside of the frame for lubricating the bogie slides. The pictures illustrates one of the difficulties often encountered when interpreting prints taken from orthochromatic film as it requires close scrutiny before the vermilion lining and countershading of the transfers can be seen.
COLLECTION R. J. ESSERY

when it was being built. The name was carried on the tank sides in about 6in high gold painted serif letters above the 'LMS'. The date of the Prince's visit, 21.2.28, was shown in very small figures immediately below the last 'E'. At first the engine carried 10in numbers but by March 1930 it had received 14in ones, still with the name on its tank sides. When it was repainted in 1933, however, the name was omitted.

In July 1932 new engines were turned out with bright metal tyres, wheel bosses and cylinder end covers. The change took effect from 2385 onwards. Repainted engines, however, had the wheels painted black. Some locomotives also had the smokebox door hinges and seating ring, sometimes called the 'dog ring', in bright metal, e.g., 2346, 2347, 2351, 2374, 2380, 2416, 2418, 2420 and 2421. Some, such as 2418, also had the tops of the frames in front of the smokebox polished.

Locomotives with side window cabs were lined out in two panels each side that included horizontal lining adjacent to the cab roof. The side tank and cab side in front of the door was one panel, with the lining interrupted by the tops of the side windows, and the cab to the rear of the door and the bunker side another. Power classification transfers were placed on the cab sides, initially to the rear of the doors and just below the lining next to the roof. In about 1934 they were moved to a position just below the division of the cab side windows.

During the early 1930s an effort was made to use up stocks of obsolescent transfers including the Midland-style 18in gold, shaded black numbers. At least one of the '2300s', No. 2322, had its number applied with such transfers together with black shaded 14in 'LMS' letters.

On 15th February 1936 a new style of sans serif, or block, lettering and numbering was introduced. Letters were 14in high, numbers 10in and both were either countershaded vermilion and glazed lake or unshaded gold. Shortly afterwards the shading was changed to all vermilion. Matching sans serif smokebox numberplates were specified to accompany them. Instructions as to which locomotives were to get which transfers were quite convoluted during 1936 and by October 1937 it had been decided to revert to the old scroll and serif style. The result for the '2300' Class was that only relatively few

The last thirty engines incorporated many more Stanier features than did their predecessors. As well as the design alterations seen in previous batches of locomotives, No. 2400 displays Stanier-pattern wheels with their characteristic triangular-section rims and the built-up balance weights on the coupled wheels. The bogie was a side bolster type, the bearers for which can be seen above the bogie frame, and the depth of the locomotive frame was reduced as a result. The cab was completely different with overhanging roof, side windows and doors, which overcame the draught problems of the earlier engines. Close examination also reveals the Stanier buffers with oval plates riveted to round heads. On this particular photograph the vermilion lining and countershaded transfers show up very well – note how the lining was interrupted by the tops of the cab side windows and the positioning of the power classification behind the cab door.
NATIONAL RAILWAY MUSEUM/REAL PHOTOGRAPHS

No. 2322 was one of the locomotives affected in the early 1930s by the instruction to use up stocks of 18in gold, shaded black transfers. At the same time it had several alterations, such as extended side tank vents, bent-up footstep corners on all but the rear steps, thicker buffer spacing blocks, and removal of bogie and pony truck brakes. It also had the cast-iron bunker tank vents replaced by longer wrought-iron pipes, the pile of coal in the bunker illustrating quite graphically why this had been necessary. V. R. ANDERSON (1382)

One of the engines to carry the 1936 block transfers was No. 2374, pictured here at St. Albans on 4th April 1937. It also had the fairly uncommon embellishments of bright metal smokebox door hinges and straps as well as the rim of its numberplate being polished. Although it appears at first glance to have been plain black, a close study of the photograph reveals that it did have full vermilion lining. It had received all the usual 1930s alterations, except for oil boxes on the upper slidebars, and its coupling rods had been replaced with flat-section Stanier ones.
A. G. ELLIS (0887)

engines ever wore the block characters and not many had new smokebox door numberplates. Locomotives we know to have received the sans serif numbers and letters were 2308, 2316, 2321, 2323, 2326, 2330, 2354, 2358, 2363, 2374, 2380, 2389, 2391, 2395–2401 and 2408. However, the only ones we know to have had sans serif smokebox door numberplates were 2316 and 2354.

From 1937 the scroll and serif transfers were changed to chrome yellow, shaded vermilion as a cheaper alternative to the gold ones. The new transfers were specified for all locomotives irrespective of livery. There were, however, stocks of the older transfers to be used up and the difference between gold and yellow characters on a dirty locomotive in a black and white photograph is extremely difficult to determine. Thus, whilst we are prepared to state that Nos. 2312, 2328, 2342, 2348, 2350, 2351, 2355, 2356, 2366, 2388, 2389, and 2424 *probably* received yellow, shaded

Relatively few engines ever wore the 1936-style sans serif letters and numbers and we know of just twenty-two of the '2300' Class so treated. One of them was No. 2308, which was photographed at Penrith on 10th August 1937. Note that the smokebox numberplate, however, was still scroll-and-serif style. Although it is extremely difficult to identify accurately the type of transfers used, from a close study we would hazard the opinion that they were shaded vermilion throughout. The narrowing of the front platform is evident in this view, as is the fact that snap-head rivets had replaced the original flush ones where the platform was attached to stays and angles.

COLLECTION R. J. ESSERY

Although sans serif smokebox door number plates were supposed to go with the 1936 block characters, the only engine we know to have received one was No. 2354. It is seen here leaving Berkhamsted on 14th October 1945.

V. R. ANDERSON (1384/39)

Once a layer of grime had been allowed to accumulate, the paint scheme of an engine could become largely academic. It is impossible to state what sort of transfers were hiding beneath the dirt on No. 2329 when it was photographed at St. Albans on 18th August 1935, although its smokebox door numberplate was in pristine condition and had been decorated with polished corners.

A. G. ELLIS (0885)

vermilion transfers and that 2377 and 2390 *almost certainly* did, we can't in all honesty be absolutely sure.

Other small variations in livery and finish that we know of during the mid- to late 1930s and 1940s included the polishing of the edges, or sometimes just the corners, of smokebox door numberplates. Locomotives featuring the former included 2374 and the latter 2320, 2328, 2329 and 2399. No. 2374 also had bright metal smokebox door hinges. Some Western and Central Division engines had white enamelled shed code plates with black side portions and figures, Central Division ones normally having a C prefix. Those we know of were 2302, 2307, 2310, 2313, 2315, 2316, 2320, 2345–2347, 2353, 2357, 2383, 2395, 2396, 2409 and 2411. No. 2397 had a cast shed code plate with the background painted white and border and figures black. Doubtless there were other variations of which we are not aware, although we have done our best to cover as much as possible.

PLAIN BLACK

During the Second World War the lining was omitted from repainted engines and gold or yellow – both shaded vermilion – or plain yellow characters were used in a variety of sizes. Since locomotives were often merely touched up rather than repainted, however, some simply had the numbers and lettering hand-painted on top of the transfers and traces of lining could possibly be seen under the grime. This state of affairs lasted until after nationalisation.

Following nationalisation on 1st January 1948, most locomotives underwent little or no immediate change to their painting, lettering and numbering and it was several years before they were all renumbered and painted in full BR livery. The first alteration for many was simply that the BR number, which was the LMS number with 40,000 added to it, was applied to the bunker sides in either unshaded 12in LMS-style scroll and serif numerals or 10in 1946-pat-

Whilst rebuilding of the '2300s' with cast-steel cylinders and outside steam pipes began in December 1943, the majority weren't altered until after the Second World War and the job was not completed until January 1954. No. 2390 was rebuilt in November 1947 and when photographed had new buffer casings with diamond-pattern steps on top, access panels in its cylinder clothing, Stanier-pattern pony wheels, and a Stanier chimney. Holes for firebox shoulder washout doors had been cut in the clothing panels but were covered with blanking plates as 2390's then current boiler didn't have the doors. The front buffer beam and platform had been fitted using snap-head rivets and its livery was plain black with chrome yellow, shaded vermilion transfers. COLLECTION R. J. ESSERY

Following nationalisation, the new British Railways numbers were applied in several different ways. A common one was that used on No. 42386 when it was renumbered on 29th May 1948, the day this photograph was taken at Derby. This new number was applied to the bunker sides in unshaded 12in scroll and serif transfers and the shading on the 'LMS' lettering was painted over in black. As is evident from the picture, the only parts of the engine affected were the newly-varnished strip along the bunker bearing the new numerals and the area around each letter on the tank side. The black paint over the previous shading is in such contrast to the rest of the filthy engine that effectively it had itself become shading. The locomotive had been rebuilt with new cylinders and steam pipes, been fitted with a protector above the rear vacuum standard, and had acquired a set of Stanier bogie wheels and a Stanier chimney. From the vertical strip of new paint starting between the 'L' and 'M', it would seem that the tank had been repaired as well, possibly due to a leak. H. C. CASSERLEY (54403)

tern sans serif straw ones without the maroon edging. Generally the type used matched the tank-side letters, i.e., serif or sans serif. At the same time any shading present on the tank-side 'LMS' letters was painted out in black. However, at least one engine, No. 42374, had the number in 1946 style 12in characters with serif 'LMS' on the tank sides. Smokebox door numberplates having sans serif numerals of a style peculiar to Derby and Bow Works were fitted to some locomotives in this condition but others were without plates until they were repainted in lined black.

A minority, e.g., Nos. 2308, 2319 and 2411, received the short-lived 'M' prefix to their LMS numbers. In these cases the pale cream characters were in the same style as the 1946 LMS livery without the maroon embellishment, the sans serif 'M' being 6in

Engines with 1936 block lettering commonly had their BR numbers applied in 10in characters similar in style to the 1946-pattern numerals but without the maroon edging, as shown on No. 42396. Power classification was carried in the later LMS position under the cab windows. The smokebox number plates on the majority of the '2300s' had numerals in a style peculiar to Derby and Bow Works that was closely similar to the 1946 cab and bunker-side characters and is well illustrated in this picture. By the time this photograph was taken, the engine's original buffer casings had been replaced by earlier-pattern ones on 2½in spacers, snap-head rivets used on buffer beam and platform, a Stanier chimney fitted and rain gutters welded to the cab roof over the side windows. It had also been rebuilt with cast-steel cylinders and outside steam pipes and access panels fitted to its cylinder clothing. NATIONAL RAILWAY MUSEUM/REAL PHOTOGRAPHS

A few engines, including 2319, carried the short-lived 'M' prefix to their LMS numbers for a while. The only other two examples known to us were 2308 and 2411. This photograph was taken a few days before the engine officially re-entered traffic in February 1948 after being rebuilt with cast-steel cylinders. It had acquired a Stanier chimney and Stanier carrying wheels, a firebox with shoulder washout doors and was painted plain black. Its power class was positioned slightly lower than normal in line with the tank top. W. L. GOOD (7691)

At least two renumbered engines, 42314 and 42322, had 10in cream Gill Sans 'BRITISH RAILWAYS' on the tank sides with 12in 1946-pattern numbers without the maroon edging on the bunker sides. When 42322 was photographed in the summer of 1948 it was still awaiting its new smokebox door number plate – a not uncommon situation in those days – and its firebox was fitted with shoulder washout doors. Whether it had just received the latter or had them since 1944 in unclear. NATIONAL RAILWAY MUSEUM/REAL PHOTOGRAPHS high, positioned centrally above the 12in numerals. The legend 'BRITISH RAILWAYS' was in cream Gill Sans 10in letters on the tank sides. Positioning of the characters varied, engines with early-style cabs having the numbers half way up the bunker side and the lettering in line with them. Side window cab locomotives, however, had the lettering half way up the deep portion of the side tanks and numbers in line with that, so the characters as a whole were slightly lower down. Whereas some other classes that received this livery had the 'M' prefix added to their smokebox door plates, that does not appear to have been the case with the '2300s'.

At least two renumbered engines, 42314 and 42322, had the same combination as the 'M' prefix locomotives, i.e., 10in cream Gill Sans 'BRITISH RAILWAYS' on the tank sides with 12in 1946 pattern numbers on the bunker. Several others, such as 42318, 42333, 42343 and 42422, had both lettering and numbers in cream 8in Gill Sans, the positioning following the same rule as described in the previous paragraph. Once again, smokebox door numberplates had Derby/Bow style numerals although some engines ran without plates for a time.

There were some instances of locomotives receiving the lettering and numbering that went with the first examples of BR lined black livery but without the lining. No. 42343 was photographed at Stoke on an unknown date in this condition. It had Stanier chimney and carrying wheels and, even though it still had its original cylinders, an access plate in the cylinder clothing. A. G. ELLIS (26780)

BR LINED BLACK

The scheme decided on in 1948 for mixed traffic and lesser passenger locomotives, including the '2300s', was based on the pre-Grouping L&NWR passenger livery. Apart from the following items, the entire engine was black inside and out:

Buffer beams and buffer casings – signal red.
Inside of cab roof – white when first painted.
Motion – bare metal.
Buffers – bare metal.
Couplings and hooks – bare metal.
Cylinder drain pipes – bare metal.

A single panel of multi-coloured lining was inset 5in from the edge of each tank side and lower cab side forward of the gangway or door. Another panel was aft of the gangway or door, inset 5in from front, bottom and rear of the lower cab side and bunker. Right-angle corners were 4in outside radius but around the lower corners of the cut-out on early cab engines the lining just followed the shape of the beading. The top of the rear lining panel on early cab and most side-window cab engines was in line with the top of the forward panel. There were, however, some side-window cab locomotives on which

The first examples of BR lined livery included the words 'BRITISH RAILWAYS' in cream Gill Sans 8in characters on the tank sides, as shown by No. 42416 at Afon Wen in July 1954. Despite the location, we think that the shallow bunker lining panel seen here was a St. Rollox variation on the official livery used for side window cab engines. Power class 4P was positioned in line with the tank-side lettering below the centres of the front windows. The locomotive had been repaired using snap-head rivets on its rear buffer beam and had received bent side tank vents in order to improve vision from the cab. Note the vacuum stand pipe protector on the rear of the bunker and the rain gutter on the edge of the roof forward of the door. The door was still full height and, according to the material at our disposal, was retained until the engine was withdrawn. A. G. ELLIS (9674)

When freshly painted in BR lined black livery with the first 'monocycling lion' emblem on the tank sides, the '2300s' could look very smart indeed. No. 42417 had most of the possible alterations by the time this picture was taken, including new cylinders, Stanier chimney, curved vents, shoulder washout doors and shortened cylinder drain pipes. It did not, however, have AWS and was one of the Northern Division engines that was not fitted with extra rain gutters on the cab roof. It was also one of a small minority to have Gill Sans numerals on its smokebox door numberplate. The shallow bunker lining panel on 'limousine cab' engines was, in our opinion, more pleasing than the usual much deeper version. Note that the number was in line with the emblem and that the power class, shown as 4P, was below it. A. G. ELLIS (7623)

the rear panel was not as deep, its top being in line with the shallower part of the forward panel below the windows. That type was, we think, a St. Rollox variation and gave the engines a more balanced aspect.[23] Going from the outside the lining was $\frac{5}{8}$in pale grey, $\frac{1}{8}$in cream, 1$\frac{5}{8}$in black and $\frac{1}{4}$in red. Whilst that was the official specification, on some locomotives the black line between cream and grey was narrower than specified. On the platform angles, the lower edges were grey with cream above and the red lines were halfway up the angle. Boiler and cylinder clothing bands were edged with $\frac{1}{4}$in red lines.

Locomotive running numbers were placed centrally on the bunker sides in 8in cream Gill Sans numerals. The cast smokebox door plates had raised, white-painted numerals, most of which were in the Derby and Bow Works sans serif style. In fact, we know of only two engines, 42415 and 42417, that definitely had Gill Sans smokebox door numbers. Comparison with the Gill Sans bunker-side numerals will illustrate the different faces. Raised characters and borders on shed code plates and water capacity plates were white. In the early days of this scheme, 'BRITISH RAILWAYS' was on the tank sides, again in cream Gill Sans 8in characters. Fairly soon, however, the smaller size of the early BR emblem with a lion astride a wheel was placed half way up the deeper tank section mid-way between the front of the cab and the step in the platform. The lion faced forwards on each side. Power classification in

Just over a year after its BR number was applied, 42390 was repainted in lined black and was photographed immediately afterwards at Derby on 25th March 1950. Its lining and transfers were typical of those applied to 'open cab' engines with the power classification shown as 4P on the cab side just in front of the cut-out. Although it had earlier been fitted with a boiler having shoulder washout doors, by the time this picture was taken, it did not have them and there were blanking plates in the clothing. As well as the modifications usual to an engine of this series at the time, it had received Stanier-pattern carrying wheels. A. G. ELLIS (31326)

The more usual BR lining style on side-window cab engines was as shown in this picture of 42415. The photograph is particularly useful as it shows the red lining quite well – something often difficult to see on prints from orthochromatic film. Note how the red line is broken by the maker's plate on the forward part of the tank side and the double red lining on the cylinder clothing band. The power classification was simply 4, rather than the earlier 4P, positioned just above the number, the normal place for side-window locomotives with large bunker lining panels.
NATIONAL RAILWAY MUSEUM/REAL PHOTOGRAPHS (R5437)

the form of small Gill Sans characters was shown, initially as '4P' but later simply as '4'. At first it was positioned on the upper cab side forward of the cut-out on early cab engines and below the windows on the Stanier cabs. When 'BRITISH RAILWAYS' was used on the tank sides, the power class was in line with it; once the lion emblem replaced the lettering, however, it was moved up to just below the lining. Later on it was placed just above the running number on early cab locomotives and those side-window cab engines with large bunker lining panels. Side-windowed engines with shallow bunker lining panels had it just below the number. There were some small variations in the BR livery; for instance, No. 42362 was seen at Macclesfield in the 1950s with polished corners to its smokebox numberplate.

There were only two other general alterations to the lined black livery of the '2300' tank engines. First was the introduction in 1956 of the BR crest in place of the earlier emblem. It was applied in the same positions as the emblem and for a short time the lions faced forward on each side. When it was pointed out by the College of Heralds that it was an approved coat of arms and that the lion should always face to the left, however, new transfers were produced for the right-hand sides. As with most things concerning locomotives, the change was a long time taking effect and some engines were withdrawn still carrying the early emblem with forward facing lions on each side. The final addition was overhead power line warning flashes that appeared on the surviving engines in 1960. They were placed at the tops of the tank fronts, firebox shoulders and, most commonly, the outside faces of the frames above the front platforms. Some engines had them on the vertical faces of the platforms instead of the frames and at least one, No. 42368, wore them in both places. A few locomotives, including Nos. 42311, 42353 and 42419, seem only to have had them on the tank fronts. They should also have been placed on the rear of the bunker but we have not seen any photographs that show the positioning.

British Railways AWS was fitted to 42409, evidenced by the protector fixed to the lower edge of its front buffer beam and the sheathed electric cable just visible behind it, when photographed at Holbeck on 19th August 1962. Apart from the conduit on the left-hand side, that was the only external evidence of AWS on the '2300s', unlike the mogul next to 42409 on which the battery box and reservoir can be seen on the platform in front of the cab. The tank engine had the common arrangement of overhead electrical warning flashes applied after 1960.
A. G. ELLIS (26474)

BR GREEN

There was also at least one engine that was painted green. The only evidence we have of this is a single colour photograph taken at Leeds City station on 8th July 1964 showing No. 42394 in charge of a parcels train. The locomotive had unlined BR green tank fronts and sides, cab front and sides, bunker sides, boiler and firebox clothing, cylinder clothing, platform angle and footstep supports. We assume that the cab and bunker rear panels would also have been green. The buffer beam was signal red and the rest of the engine appears to have been black. The smokebox door numberplate had white Derby or Bow Works style numerals but the shed code plate was all black. The later BR crest was on the tank side and the running number was on the bunker in 8in cream Gill Sans numerals. Warning flashes were on the firebox shoulders and tank fronts but absent from the front frames or platform. The engine had a Stanier chimney, snap-head rivets on its front buffer beam and platform, and washout doors on the firebox shoulders. It was not AWS equipped. Apart from the above, we can add no more detail and know of no other engines so treated, nor can we find any documentary evidence of '2300s' being painted green.

This is the picture referred to showing 42394 at Leeds City painted green. The original colour print shows the shade unmistakably as well as the fact that there was no lining. R. J. ESSERY

As can be seen from the above, there were many and often subtle variations in the livery details of the locomotives throughout their lives. Thus, we would once again urge the use of photographs of a specific engine at a particular time when depicting one in model or picture form. For further details of the painting techniques and materials used by the LMS, see *Locomotive Profile No. 2 – The Horwich Moguls.*

APPENDICES

APPENDIX A – BUILDING, MODIFICATION, RENUMBERING AND WITHDRAWAL DATES

Information in this table was collated mainly from the engine history cards. Unfortunately, some of the history cards, particularly ex-Northern Division ones, are incomplete. An asterisk indicates that the history card is incomplete and the information comes from a secondary source that we consider accurate. A dash indicates that the history card is incomplete but we do not have reliable information from another source. We can, however, confirm that all the engines were rebuilt with cast-steel cylinders and outside steam pipes.

Building dates are actual calendar days on which the locomotives were put into traffic. Cylinder replacement dates are the week endings in which they were officially returned to traffic; the work may have been completed a few days earlier so there could be as much as two or three weeks difference between the actual date of completion and the official date shown. Renumbering and withdrawal dates are also week endings.

No	*Built*	*New cyls.*	*BR No. applied*	*Withdrawn*
2300	9 Dec 27	16 Jun 46	26 Jun 48	26 Nov 60
2301	20 Dec 27	19 May 45	6 Nov 48	19 Oct 63
2302	22 Dec 27	25 Feb 51	10 Jul 48	30 Sep 61
2303	30 Dec 27	20 Apr 46	16 Oct 48	27 Oct 62
2304	6 Jan 28	25 Dec 43	25 Dec 48	8 Sep 62
2305	13 Jan 28	22 Apr 50	22 May 48	1 Sep 62
2306	19 Jan 28	15 Apr 44	25 Feb 50	29 Dec 62
2307	26 Jan 28	8 Jul 47	2 Oct 48	29 Jul 61
2308	28 Jan 28	21 Feb 48	19 Nov 49	29 Aug 59
2309	3 Feb 28	12 Jul 52	3 May 50	26 Sep 64
2310	10 Feb 28	30 Sep 44	26 Feb 49	9 Mar 63
2311	22 Feb 28	15 May 48	1 May 48	Apr 64*
2312	23 Feb 28	17 May 47	23 Oct 48	14 Nov 59
2313	1 Mar 28	23 Feb 52	12 Nov 49	23 Nov 63
2314	3 Mar 28	19 Feb 44	10 Jul 48	29 Dec 62
2315	10 Mar 28	24 Feb 51	9 Oct 48	29 Dec 62
2316	14 Mar 28	26 Jan 46	20 Nov 48	16 Feb 63
2317	22 Mar 28	14 Jul 51	29 Jan 49	Sep 65*
2318	30 Mar 28	18 May 46	27 Nov 48	8 Sep 62
2319	13 Apr 28	21 Feb 48	11 Jun 49	19 Oct 63
2320	27 Apr 28	15 May 48	15 May 48	17 Nov 62
2321	2 May 28	13 May 44	17 Sep 49	7 Nov 59
2322	19 May 28	8 Jul 44	8 May 48	31 Jul 65
2323	4 Jun 28	19 Feb 44	29 Aug 49	23 Jun 62
2324	22 Jun 28	16 Jun 45	9 Oct 48	17 Nov 62
2325	21 Jan 29	24 Jan 48	14 May 49	30 Sep 61
2326	29 Jan 29	31 Dec 49	30 Oct 48	2 Jul 60
2327	2 Feb 29	8 Jul 44	8 Jan 49	28 Aug 65
2328	9 Feb 29	30 Sep 44	4 Sep 48	9 Sep 61
2329	15 Feb 29	13 May 44	31 Dec 48	30 Sep 61
2330	20 Feb 29	25 Mar 46	4 Jun 49	9 Dec 61
2331	25 Feb 29	5 Aug 44	26 Jun 48	1 Sep 62
2332	28 Feb 29	2 Dec 50	30 Apr 49	30 Sep 61
2333	6 Mar 29	24 Jan 53	26 Feb 49	4 May 63
2334	12 Mar 29	16 Jun 51	11 Sep 48	25 Dec 65
2335	20 Mar 29	22 Feb 47	2 Oct 48	25 Apr 64
2336	6 Apr 29	8 Sep 51	5 Nov 49	20 Oct 62
2337	23 Mar 29	29 Jan 49	29 Jan 49	21 Dec 63
2338	2 Apr 29	27 Dec 52	15 Jan 49	11 Jan 64
2339	6 Apr 29	6 Oct 45	10 Jul 49	28 Jul 63
2340	11 Apr 29	12 Aug 50	16 Oct 48	9 Jun 62
2341	16 Apr 29	13 May 44	2 Jan 50	17 Oct 59*
2342	23 Apr 29	20 Apr 46	19 Feb 49	2 Jun 62
2343	26 Apr 29	19 May 51	15 Jan 49	30 Oct 65
2344	2 May 29	4 Nov 50	24 Apr 48	27 May 61
2345	8 May 29	15 Jun 46	4 Sep 48	21 May 60
2346	14 May 29	19 Apr 52	3 Jul 48	10 Sep 60
2347	17 May 29	18 May 46	10 Jul 48	15 Sep 62
2348	23 May 29	–	19 Mar 49	30 Sep 61
2349	30 May 29	25 Nov 44	11 Dec 48	22 Jul 61
2350	4 Jun 29	28 Dec 46	30 Oct 48	13 Dec 65
2351	6 Jun 29	3 Nov 51	5 Feb 49	25 Aug 62
2352	11 Jun 29	18 Jul 47	11 Feb 48	28 Apr 62
2353	14 Jun 29	13 Aug 49	2 Jul 49	13 Jun 64
2354	20 Jun 29	27 Dec 47	26 Nov 49	14 Nov 59
2355	27 Jun 29	–	27 Aug 49	30 Nov 63
2356	2 Jul 29	16 Jun 51	1 Oct 49	30 Sep 61
2357	7 Jul 29	26 Feb 49	12 Feb 49	13 Mar 63
2358	8 Jul 29	19 May 45	12 Jun 48	27 Oct 62
2359	12 Jul 29	24 Mar 45	14 Jan 50	24 Oct 64
2360	18 Jul 29	16 Jun 45	28 Aug 48	19 Aug 61
2361	23 Jul 29	18 May 46	1 Oct 49	8 Feb 64
2362	26 Jul 29	12 Jul 47	16 Apr 49	2 Jun 62
2363	1 Aug 29	28 Jan 50	29 May 48	23 Dec 61
2364	9 Aug 29	2 Dec 50	11 Sep 48	30 Sep 61
2365	14 Aug 29	5 Aug 44	11 Feb 50	8 Oct 60
2366	27 Aug 29	21 Feb 48	27 May 50	11 Apr 64
2367	2 Sep 29	20 Mar 48	1 Apr 50	25 Aug 62
2368	6 Sep 29	19 May 45	5 Nov 49	19 Jun 65
2369	11 Sep 29	4 Oct 47	7 May 49	15 May 65
2370	16 Sep 29	15 May 48	13 Mar 48	30 Jun 62
2371	19 Sep 29	30 Oct 48	16 Oct 48	28 Apr 62
2372	24 Sep 29	18 Jul 47	5 Nov 49	29 Dec 62
2373	27 Sep 29	21 Apr 51	21 May 49	19 Nov 60
2374	3 Oct 29	13 Jul 46	7 Aug 48	2 Oct 65
2375	13 May 32	24 Mar 45	5 Feb 49	24 Feb 62
2376	18 May 32	23 Apr 49	23 Apr 49	17 Nov 62
2377	25 May 32	23 Mar 46	26 Mar 49	6 May 61
2378	1 Jun 32	29 Nov 47	29 Oct 49	18 Apr 64
2379	8 Jun 32	6 Oct 45	17 Sep 49	1 Aug 64
2380	15 Jun 32	27 Jan 51	7 Jan 50	10 Dec 60
2381	22 Jun 32	2 Oct 48	11 Sep 48	8 May 65
2382	29 Jun 32	14 Jun 47	26 Mar 49	30 Sep 61
2383	7 Jul 32	–	1 May 48	30 Sep 61
2384	15 Jul 32	14 Jul 45	29 May 48	18 Oct 63
2385	4 May 33	17 Apr 48	6 Aug 49	8 Sep 62
2386	11 May 33	23 Feb 46	29 May 48	30 Sep 61
2387	22 May 33	18 Jul 47	2 Jul 49	3 Nov 62*
2388	25 May 33	25 Dec 48	6 Nov 48	23 Mar 63
2389	31 May 33	25 Dec 48	14 Aug 48	23 Mar 63
2390	31 May 33	29 Nov 47	12 Feb 49	10 Sep 60
2391	5 Jun 33	16 Jun 45	14 May 49	2 Mar 63
2392	13 Jun 33	12 Jun 48	22 May 48	9 Feb 63
2393	20 Jun 33	18 Jul 47	5 Feb 49	26 May 62
2394	22 Jun 33	24 Mar 51	4 Jun 49	To WR 1953
2395	28 Aug 33	2 Oct 48	25 Sep 48	18 Nov 61
2396	29 Aug 33	12 Jul 47	18 Jun 49	7 Jul 62
2397	31 Aug 33	–	25 Sep 48	21 Jan 61
2398	4 Sep 33	22 Feb 47	13 Nov 48	3 Dec 60
2399	6 Sep 33	23 Dec 44	4 Dec 48	3 Sep 60
2400	13 Sep 33	25 Mar 51	–	Jan 65*
2401	13 Sep 33	23 Feb 46	22 Oct 49	29 Jun 63
2402	20 Sep 33	25 Nov 44	22 Jan 49	13 Oct 62
2403	26 Sep 33	18 Jul 47	2 Apr 49	29 Dec 62
2404	29 Sep 33	20 Apr 46	18 Sep 48	21 Oct 61
2405	5 Oct 33	10 Jul 48	10 Jul 48	Oct 64*
2406	10 Oct 33	25 Dec 48	4 Dec 48	Sep 65*
2407	12 Dec 33	2 Apr 48	22 Apr 50	17 Nov 62
2408	18 Oct 33	–	24 Dec 49	Apr 64*
2409	19 Oct 33	18 Jun 49	18 Jun 49	Jan 64*
2410	25 Oct 33	2 Oct 48	11 Sep 48	Sep 66*
2411	28 Oct 33	11 Jul 53	15 Oct 49	Aug 64*
2412	1 Nov 33	16 Jun 45	14 Aug 48	Jan 62*
2413	4 Nov 33	20 May 50	19 Feb 49	Jun 64*
2414	8 Nov 33	27 Jan 45	25 Sep 48	10 Oct 64
2415	13 Nov 33	23 Apr 50	–	29 Dec 62
2416	15 Nov 33	9 Oct 49	–	27 Jun 64
2417	20 Nov 33	9 Sep 51	–	11 Apr 64
2418	22 Nov 33	5 Nov 50	–	9 Apr 60
2419	28 Nov33	16 Jul 49	–	30 Nov 63
2420	1 Dec 33	23 Apr 49	–	19 May 62
2421	6 Dec 33	15 Jul 51	–	22 Aug 64
2422	11 Dec 33	30 Jan 54	–	22 Dec 62
2423	19 Dec 33	5 Mar 49	–	30 Sep 61
2424	15 Jan 34	16 Jun 45	22 Oct 49	26 Sep 64

APPENDIX B – SHED ALLOCATIONS

As in our previous works, we have not tried to show where every engine was at all times throughout its history but have provided a series of allocations on 'snapshot' dates. Although some locomotives remained at one shed for many years, others moved many times, often staying at a particular location only a few weeks. This was partly due to a desire not to leave engines too long in a hard water area where the water wasn't treated, although there were other reasons as well. To try and show the movements of every locomotive during its lifetime would take too much time and space for a volume such as this. As a result, some sheds that had one or more '2300s' at some time do not feature in the tables but are noted at the end of each one.

The information given for 1935 and 1948 has been gleaned from LMS stock lists and the engine history cards. The 1960 list was collated from various sources. We have chosen the dates for two reasons. Firstly, they are ones for which we have what we think is reliable information and secondly they represent what we believe to be popular periods for modellers. In the 1935 list we have been unable to determine at which of the sheds the five engines allocated to Crewe were actually stabled. For more information on LMS locomotive sheds we would recommend the *LMS Engine Sheds* series by Chris Hawkins and George Reeve published by Wild Swan. A comprehensive list of shed allocations for 1945 is contained within the series.

28th September 1935

Shed	*Locomotives allocated*
Accrington	2310–2312, 2407, 2411
Barrow	2349, 2359
Burton	2333
Buxton	2365–2371, 2381
Carnforth	2308, 2313, 2316, 2317, 2386
Colne	2412–2414
Crewe	2390–2394 (2392 was on loan to Derby)

Shed	*Locomotives allocated*
Cricklewood	2380
Derby	2392 (on loan from Crewe)
Edge Hill	2302, 2402
Greenock	2309, 2419–2422, 2423 (2419–2422 actually stationed at Portpatrick)
Kentish Town	2374
Lancaster	2361
Leicester	2330, 2331, 2334, 2335
Longsight	2314, 2319, 2355–2358, 2382, 2388, 2395-2399
Macclesfield	2301
Millhouses	2337
Newton Heath	2383, 2384, 2406, 2408
Nottingham	2338–2342
Polmadie	2415–2418
Preston	2401
St. Albans	2300, 2302, 2325–2329
Saltley	2336, 2372, 2373
Shrewsbury	2351, 2404
Speke Jct.	2360
Stafford	2307, 2320, 2387, 2400, 2403
Stockport	2315, 2322, 2332, 2350, 2352, 2353, 2385
Stoke	2303–2306, 2323, 2343–2348, 2363, 2364
Swansea	2321, 2354
Tebay	2318
Wigan	2405, 2409, 2410
Willesden	2323, 2324, 2375–2379, 2389, 2424

Other locations to which we know '2300' Class engines were allocated or loaned in the 1930s were Agecroft, Aston, Bangor, Bank Hall, Bournville, Bradford, Bushbury, Kettering, Llandudno Junction, Manningham, Monument Lane, Normanton, Northampton, Plaistow, Rose Grove, Uttoxeter, Walsall, Warrington and Watford.

31st December 1947

Shed	*Locomotives allocated*
Alsager	2348
Barrow	2321, 2359, 2386, 2392, 2393
Bournville	2327, 2338, 2339, 2342, 2373
Burton	2336
Buxton	2306, 2315, 2318, 2365–2368, 2370, 2371
Carnforth	2379
Crewe North	2309
Derby	2340,2341
Greenock	2400, 2415–2423
Huddersfield	2310–2312, 2324, 2384, 2408, 2410–2414
Kentish Town	2325, 2329, 2331, 2383
Leicester	2330, 2334
Longsight	2322, 2350, 2351, 2395–2399, 2401, 2402
Low Moor	2406, 2407, 2409
Macclesfield	2305, 2319, 2323, 2349, 2355–2357, 2369, 2382
Manningham	2377,2380
Mirfield	2405
Nottingham	2328, 2333, 2361
Oxenholme	2301, 2313, 2314, 2317
Saltley	2326, 2337
St Albans	2300, 2302, 2335, 2374
Springs Branch	2303
Stafford	2345–2347, 2391
Stockport	2332, 2352-2354, 2360
Stoke	2320, 2343, 2344, 2364, 2375, 2376, 2378
Swansea	2307, 2385, 2387, 2388, 2390, 2394
Tebay	2308, 2403, 2404, 2424
Uttoxeter	2358, 2363
Watford	2304, 2389
Wigan Central	2362, 2381
Willesden	2316, 2372

Other locations to which we know '2300' Class engines were allocated or loaned in the 1940s and 1950s were Accrington, Bangor, Bank Hall, Birkenhead, Bletchley, Brunswick, Bushbury, Carlisle, Chester Midland, Chester Northgate, Corkerhill, Farnley Junction, Goole, Gorton, Hasland, Holyhead, Lostock Hall, Lower Darwen, Monument Lane, Neasden, Newton Heath, Northwich, Polmadie, Royston, Rugby, Shrewsbury, Southport, Sowerby Bridge, Stourton, Walton on the Hill, Warwick and Woodford Halse. Some were loaned to the Eastern and Western Regions after nationalisation.

1st January 1960

Shed	*Locomotives allocated*
Annesley	42333, 42339, 42361
Barrow	42320, 42332, 42364, 42392, 42397, 42401
Buxton	42306, 42370, 42371
Derby	42352
Goole	42311, 42324, 42407
Gorton	42326, 42328, 42373, 42374
Holbeck	42377, 42409
Huddersfield	42310, 42312, 42384, 42410, 42412–42414
Kentish Town	42325, 42329, 42334, 42342
Landore	42388, 42390
Leicester	42330, 42331, 42338
Longsight	42304, 42369, 42381, 42395, 42398, 42399, 42416
Macclesfield	42318, 42347, 42348, 42355, 42363, 42382
Manningham	42380
Mirfield	42406
Northampton	42353
Northgate	42303, 42308, 42317, 42415, 42417
Northwich	42319, 42356, 42359, 42365, 42386, 42387, 42393, 42423
Oxenholme	42301, 42313, 42314, 42345
Royston	42408
Speke Jct.	42389
St. Albans	42300, 42302, 42341
Saitley	42327, 42337, 42340, 42383
Sowerby Bridge	42405, 42411
Stafford	42309, 42400, 42402
Stockport	42316, 42322, 42343, 42354, 42357, 42372, 42391, 42404
Stoke	42315, 42323, 42344, 42346, 42362, 42378, 42418, 42420, 42421
Swansea	42385, 42394
Tebay	42396, 42403, 42424
Trafford Park	42419
Uttoxeter	42358, 42375
Willesden	42321, 42350, 42351, 42360, 42366–42368, 42376, 42379, 42422
Woodford Halse	42335, 42336, 42349

Nos. 42305 and 42307 had been transferred to the Western Region in 1953.

Other locations to which we know '2300' Class engines were allocated or loaned in the 1960s were Bangor, Birkenhead, Bletchley, Carlisle Kingmoor, Carlisle Upperby, Carnforth, Chester, Crewe South, Rowsley, Toton and Watford.

NOTES IN TEXT

1. Although the '483' Class 4–4–0s were counted as rebuilds by the Midland, this was an accounting exercise and the engines were, in fact, virtually new with only a few parts from their supposed donor locomotives used. See *Midland Engines No. 3* by the same authors, published by Wild Swan.
2. These figures were taken from a book entitled *Locomotive Engineering* published in 1922. Among its contributors was Sir Henry Fowler.
3. The '1883' and '2228' Class 0–4–4Ts were the subjects of the first of the companion *Midland Engines* series. They were the last 80 of the Johnson bogie tank engines built and were in service until 1959.
4. The eight LT&SR Baltic tanks had been something of an embarrassment for Whitelegg. He had failed to get approval from the Great Eastern Railway's Civil Engineer before they were built for running them into Fenchurch Street, which was a grave mistake as subsequently they were not allowed over the viaduct leading into the station.
5. Hughes was persuaded by the LMS board to remain in a supervisory capacity and resisted attempts by Fowler to alter the mogul design. A few Midland features, such as the narrow tender, bogie brakes, bye-pass valves, combined injectors and steam brakes, were fitted. See *LMS Locomotive Profile No. 2 – The Horwich Moguls* for further details.
6. It is somewhat ironic that the same J. E. Anderson later became Superintendent of Motive Power for the LMS and was largely responsible for the spread of the notorious 'small engine policy'. He also seems to have been instrumental in getting the Fowler Pacific cancelled and in having short-travel valves and small axleboxes fitted to the 2–6–0 + 0–6–2 Beyer-Garratts. Despite the comments made by some writers, however, Anderson was not an imbecile who did not understand the principles of steam engines, but was an extremely capable draughtsman and railwayman who made decisions for, as he saw them, sound economic reasons. For example, he was against the introduction of the Fowler Pacific partially because it would involve the expense of installing new turntables. That he failed to make the best decisions all the time hardly sets him apart from the majority.
7. The all-powerful position of the Civil Engineer who, because of the existence of a few problematic platforms or bridges along an entire route, could insist on major alterations to the dimensions or weight of a design, or even reject a scheme completely, was patently ridiculous. This state of affairs persisted until Stanier insisted on proper studies being undertaken, the result of which was that many of the previously inviolate rules were found to be quite unnecessary.
8. This problem was common to many LMS locomotives and in 1930 it was decided to initiate a widespread modification programme to replace Schmidt rings with multiple ones.

9. In a paper read to the Institution of Locomotive Engineers in 1946, E. S. Cox stated that there were real benefits in the decision to standardise throughout the LMS the general design features and details of Midland locomotives. By doing that and not perpetuating non-standard designs, in 1932 no less than 46% of the company's locomotive stock took standard parts. The savings that resulted from reduced stores holdings and simplified maintenance and repair schedules was substantial.
10. Heated controversy followed the Sevenoaks accident with many claims and counterclaims about the safety, not just of 2–6–4 tank engines, but of large tank engines in general for fast passenger traffic. The destabilising effects of water surging in part-empty side-tanks, increased lateral oscillations and many other arguments were advanced against their use. Some trials were conducted with the 'River' tanks in which the state of the track was found to be a highly significant factor in their behaviour and a large body of opinion held that there was nothing intrinsically wrong with them. Eventually, however, they were rebuilt as 2–6–0 tender engines. It is ironic in view of the speeds they regularly attained that the LMS 2–6–4Ts were regarded as inherently safer because they were intended for hauling suburban trains. It is also interesting to read the opinion of Tom King, an ex-Midland and LMS driver, on the derailments of the 0–6–4T 'Flatirons' that led to their withdrawal from fast passenger and mail train duties in the 1930s. Tom had experience of working on the engines and thought that track imperfections were more to blame than any shortcoming on their part. See *Midland Record No. 11* for more details.
11. Johnson started the system of alphabetic nomenclature for Midland boiler types in the 1890s. When the letter 'G' was reached it happened to coincide with the introduction of the first Belpaire boilers and from then on 'G' indicated a boiler with a Belpaire firebox. The number was the nominal firebox length, so 'G8' meant a boiler having an 8ft long Belpaire firebox. When superheating was adopted, it was shown by an 'S'. An 'X' indicated that the boiler was different in some way from the main group, e.g., HX boilers had different arrangements of back plate fittings and valve mountings whereas G7X was the designation for G7 boilers with steel inner fireboxes. The original G boiler was only used on a small number of engines and became the GX. The suffixes 'A' and 'B' were used to sub-divide otherwise closely similar boilers, such as the G8A of the last batch of 'Belpaire' 4–4–0s that had fewer tubes than the standard G8 and an altered front tubeplate. Thus the 2–6–4T's G8AS boiler had an 8ft long Belpaire firebox, was modified from the basic G8 and was superheated. The system was carried on into the LMS with such designations as G10½S for the 'Royal Scots' or G9HS (the 'H' indicating Horwich) for the parallel boiler 2–6–0s being used. When Stanier took over he introduced his own system for new boilers but left the old designations in place.
12. Quoted heating surfaces varied between drawings and documents, even for boilers from the same order. The figures we have used were taken from the 1927 general arrangement drawing.
13. Exhaust steam injectors were first tried on the LMS with the 'Royal Scots' and showed that worthwhile economies could be achieved by fitting them. As well as the 2–6–4 tanks, later batches of Horwich moguls were built with them and in 1931 it was decided that over 1200 existing LMS locomotives would receive them. They also became standard fittings on Stanier locomotives. In 1937, however, Stanier wrote that, 'Due to the introduction of larger types of engines for working the more important passenger and freight services, it is considered that the provision of this fitting does not afford the savings previously anticipated.' As a result, the work of fitting them was ended in November 1938 and not all the engines earmarked actually received them.
14. The only other Derby designs with Walschaerts' gear to predate the 2–6–4Ts were the Deeley 0–4–0 shunting tanks of 1907, the S&DJR 2–8–0s and the one-off 0–10–0 Lickey Banker. Ahrons suggested that one of the reasons for the use of Walschaerts' motion on the 0–4–0s was to try it out from both a manufacturing and maintenance viewpoint before its adoption for main-line engines.
15. Some writers have cited this as 'blind adherence to established Derby practices' and other, similar, phrases. It strikes us that anyone rising to the position of Chief Locomotive Draughtsman for the largest joint stock company in the world would probably know something about locomotive theory and design and that Chambers had reasons for his policies. That he didn't make them widely known for the benefit of later enthusiasts is certainly regrettable but hardly evidence of stupidity. The same exhaust clearance was later adopted for the 'Coronation' Pacifics and rebuilt 'Royal Scots' so maybe there was something in it.
16. The statements of E. A. Langridge that we have used are taken from correspondence between him, one of the authors and Arthur Cook, author of the RCTS books on LMS locomotives. Langridge started work at the Midland Locomotive Drawing Office in 1919 and remained at Derby until 1959, becoming head of the Development Section, where he was known to one of the present authors.
17. Flat-section rods fitted later to some rebuilt 'Royal Scots' were replaced after a few years with fluted ones, although we have been unable to ascertain why this was so. For more details see *LMS Locomotive Profile No. 1* on those engines.
18. Pony truck and bogie brakes were, by this time, at the end of their fashionable status and it is somewhat surprising that Derby was still using them. One of the alterations that Hughes had allowed Fowler to make to the mogul design in 1925 was the addition of pony truck brakes because the latter considered that the engine was lacking brake power. Whilst there may have been some merit in this argument for an engine that would be called on to operate loose-coupled unfitted goods trains, the same can hardly be said for one intended for suburban passenger duties. In 1922 Hughes had submitted a report to the Congress of the International Railway Association on the reasons for the removal of bogie brakes from the 1908 L&YR 4–6–0s. In it he wrote that, 'The brake tended both to stiffen the bogie wheelbase and impede the free rotation of the wheels, thus increasing the tendency for them to mount the rail. As one of the functions of the bogie is to guide the engine round curves, it was considered advisable to keep it as flexible as possible.' Obviously his opinion was not shared by the management at Derby and although Stanier had the brakes removed from all locomotives when he took office, it has to be said that there were, as far as we know, no accidents or derailments attributed to them.
19. For further details of the development and construction of the Bissell truck and history of the Midland's American locomotives, see *Supplement No. 1 to Midland Record* by David Hunt published by Wild Swan.
20. Stanier locomotives built after 1935 had Ferobestos linings on the bogie and pony truck slides when new. The instruction to carry out the modifications to earlier engines was considered urgent and accompanied by a memo from Stanier ordering its completion as soon as possible. It nevertheless took nearly 13 years.
21. For a more comprehensive description of the BR AWS see *LMS Locomotive Profile No. 2* on the Horwich moguls. That volume also contains an installation drawing of the system on those engines.
22. Some LMS documents refer to the colour of crimson lake engines as 'Derby Red' or 'Midland Red' right up to the Second World War. For a detailed discussion of the colour of LMS locomotives, see *An Illustrated History of LMS Locomotives Volume 1* by Essery and Jenkinson published by the Oxford Publishing Co.
23. St. Rollox had a tendency to go its own way as far as interpreting livery styles was concerned and most 'Scottish' engines had some departure from the norm at some stage. It comes as no great surprise, therefore, that it seems as though this particular alteration came from north of the border.

POSTSCRIPT

Withdrawal of the '2300' Class began with No. 42308 in August 1959 and by the end of 1963 there were just 32 of them left, with several of the survivors stored out of use. The last one, No. 42410, went in September 1966 and, sadly, none was preserved. It was a testament to their soundness of design that not only was their withdrawal concurrent with later designs of the same wheel arrangement but they remained for the most part on their design duties until the end. They were arguably the best locomotives to have emanated from the Derby Drawing Office during its days of pre-eminence and represented the first examples of one of the most successful groups of engines to run on any British railway. They were also a link between the pre- and post-Stanier days of the Midland, LMS and British Railways and were, to our way of thinking, worthy of preservation ahead of many other types that did survive. That none of them did is a great pity.

Caption continued from page 5

The faces of the original one-piece buffers were relatively flat compared with the later variety, the buffer beam was flush-riveted, and the buffer casings were mounted on 1in spacing blocks. The footsteps were flat and flush-riveted to their supports and there were no lifting holes in the front frames. The chimney had a broad and sharply undercut rim and there were no access holes with covers in the cylinder clothing. The tank vents protruded only a few inches above the tank sides, and tanks, cab and bunker were flush-riveted. The engine was fitted with pony truck and bogie brakes. Note that the exhaust injector was not visible when this photograph was taken as it was still positioned between the frames behind the ashpan. The oil boxes on the tank fronts supplied oil to the leading coupled wheel axlebox slides.

D27-10651 – Frame arrangement *(from pages 20/21)*

This 1927 drawing was initialled by W. Armin, the draughtsman who designed the frames, and shows those used on all except the last batch of 'Stanier' engines. There was, however, no frame arrangement issued for those locomotives but just a series of detail alteration sketches referred to on this one, the main differences being to the bogie centre and pony truck mountings and the depth of the portion between the bogie wheels. It shows the longer buffers and the later addition of lifting holes and stiffening plates above the front platform. At the top of the drawing is a side elevation of the platform angle, footsteps and supports. The steps drawn have been altered to show the turned-up ends fitted to engines built in the 1930s, i.e. 2375 onwards, and to a few others when replacements were required. Below the platform angle is a side elevation of the main frames and between the two are a series of cross sections. From left to right these are taken through: the front footsteps, footstep support and left-hand side of the front platform with, below that, the fabricated pony truck bearer; the front platform and stretcher; the stretcher below the front of the smokebox saddle, the saddle, and the raised platform; between the rear of the steam chest and the leading coupled axle; three frame stretchers; cab footsteps, support and stays; bogie centre plate and stretcher. Below the side elevation is a split plan view from above and below the platform with front and rear elevations to left and right respectively. The front elevation is also split with an external view above the centreline, showing some internal details dotted, and a section behind the buffer beam below it. The note on the lower edge referring to alterations for job number 5234 concerns the fitting of cast-steel cylinders in the 1940s and 1950s.

D28-10985 – General arrangement 2–6–4 tank engine *(from pages 31/32)*

The locomotive depicted in this drawing is one of the 2300-2324 series before most of the modifications described in the text were made. The exceptions are the 2½in thick buffer spacing blocks, that increased the overall length to 47ft 2¾in, and the repositioning of the exhaust steam injector. There are no lifting holes in the front frames, the side tank vents are short, bunker tank vents are the cast-iron mushroom type, the cab has long rear cut-outs and the engine still has bogie and pony truck brakes. As we have written before, GAs can be difficult to interpret as well as to describe. The layout of them and the amount of detail shown varied not only from drawing office to drawing office, but also between individual draughtsmen. This one is a good example of the genre and has a wealth of detail without being too cluttered. The side elevation is as though the engine has been cut in half and we are looking through the structure towards the outside. The bogie, however, has a different sectional plane to the rear of its centre, which shows the outside of the frame and equalising beam with a section through the brake mechanism. Some details, such as all but one of the boiler tubes, have been omitted for clarity, although the three rows of superheater flues and an element in the top one are shown. The brass ends at the rear of the superheater flues can be seen, as can the narrowing of the small tube at the rear and widening at the front. Some of the firebox roof stays are shown, including the front two rows of sling stays described in the text, and details of the regulator linkage, valve and main steam pipe in the dome can be seen. The water scoop is depicted in the down position with its flap valve to the rear for pick-up in the chimney-first direction. The plan is in two portions. Below the centreline is a view from above the engine with the boiler removed and the top of the cab and firebox sliced off. A portion of the platform above the left-hand cylinder has been removed and the cylinder itself sectioned to show details of the piston and gland. Some details below the tank top, platform and frame are shown dotted. Above it is a series of horizontal sections through components below the platform. There is, however, no common plane. Sections through cylinders, wheels and firebox are all taken on different planes whilst some items are not sectioned. Actual construction of the locomotives would have been undertaken using a series of detail and sub-structure arrangement drawings, some of which we have included. The overall GA was just to illustrate how it all went together and interpretation will be aided by reference to other drawings.

D27-10670 – Cab, side tank & bunker arrangement

(from pages 40/41)

This rather complex-looking drawing shows the arrangement of tanks, cab and bunker on engines 2300-2394. Along the top of the sheet is a side elevation of the structure sectioned along the centreline, i.e. we are looking from the middle of the locomotive out through the right-hand tank. Internal details of the tank are shown dotted. In front of the cab, above the tank, is a scrap plan view of the cab roof showing the ventilator. Below the front of the tank is a half-size (on the original) sketch of the slot that was cut in the inside lip of the tank to enable water to drain away rather than being trapped on the top. In the middle of the drawing is another side elevation, this time an external view from the left-hand side with the upper part of the cab omitted and internal detail dotted in. Below that is a plan view split along the centreline and with the upper part of the cab removed. The top half shows an external view of the right-hand tank and right-hand half of the bunker with internal detail dotted. The lower half of the plan is a horizontal section through the left-hand tank and left-hand half of the bunker with details of the bottom shown. Between the tanks is a plan of the bottom plate of the right-hand tank. The V-shaped structure seen in the two side elevations near the front of the tank was the anti-splash device referred to in the text, designed to stop surging water from bursting out of the forward filler when the engine came to a stop. The mechanism in the left-hand side tank at the front of the cab was the float that drove a water level indicator in front of the driver's spectacle. Just above and to the rear of that, the reversing screw bracket and handle are shown chain dotted. Note the lifting brackets on the tops of both side and bunker tanks and that the drawing shows the early arrangement of cast-iron bunker tank vent. It has, however, been amended to show the extra angle between the roof and front and back plates.

D33-12958 – Cab, side tank & bunker arrangement end views *(from page 28)*

This drawing accompanies D27-12957 and shows sections of the 'limousine cab' engines. At the top left is a view looking forward from inside the cab structure. To the left of the centreline the section is taken in the doorway and shows the rear of the side tank and the cab front without any fixings. To the right is a section taken forward of the door through the side tank with the window frames shown on the cab front. Superimposed on it are the Midland and Caledonian loading gauges, which show just how tight to gauge the engines were. Alongside is a view looking rearwards, to the left of the centreline, being taken from behind the door with the rear spectacle frame omitted. Right of the centreline the section is taken at the doorway and shows the spectacle frame. In the middle of the rearwards view we can see the frame for the coal door that was added from No. 2324. Below the rearwards view is a split rear elevation of the bunker. To the left of the centreline is an external view of the rear of the bunker with internal detail dotted in. To the right is a section taken partway into the bunker. At the bottom left of the drawing is a series of lateral sections taken on various vertical planes. From left to right they show sections at the front splasher, in between the splashers, at the rear splasher, and an external view of the tank front. Once again the drawing was developed from an earlier one showing the arrangement of Nos. 2300-2394 and the draughtsman has made the mistake of showing a cast-iron bunker tank vent. Nos. 2395-2494 were all built with 2in wrought-iron pipes running up to the cab roof. The drawing has been amended to show the extra angle at the join between the roof and front and rear plates as well as the rain gutters at the edges of the roof above the side windows. Between the front and rear views is a full-size (on the original) section through one of the gutters and the weld.

Most 'limousine cab' engines had the larger of the two lining panels on their bunkers with the power classification characters above the number, which was still in line with the emblem or crest. No. 42406 had the latter on its tank sides when photographed at Wakefield in July 1964, just over a year before it was withdrawn. The engine had all but one of the standard '2300' Class modifications including BR AWS – note the electrical conduit clipped to the lower edge of the platform angle and turning through it below the cab. The exception was that it retained full-height cab doors throughout its life. The rear buffer beam had been fitted with snap-head rivets following a repair and the locomotive had a 'full set' of Stanier wheels.
R. J. ESSERY (376)

These three photographs, again taken at Wakefield in July 1964, are included to show details of a 'limousine cab' engine, No. 42406, with extra rain gutters above the side windows and full-height cab doors. Note that none of the footsteps was as originally fitted; whilst the bunker and cab ones had turned-up ends, they were flush-riveted and those at the leading end, although fitted using snap-head rivets, had bent-up corners. Such things were not wholly uncommon in BR days. R. J. ESSERY (376A, 376B & 376C)

A Magic[illegible] Practical Guide To the Weird and Wonderful World of Popular Culture

---

"Asking yourself these deeper questions opens up new ways of being in the world. It brings in a breath of fresh air. The real trick to life is not to be in the know, but to be in the mystery."
—Fred Alan Wolf

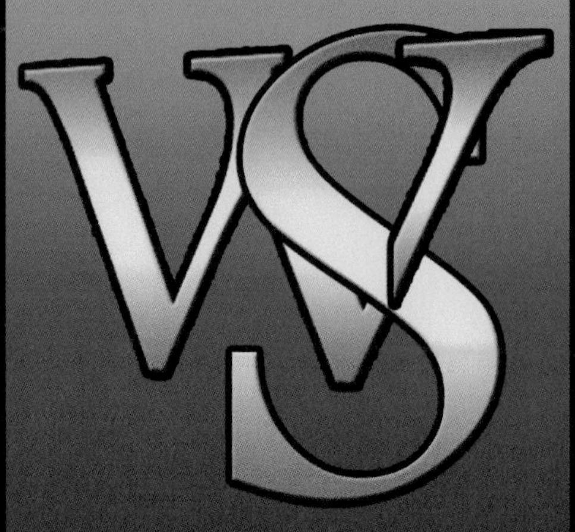

Weird Stuff

Winter 2013

Vol 1 #1

Co-Publishers
Freeman Fly
Jamie Hanshaw

Co-Editors
Freeman Fly
Jamie Hanshaw

To order more copies or get Operation: Culture Creation #2 write to:

Weird Stuff
P.O. Box 25186
Greenville, SC
29616

freeman@freemantv.com

An Exegesis on the Cover Art by Freeman

A shadowy pope-like sorcerer dangles a robot made from ipads and iphones, a commentary on the epidemic of screens being placed in front of our faces from birth. The robot is covered in corporate logos. The two small children are watching Donald Duck read from Adolph Hitler's book, *Mein Kampf*. Behind the sorcerer a cathedral column depicts catastrophe scenes of New York City. The path to the left represents nature, our source of happiness and a way to transcend the electronic mind control. The photo is from the Palenque Mayan ruins, a winding staircase leads down the mountain from the pyramid.

WeirdStuffMagazine.com FreemanTV.com

ISBN 978-0-9890988-0-9
ISSN 2326-1048

Contents

Written by
Jamie Hanshaw
Freeman Fly

The Vision of Ezekiel - 16th Century German Woodcut

The world is magical but designed to make us believe we are not magi.
-Pete Carroll

Once upon a time, the concept of magic was considered the synthesis of all arts, sciences and religions. Magic was, for the practitioners of it, their way of knowing God. It has been said that the twentieth century has been a time of everything losing its magic. Some may wonder, in the age of science and reason, of what value is magic when the natural has been deemed mediocre and the supernatural to be non-existent? Cold hard science has become the religion of our era. However, the human mind is reaching a crucial point in its evolution, rediscovering latent powers and preparing to develop new powers that would have once seemed supernatural. Magic is not the superstition of the past, it is the science of the future.

Now, magic is back in a big way because we as a species are becoming aware of some suppressed abilities that can only be described as magical. We are in the midst of a magical revival, the revealing of occult secrets that have come to the attention of the general public. The word 'occult' does not mean inherently evil. It simply means that which has been hidden. These ideas have been hidden from common people, in secret documents and secret meetings and private libraries; passed down through mystery schools, fraternities and through specific dynasties. These secrets are now coming to light.

For thousands of years, the brightest minds of humanity have sought to understand these arcane concepts of magic and alchemy. Now we are discovering that these were probably better understood by our ancient ancestors and were something we already knew how to do all along. We are now more genetically different from the people of 5,000 years ago as they were from the Neanderthals. At the same time studies show that in many ways, such as the nature and strength of our belief in the supernatural, we have not changed so much after all.

From the very beginning of human civilization there have been shamans, healers, dream interpreters, diviners, bards and astrologers. Their activities are among the first documented in history. For primitive people, magic was basically the use of man's latent abilities to influence the hunt or perhaps the battle using creative play. Of all the art forms practiced on the planet, Paleolithic cave paintings, known as the Magdalenian art system, is the least understood, the longest lasting and was the first in recorded history. When we study the hunting habits of the aboriginal peoples that are still around today, like the Pygmies of the Congo who will draw a picture in the sand of the animal they intend to hunt, or the Tungus of the Siberian tiaga, who will carve a wooden likeness of an animal they intend to capture, we discover that these rituals took place *before* the event. These cave drawings recorded somewhat of a prophesy and they depicted not what the men had *done*, but what they were *going* to do. Humans possess the unique ability to look upon the world and not only see it as it is, but what it could be and we call this ability the imagination. Everything that exists was once a figment of someone's imagination. Have a look at all the objects surrounding you, what you are seeing are thoughts that have come into materialization through creative work. Imagination is the soul's eye where forms are first outlined.

The instructional documents of one occult fraternity state that magic is an exercise that involves the use of will power and the visual imagination, emphasizing the indivisibility of the two in effective magical workings. *"To practice magic both the Imagination and the Will must be called into action, they are co-equal in the work...the Imagination must precede the Will in order to produce the greatest possible effect...When, however the two are conjoined, when the Imagination creates an image, and the Will directs and uses that image, marvelous magical effects may be obtained."* [1]

When a Cro-Magnon or Neanderthal man used his imagination and will-force to set out and slay an animal, this cave art became not just art, but the primitive idea of a magical sigil. Early man must have felt himself wholly surrounded by the supernatural almost every moment of the day. When an Azande tribesman of North Africa sets out to cultivate his crops in the morning, he will carry a charm to assist his hoe. In the afternoon when he goes for a hunt, he will leave behind a protective spell to guard his fields and take with him a medicine to guide his spear. For most primitives, magical rites are indispensable for enterprises ranging from hut building and cooking to funerals and war. "Savages" have preserved what science is rediscovering today. The farther we go back into the origins of the world, and the more closely we study primitive peoples, the more often we discover their traditional magical secrets coincide with the present state of scientific research.

Lascaux Cave in France

***

Quantum Physics

It has been said that anyone who claims to understand quantum physics doesn't really understand quantum physics because it is *that* strange. The theory states that subatomic particles cannot be pinned down in time or space and may be in two or more places at once. The same object may appear to be a particle, locatable in one place, or a wave, spread out over space and time. In quantum physics, the observer influences the object observed. There are no isolated eyewitnesses of a mechanical universe but everything participates within the universe. What exists beyond our five sense perception are infinite possibilities. *"A sizeable body of research exploring the nature of consciousness, carried on for more than thirty years in prestigious scientific institutions around the world, shows that thoughts are capable of affecting everything from the simplest machines to the most complex living beings."* [2]

What is the secret that masters of industry pay tens of thousands of dollars to hear from elite members of illuminati societies? It is that reality is built from thought and it behaves in accordance with the expectation of the observer. This is the driving force behind concepts such as the Law of Attraction which argues that thoughts, both conscious and unconscious, can affect changes in the material plane. The "Secret" in this case is that our imagination gives birth to creation.

What does the word "Magic" mean to us today? *Webster's Dictionary* gives four definitions....

Magic: from *magoi;* the magi or priests of the Medes and Persians skilled in astrology who predicted the Star of Bethelhem.

a. the use of means such as charms or spells believed to have supernatu-

Whatever it is that you are
feeling is a perfect reflection
of the process of what is becoming.
What you think and what you feel,
and what manifests is always a match.
~Esther Hicks,
The Teachings of Abraham

Finally, brethren, whatsoever things are true, whatsoever things are honest, whatsoever things are just, whatsoever things are pure, whatsoever things are lovely, whatsoever things are of good report; if there be any virtue, and if there be any praise, think on these things.
Philippians 4:8 KJV

Photo: Aleister Crowley's Thoth Tarot

ral power over natural forces

b. an extraordinary power or influence seemingly from a supernatural source

c. something that seems to cast a spell or enchantment

d. the art of producing illusions by sleight of hand, prestidigitation, or stage magic.

According to the infamous occultist, Aleister Crowley, one whose philosophy has shaped the 20th century, "Magic is the science and art of causing change to occur in conformity with the will." This was stated in the early 1900's when science agreed that there was plenty to discover about the universe, but that it was a fundamentally dead and mechanical universe. 21st century rediscoveries have made us aware that the universe is stranger and more interesting than our ancestors realized and may turn out stranger than even scientists are willing to admit.

***

Consciousness

According to the classic magicians, the secret of magic was the absolute understanding of the four elements and human mastery over them, but then a new buzzword entered into the vocabulary and that word was "consciousness" and we were all suddenly very conscious of our consciousness. Consciousness or "wakefulness" is the state of being aware of one's own existence, sensations, emotions, thoughts and surroundings. It is information received and decoded by the brain. To understand consciousness you would have to come to terms with the idea that the 'world' is in your 'head'. So the definition of magic changed in accordance with the magical axiom of Hermetic Philosophy, "As Above, So Below" and we discover that the universe is mental and we are but a microcosm in the macrocosm. Now we have a more contemporary definition which states that: *"Magick is the science and art of causing change in consciousness to occur in conformity with the will, using means not currently understood by traditional western science."*[3] In other words, anything you can imagine, anything you can symbolize can be made to produce a change in consciousness and therefore changes in your environment. Any adjustment in the way in which we perceive the world is a transformation in the world itself and this is the essence of magic.

Magic rituals are sort of like virtual reality, hacking into the five senses and manipulating them to decode a different reality to the one they normally would. Mind very much resembles matter, both in degrees of density and in its peculiarity of design. Mind and matter are mirror images of one another. The idea of the universe as a 'giant brain' has been proposed by scientists and science fiction writers but now physicists say there may be some evidence that it's actually true. According to a study published in *Nature's Scientific Reports*, the universe may be growing in the same way as a giant brain with the electrical firing between brain cells 'mirrored' by the shape of expanding galaxies.

The mysteries of Quantum Physics coalesce with another modern discovery called String Theory which is the discovery that the universe is a symphony of vibrating strings. In Genesis it says that God created the world with his voice. All physical matter is a result of frequency. If you amplify the frequency, the structure of the matter will change. There is a physical phenomenon called "harmonic resonance." We have all seen how a wine glass will shatter if you place it near the correct fre-

"Magic is the art of effecting changes in consciousness at will."
~William Butler

"All that we are is the result of what we have thought."
~Buddha

quency. If one object vibrates powerfully enough, another object nearby will start to vibrate (or resonate) with the first *if* they share a natural vibratory rate. For example, if a violin string is played near a piano, the piano strings that have a harmonic relationship to the violin note will begin to resonate. Magicians know that if you can control the vibratory rate of an object, you can cause reactions in other objects. Therefore, the knowledge of how to vibrate certain words becomes essential.

The study of visible sound and vibrations' effect on matter is called Cymatics. One of the earliest to record that an oscillating body displayed regular patterns was Galileo Galilei. By placing sand, crystals, water or oil on a flat surface and vibrating that surface at different frequencies, you will see complex patterns begin to appear. Depending on the frequency, emerging patterns perfectly resemble many religious symbols like the Star of David or the Hindu Mandala. Ancient Hermetic philosophers all taught the theory of vibration. The great geometrician, Pythagoras, also held that everything that exists is a vibration. This allowed him to be the first to demonstrate the mathematical foundation of music.

So, the subatomic particles we see in nature, the quarks that form hadrons are nothing but musical notes on a tiny vibrating string. Physics is nothing but the laws of harmony that you can write on those strings and chemistry is the melodies you can play on interacting strings. We are nothing but cosmic music played out on vibrating strings and membranes. Everything that exists is an energy field, a unique vibrational pattern of energy created by thought and emotion. We do not live in a solid physical world. Atoms are virtually empty. Waveform is the prime reality in the universe and the base construct is waveform information encoded as vibrational resonance.

You are not only your physical body, you are a standing wave. Your consciousness uses your body to interface with the three dimensional world much like a person uses

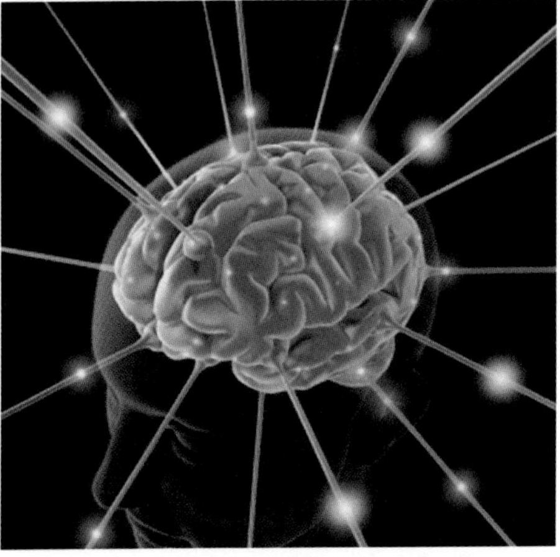

a computer to interface with the internet. The mind-body computer is an incredibly advanced biological system which decodes information and allows our infinite awareness to interact with this range of frequencies that we call the world. This is how our five senses work. When we hear a noise, it comes to us through sound vibration. We see a green leaf but it is merely the color vibration gathered by the eyes and transmitted to the brain. There are many vibrations which are pitched so high or so low that our five senses cannot decode them. Our visual range as shown in the electromagnetic spectrum chart in any school points to the existence of many other frequencies beyond the human range—ultraviolet, radiowave, infrared, microwave and gamma. Occult lore has insisted that there are various other forms of consciousness that exist in these realms.

"There is no matter as such – All matter originates and exists only by virtue of a force which brings the particle of an atom to vibration and holds this most minute solar system of the atom together. We must assume behind this force the existence of a conscious and intelligent mind. This mind is the matrix of all matter."
– Max Planck

The secret that the powerful people of history have kept hidden is that there are ways to 'hack' this three dimensional reality. The Law of Attraction is a cornerstone of occult teaching. It is the belief that "like attracts like" meaning you attract those things that you are in vibrational resonance, or 'in tune' with. Thoughts are vibrations and every thought you have becomes somewhat of a "wish." The more you experience the feeling of having something, the more likely you will have it. This can be a good thing or a bad thing depending on what you've been thinking about. The genetic material of the body is

"Imagination is everything; it is the preview of life's coming attractions."
~Albert Einstein

a highly sophisticated transmitter and receiver of frequencies. Amino acids act as a micro antenna. These antenna on our DNA are activated or closed down by the wave lengths of emotion which constantly pass through them.

The outstanding thinkers, Einstein, Tesla, and Edison all agree that every time you think a thought, your brain transmits a frequency. The more intensity of emotion you put into that thought, the more will material connections will be attracted to it. Thoughts transmit vibration and it is always attracting similar vibrations. Moments when everything seems to fall together have a quality of hinting that there is someone "up there" who either likes you or hates you. That is only yourself manifesting what you've been dwelling on. There is no punishment, only cause and effect.

***

Emotions

All magic seems to be the result of associations, or changes in consciousness, powered by emotions. These emotions play a vital role in knowing what we are creating. Our emotions help to chemically reinforce data into long-term memory and we can observe how our thoughts plus emotions create reality at a cellular level.

A cell is the smallest unit of consciousness in the body. The part of our brain that regulates emotion is called the hypothalamus. It assembles small chain amino acid sequences called neuro-peptides that match every emotional state we experience. These peptides are released into the blood stream through the pituitary gland and travel to different parts of the body looking for cells to bond with. A single cell has billions of receptor sites. When a peptide docks into a receptor, it sends a signal into the cell setting off a biochemical reaction that can change the nucleus of the cell itself in many ways. If a cell is constantly bombarded with the same emotional chemistry, when it divides, the new cell will have more receptor sites specifically designed to receive that particular neuro-peptide.

Emotions play a fundamental role in a person's moral life. They transform values into actions. Emotions reinforce strength of will and courage of convictions. When researchers have studied unemotional people, they find out that their dealings with others are shallow, lifeless and mechanical. Without emotion you are a robot. *"Magic is a science and art comprising a system of concepts and methods for the build up of human emotion, altering the electrochemical balance of the metabolism, using associational techniques and devices to concentrate and focus this emotional energy, thus modulating the energy broadcast by the human body."*[4] In magic, a wave of powerful emotion is projected with calculated intent by someone who has developed his powers to an abnormal pitch and according to occultists the results can be far reaching.

In the world of Harry Potter there are two types of people, the magicians and the muggles. This implies that there are some people who can perform magic and others who cannot. The chosen few, who are of a certain ancestry, must be initiated and indoctrinated by a priest craft in order to perform miracles. We hold that in reality this is simply not true. Magic is a change in consciousness and a change in consciousness is a change in reality. Any deliberate action which produces a visible ripple

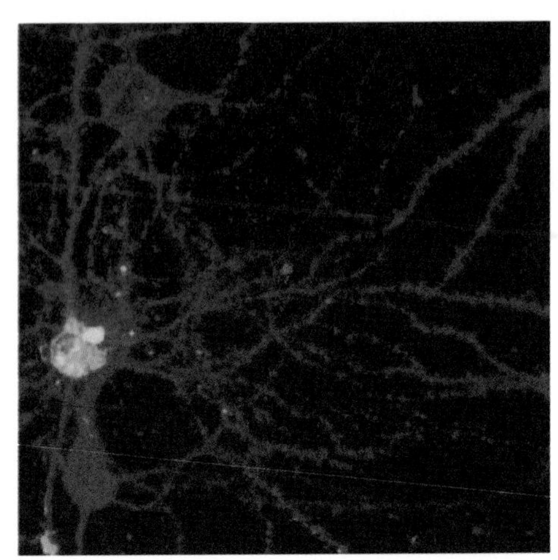

over the surface of our existence can be considered a magical act. If working magic is as simple as combining our free will with imagination, it seems that we are all magicians. *"Since everyone who lives is possessed of the magical ability to transform matter and to produce mental worlds, then everyone is a magician."*[5] The idea of God answering prayer could also be described as an extraordinary power or influence from a supernatural source. Modern philosophers would call this experience "co-creation." In its broadest sense, magic is

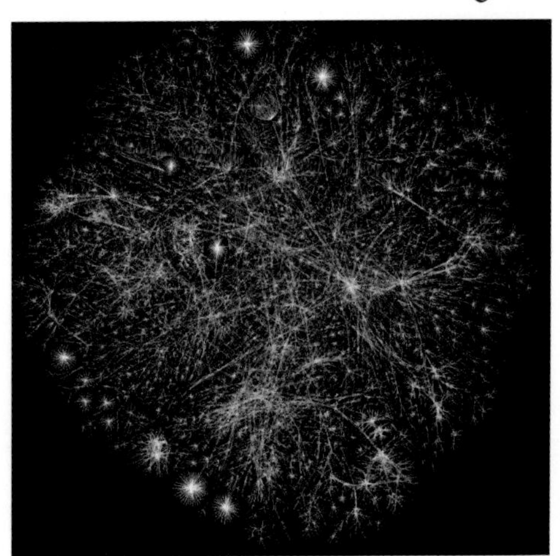

the art of making things happen.

So, if we are constantly practicing magic by co-creating our own reality, how can we tell if our works will bear the fruit of good or evil? *Modern Magick* gives us examples of three different types of magic:
1.White Magick, which is "for the purpose of obtaining the Knowledge and Conversation of your Holy Guardian Angel." A curious goal for a phenomenon that has always been deemed by the church as dangerous heresy.
2. Black Magick is done "for the purpose of causing physical or non-physical harm to yourself or others, and is done either consciously or unconsciously."
3. Grey Magick is a mixture of black and white magic and is done "for the purpose of causing physical or non physical good to yourself or others." This is also done consciously or unconsciously. Isaac Bonewits states that "There is nothing that we as scientists (and all magicians are scientists) can label "Black Magic" or "White Magic" just as we cannot as scientists label anything "Good" or "Evil." That is the job of ethics, not science." Some magicians disregard the monochromatic idea of black and white magic altogether and adhere to a full color spectrum where Green magic is done for the earth and fertility; Blue magic is for emotions; Red magic has to do with matters of the body and so on. Aleister Crowley's successor, Kenneth Grant, states that "There is only Magick; whether it is 'black' or 'white' in the moral sense depends solely on the intent of the operator." In truth, there are as many systems of magic as there are people on the planet for no two magicians are the same and the magic works best if it is your own.

One way of knowing if we are manifesting good is simply by being sensitive to our emotional guidance system otherwise known as our conscience, which is the root word for consciousness. The Latin, *conscientia*, primarily means moral conscience, suggesting that simply by being aware, we can also inherently distinguish between good and evil. You don't need a religion to have morals, if you can't determine right from wrong, you lack empathy, not religion.

Many people believe that the creator left us a book to help humanity discern good from evil, but we believe that this information is encoded within our very DNA. The physical body has set up defense mechanisms to keep itself from harm. So does the spiritual body. In physical form we call this warning sign pain. If you put your hand in a fire the body sends signals of pain to teach you that this is damaging and should be avoided. So it is with our conscience. If we are feeling emotional distress at a certain activ-

"If the magician uses his powers for good purposes, he may choose for himself, the expression "white magic"; if he uses his faculties for bad purposes he may talk about "black magic"; but no matter whether the actions of a magician are morally good or bad, they are brought about by exactly the same laws." —Franz Bardon, *The Practice of Magical Evocation* ity this is a clear indication that we should probably stop. In the literal sense, "conscientia" means knowledge-with, that is, shared knowledge meaning every single person, deep down, some deeper than others, has the God given ability to know right from wrong. It's really very simple, when you are doing right, you feel good. You are positive about the outcome. You are excited and looking forward to things ahead. Positive thoughts coupled with good feelings equal good works. The thoughts that we offer formulate our and others' future experience in life.

The psychological and moral orientation with which one embarks on the process of shaping reality will determine whether the magic they practice is 'white' or 'black.' When you are feeling negative emotions, when you are in fear, jealousy, worry, vengefulness or self-pity, you are unwittingly practicing black magic. It's extremely emotionally taxing to be evil. Why do you think all presidents age so rapidly when they come into office? Any incantations addressed to the angels are not essentially different from those for invoking demons. The difference is solely one of intention. Any magical operation that taps the universes' occult power can do so for good or evil ends, depending on the magician.

It is a very interesting study when one attempts to reconcile occult mysticism and Christianity. One man who tried to do so was the Catholic saint Albertus Magnus. He was the Dumbledore of 13th century. According to legend, Magnus is said to have discovered the philosopher's stone and passed it to his pupil, Thomas Aquinas. As a German Dominican friar, bishop and instructor in Paris, Magnus endeavored in particular to find some species of accommodation between magic and Christian theology. He believed the 'three wise men' or magi of the Bible were practitioners of a kind of 'natural magic' which relied on inherent principles of nature and the supernatural influence of the stars. Church fathers could not disregard the cohesion Magnus put forth in his numerable works and long after he died, he was sainted in 1931 as Saint Albert the Great.

Christian theology plays a large role in the history of magic. In his letter to the Philippians apostle Paul hits upon the Law of Attraction when he writes "Be careful for nothing; (i.e. don't worry) but in every thing by prayer and supplication with thanksgiving let your requests be made known unto God." When we meditate with gratitude and have faith that the universe or God is working in our favor we can co-create the world that we desire. What we dwell upon, positive or negative, will be manifested in reality. You will always get what you think about most of the time. At the subatomic

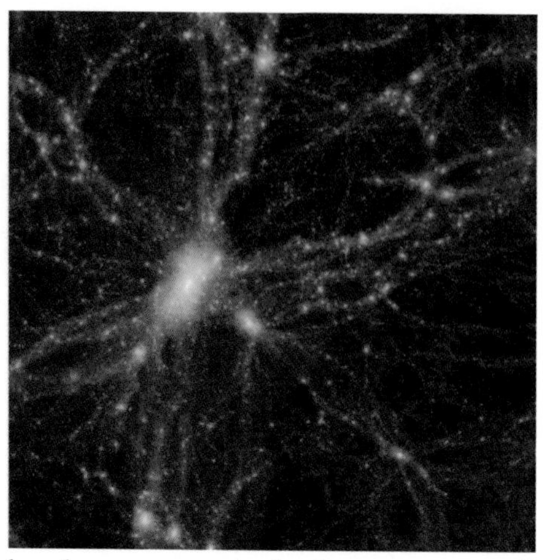

level we are actively "imagineering" the material world into existence. Maybe the concept of magic isn't so hard to understand after all.

This simplification of good and evil may seem childish at first but Christ tells us in the gospel of Matthew that this is the only way we can experience the Kingdom of Heaven or the true Magic Kingdom. The best investigator of the occult, or of almost anything else, has a childlike sense of curiosity and wonder about seemingly mundane things. To understand magical thinking it

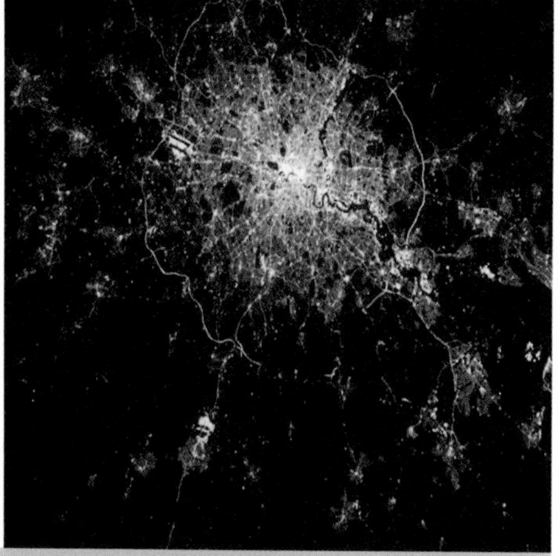

Physicists have discovered that the stucture of a brain cell is the same as the entire universe. The image on the top left shows three neuron cells of a mouse's brain. An international group of astrophysicists used a computer simulation to re-ceate how the universe grew and evolved. The image on the top right is a simulation snapshot of the present universe that features a large cluster of galaxies, surrounded by thousands of stars and dark matter. The image at bottom left shows a graphical representation of the internet and bottom right is a photo taken from space of London at night.

Albertus Magnus

might be helpful to recall a time in your life when there was no clear dividing line between the inner world and the outer; between the real and imaginary; when everything in the physical world seemed to possess a mysterious power of its own; when angels, demons, fairies, and ghosts were as real as the living room furniture—in other words: childhood.

In Matthew, chapter 18, the disciples came to Jesus with an interesting question. They wanted to know who understood Jesus' teachings the best. Who was living and thinking in a way that pleased God the most? "At the same time came the disciples unto Jesus, saying, Who is the greatest in the kingdom of heaven? and Jesus answered: Verily I say unto you, except ye be converted, and become as little children, ye shall not enter into the kingdom of heaven. Whosoever therefore shall humble himself as this little child, the same is greatest in the kingdom of heaven." Jesus instructs his disciples to work magic in Matthew 10:7-8: "And as ye go, preach, saying: The kingdom of heaven is at hand" meaning it is available to us at any time, not just upon death. We can make the world into a heaven or a hell depending on how we choose to see it. He goes on to tell the disciples to perform their own miracles. "Heal the sick, cleanse the lepers, raise the dead, cast out devils, freely ye have received, freely give." In John 14:12 Christ tells us "Verily verily I say unto you: He that believeth on me, the works that I do shall he do also and greater works than these shall he do." So, now we are at a point in our evolution where there is the potential to see millions of Christs, millions of Buddhas and millions of Gandhis.

Why should magic be at odds with science or religion? Science is supposed to be the absolute and complete possession of the truth. Pioneer scientists were also magicians. Chemistry comes from alchemy, astronomy comes from astrologers. Several hundred years ago the magician represented and reconciled many different practices. He possessed the knowledge of magical arts, he was a physician, theologian, and philosopher. One of the most notable examples of this kind of magician was the Swiss alchemist and physician, Paracelsus. He was called "the golden doctor" because he used alchemical methods to examine the magical properties of minerals. He was one of the first physicians to make use of magnets and magnetism in treating patients and paved the way for Mesmer and Freud. Paracelsus, stated that "*The existence of true magic does not require any ceremonies or conjurations, or the making of circles and signs; it requires neither benedictions nor maledictions in words, neither verbal blessings nor curses.*" He believed that an experienced magician would be able to influence the physical health of a person, for good or bad, simply by thinking about them. "*It is possible that my spirit, without the help of my body, and through the ardent will alone, and without a sword, can stab and wound others. It is possible that I can bring the spirit of my adversary into an image and then fold him up and lame him at my pleasure.*"

One does not need to be an occultist to perform magic, as we have seen; we do this naturally on a daily basis without even knowing it. "*A person can be a superb occultist and a lousy magician and vice versa; the basic talents involved are not the same and only rarely do they show up in the same individual.*"[6] We can equate an occultist as a scientist and a magician as the engineer. Those who do not know what they are doing are compelled to perform magic strictly through the observation of rituals, those who understand its real nature and purpose can move directly to its center and act from there without the need for incantations. The ability to bestow blessings or curses upon others lies not in the secret chamber of the ceremonial magician, but only in the intent of the emotion put forth into the universe. Such is the power of thought.

Paracelsus

"The art of artistic creation is nothing less than a magical operation. The finished work itself is a magical object, a species of talisman, capable of invoking and concentrating occult or cosmic energies."

— *The Elixir and the Stone*

The Laws of Magical Thinking Will Be Crucial To Your Comprehension. The magician knows that somewhere in nature there is a cause for every effect. However, there are many effects which continue to confound our understanding. Magic is a science dedicated to the perception and classification of these invisible causes. *"To be a magician one must learn to investigate all phenomena with the eye of a scientist who scorns no possible hypothesis nor neglects to take into the fullest consideration the complete structure of our actual and potential being."*—Bernard Bromage. Magical thinking is not random, it has its own laws and logic but it is poetic rather than rational.

The Law of Knowledge states that understanding brings control. If you can know all there is to learn about something then you have absolute and total control over it. The more you learn, the stronger you become. Knowledge is power, information is energy. To the magician, the goal and purpose of existence is knowledge and experience. The notion that knowledge is power is true for both the outside world and the inner man, which is why its sub-law is **The Law of Self Knowledge.** Across the portico of the Temple at Delphi and other ancient mystery schools can be seen the phrase "Know Thyself." One of the best ways to begin your magical path is to begin to learn about yourself beginning from the inside out. Start with the smallest thing and work your way up. Ask yourself these questions... What am I? What am I made of? What are cells? How do they work? What blood type am I? What do blood cells do? How does digestion work? How do different foods affect me?

The Law of Names states that knowing the complete and total true name of something gives you control over it. The belief that the name of a thing contains the essence of its being is one of the oldest in magic. In fact "to name" in Hebrew means "to make appear" and in English to "in-form" means the same, to give form to something that was previously vague. There is a common belief throughout the world that if you give a person a new name you give him a new soul. Do you remember the plot of the children's movie, *The Never Ending Story*?

There is an Egyptian legend which describes how the goddess Isis tried to capture the power of

The Lesser Banishing Ritual of the Pentagram

The Jews have an ancient prayer called the Kadish which is exactly like the Lord's Prayer in the Book of Matthew. The prayer is divided into a series of separate statements each of which is believed to be a veiled reference to the secret cosmic sciences. It was taught that the very words and sounds were capable of producing strange and wonderful things. The LBRP is the beginning and ending of many Kabalist magician's ceremonies and its main purpose is for purification.

Part One: The Kabalistic Cross

1. Touch the forehead and vibrate (say)
ATEH (thou art)
2. Touch the middle of the solar plexus and vibrate
MALKUTH (Kingdom)
3. Touch the right shoulder and vibrate
VE-GEVURAH (and Power)
4. Touch the left shoulder and vibrate
VE-GEDULAH (and Glory)
5. Clasp the hands before you and vibrate
LE-OLAHM (forever)
6. Hands as before, with the dagger between fingers, point up, vibrate **AMEN**

Part Two: The Formulation of the Pentagrams

The magician moves in a clockwise circle while vibrating (reciting) four of the Hebrew names of God towards the four corners.
To the East: **YHVH (Yahweh)**
To the South: **ADNI (Ahdohnye)**
To the West: **AHIH (I am)**
To the North: **AGLA**
(Thou art great forever my lord)

Part Three: The Evocation of the Archangels

Extend the arms in the form of a cross, say:
Before me, Rah-Fay-El (RAPHAEL)
Behind me, Gahb-Ray-El (GABRIEL)
On my right hand, Mih-Chai-El (MICHAEL)
And on my left hand, Ohr-Ree-El (AURIEL)
For about me flames the pentagram,
And within me shines the six-rayed star.

the sun god, Ra, by discovering his secret name. She mingled together some of his spit with the earth to create a venomous snake that bit him. When every remedy had been tried and failed he agreed that Isis should take his name, his identity and his powers. In Indian and Egyptian culture, during the naming ceremony, each infant receives two names, one of which must remain secret. Mormons also do this in their wedding ceremonies. In Genesis, Adam performs the essentially magical act of naming the plants and creatures. Through this act he obtains God's gift to him of dominion over the earth. To name a thing is to impose form upon it. Individuals undergoing initiation rites in many diverse cultures acquire new and often secret names which potential enemies do not know and cannot exploit.

The New Testament makes it clear that people could use the name of Jesus to cast out demons and perform other miracles even if they did not follow him or accept his teaching. This is an example of **The Law of Words of Power** saying that there are certain words that are able to change the inner and outer reality of those saying them. For this reason it is not surprising that in magic, certain words were thought to have such enormous power that they were taboo. The most notorious magic word being "ABRACADABRA" which derives from the Aramaic Avrah KaDabra, meaning "I create as I speak." In Eastern mysticism these are known as mantras and the power is believed to lie in the very sounds of the words themselves.

The root of all magic is The Word. "In the beginning was the Word, and the Word was with God, and the Word was God." John 1:1. In every culture the shaman is the one with the biggest vocabulary, that's why we call them spell-ing words. In western occultism there is a great deal of emphasis on the names of God as words of power. The Bible and the Talmud are full of rules concerning the name YHVH or the "Tetragrammaton." This is the original four letter word that was never to be spoken out loud, except by the high priest in the holy of holies. Instead of the

sacred name being intoned it was changed to become Yahweh or Jehovah. *"With the name Jod He Vau He one commands Nature; kingdoms are conquered in the name of Adonai, and the occult forces which compose the empire of Hermes are one and all obedient to him who knows how to pronounce duly the incommunicable name of Agla."*[7] The Kabbalistic magician believes that physical matter can be transformed molecule by molecule through incantation of ancient Hebrew letters and numbers and that the nature of reality is merely an illusion. In Hermetic belief, individual letters can be the equivalent of storage cells, repositories charged with a form of divine or magical power as a battery is charged with electrical energy.

Russian scientist, Pjotr Garjajev, a biophysicist and molecular biologist confirmed that DNA can be programmed by words and frequencies. Words *are* frequencies. Experiments showed that DNA can be healed simply through vibrations and spoken sound. The human DNA is a biological internet and superior in many aspects to the artificial one. This greater understanding of DNA's role as a crystalline receiver-transmitter can explain intuition, clairvoyance, telepathy, and spontaneous healing.

The Law of Association states that if two things have something in common, anything, that thing can be used to control both and they mutually influence each other. It is also interesting that the major function of the human brain seems to be association. According to **The Law of Similarity**, effects resemble causes and the magician infers that he can produce any effect just by imitating it. Therefore, if you want to make something fly, you must put feathers or wings on it, chirp over it and so forth. In magic, look-alikes *are* alike. Nutritionists are finding evidence of this law in the ways that different foods work in our body. A sliced carrot looks like an eye and it enhances blood flow to the eye and improves vision. A tomato has four chambers and is red like a heart; they are also loaded with lycopene that is good for the heart. A walnut looks like a brain and helps develop neurons to enhance brain function.

The Law of Contagion states that things that have once been in contact with each other continue to act on each other at a distance even after physical contact has been severed. A Maasai warrior from east Africa wears a lion's mane to acquire the animal's strength and bravery. British Columbian Indians rub a baby girl with the body of a beaver to make her industrious. The pueblo Indians of New Mexico believe that rain can be summoned by means of imitative magic, which is a form of sympathetic magic. In traditional rain dances, priests will roll round stones on a floor to stimulate thunder, sprinkle water on the ground like rain, and place a bowl of water on the alter to simulate full springs and pools. Most magical thinking involves the idea of transmitting qualities and attributes. This forms the basic idea of what is called "contagious" magic.

Early man must have reasoned that if ice is cold and makes you cold and if fire is hot and makes you hot, the beaver's industriousness or the lion's strength will rub off as well. In some primitive tribes, the heart of a valiant enemy might be eaten to gain his courage; but more often the transmission works through symbols. A man in a motorcycle gang might feel he has assumed some of the "devilry" of the face on his jacket. Similarily, a young girl is a princess when wearing a tiara.

Another way of observing this principle is the concept of quantum entanglement. Bell's theorem states that: "Particles once in common continue to influence one another instantaneously, even across the light-year stretches of galaxies." Einstein called this "spooky action at a distance." Contagious magic shades into Sympathetic magic which is based on the idea that whatever happens to part of something, or its image, will happen to the whole. Thus it was always a good idea to keep your nail clippings, hair, saliva and other bodily cast-offs out of the hands of those who wish to do you harm. These are thought to retain the qualities of the person over which the sorcerer gains power. Pop star, Madonna even has an entire clean up crew to erase all traces of her DNA from backstage and concert venues!

The Law of Imitation is where one entity assumes the characteristics of another. Magic and sorcery depend heavily on mimicry. When a high priest of the O.T.O. dons the mask of an ibis in a ritual, he is the conduit and becomes the god Thoth for the duration of the ritual. Sorcerers know that if you show people something they will inherently imitate it. It is our nature. People learn from one another through the process of imitation. Babies learn to speak by imitating adults. In this way, the origins of deviant behavior are very similar to the origins of fads and fashions. Each is a socially learned acquisition. The law of imitation spreads from the top down; consequently, youngsters imitate older individuals, the poor imitate the rich, peasants imitate royalty, and so on. Many of our cultural customs come from peasants copying the rituals of royalty. Crime among young, poor or low-status people is really their effort to imitate wealthy, high-status people. This law suggests perhaps people follow the model of high-status in hopes that their imitative behavior will procure some of the rewards associated with being of a "superior" class. The motto for this is "monkey see monkey do."

The Law of Synthesis or **The Law of Opposites** states that the synthesis of two conflicting ideas will produce a new third idea that will not be a compromise of the original two. **The Law of Polarity** says that anything can be separated into two opposite parts with each part having its own essence and that everything contains its opposite. This doctrine of opposites grew from Greek philosphers' impression that pairs of opposites in nature had a journey to become One; the "something" that underlies all of creation connecting the opposites and reconciles all diversity. They called the perfect balance between opposites "Justice." The Yin Yang is a Chinese symbol for the Laws of Synthesis and Polarity. The most famous phrasing of this law in Western occultism is "As above, so below."

One Kabbalistic legend says that God wished to behold God. In other words, God wanted to re-create himself. However, that posed a problem because for something that was absolute, omnipotent, omniscient and omnipresent to create "an- other" it first had to create the idea of duality.

The Law of Balance states that if you wish to survive, you must keep all aspects of your universe balanced. Fanaticism is to be avoided because the further you go towards extremes, the less flexible and adaptable you become.

The Law of Infinite Data states that there is always new information to be discovered on every subject. The sources of knowledge are limitless if one wishes to tap them. Although, within **The Law of Finite Senses** they are limited to the amount of information which one can absorb and process at any given time. **The Law of Infinite Universe** states that because there are an infinite number of ways to perceive the world, there are an infinite number of worlds we may assemble from our awareness. Each person sees his universe or world a different way; therefore, no two people have identical views of the world. All people do not receive the same information or data; if they do, they view it differently, thus making for an endless number of universes. Every being inhabits a different sphere of consciousness, a butterfly lives in a butterfly universe and a fish lives in a fish universe and so on. The theory of the Multiverse says there are infinite parallel universes containing every possible situation.

The Law of Personification states that any object or phenomenon may be considered to be alive and to have a personality. By complete association between yourself and that personality or "entity" you can *become* that entity. A true Vampire would tell you that in order to become a vampire you must first identify yourself a vampire, study vampires, behave like a vampire, associate with other vampires and in the end you will be one. You will always become what you imitate. Its sub-laws are The Law of Invocation and Evocation in which the magician can conjure up from the inside and outside, real entities. The key phrase for these two laws is: "Beings within, beings without." The process of dealing with external powers is called evocation and that of dealing with internal powers is called invocation.

***

The Magician

In the Tarot, the number of the Magician is I. The "All One" concept that many religions speak of is really the infinite, eternal consciousness of God having separate experiences in a tiny range of frequencies called the physical world. The duality or "otherness" of our ego enwraps each of us in a lonely mental prison but the magician sees all of creation in his own body and vice versa. To die without dying is one of the great ordeals of the magical path and this is primarily symbolic of the death of the solitary ego.

We are all a part of God experiencing itself from different points of view. You are me and I am you. Your happiness is my happiness, and your pain is my pain. Your success is my success and any harm done to one is a detriment to all. Whatever affects one directly affects all indirectly. This is the interrelated structure of reality. John Donne caught it years ago and placed it in graphic terms. *"No man is an Island, entire of itself; every man is a piece of a Continent, a part of the main. Any man's death diminishes me because I am involved in mankind; and therefore never send to know for whom the bell tolls; It tolls for thee."*

There are always different ways of being in the world, no matter how scarce they tell you things are. There is a story about an anthropologist who proposed a game to the children of an African tribe. He put a basket full of sweet fruit near a tree and said that whoever could get there first would win the fruit. When he told them to run they all took each other's hands and ran together, then sat together enjoying their treats. When he asked them why they had run like that they said: "UBUNTU, how can one of us be happy if all the other one's are sad?" 'UBUNTU' in the Xhosa culture means: "I am because we are."

Magic itself is a symbol of the greater unity and the object of magic is the raising of consciousness or "enlightenment." This is known as High Magic and is intended to bring about the spiritual transformation of the person who practices it and is designed to channel the magician's consciousness toward God. The aim of high magic has been described as communication with one's Holy Guardian Angel or higher self. This is also known as theurgy which means "divine work" or the use of magical means to attain religious salvation.

As magicians and co-creators of reality we have a great responsibility to protect our mind and imagination from dark forces. If you do not understand the way reality works you will remain a passive victim, a powerless slave to circumstance. Almost since the beginning of the human race, the molding of men has been done by those who knew something of thought's great power. If you do not learn how to use your imagination correctly, it will be used against you. We must always be careful of who we grant access to effect changes in our consciousness. When you enter the magic kingdom of Disney, Dreamworks, or any other corporate social engineer, therein lies an agenda to capture your imagination. In a place where dreams come true, whose dreams are we manifesting into reality? The borders of the kingdom of magic do not stop at the walls of Disneyland. Whether you believe our world belongs to the good or the evil, it is a world of magic none the less.

***

1. *The Rebirth of Magic*, Francis King & Isabel Sutherland
2. *The Intention Experiment*, Lynn McTaggart
3. *Modern Magick*, Donald Michael Kraig
4. *Real Magic*, Isaac Bonewits
5. *The Magician's Dictionary*, E.E. Rehmus
6. *Real Magic*, Isaac Bonewits
7. *The Key of the Mysteries*, Eliphas Levi

Books:

Man, God and Magic, Ivar Eissner

The Holographic Universe, Michael Talbot

The Occult, A History, Colin Wilson

Movies:

What the Bleep Do We Know?, Betsy Chasse, Mark Vicente

Down the Rabbit Hole, Betsy Chasse, Mark Vicente

The Secret, Drew Heriot, Sean Byrne

Other Resources:

Your Wish is Your Command, Kevin Trudeau

A ride at EPCOT called "Imagination" sponsored by Kodak

"The art of divine Magic consists in the ability to perceive the essence of things in the light of nature and by using the soul-powers of the spirit to produce material things from the unseen universe, and in such operations the Above and the Below must be brought together and made to act harmoniously. Magic is spiritual wisdom. Arcane knowledge misapplied is sorcery."

—Helena P. Blavatsky
The Secret Doctrine

1	2	3	■	4	5	6	■	■	7	8	9	10
11			■	12			■	13				
14			■	15			■	16				
17			■	■	18		19		■	■	■	■
■	20		21	■	22			■	■	23	24	25
■	■	■	26	27		■	28	29	30			
31	32	33			■	■	■	34				
35					36	■	37			■	■	■
38			■	■	39	40				41	42	■
■	■	■	■	43				■	■	44		45
46	47	48	49		■	50		51	■	52		
53					■	54			■	55		
56				■	■	57			■	58		

Across:

1. Norse Underworld Goddess
4. Government group controlling substances
7. Anonymous does it for these
11. Sumerian sky god
12. NewYork time
13. pretty gal
14. Beastie Boys' "License to ___"
15. class for an immigrant
16. a treat for a squirrel
17. tiny (slang)
18. "_____Rider"
20. Albert Hoffmann's discovery
22. government eavesdroppers
23. tree of Druids
26. companion of 28 across
28. Ibis headed deity
31. an alchemist's concoction
34. heart vessel
35. The Cranberries' hit (1994)
37. snake of the Nile
38. suffix for a lifeform
39. Valentine Michael Smith, for one
43. mobile dwelling
44. hive dweller
46. September sign
50. bored replies
52. Ain Soph ___ (Kabbala)
53. Homer's epic
54. son of Akhenaton
55. prefix meaning "three"
56. feline comment
57. before, to a poet
58. Goddess of the Dawn

Down:

1. with 45 down, a Discordian cry
2. son of 11 across
3. calms
4. John _____, astrologer to Queen Elizabeth I
5. member of ascetic Jewish sect
6. he carried the world on his shoulders
7. Latin prefix meaning "light"
8. Organization once headed by Aleister Crowley
9. Manannan mac ___, Irish sea god
10. "____and the Art of Motorcycle Maintenance"
13. small island
19. college admission exam
21. apply make-up
23. "this is ____time!" (quote from *The Goonies*)
24. phone company
25. Austin O. Spare's philosophy, or Korean Car
27. tire measurement
29. "One Star in the ____"
30. Kachina tribe
31. "Blizzard of___" (1980 album)
32. Pooh's pal
33. UFC fighter's skills
36. Australian bird
37. The once and future king
40. Greek word meaning "excellence"
41. to end or reduce
42. ______linguistic programming
43. Hebrew letter whose value is 10
45. with 1 down, a Discordian cry
46. ____ and vigor
47. French word for "island"
48. Duran Duran album (1982)
49. "gew___", a trinket
51. postal abbr. or French saint

*Puzzle Author: Monty Kayser

The Pentagram

The pentagram is the time-honored symbol of the magical arts. It is used in nearly every system of magic and is a part of the iconography of every religion. The early Christians associated the pentagram with the image of Christ because this symbol represented another form of Alpha and Omega, esoterically expressing the living Christ. *The Magician's Dictionary* states that, *"in a general sense it stands for all magical symbols and talismans. It is the magician's sine qua non."* The first known use of the pentagram was found in Mesopotamian texts, dating from around 3000 BC. The Sumerian pentagrams served as pictograms for the word "UB" meaning "corner, angle, cubicle, cavity, or pit."

Many types of ceremonial magic require the use of a pentagram ritual before any other ritual is to take place. It is considered by occultists to be the most potent means of conjuring spirits. Paracelsus proclaimed it to be the greatest and most powerful of all signs. To Cabalist magicians it is the Sign of the Microcosm called the Microprosopus. Microcosm and macrocosm are two aspects of a theory developed by ancient Jewish and Greek philosophers to describe human beings and their place in the universe. They viewed the individual human being as a little world (micro) whose composition and structure mirror the universe, or great world, (macro). They taught that the body of a man is a miniature universe and the complete comprehension of the pentagram is the key to the two worlds. A true pentagram has strokes through the center and five equidistant points. A pentacle is a pentagram inscribed on a pendant or disc, with a circle around it.

The points represent the five elements, Earth, Air, Fire, Water and Spirit. In many interpretations the pentagram is the symbol of Man. It has five points and the human brain has five parts: brain stem, cortex, neo-cortex and the left and right hemispheres. As a man's body has five distinct extremities the ancients would often depict a pentagram with the body of a man or woman and its head at the top representing spirit and the other four points representing the other elements. An upright pentagram means that the fifth element, spirit, is raised to the most significant position which controls and unites the other four. It symbolizes balance and a person who can understand their divine nature.

Photo Underlay: Heinrich Cornelius Agrippa's pentagram from his 16th century work, *Three Books of Occult Philosophy*

Pythagoras

The pentagram is the symbol of the Pythagoreans, a monotheistic religious sect that originated in ancient Greece around 530 BC. It was built on the principles of the philosopher and mathematician, Pythagoras. He was known to have traveled all over the ancient world and study at the feet of many masters and was initiated into the mysteries by Rabbis, Egyptians, Babylonians, Chaldeans, Persians, Hindus and more. Pythagoreans used to meet in secret to discuss their mathematical discoveries and they would draw the sign of the pentagram on their right hand to know one another. They considered the pentagram the union of man with the universe, the soul merging with the spirit. They declared the number five the number of man, representing the microcosm.

Pythagoras taught that the pentagram was full of math-magic. It contains the proportions that he used to create the diatonic scale of music that we use today. Also, hidden within it is the secret to creating the golden rectangle, a mathematical law of beauty, which the Greeks admired for its pleasing proportions and magic qualities. The Parthenon, Notre Dame and the Mona Lisa all contain many golden rectangles as does the human body itself. The intersections of a pentagram form the golden ratio of about 1.618 or phi. This was called the divine proportion, and is very close to the orbital resonance of Earth to Venus. The pentagram contains the golden rectangle many times over which can mathematically reproduce itself indefinitely. This ratio also contains a magic spiral called the Fibonacci sequence which repeats the proportions of the golden section into infinity. Fibonacci spirals can be found everywhere in nature from the shape of galaxies, to the shell of a snail. Many types of flowers, ferns, pinecones, pineapples, hurricanes, the tail of a sea horse, and other sea creatures like the chambered nautilus are visible examples of the sacred spiral.

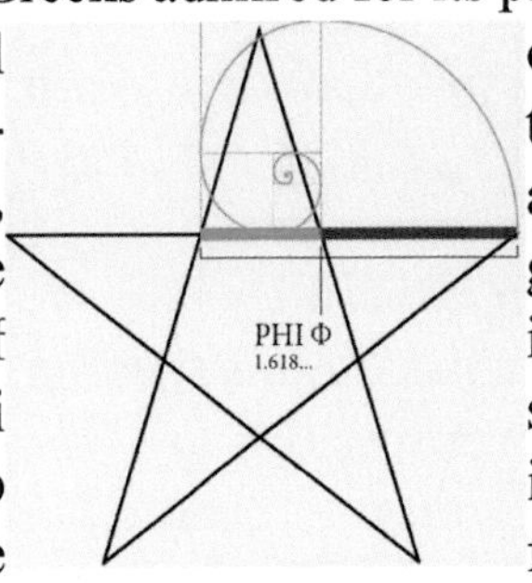

PHI Φ
1.618...

Pythagorean Signet Ring

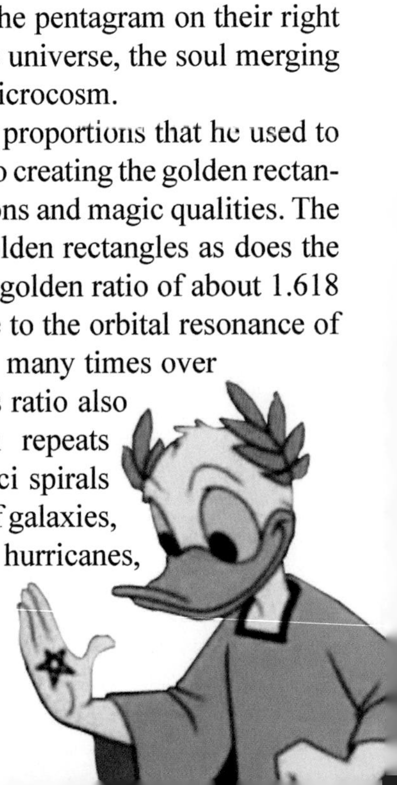

"We proceed to the explanation and consecration of the Sacred and Mysterious Pentagram. At this point, let the ignorant and superstitious close the book; they will either see nothing but darkness, or they will be scandalized. The Pentagram, which in Gnostic schools is called the Blazing Star, is the sign of intellectual omnipotence and autocracy. It is the Star of the Magi; it is the sign of the Word made flesh; and according to the direction of its points, this absolute magical symbol represents order or confusion, the Divine Lamb of Ormuz and St. John, or the accursed goat of Mendes. It is initiation or profanation; it is Lucifer or Vesper, the star of morning or evening. It is Mary or Lilith, victory or death, day or night. The Pentagram with two points in the ascendant represents Satan as the goat of the Sabbath; when one point is in the ascendant it is the sign of the Saviour. The Pentagram is the figure of the human body, having the four limbs and a single point representing the head. A human figure head downwards naturally represents a demon— that is, intellectual subversion, disorder and madness. Now, if Magic be a reality, if occult science be really the true law of the three worlds, this absolute sign, this sign ancient as history and more ancient, should and does exercise an incalculable influence upon spirits set free from their material envelope."

— Transcendental Magic, Eliphas Levi.

The Averse Pentagram

"The black magician cannot use the symbols of white magic without bringing down upon himself the forces of white magic, which would be fatal to his schemes. He must therefore distort the hierograms so that they typify the occult fact that he himself is distorting the principles for which the symbols stand. Black magic is not a fundamental art; it is the misuse of an art. Therefore it has no symbols of its own. It merely takes the emblematic figures of white magic, and by inverting and reversing them signifies that it is left-handed."
–Manly P. Hall

In symbolism an inverted figure represents a distorted power. The reason black magic works is because it draws upon a fundamental power source while at the same time perverting it. One of the most commonly practiced ceremonies in LaVey's Satanism is the Black Mass which incorporates an inverted cross and pentagram, a dark priest, a nun and a nude woman as the altar.

The pentagram is used extensively in black magic, but always differs in one of three ways: by having two points up, by elongating the points to various lengths, or the star may be broken so that the converging lines do not form a point. Since the pentagram is an example of mathematic and organic perfection, altering it is the desecration of a universal language and would also represent something in-organic or synthetic.

Black magic is a combination of sacrileges designed to profane the human mind. When the pentagram is averse it represents Mind sinking below the elements, suppressed by the weight of the lower principles and being submerged and conquered by them. If employed in this way, it is for the purpose of crushing the mind of a victim under the weight of the desires of the body. It would be used for the definite purpose of causing one to go insane.

"In Satanism the pentagram is also used, but since Satanism represents the carnal instincts of man, or the opposite of spiritual nature, the pentagram is inverted to perfectly accommodate the head of the goat, its horns representing duality, thrust upwards in defiance, the other three points inverted or the trinity denied." —Anton LaVey

The averse pentagram is also known as the Star of Set. It is often inscribed in a double circle, with the head of a goat inside the pentagram. This is called the Sigil of Baphomet, the "God of the Sabbath of Sorcerers." This Baphomet represents the generative fertility of the goat combined with the powers of darkness. Goat worshipping cults existed in ancient Egypt and thrived on the Nile Delta. The goat-headed god of Mendes—the Greek name for the ancient city of Djedet, Egypt—was depicted with a goat's face and legs. The Greek historian Herodotus wrote that all male goats were held in great reverence by the Mendesians and in that time and place, women were known to publicly copulate with them. At several places the god Pan and a goat were worshipped as gods of generation and fertility, they called them both Mendes.

The Hebrew letters in the Satanic pentagram form the name Leviathan, a sea creature from Hebrew mythology who is a symbol of man's lower nature. Leviathan was the great dragon of the abyss, a powerful figure that even Yahweh was afraid of. The Pythagoreans, knew him as "Tartaros" literally translated from Greek as a "Pit" or "Void" and said to be where the fallen angels are from. Even in the Thelemic system of magick an inverted pentagram represents the descent of spirit into matter. Agrippa considered this orientation of the symbol evil because it attracts sinister forces by overturning the natural order of things. It is associated with the triumph of matter over spirit and is referred to as "the goat of lust attacking the heavens with its horns."

The foundation of black magic is the pact or contract. It is primarily focused on the art of conjuring up spirits from the lower planes by means of a secret process of ceremonial magic in order to gain their help. True black magic is a contract with a spirit, where, for a time, the magician becomes the master of the spirit he has summoned. The demon agrees to serve the conjurer for the length of his earthly life, and after death he will become the servant of the demon. The magician would sign the contract with his own blood according to the magic axiom: "he controls the soul who controls the blood of another." When the magician binds an elemental to his service, a battle of wits ensues, which the demon eventually wins. For this reason the black magician will attempt to prolong his life as much as possible.

Photo: *The Secret Teachings of All Ages*

Sorcerers & Robots
A Love Story

"We are caged by our cultural programming. Culture is a mass hallucination, and when you step outside of the mass hallucination you see it for what it's worth."

—Terrence McKenna

Do you ever get the feeling that you're surrounded by a population of mindless robot zombies, blindly being led through life like sheep and not capable of a single original thought? Well, maybe you are. Perhaps you've always felt like an outsider, estranged and isolated from others, struggling to comprehend the mentality of those around you, like an anthropologist in your own culture. Or maybe, from time to time, you find yourself, incredulously asking the question: "What is *wrong* with people?" When we start to view the world as a spiritual domain there may be an answer to some of your questions. Philosopher, Colin Wilson, states that "*Modern civilization induces an attitude of passivity. When a stone age hunter set out to trap wild animals he was aware of his will as a living force... When a modern city dweller walks down a crowded thoroughfare, he feels no sense of challenge or involvement. This city was built by other people. He can go through an ordinary day's work in a state approximating sleep. Most of his routine tasks are carried out by the 'robot.' There is neither the need or the opportunity to use the will.*"[1]

Aleister Crowley c. 1910

The Imagination and the Will are two of the most important mental faculties required for the art of magic. When rituals are performed the will and imagination must both be directed through acutely focused attention toward the desired goal, altering reality to produce a magical act. These forces are the two most valuable commodities up for grabs in the war for your mind.

The **magician** calls upon his divine guiding force with prayer and gratitude, seeking enlightenment according to his conscience, or the Holy Spirit and he has surrendered his will to a higher spiritual authority. The magician loves humanity and his efforts are for the benefit of all. He has no ambition to impose his beliefs upon others but aspires to respectively learn from and teach those who have ears to hear. The magician realizes that every change

Mickey Mouse is the Sorcerer's Apprentice. In *Fantasia*, the Sorcerer's name is Yensid, which is "Disney" spelled backward.

he wishes to see in the world must begin with himself and radiate outward.

The **sorcerer** seeks to enforce change in consciousness on a grand scale. He wants to produce a "Mass Effect." He attempts to master command over the laws of nature according to his own will. His philosophy favors the desires of the few pitted against the good of the many and his obsession is the quest for private power. Carried to its furthest extreme, the sorcerer's ambition is to wield supreme authority over the entire universe, to make himself a god. The driving force behind black magic is the hunger for private power. Black magic is occult techniques used for evil ends and for the sorcerer's self-aggrandizement.

An infamous sorcerer, Michael Aquino, explains that rather than seeking acceptance from a higher power, *"The Satanist, the black magician, does not seek that kind of submergence of the self. We do not seek to have our decisions and our morality validated by any god or higher being. We take responsibility unto ourselves."* Aquino believes that the governing principle of magic is the ability to *"control people without their realizing how or why they are being controlled."*[2]

The sorcerer seeks to misuse that which he does not understand. The term bewitchment expresses exactly what it means: the act of enveloping someone into a formulated will. Witchcraft, in this sense, is a ceremonial operation with the intent to bewitch someone and serves to fix and confirm the sorcerer's will.

***

Aleister Crowley

The Magician's Dictionary states that, *"Sorcery is the invocation of the gods to use them to work one's will."* The Greek word for "will" is

THELEMA and the Temple of Thelema is a religion based on Aleister Crowley's *Book of the Law*. Its philosophy states that "Do what thou wilt shall be the whole of the Law. / Love is the law, love under will. / Every man and woman is a star."

Born in England in 1875, Crowley became arguably the most infamous sorcerer of all time. It is claimed that as a child Aleister was so defiant that his own mother nicknamed him "the beast." His father traveled the English countryside preaching the doctrines of a strict fundamentalist group known as the Plymouth Brethren. Aleister's self-proclaimed life's mission was to destroy Christianity and build the religion of Thelema. Crowley was the twentieth century's leading black magician, philosopher and occultist. He was an agent in British Intelligence, a poet, a prophet and self proclaimed "Beast 666." He also considered himself a reincarnation of the famous magician, Eliphas Levi.

In 1903, as a young man of twenty eight, Crowley and his new wife, Rose, took a long honeymoon. On their first visit to Egypt they performed a ritual called "Liber Samekh" in the King's Chamber of the great pyramid. They returned to Cairo the next spring, and while he was practicing his Preliminary Invocation ritual, his wife began to say strange things like "they are waiting for you" and "it is all about the child." He ignored her behavior until she told him that the god, Horus, was waiting to talk to him and was offended that he had not been invoked yet. Crowley began testing his wife who had no knowledge of Egyptology. He asked her to point out the god whom she was in contact with and she led him into a museum where she showed him a mortuary stele of Horus in his form of Ra-Hoor-Khuit. Crowley was astounded by the exhibit's number: 666, and called it the "Stele of Revealing." Later in his room, he took dictation from an entity named Aiwass. For an hour precisely, from noon to 1:00pm on April 8, 9 and 10, Rose channeled Aiwass and dictated the substance of the book which forms the most important magical document of the sorcerer's new aeon, *The Book of the Law.* Aiwass told Crowley that he was especially chosen to establish a new epoch in the evolution of consciousness on this planet over which the god Horus will preside. A full account of this story can be found in two of Crowley's books called *Confessions* and *The Equinox of the Gods* Vol: I #7.

During WWI, Crowley transferred his activities to America where he became the first kind of tabloid celebrity. The press proclaimed him "The wickedest man in the world." He shocked the west by his newspaper accounts of Black Masses and sexual orgies. In the headlines he was named "the king of depravity." He was obsessed with red-heads and he initiated a large number of women, whom he called Scarlet Women, and branded them with the mark of the beast. He also spent time in Italy but was expelled by the government due to suspicion of human sacrifice. Crowley was the epitome of a sorcerer. His ties with the political elite facilitated the propagation of the doctrine of Thelema worldwide and he was recognized by the BBC as the 73rd greatest Briton of all time.

Crowley's impact on today's popular culture is colossal. Whether it is through direct references to his persona or through Thelema inspired works, Crowley is everywhere. Rapper Jay Z's clothing line sports hoodies that say, "Do what thou wilt" "Masters of the Craft" and other esoteric phrases. Crowley can also be found in odd places such as the anime Yu-Gi-Oh! where one of the characters of the series is named Alister in honor of him.

***

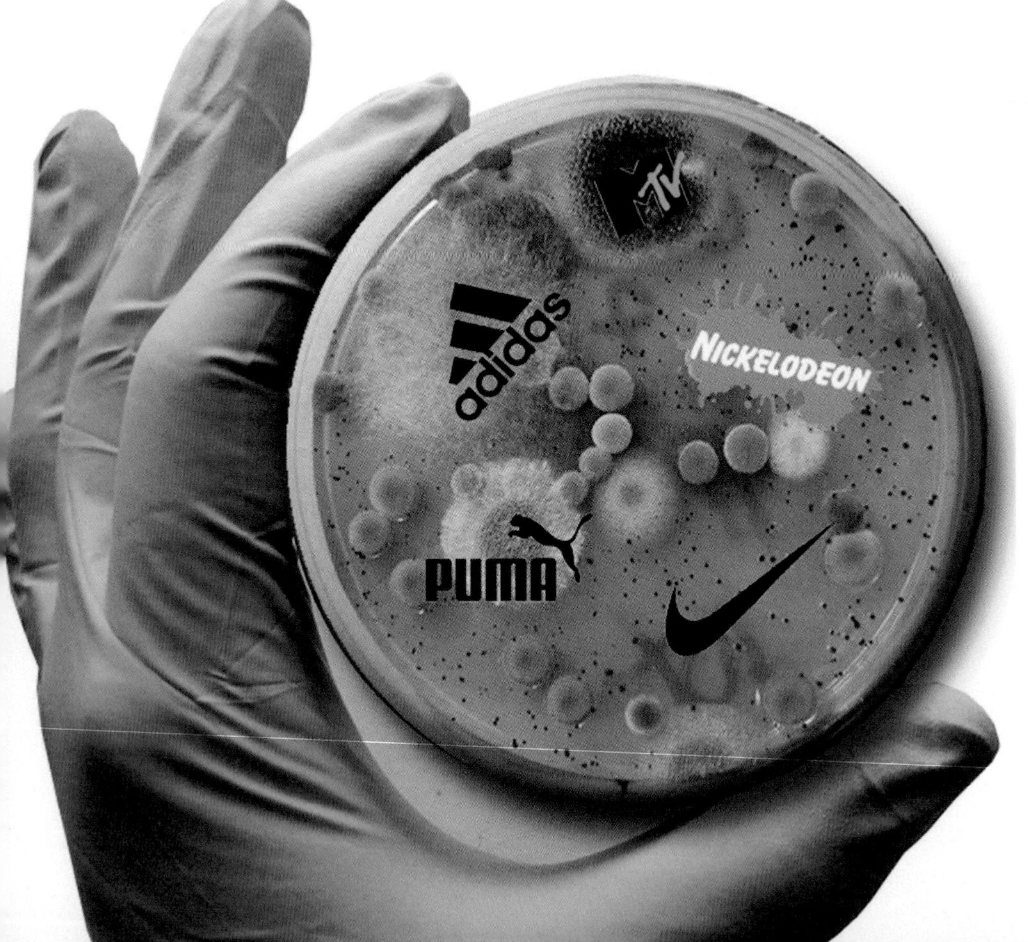

Culture

We define ourselves with logos and attitudes to create something we call culture, but where does it come from? Thomas Mann says at the root of culture lies cult. The arts of a culture have always been associated with religion. The earliest music, painting, drawing, sculpture, dance, literature, were almost all inspired with religious principles, doctrine and ritual. Culture is defined as the set of shared attitudes, values, goals, and practices that characterizes an organization or group. The very word culture comes from the Latin *cultura* stemming from *colere,* meaning "to cultivate." But who is doing the cultivating now?

In biology, culture is the growth of populations of microbes in an artificial environment such as a Petri dish known as the "culture media." By including or excluding particular substances into the media, the scientist can control what cells will and won't develop and what directions those groups will go.

By use of ritual and symbolism, a sorcerer can enchant others and subconsciously conform their will to match his own. A pentagram on your shoe or a swastika on your jacket, these symbols have been manipulated by mystery schools for centuries. Did you know that the founder of the sports brand Adidas is Adolf "Adi" Dassler and the founder of Puma was his brother, Rudolf? They were both passionate Nazis and they manufactured clothes for the Wehrmacht—the unified armed forces of Germany. Do you know what it means when you put on your Converse every morning? By being ignorant of the meanings of certain symbols, we unwittingly participate in a ritual, manifesting reality to the whim of the sorcerer.

***

Symbols

For magicians, the correspondences connecting the diverse skins of the universe are best expressed by symbols. Such symbols are like letters and words in Egyptian or Hebrew, batteries holding a latent charge of energy. These symbols were often called 'seals' or 'signatures' and were thought to be the cross stiches in the fabric of reality. They could be manipulated or activated, like elements or molecules in chemistry, to form new compounds of possibility.

The language of symbols works on the subconscious level of the mind as they are easy to grasp and meditate upon. The only magically effective symbols are those charged with the peculiar vitality of the subconscious. The subconscious mind is the repository of all images, all ideas, and all concepts. Communication with it is only possible through a symbolic language. Psychology has found that people, and even animals, can respond to symbols as if they were the objects they represent. There is no set interpretation of any symbol and for each human being a symbol, whatever it may be, will convey a unique meaning. Symbolism is constantly used to represent concepts that we cannot define or fully comprehend. These symbols are hidden in plain sight and go unnoticed to the conscious mind. Carl Jung stated that this is how cultural symbols *"have been used to express 'eternal truths' and that are still used in many religions...Such cultural symbols nevertheless retain much of their 'spell.' One is aware that they can evoke a deep emotional response in some individuals, and this psychic charge makes them function in much the same way as prejudices... Such tendencies form an ever-present and potentially destructive 'shadow' to our conscious mind...Our times have demonstrated what it means for the gates of the underworld to be opened. Things whose enormity nobody could have imagined in the idyllic harmlessness of the first decade of our century have happened and have turned the world upside down. Ever since, the world has remained in a state of schizophrenia."*[3]

The basis of magical suggestion is that a thought generated from a sigil, or symbol, may be projected into a person's aura and there, breed further thoughts. The target may be unaware of his activities, may not in the least suspect that the "thought" born within him is not his own. The idea of controlling humanity with esoteric words and symbols encoded within a play, a media spectacular or as a ritual, is one of the most difficult for people to comprehend.

***

"Symbols are oracular forms—mysterious patterns creating vortices in the substance of the invisible world. They are centers of a mighty force, figures pregnant with an awful power, which, when properly fashioned, loose fiery whirlwinds upon the earth."[4]

The Tavistock Institute

So where do we get our cultural symbols? Today it has been refined into the modern science of the mass manipulation of public opinion. Few people have heard of something called "the mother of all think tanks"—the Tavistock Institute. This is the world's premier firm in brainwashing and social engineering. In 1921, the Duke of Bedford, Marquess of Tavistock, donated a building to study the effect of shellshock on British soldiers who survived World War I. Its purpose was to establish the "breaking point" of men under stress.

During WWII it was the headquarters of the British Army's Psychological Warfare Bureau and through MI6 it dictated the policy to the United States in matters of psychological warfare. Tavistock is a globally-active council that has influenced just about every social and political movement of note throughout much of the world for the past fifty years. Without the Tavistock Institute there would have been no world wars. Partially funded by the Rockefeller and the Rothschild family its aim was to manipulate society through social crisis. Times are being made to change according to a very carefully laid out Tavistock formula. It is generally seen as the nerve center for global manipulation and Hollywood is just one arm of that. Closely affiliated with Stanford, MIT and NASA it is headquartered in London and operates a six billion dollar a year network of foundations in the U.S. Ten major institutions are under its direct control, with 400 subsidiaries, and 3,000 other study groups and think tanks which specialize in organizational behavior, political science, psychoanalysis, psychology and sociology. Tavistock's pioneer work in behavioral science, along Freudian lines of "controlling humans", established it as the world center of cultural ideology. Tavistock Institute developed the mass brain-washing techniques which were first used experimentally on prisoners of war in Korea and its experiments in crowd control methods have been widely used on the American public to this day. All Tavistock foundation techniques have a single goal: to break down the psychological strength of the individual and render him helpless to oppose the dictators of the New World Order.

Any technique which helps to break down the family unit, and family inculcated principles of religion, honor, patriotism and sexual behavior, is used by the Tavistock scientists as weapons of crowd control. The institute has developed such power in the world that hardly anyone achieves prominence in their field unless they have been trained in behavioral science at Tavistock or one of its subsidiaries.

***

"THE MOST DANGEROUS OF ALL SCIENCES IS THAT OF MOLDING MASS OPINION, BECAUSE IT WOULD ENABLE ANYONE TO GOVERN THE WHOLE WORLD."—Talbot Mundy

Behavior

An effective sorcerer is also a good behaviorist. In order to manipulate someone you must learn how to control their emotional state and response. One way to do this is to keep people thinking with their R-complex or reptilian brain. The first part of our three part brain, the brain stem, or basal ganglia is what we have in common with all other animals that have a backbone. It controls basic motor functions of the body that we never think about such as breathing, heart rate, blood pressure and other automated systems of the body. The R-complex is responsible for rage and basic survival fight-or-flight responses; it is also where ritualistic behavior comes from. It can override the more rational function of the brain and result in unpredictable, primitive behavior in even the most sentient of creatures. One result of a person thinking with their reptilian brain is the constant need for procreation. This is why sex and violence sell so well. The reptilian brain is in a constant state of agitation and hyper-vigilance to threat. This is why we are bombarded daily with negative messages that frighten us. It suspends our conscious processing and keeps our subconscious mind open to suggestive programming.

Reptiles are able to greet one another, forage for food, establish territory and work in social groups. Reptiles also have awe for authority and understand social hierarchy because that is associated with that level of thinking. A great deal of the reptilian brain's actions are pre-set and work very mechanically. Most reptiles can be hypnotized easily if you know how. In India and Africa snake charming is a common phenomenon. The reptilian brain is only concerned with survival and security. Its basic thinking is "what is safe/what is not safe?" The reptilian brain has the ability to shut down the other "brains" if it senses danger. Capable of paranoia, it is our reptilian brains that allow persecution of minorities or slaughter foreigners whom we have been convinced pose a threat to our "nation" or survival. *"At least five human behaviors originate in the reptilian brain…they find expression in: obsessive compulsive behavior; personal day to day rituals and superstitious acts; slavish conformance to old ways of doing things; ceremonial re-enactments; obeisance to precedent, as in legal, religious, cultural,… and all manner of deceptions."* —Skip Largent

***

Hollywood the New Religion

Today, the most powerful sorcerers appeal to our reptilian brain and wield their wand through Hollywood. The film industry is inarguably the most prolific culture creator on the planet today. The ancient Druid magicians used the sacred branches of the holly tree to make their magic wands. Thought to have supernatural powers, the holly tree has been a symbol of death and resurrection, eternal life and fertility dating all the way back to Nimrod of Babylon. The wand itself was a symbol of the will and also of the phallus. In Wicca, Holly is used at Lammas, the first harvest of the year. The Holly King in the new Pagan tradition is the god of the dark half of the year, who is in eternal struggle with the Oak King, the god of the light half of the year.

For many people, spirituality has been usurped and replaced by Hollywood and this process has many examples throughout history. Youth film hours replaced Sunday school in Nazi Germany. For more than a century after Henry VIII broke with the Church of Rome, no churches were built in England. Instead they built theaters. The English theater became a new species of church and temple. Within these structures the rites and mysteries of magic were performed for the public. These wooden playhouses, laid out to astrological specifications, created a Hermetic microcosm. A theater such as the Globe of Shakespeare's company, became magical, cosmic and religious. The modern concept of theatre originated in divine dramas staged at religious festivals in ancient Greece. Such performances were more than mere play acting. These actors were seen as living embodiments of the gods and goddesses they portrayed and also as

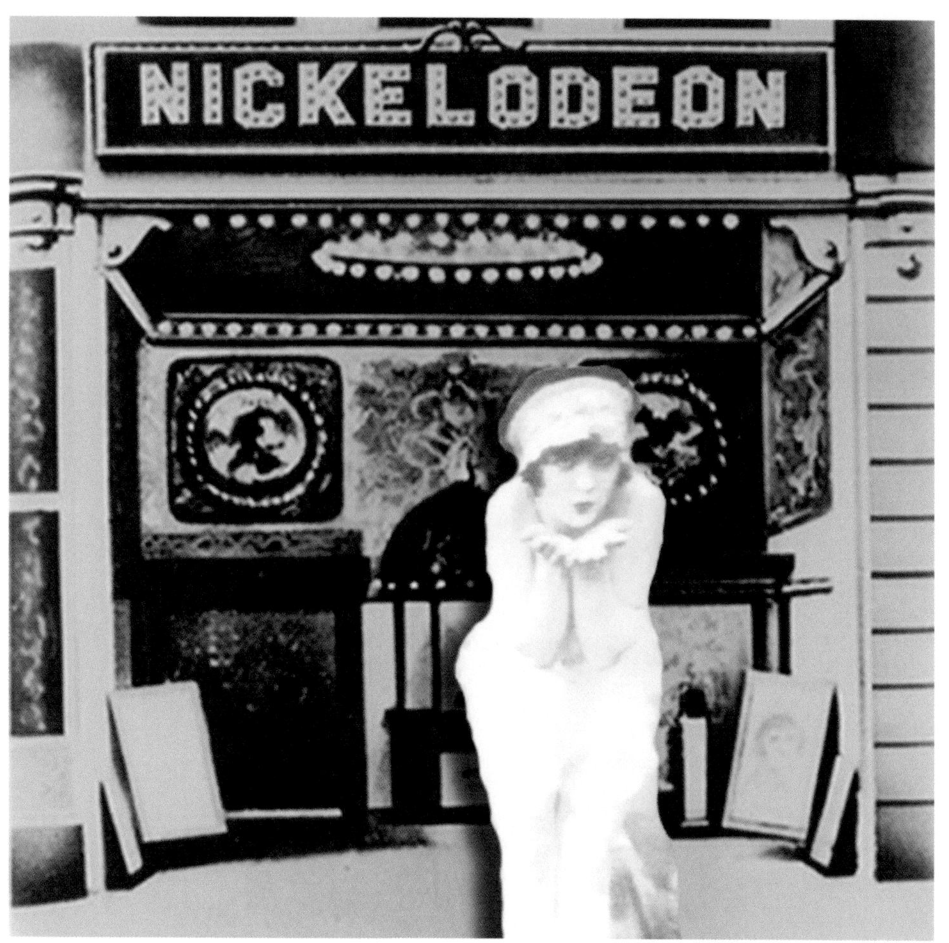

channels for their powers.

The history of the movie industry begins in New Jersey, in 1888 with the invention of the Kinetograph, a motion picture camera; and the Kinetoscope, a peep-hole motion picture viewer, by "the wizard of Menlo Park," Thomas Edison. New Jersey was where many early film studios in America's first motion picture industry were based at the beginning of the 20th century. For more than a decade Edison was the premier maker and distributor of esoteric, silent motion picture studies. He felt that by producing wholesome films they were helping to preserve the nation's morals.

Seeing the growing popularity of a new form of entertainment called "movies," a Jewish immigrant named Carl Laemmle bought a nickelodeon and in 1906, he opened the White Front Theater in Chicago. The nickelodeon was the first type of indoor exhibition space dedicated to showing projected motion pictures. The name derived from the cost of admission which was a nickel and the Greek word for theater: odeon. Before Edison had perfected his camera, other individuals had developed a system of rapidly moving cards which depicted short scenes. The pictograph system, as it was called, were movies of naked women or sex acts by couples. The earliest films had been shown in peep show machines or projected in vaudeville theaters as one of the acts. Nickelodeons drastically altered film exhibition practices and the recreational habits of the American public.

To exploit the pictograph market Laemmle and his investors used their homes and buildings in New York to set up nickelodeons, which turned their real estate into a means of making money on this early form of pornography. Today Nickelodeon™ is a popular kid's network who is famous for "sliming" children and their corporate logo looks exactly like ejaculation. The nickelodeon system spread from New York and Carl Laemmle used them as a framework for organizing his own distribution system nationwide. By 1909 it had grown into the largest non-Edison film exchange in the country.

To avoid paying royalty fees to Edison for his patented camera design, Laemmle reformed his company as Universal Studios and headed to California. The migration west was partly to escape agents from Edison's Motion Picture Patents Company, but the booming outskirts of Los Angeles offered several advantages the east coast didn't have. Plenty of natural sunlight for filming, cheap land for large studio lots, a variety of outdoor settings within a short drive and a climate that allowed for year-round production proved the ideal environment for making movies.

Edison's Trust and the Federal Government attempted to regulate the moral content of the new film industry on the west coast but the guiding hand of movie content was profit. Hollywood's early moguls had no idea of what was meant by "socially acceptable," if the film made money, it was a good film.

"Unlike their early East Coast counterparts, the heads of Hollywood's studios were less interested in artistic experimentation than profit. They put on the screen what sold the most. The public was willing to pay to see films with sex and violence, and Hollywood was more than happy to make them."[5]

"Although for long periods your mind may not be generating any thoughts, it has linked into the thought activity of the television show. It has linked up with the TV version of the collective mind, and is thinking its thoughts. Your mind is inactive only in the sense that it is not producing thoughts. It is, however, constantly absorbing thoughts and images that come through the TV screen. This induces a trancelike, passive state of heightened susceptibility, not unlike hypnosis." —Eckhart Tolle

WeirdStuff!

The Television Ghost:

The Television Ghost was a horror television series that aired in New York from 1931 until 1933 on a station of the Columbia Broadcasting System. It is one of the first dramatic television series ever made and each episode lasted for only fifteen minutes. The only actor was George Kelting who played a ghost, with his face painted white and a sheet wrapped around him who would tell scary stories in close-up. The premise of the show was that the spirits of the victims of murder would tell the gory tale of their death.

Television

Nothing has done more to aid the sorcerer in his hypnotism than that little domestic terrorist in every house, the television. The American Medical Association reports that the combined hours spent in front of a television or video screen is the single biggest chunk of time in the waking life of an American child. One ad for a technology called Ultraviolet brags that you can take your programs with you anywhere you go, from your DVD player to whatever portable media device you want so your child never needs to tear his eyes away from the programming and interact with other humans. There was a time when a family traveling in a car might entertain itself by talking, singing or playing games. Now, however, many kids have their own laptops or cell phones and many family vehicles come equipped with DVD players. Family members no longer look to each other or the outside world for entertainment when a constant stream of media sources is at their fingertips.

The American inventor and television pioneer, Philo Farnsworth, stated, *"I know the secret of making the average American believe anything I want him to. Just let me control television."* Humans are wired into their television sets. They have come to look at the images on the screen as reality. If you put something on television, it becomes reality. When the world outside the television set contradicts the images, people start changing the world to make it more like what they see on TV. You lose your sense of what is being done to you, but your mind is being shaped and molded. When asked about his family's TV viewing habits Farnsworth said, *"There's nothing on it worthwhile, and we're not going to watch it in this household, and I don't want it in your intellectual diet."*

Even the founder of the Church of Satan, Anton LaVey, saw that the minds of men were being anesthetized and controlled through the manipulation of electronic media; in particular, television. He believed that the ultimate goal of the political technocrats was to create, through TV, a uniform society in which individualism is stifled and the masses are programmed to march to whatever tune was played.[6]

Watching television induces low alpha waves in the brain. These are completely different than relaxed alpha states created by meditation. These are states associated with suggestibility and too much time spent in the hypnotic low alpha wave state can cause unfocussed daydreaming and inability to correctly perceive reality. The flicker rate of the television was specifically timed to match our Alpha state. This is why people, especially children, "tune out" when the TV comes on. Thier mouths drop open, eyes become glassy and they can't hear anything you say to them.

Researchers have said that watching television is similar to staring at a blank wall for several hours and watching TV only trains your brain to watch more TV. In less than one minute of viewing, a person's brainwaves switch from Beta, brainwaves associated with active, logical thought, to primarily Alpha waves. These trance states can last up to 45 minutes after the television is turned off and even longer if you've been watching in HD. Why would a president mandate that all TV's must go high definition?

Most parts of the brain responsible for logical thought, tune out during viewing. Advertisers have known about this for a long time and they know how to take advantage of this passive brain state. The brain is in a hyper-receptive state, ready to absorb suggestions, within just a few seconds of the television being turned on. All advertisers have to do is flash a brand on the screen, and attempt to make the viewer associate the product with something positive. But you don't need us to tell you that watching TV is bad for you, so here's something interesting you might not have heard...

The story of the invention of the television is weird stuff. Classic magicians call the spirit world "the aether." In the early 1870's a British physicist named Sir William Crookes, was a member of The Golden Dawn and president of the Society for Psychical Research. He believed that the spirits of the aether were capable of moving tiny particles. During his inventions of devices to measure the existence of electrons, he invented the Crookes tube, the first cathode ray tube. By firing electrons at glass covered in phosphorus he was hoping that that spirits would arrange the particles on the screen to give visions of the other side. He experimented with projection by placing an object inside the tube and bombarding it with electrons to pro-

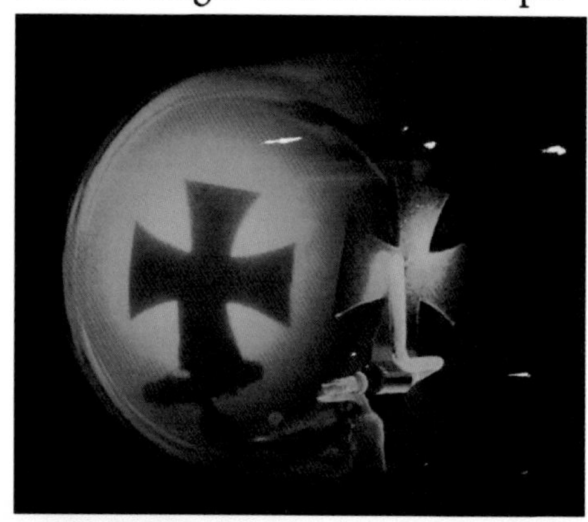

image. He used the Maltese cross as the first image projected, which is a rich esoteric symbol used by magicians, Kabalists, Templars and most famously, the Nazi's.

***

The Stars

The spell of Hollywood has a foothold in the human being's natural instinct to follow the stars. Since the dawn of time, man has studied the stars for navigation, for signs and for seasons and to keep time. It is no coincidence that the magicians or Magi of ancient Persia were called The Star Gazers. Stellar worship is one of the oldest forms of religion practiced by the ancients. Constellations were anthropomorphized and deified with elaborate myths involving their movements and relationships. Each star was seen as the abode of some hero or god once incarnate on Earth. *"All mythologies find their explanation in this starry language, and every religion is founded upon the movements of our solar system. The rise and fall of empires and races of men are written in its pages."*[7]

The pagans looked upon the stars as living things, capable of influencing the destinies of individuals, nations and races. Albertus Magnus said *"The second great wisdom... is the science of the judgments of the stars, which provides a link between natural philosophy and metaphysics... No human science attains this ordering of the universe as perfectly as the judgment of the stars does."*[8]

Studying the stars is in our blood, but today most people are looking at the stars in the tabloids and not in the sky. They are mindlessly obsessing over their every movement in the newspapers, magazines, and television shows like Access Hollywood and Entertainment Tonight. Hollywood is the new home of the heavenly bodies that man looks to for direction. *"The ancestors of the present day sorcerers were disciples of power rather than lovers of knowledge...The power of their spiritual office went to their heads and dominion over the minds of men became their obsession. They were students of the heavens and they knew when eclipses were going to occur and when enormously long cycles were opening and closing. They knew when constellations and special stars arose and set and*

CARL LAEMMLE

when significant conjunctions were about to happen. Furthermore, their ability to read the stars enabled them to read men."[9] Hollywood controls the movements of the "stars" and the hearts and minds of men follow, however, worshipping these celebrities is probably one of the most deluded and destructive things a person could do.

***

Subliminal Messages

The origin of the word "mesmerize" comes from the work of Franz Anton Mesmer, who developed the theory under the influence of experiments in electricity and magnetism. He is an early example of the psychologist as a magician. Fashionable in Paris during the 1780's, mesmerism was often known as animal magnetism or electro-biology. Although he could not have named it, Mesmer was working with the psychological principle which we would today call 'the power of suggestion.' He discovered 'mesmerism' or 'hypnotism' having put his patient into a hypnotic trance, he could plant suggestions in the mind which produced dramatic changes in behavior.

Successfully modifying human behavior requires brain manipulation techniques that when expertly applied become a form of soft mind control. One of the most important methods for manipulating human beings is the power of suggestion and nowhere is this power exploited more deliberately than in the world of advertising. It is the continued and repeated suggestion that first makes you believe and then eager to buy. The founders of all great religious movements knew much of the power of repeated suggestion. Teachings are hammered in, beginning at birth and into our mothers and fathers before us, and back down through the centuries. Whether we know it or not, we are all victims of suggestion, in many cases almost to the point of being hypnotized. In the course of a single day, we are saturated, through radio, television, newspapers, and magazines with a bewildering amount of advertisements. They have gone way past the suggestion to outright bullying. We see them on cars and buses and blimps and every website we visit. But are we really seeing all the things we are looking at?

Among the most sinister of techniques for advertising is subliminal messaging. The most powerful forms of suggestion are 'below threshold' and they bypass the conscious mind. Most of what we perceive, we have no conscious awareness of having perceived. Later these images seep into the conscious mind as apparently the person's own thoughts, desires and ideas. These can be audio, visual or both. In audio form, the message would be 'buried' in an otherwise innocent sound track. In visual form, it would be an image or caption flashed at regular intervals during a film at speeds too rapid to be registered by the eye. These messages work with the effect of a hypnotic suggestion. Subliminals allow the ability of media to manipulate people to produce deep, visceral responses.

In 1919, Dr. Poetzl, an Austrian neurologist, published a paper describing his experiments with the tachistoscope, a viewing box into which the subject looks at an image that is exposed for a small fraction of a second. In the experiment Poetzl required the subjects to draw a picture of what they consciously remembered about what they had seen. He later had them make drawings of the dreams they had after viewing the tachistoscope pictures.

It was shown unmistakably that the details of the picture which had not been in the first drawing provided material for the construction of the dream. The conscious mind forgot the details but all the information was stored instantly for the subconscious to bring out later during sleep.

The first public application of this scientific discovery was in 1956, when a special projector was installed in a New Jersey movie theater by a firm called Subliminal Projection Co. For six weeks they flashed the words "Drink Coca-Cola" and "Hungry? Eat Popcorn" across the screen every five seconds at the subliminal level of 1/3000th of a second. Sales reportedly increased by over 50%. It was not long until legislatures in Washington DC, along with the FCC and the CIA became interested with this new form of advertisement. Due to their unpopularity with the public, companies such as Vicary's Subliminal Projection Co. soon went out of business. The FCC eventually sent out a public service announcement stating that all uses of subliminal messages would only be used in the best interest of the public, and if used, would be highly regulated.

Today, the British mentalist and hypnotist, Derren Brown, makes a living proving just how well these techniques work on us. In shows such as *Mind Control* and *Trick or Treat,* Brown uses hypnosis, neural linguistic programming and subliminal messages to prove that you can quite easily get someone to suspend their free will and do something that they would otherise object to.

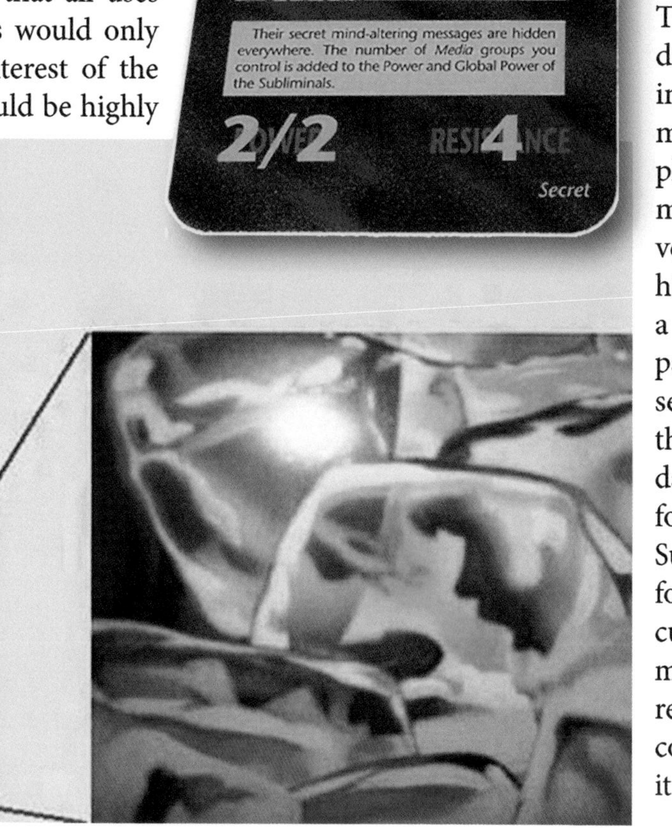

The most obvious hidden messages that are easy to recognize are sexual. The simple three letter symbol, usually invisible to consciousness, appears instantly perceivable at the unconscious level. The word "sex" is spelled out in the dust in the movie The Lion King and in Rapunzel's hair in an ad for the movie Tangled and countless other places, but many times the overt message in the movie is just as perverted. The word "sex" is frequently hidden in political propaganda. In a 1976 congressional election campaign in Virginia's 10th District, sexual embeds were discovered in the campaign literature of all candidates except one who could not afford to hire an advertising agency. Subliminal stimuli probably account for much of the behavior we see in culture today. Sexual symbolism and metaphor in advertising is easily recognized to the point of cliché, but continues to be exploited because it still works. While you might not think a hidden penis will get you to buy a Coke, it can surely give you a glimpse into the advertiser's psyche.

***

"I FORESEE A TIME WHEN WE SHALL HAVE THE MEANS AND THEREFORE, INEVITABLY, THE TEMPTATION TO MANIPULATE THE BEHAVIOR AND INTELLECTUAL FUNCTIONING OF ALL PEOPLE THROUGH ENVIRONMENTAL AND BIOCHEMICAL MANIPULATION OF THE BRAIN."
—Dr. David Krech of UC Berkley, 1968

Technology

The methods of subliminal messages and suggestion, while still heavily employed, will soon be obsolete. Why mess around with suggestion when there are ways to just make someone think exactly what you want? The sorcerers have always used their technological prowess to hypnotize and control the masses. One techno-wizard is National Security Agency General, Michael Aquino. He was involved with military intelligence in Vietnam, Germany and at the Presidio in San Francisco. As a Defense Intelligence Agency attaché he taught political science on the university level. He reported directly to the Joint Chiefs of Staff and worked one on one with Dick Cheney. He was also the former national commander of the Eagle Scouts Honor Society. During his time as a Satanic chaplain for the U.S. Army, he was also working on audio warfare. During battles they would broadcast demonic sounding screams from helicopters to scare the Vietnamese.

As an army specialist in intelligence and psychological warfare, Aquino became the Executive Officer of the 306th Psychological Operations Battalion. His thesis was called "From PSYOP to MindWar the Psychology of Victory." In it he states that enemy populations could be subdued by inflicting a state of terror and feelings of imminent destruction. Outbursts of violence could be induced by Extremely Low Frequency, or ELF waves piggybacked on broadcasts of radio, television or microwave communications to manipulate the thoughts and feelings of target populations. Microwave radio frequency radiation weapons, also known as Psychotronics, are designed to influence the central nervous system. This technology can slowly drive a target crazy via silent sound coupled with subliminal suggestion. One can broadcast rage or fear to an individual target to direct and control them. Hallucinations can be induced by electromagnetic frequencies of 500 Megahertz.

Naval Intelligence and other groups have conducted research into the ELF waves' effect upon the human body and mind. Some of the many things that can be done with this technology include, put a person to sleep, make a person feel tired or depressed, create a zombie state, a violent state, a sexually aggressive state, change cellular chemistry, change hormone levels and much more. Unfortunately, ELF waves can penetrate almost anything.

At the beginning of the 19th century, Nikola Tesla began studies on the effects of electromagnetic frequencies on humans. His research, originally designed to liberate mankind through free energy, was stolen and corrupted by the military industrial complex. He discovered that *"Alpha waves in the human brain are between six and eight hertz. The wave frequency of the human cavity resonates between six and eight hertz. All biological systems operate in the same frequency range. The human brain's alpha waves function in this range and the electrical resonance of the earth is between six and eight hertz. Thus, our entire biological system-the brain and the earth itself- work on the same frequencies. If we can control that resonate system electronically, we can directly control the entire mental system of humankind."* —Nikola Tesla

Dr. Alan Fry, a biophysicist at GE's Advanced Electronics Center and contractor for the Office of Naval Research discovered in 1958 that the human auditory system responds to electromagnetic energy in a portion of the radio frequency spectrum. He stated that: "The human auditory system and a table radio may be one order of magnitude apart in sensitivity to radio frequency energy." He experimented with microwaves seeking to transmit spoken word directly into the audio cortex and also developed the induction of heart seizures by beamed electromagnetics. His work was carried on by Dr. Michael Persinger who stated that *"All consciousness is due to electromagnetic patterns generated within the brain. What we do is imitate what the brain normally does and apply it experimentally."* He perfected a means to make subjects feel like they had been abducted by aliens, or had an encounter with angels or God.

Captain Paul Tyler, Director of the U.S. Navy's Electromagnetic Radiation Project stated, "With the right electromagnetic field, for example, you might be able to produce the same effects as psychoactive drugs." Using the technologies of ESB (Electrical Stimulation of the Brain) one could evoke hallucinations as well as fear and pleasure. It could literally manipulate the human will at will.[10]

Dr. Jose Delgado has researched the human brain and published his results in professional papers since 1952. As Professor of Physiology at Yale, his research included behavior modification, altering migratory movements, and genetic mutations caused by ELF frequencies. Delgado began with electrodes but discovered that wireless effects were possible. He found that by changing the frequency and waveform on an experimental subject, he could completely change their thinking and emotional state. In his book, *Physical Control of the Mind*, Delgado quoted UNESCO's Constitution stating, "Since war begins in the mind of men, it is in the minds of men that the defenses of peace must be constructed."

Meanwhile the Soviets had moved way ahead of the United States in their development of mind war technologies. They had perfected a device called Lida which produced an ELF pulsing field. Lida was used to put prisoners of war into a trance, so that secrets could be extracted from them more easily. The Soviets went on to discover that by slight manipulation—by reversing brain polarity—they could induce "Telepathic Hypnosis."

Don't think this type of technology doesn't have its practical applications. In 1958, at the age of 14, Patrick Flanagan entered the United States Patent Office with what he called the Neurophone; a device that transmits acoustic information directly into the brain by means of an electromagnetic field. They laughed him out of the building until in 1967, he showed that he could make the deaf hear. The neurophone has many applications as an enhanced learning machine or as a brain to computer interface, but the potential misuse is even greater. The neurophone is now in the hands of the military ELF array known as HAARP which stands for The High Frequency Active Auroral Research Project. HAARP is the largest ionospheric heater in the world, a reversal of a radio telescope, transmitting instead of receiving ELF waves. HAARP can manipulate global weather patterns, hurt ecosystems, and knock out electrical systems and communications while altering moods and mental states. The equipment beams focused energy up to the ionosphere and from there it can manipulate Earth's resonance field and all beings within it. In the foreword to the book, *Angels Don't Play This HAARP,* Flanagan states that, *"As a result of these personal research*

With knowledge of the brain, we may transform, we may shape, direct, roboticize man. I think the great danger of the future is that we will have roboticiced human beings who are not aware that they have been roboticized. —Jose Delgado

By implanting electrodes in the brain and anchoring them to skull, Delgado and his team were able to remotely control the behavior of these rhesus monkeys. Photos: *Physical Conrol of the Mind*

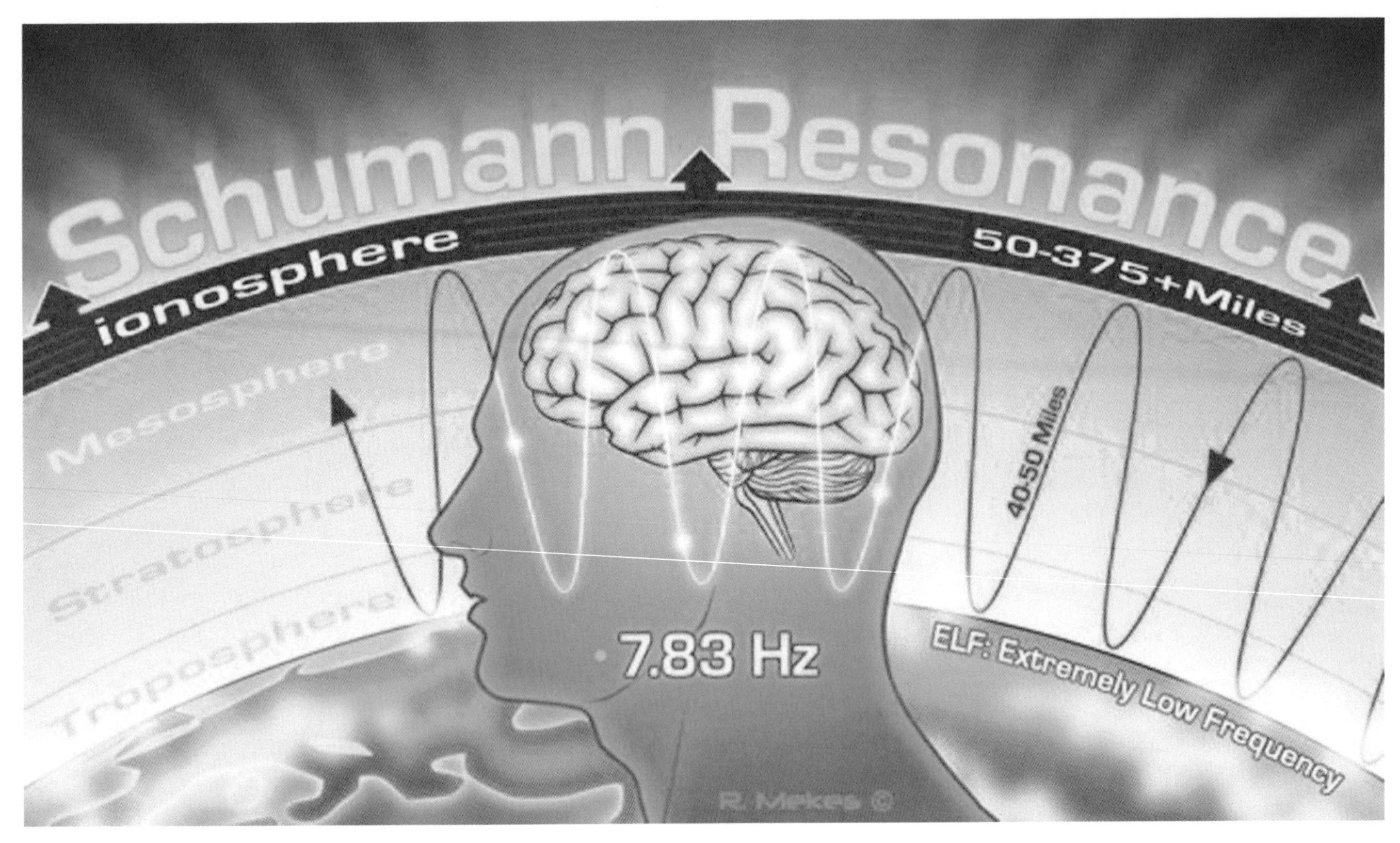

experiences I am acutely aware of the potential misuse of HAARP technology for the implementation of electronic global mind control."

Earth is wrapped in a doughnut shaped magnetic field known as the ionosphere. Dr. Bernard Eastlund discovered a method of manipulating this energy. His patent "Method and Apparatus for Altering a Region in the Earth's Atmosphere, Ionosphere, and/or Magnetosphere" was applied for in 1985 and the Department of Defence sealed it under a "Secrecy Order" using the National Security Act.

The Schuman Resonance is the wave frequency created by the cavity or sphere within a sphere of the electromagnetic field around the Earth and the Earth itself. The shape and amount of energy create a particular frequency. This was predicted mathematically by Winfried Otto Schumann in 1952. The limited dimensions of the Earth cause this waveguide to act as a resonant cavity for electromagnetic waves in the ELF band. Normally, this standing wave within the Earth/Ionosphere cavity is approximately 7.83 Hz. This frequency can alter slightly due to perturbations for example when solar flares strike our planet. These "earth brainwaves" are identical to the spectrum of our brainwaves as Tesla also discovered.

Isaac Bonewits in his thesis on "Real Magic" for which he earned the first and only degree in magic and thaumaturgy from the University of California, describes a machine that "will be able to read minds and send out thoughts of its own!" The device he describes is identical to the HAARP antennae array. He was discussing "Psi War" and his thesis was written more than 20 years before the creation of HAARP.

His theories rest solidly on Professor I. M. Kogan, Chairman of the Bioinformation Section of Moscow. In his highly technical paper "The Information Theory Aspect of Telepathy," Dr. Kogan shows mathematically that the human body produces more than enough energy to create long standing radio frequency waves that reach the ionosphere which act as a carrier for telepathic information.

Advertisers are now using directed radio frequencies to put their message directly into your head. An outdoor billboard that displays an ad for *Paranormal State*, a ghost-themed series premiering on A&E, uses special technology to transmit sound so close to you that you think it's inside your head. As you walk by, the sound of a woman's voice whispers a chilling message, "Who's that? Who's there?" It's not your imagination. The technology is created by Holosonic and the device is effectively an 'audio spotlight' that can project sound literally right into your ears.

One genre of magic, ESP or telepathy, operates upon the same electromagnetic spectrum as radio waves. *"Basically, every human body is a walking radio station, broadcasting and receiving on ultra-long wavelengths of the standard electromagnetic energy spectrum...And 99 percent of all instructions for casting spells are ways of changing your neural system!"*[11]

These neural patterns link together creating something called a "switchboard," a "metapattern" or mass mind which is the common sea of consciousness shared by all individuals linked together like an invisible psychic internet. Jung called this the "collective unconscious" and it is in this realm that the sorcerer can do his best work. The collective thought waves of the seven billion people on planet earth also create an atmosphere and it affects everyone either consciously or unconsciously. Like the Borg in Star Trek, you can tune into this "collective consciousness" and broadcast ideas to others who will receive and act on them. The French adept Antonin Artaud, forecasted this type of mass public sorcery from the 1940's, *"Aside from trifling witchcraft of country sorcerers, there are tricks of global hoodoo in which all altered consciousnesses participate periodically...That is how strange forces are aroused and transported to the astral vault, to that dark dome which is composed above all of...the poisonous aggressiveness of the evil minds of most people ...the formidable tentacular oppression of a kind of civic magic which will soon appear undisguised."*

***

The Robot

In Mary Shelly's cautionary tale of the disasters of will and ambition, a fanatical scientist steals dead bodies from their graves and assembles from them a creature that he activates by electromagnetism.

Frankenstein's monster was simply a modern version of the "golem" or the primitive idea of a robot or mind controlled slave. Golem is a Hebrew word for "shapeless mass." The golem of the ancient Cabalists was an artificial manlike being created either by carving wood, clay, wax or mud or by screwing together pieces from assorted dead bodies. It was brought to life by carving a sacred name into it. When the planets are aligned properly the rabbi will summon the demon, Astaroth, to recieve the magic word to animate the

Photo: From the 1920 movie, *The Golem: How He Came Into the World*
Background: Ionospheric heater known as HAARP

golem by writing on its forehead the word "emet" which means "truth" or "reality." When he rubs out the first letter, the remaining word means "dead" and would cause the golem to crumble into dust. The golem had no mind and was a perfect slave for the magician who had created him. In the Talmud, Adam was initially created like a golem when his dust was "kneaded into a shapeless husk."

In 1915, writer, director and actor Paul Wegener told the story of *The Golem* in three films that make up the first horror series ever created. They are based on a legend in Jewish mysticism about an astrologer, Rabbi Loew who predicted doom for the Jews in 16th century Prague. According to a decree from the Emperor, they were to be expelled from the city or killed for practicing black magic. To protect the Jewish community, the rabbi constructed the Golem out of clay and brought it to life through rituals and Hebrew incantations. As the golem grew, it became increasingly violent, killing gentiles and spreading fear. In the end, the Emperor begs the Rabbi to destroy the Golem, promising to stop the persecution of the Jews.

Many scholarly books leave out the dark side of the Kabbalah which concerned black magic, dealing with demons and blood sacrifice. Attempts to create golems, zombies, robots, soulless bodies or slaves out of people are perhaps the most famous examples of practical sorcery. Sorcerers love robots, they *need* them. They need to create a planet of illusions where your thoughts, ideas and creative force are subject to their command. Their world is a constant battle to control our unconscious mind through sound, symbols and words. From hidden symbols to invisible weapons technology, the modus operandi of the sorcerer is mind control. His main source of power is YOU. It is your mind, will, and creativity under his control. A planet where his thoughts are your thoughts and each individual is merely a robot on Planet Hollywood.

***

1. *The Magician's Dictionary*, E.E. Rehmus
2. *Satan Wants You*, Arthur Lyons
3. *Man and His Symbols*, Carl Jung
4. *Lectures on Ancient Philosophy*, Manly P. Hall,
5. *Walt Disney - Hollywood's Dark Prince*, Marc Eliot
6. *Satan Wants You*, Arthur Lyons
7. *The Light of Egypt*, Thomas H. Burgoyne
8. *Speculum Astronomiae*, Albertus Magnus
9. *Astro-theology and Sidereel Mythology*, Michael Tsarion
10. *Journey into Madness, The True Story of Secret CIA Mind Control and Medical Abuse*, Gordon Thomas
11. *Real Magic*, Isaac Bonewits

Books:

The Tavistock Institute of Human Relations, John Coleman
The Elixir and the Stone, Michael Baigent & Richard Leigh
Media Sexploitation, Wilson Bryan Key

Movies:

Spiritworld, Christopher Everard
Monarch: The New Phoenix Program, Marshal Thomas

Do You Have Feelings?

Do you occasionally suffer from emotions of an almost human nature? Zombitol can help. Maybe you find yourself feeling sad some days and happy other days? Do you sometimes get nervous when meeting new people? Are the dishes piling up in the sink with no end to laundry in sight? In this fast paced world, who has time to figure out what's actually depressing you?

If you find yourself admiring the logic of Dr. Spock, Dexter, or Agent Smith, tell your doctor that Zombitol is right for you. Zombitol is there when you want to feel nothing. From the makers of Repressitol. Helping people feeling "meh" since 1992.

Side effects may include, but are not limited to: nausea, vomiting, headaches, dizziness, runny nose, nasal sores, nasal fungal infection, heartburn, hair loss, diarrhea, gloucoma, cataracts, dry mouth, water retention, increase in semen, decrease in semen, painful rectal itch, gas with oily discharge, an increased number of bowel movements—an urgent need to have them—and an inability to control them, coma, death and trouble swallowing. The way Zombitol works is not entirely understood. Psychological effects may include hallucination, depression, sociopathic behavior, confused morality, homosexual sex addiction, or other overpowering urges such as increased gambling and the zombie apocalypse. Other patients have reported psychotic nightmares, suicide ideation, sleep eating and narcolepsy.

Ceremonial magic is the ancient art of evoking and controlling spirits by a scientific application of certain formula. A magician enveloped in sanctified vestments and carrying a wand inscribed with hieroglyphic figures could by the power invested in certain words and symbols control the invisible inhabitants of the elements and of the astral world. While the elaborate ceremonial magic of antiquity was not necessarily evil, there arose from it perversions several false schools of sorcery or black magic.

In Egypt, the black magicians of Atlantis continued to exercise their superhuman powers until they had completely undermined and corrupted the morals of the primitive mysteries. Thus, black magic dictated the state religion and paralyzed the intellectual and spiritual activities of the individual by demanding his complete and unhesitating acquiescence in the dogma formulated by the priestcraft.

–Manly P. Hall

The Secret Teachings of All Ages

Littlefield Fountain—The University of Texas Tower

A Treatise on Slack Magic

How to survive and/or bring about the end of the world as we know it.

For those who have been enchanted, mesmerized, lobotomized, or roboticized, there is still hope. We will offer a new system of magic for the meek magician. For the un-ambitious, the dreamers, the artists, the empathetic; for the compassionate and merciful, the peacemakers and for the clean of heart. It is for the lights of the world. This magical system is founded on the principle that a loving creator designed nature to care for us and life is to be relatively stress free. The idea of scarcity has no place in this practice for we believe that all people, individually and collectively are entitled to life in all abundance. "That they may have life, and that they might have it more abundantly."[1] That is the law. There is no exploitation in Slack Magic, only a showering of gifts, easily bought by free spirits and generously scattered on all hands.

Magic has always been synonymous with effortlessness, but anyone who has witnessed a ritual can argue that there is a great amount of physical, emotional, spiritual and mental effort being put in to produce a desired effect. Constantly performing rituals can be downright robotic! Instead of another revolution, which is just one more turn around the same wheel, let's show those sorcerers who would oppress us that we will thrive with non-compliance. Let's counter black magic with Slack Magic!

***

Slack

*"Slack that can be described is not true slack."**

The Church of the Subgenius is a parody religion with some powerful insights. They believe that the ultimate conspiracy is to rob us of our Slack. Slack equals freedom. What is this idea of freedom that Americans hold so dear but the ability to do what you want, when you want? Who in the world can honestly say that they have this? Slack is the hour that is not scheduled. It is the lack of stress, deadlines, and fear of time. *"Slack is absolutely 'free' time, devoid of all stress, to do whatever you damn well please for eternity."*[2] You would think that without deadlines that humans would postpone everything forever and ultimately end up doing nothing. On the contrary, slack manages to be a great motive without the sense of impending doom. People want to work, they love it. Slack is simply being allowed to do the kind of work you love. False work, done only for money, without fun is a sin against yourself.

First man learned to work, then he learned to slack. If we must work hard let the effort be equal to universal laws and be able to reproduce itself exponentially. The true nature of the universe is abundance. The act of planting a tiny seed has the potential to regenerate itself forever. The right kind of work and effort should bring infinite rewards. Let our ultimate goal of work be to help other people have slack. The world is full of hardworking people that have little or nothing to show for it. Tonight, hundreds of millions of men and women will struggle to get to sleep because they are stressed out about not making enough money even though they are working as hard as they possibly can. They are called "the working poor," and their numbers are absolutely exploding. In Japan they are working so hard that they literally drop dead on the job. This is so common that there is even a word for it—Karoshi, which means "death from overwork." The hard work that we do in the present *should* equal less work in the future, but this can never be realized with the system designed the way it is today. Something more than hard work is necessary.

The successful people of history have become so through creative thinking. Slack is the starting point of creativity. It is the feeling that everything is in its place and you are free to produce anything from your imagination or study any subject that interests you. Technology will not help you have slack. What good is an iphone 5 when your daily existence is still one of survival? The majority of your brain power is wasted trying to procure the very basics: food, water and shelter. It was not designed to be that way. The time in your life when you came the closest to knowing what slack is was probably in grade school, between the hours of 3pm and 6pm. After school, but before dinner, when you had no responsibilities and food was being prepared for you. In this magical time to yourself, a minute was an eternity. You felt like you could do anything and you were right.

Slack is the ability to effortlessly achieve your goals. Jesus' most famous speech, the Sermon on the Mount, reflects this attitude when he says: Behold the fowls of the air: for they sow not, neither do they reap, nor gather into barns; yet your heavenly Father feedeth them. Are ye not much better than they? ...Consider the lilies of the field, how they grow; they toil not, neither do they spin: And yet I say unto you, That even Solomon in all his glory was not arrayed like one of these.[3] Enlightened beings, superior magicians and emerging robots REPENT! QUIT YOUR JOB! SLACK OFF!

"We must do away with the...notion that everybody has to earn a living. It is a fact today that one in ten thousand of us can make a technological breakthrough capable of supporting all the rest. The youth of today are absolutely right in recognizing this nonsense of earning a living. We keep inventing jobs because of this false idea that everybody has to be employed at some kind of drudgery because, according to Malthusian-Darwinian theory, he must justify his right to exist...The true business of people should be to go back to school and think about whatever it was they were thinking about before somebody came a long and told them they had to earn a living."

—R. Buckminster Fuller

7 Slack Magic Formulae:

I. Have No Fear!

"Fear is the path to the dark side. Fear leads to anger, anger leads to hate, hate leads to suffering." —Yoda

Fear is like a magnet and it is always guaranteed to attract that very thing you are most afraid of. All negative things in the world are ultimately manifestations of fear. Hatred, resentment and violence all stem from the reptilian brain in its fight or flight mode. Fear is a long slow wavelength and activates very few of our DNA 'antennas' which connect us to the Cosmos. Only by de-linking this knowledge has it been possible for sorcerers to orchestrate the agenda over thousands of years. When we are under a spell of fear we will give our power away to anyone we believe will protect us. Fear clouds the mind so that the survival part of the brain clicks in the higher areas of thinking are shut down. Because fear is a lack of faith we remove, by our own free will, God's protection. When Bobby McFerrin sings "Don't Worry, Be Happy" we cannot think of a state of mind more conducive to working slack magic than this. Worry is anti-magic. How many times have we worked ourselves into a frenzy worrying about something that never came to pass? This is a tremendous waste of energy that makes us less equipped to deal with real problems as they arise. All worry is fear of the future and spells that are cast from this mental state are the essence of a destructive kind of magic. Take therefore no thought for the morrow: for the morrow shall take thought for the things of itself.[4]

We must never find ourselves being paranoid and in fear...instead let's learn to practice Pronoia! Try to believe that in the magical universe there are mysterious forces at work, moving outside of your perception like the invisible currents of the sea. Pronoia is the understanding that these forces are fundamentally friendly and are conspiring behind your back to help you. Foster the outlandish perception that the universe is trying to shower you with blessings. Pronoia is your belief that life is a sublime game created for our amusement and illumination. The core principle is that all of creation is on our side; that the very structure of reality ensures our eventual liberation from suffering. When we believe this we awaken to our divine nature and become co-creators. *"The most important decision we make is whether we believe we live in a friendly or hostile universe."* —Albert Einstein

II. Everything is Play!

"Work and play are words used to describe the same thing under differing conditions."
—Mark Twain

Life is what you make of it. It can be drudgery, or it can be play. The key to effortless manifestation is to think of it as a game. Mankind's genius is creative play. It's what separates us from all other species on the planet and makes us the most amazing and the most dangerous thing. As a child, creative play is the foundation of learning, critical thinking, problem solving and empathy. Experts in the field of creativity tell us we need a playful attitude to allow the "juices" to flow, and to bring enjoyment and a sense of adventure to our endeavors. Creative play also helps us have the stamina to follow through on our goals by helping us trust in the uncertainties that come with the creative process. Play is born from curiosity and exploration. A spirit of play engages us and brings us into the moment. When we are in this state of play, this is the cosmic "sweet spot" or "luck plane" when we are connected to Source Energy, the vortex of creation.

We must give up the notion that play is not serious. Work or study and play are not opposites, they are inexorably linked. When Mary Poppins sings "A Spoonful of Sugar," she is trying to get the children to forget they are actually cleaning the room by making it a game. By using animals as the model she illustrates how things seem to magically happen in nature. The birds build their nests with a happy tune and the bees get the job done by dancing and enjoying the nectar along the way. P.L. Travers, creator of Mary Poppins, was a disciple of Russian mystic, G.I. Gurdjieff, who was influenced by Sufi and Tibetan Lamas. The character of Poppins in the books, is that of a Sufi adept in the way she is able to turn the world inside out and upside down and bend the laws of nature.

Dr. Stuart Brown, president of the National Institute of Play, reminds us that "The opposite of play is not work, it's depression." He created the institute in 1996, after more than twenty years of psychiatric practice and research persuaded him of the dangerous long term consequences of play deprivation. Brown states, "If you look at what produces learning and memory and well-being, play is as fundamental as any other aspect of life, including sleep and dreams." A committee investigating the life of the University of Texas shooter, Charles Whitman, unanimously identified his lifelong lack of play as the key factor to his homicidal actions.

Studies on the brains of cats, rats and mice at play have shown some interesting results. Play is related to growth of the cerebellum, a critical region of the brain which is the area that coordinates movements originating in other parts of the brain. A graph showing the growth curve of the cerebellum of a mouse was nearly identical to a graph curve depicting the mouse's playfulness. Rats and cats showed the same relationship as mice: a match between when they were playing and when the cerebellum was growing.

"We don't stop playing because we grow old;
we grow old because we stop playing."
—George Bernard Shaw

Why would a child want to play with a toy vacuum or plastic lawn mower? Anything is fun for them because they have not learned to associate these activities with negative feelings. It's not the activity that is the problem—it's your attitude towards the activity. Remember that there is no such thing as serious business; this is Earth, after all, and no one gets out alive. In ancient China, before communism, Taoism was largely the religion of the merchant. They proceeded to stop thinking of business as business and began to think of it as pleasure. Instead of resenting every minute, and wishing he could make more out of every transaction, the Taoist merchant settled down to a quiet game of buying and selling. It gradually reached a point through Asia where it wasn't about the actual buying or selling, but about the game of bargaining. In the east, merchandising is seen as a pleasant occupation, a game in which each person tries to outwit the other.

A spirit of play connects us and creates a relaxed feeling of togetherness. If you want people to join in your activities you must show them that you are having fun. Play fosters a collective experience of engagement with the content. The basis of human trust is established through play signals and even dogs do an unmistakable "play bow" to show non-aggression.

"The master of the art of living makes little distinction between his work and his play, his labor and his leisure, his mind and his body, his education and his recreation, his love and his religion. He simply pursues his vision of excellence in whatever he does, leaving others to decide whether he is working or playing. To him, he is always doing both." —Lao Tzu

III. The Glad Game.

"When you focus on the things that you're grateful for, then it opens you to the source of all those things that came into your life for which you are grateful." —Deepak Chopra

The classic movie, *Pollyanna* was about an annoyingly chipper little girl who helped people turn their lives out of misery using what she called "The Glad Game." By doing this, she unknowingly happened upon the cornerstone of success—and attracting more things that make you happy. The attitude of gratitude is the most magical one of all. Gratitude creates abundance consciousness. It is the antidote for two root sufferings that we experience. The first is the feeling of insufficiency, not having enough or not being enough. This sense of dissatisfaction opens the way to the second kind of suffering, being incessantly busy trying to get more or be more in order to somehow fill this inner feeling of discontentment. Seeking inner satisfaction from external sources keeps us on a never-ending loop of pursuits and distractions, always waiting for and expecting happiness to come to us from the outside.

After the temporary pleasure or sense of accomplishment wears off we find ourselves once again pursuing the next "fix." How many times have we worked so hard for something that when we finally achieved it, it was a total emotional letdown and you find yourself asking "what's next?" The miracle of gratitude is that it reverses this pattern and instantly puts us in touch with all the many gifts and blessings that we already have. Instead of letting circumstances dictate our happiness we can learn to generate happiness from the inside-out.

Ancient teachings and modern medical research agree that one of the fastest ways to restoring harmony and balance in our lives is to foster gratitude and appreciation. The moment you do, brain function becomes more balanced, harmonized, your heart begins to pump in a much more harmonious rhythm; and biochemical changes trigger a host of healthful responses throughout your body. In the Jewish spiritual tradition, the very first words of prayer spoken upon waking up in the morning express gratitude for the gift of another day of life: "I am grateful. Thank you for returning my soul to me with great compassion." An important part of Buddhist practice, too, is to begin each day with appreciation for the rare gift of a precious human birth and to contemplate its ever changing nature. Every year Americans celebrate a day of Thanksgiving. We give thanks for our abundance, with the hope of avoiding scarcity in the year ahead. It is not just an act of appreciation for what has past, but hope for the future as well. Unknowingly, with thanksgiving we are practicing the law of attraction. By giving thanks for what we have with confidence for better days ahead, we may cause this to occur. The opposite is true, if we complain about the present with grim expectations for the future, then that will likely be our fate as well.

Some magicians say that in order to obtain that which you desire, you must be obsessed with it. You must be willing make the objective the burning desire of your entire life. Why not cut to the chase and be obsessed with just being happy? The tiny Himalayan kingdom of Bhutan is taking a radical approach to foster happiness in their citizens. Since 1971 the country has rejected GDP as the only way to measure success. Instead, their approach to new development measures prosperity through principles of Gross National Happiness (GNH) and the spiritual, physical, social and environmental health of its people and natural environment.

Happiness is sought by so many and found by so few because it is a matter entirely unto ourselves. It is the one thing that we have direct control over. Our environment and circumstances of life ultimately have no effect on our happiness except what we allow from the outside to enter our consciousness. True happiness is independent of position, wealth, or material possessions. It is a state of mind which we ourselves have the power to control and that control lies within our thinking. Train yourself, like a Jedi master honing his skills, to find happiness no matter what.

IV. Have Faith!

"Through faith the imagination is invigorated and completed, for it really happens that every doubt mars its perfection. Faith must strengthen the imagination, for faith establishes the will."
—Paracelsus

The science of the nineteenth century called itself organized common sense but was actually based on Descartes' method of doubting everything that could be doubted and hoping that what was left over would be the truth. This "Cartesian" division allowed scientists to treat matter as dead and completely separate from themselves, and to see the material world as a combination of different objects assembled into a huge machine. So science was based on doubt where magic was based on faith.

Why do Christians believe that Jesus was the son of God? Because they believe in his testament of miracles. If working miracles (magic) is proof that God is with you, then why don't we see more people applying this like Jesus said they could and would do? One reason is because of money. Money is an illusion that usurps the miraculous nature of the universe. This is why Jesus said that it would be easier for a camel to pass through the eye of a needle than for a rich man to enter the kingdom of heaven, a realm where miracles happen. A person with money can manifest anything he wants to through his own god (money) and therefore has no need, desire or opportunity to know the real God. The catch is that his experiences, had by money, are restricted to only the things he can think of.

In order to produce a miracle you must believe one is possible in the first place. Only belief enables a person to do what others think is impossible. All the great things in the world have been done by people who were dreamers and believers in their dreams coming true. The power of belief is by far the most powerful and creative force in the universe. All the great sages and prophets taught a fundamental idea that is found in all religions, cults, creeds and sects. The gist is: if you believe it, it is so. As a man thinketh in his heart, so is he. This idea reduced into one word is faith. Even Jesus could not perform miracles without faith. While he was traveling and healing with his disciples, he found himself back in his own country. When he tried to preach at the synagogue the priests there did not receive him well and were offended. They did not believe that the Jesus they knew, the carpenter, son of Mary and Joseph, was capable of doing such miracles. But Jesus said unto them, "A prophet is not without honor, but in his own country, and among his own kin, and in his own house. And he could there do no mighty work, save that he laid his hands upon a few sick folk, and healed them. And he marvelled because of their unbelief. And he went round about the villages, teaching."[5]

Believing that now is always a perfect moment is an exercise in training your senses and intellect so that you're able to perceive the fact that life always gives you exactly what you need, exactly when you need it. You must have faith that everything is going to work out for you in the end. You must believe that life is always going in your favor, no matter what. Whatever disasters or misfortunes befall you, always trust that they are happening for your greater good. An easy example of this would be that you missed the plane flight that crashed. At the moment you couldn't board your plane, you thought that you had the worst luck in the world, but then you discovered that all these seeming "misfortunes" were all a part of your protection. In Goethe's *Faust*, the Devil in the form of Mephistopheles, introduces himself as a principle which constantly intends wickedness, but inadvertently achieves goodness by performing his required role in the moral and cosmic drama of reality.

V. Don't Force It~Use the Force!

"Those that flow as life flows know they need no other force." —Lao Tzu

Slack is the lack of tension. Nearly everyone today is functioning under massive amounts of stress and tension. Stress depletes us mentally and emotionally because it is physically exhausting and can lead to serious mistakes of judgment. Our bodies are designed to bear a certain amount of stress in critical periods of survival. Nature provides a defense in times of emergency but we cannot survive under continuous tension. Stress is a disease as much as any other physical ailment and unless we can cope with it, it can undermine our entire life. Man is simply not equipped, physically or emotionally, to stand the kind of world he is creating for himself. There can be no success if the person does not survive to enjoy it.

The slack magician is relaxed at all times, he goes with the cosmic flow. If you believe that you are always in the right place at the right time, you are correct,—*if* you came there with a good attitude. When Parsifal, the hero of a great soul myth, first visited the Castle of the Grail, he was asked how he had come there and he answered "I know not." He just happened to enter the holy place. Central to Taoist teachings is the concept of Wu-Wei, or the action of non-action. Wu-Wei refers to the state of being in which our actions are quite effortlessly in alignment with the ebb and flow of the elemental cycles of the natural world. This kind of "going with the flow" is characterized by a great ease and awake-ness, in which, without even trying, we are able to respond perfectly to whatever situations arise. At the same time it is not to be considered inertia, laziness, or passivity. Rather, it is the experience of going with the grain or swimming with the current. The practice of Wu-Wei is considered to be one of the highest forms of virtue.

The beauty of Slack Magic is that you don't have to try so hard. The moment when life becomes competitive it becomes stressful. Wise men know that the benefits of cooperation far outweigh the benefits of competition. Only ignorant people thrive on the winner/loser mentality. If other people want to be more ambitious, then good for them, let them be; but realize we do not have to compete with them. Any attitude of competition is inferior and the person who is obsessed with dominating other people is the unhappy one. *"Lesser religions demand that 'direct your will' and 'focus your energies'. Dobbs preaches the opposite although you must know of your power to begin with, the real key is to NOT TRY."*[5]

Let go of others' ideas of "success" and the need for their approval. Success is something that's ingrained in our culture, and almost every moment of our childhood and schooling are geared towards success, but it is a hollow concept. Who defines success? What happens when we don't achieve it; and what happens when we do, and still want more, or realize it wasn't worth all the effort, and that we've wasted our lives trying to please other people?

If you want to be happy you must learn to detach yourself from your competitive ego. Ego-lessness is a condition which many religious philosophies regard as a supreme state. The first and simplest way to tell whether you are acting from your ego is whether things have to be done *right now*. The ego thrives on control and the idea of feeling important and superior to others. We try to control our environment, control other people, control the outcomes and yet, it's all an illusion: we have no control over what happens. Things go wrong all the time, plans fail, we fail, and we feel like failures because of it because we thought we could control something and it didn't happen. Trying to control other people is a huge source of conflict and a waste of your vital energy. We must try to relinquish control of employees, co-workers, bosses, team members and loved ones. Let them do what they want and work with you how they will.

How can we know when the force is strong with us? It has long been the intuitions of poets, mystics and occultists that there are hidden "meanings" floating around us which we are normally cut off from by habit, ignorance and the dullness of the senses. It is as if the intelligent universe were trying to communicate with us. Esoteric tradition may be no more than the superstition of ignorant savages but it could also be an attempt to explain one of those accidental glimpses of a meaning that goes beyond everyday banality. The capacity to enjoy subtle vibrations or "intuition" is an important part of our energy outlets. Modern mystics call this force Syncronicity. The word was first used by Carl Jung and described as "temporally coincident occurrences of acasual events" in other words, a meaningful coincidence. It is the assumption that accidents and co-incidences and déjà vu are in some way linked with the unconscious side and events that seem to be much more than sheer coincidence. The concept of synchronicity did not escape Albert Einstein who was fascinated by this principle of connectivity of events that could not be explained by scientific means. Jung stated that these synchronicities served to link the subjective world to the objective world. When you experience a synchronicity it is evidence that the Force is with you.

VI. Wish With Your Heart~Not Your Will!

The human being is capable of two kinds of knowledge, called the rational (science, research) and the intuitive (religion, meditation) and in the West, intuitive knowledge is often devalued. In the East, the opposite is true. The *Upanishads* speak of a higher and a lower knowledge and associate the sciences with lower and religious awareness with the higher. The main purpose of the mystic schools and many aspects of the Eastern way of life are to teach techniques to silence the thinking mind and to shift awareness from the rational to the intuitive modes of consciousness through meditation in various forms. Yoga, T'ai Chi, Chinese calligraphy or a Japanese tea ceremony are all examples of meditation. Anything that produces a feeling of peace and serenity and still the mind can produce an experience of oneness with the surrounding state and put us in touch with our intuition.

In the beginning of the 2011 movie, *The Green Lantern*, the narrator says "Billions of years ago a race of immortals harnessed the most powerful force in existence: The emerald energy of willpower." The Guardians of the Universe sent rings powered by the energy of will out to the 3,600 different sections of the universe to select recruits. The ring works by focusing the will which turns thought into reality. In order to be chosen by the ring, it was said one must be without fear. These recruits were intergalactic peacekeepers known as the Green Lantern Corps. Of all the threats they ever faced, the strongest was an entity of fear.

This movie confuses the topic in two ways. First, green is not the color of willpower. In the traditions of Hinduism and Buddhism they teach of the chakras, which are wheels or vortexes, and are the centers of Prana, their word for the life force. Each chakra is assigned to a color in the rainbow spectrum. The chakras rainbow energy wheels are arranged starting from the bottom of the spine to the top, going from red to violet, from low to high frequencies. The Anahata or Heart chakra is right in the middle, its color is green, and its symbol is the six pointed star. On the color vibration scale of the visible spectrum of light, green is in the center and it represents balance. Green is the true color of love and nature provides this color for us in the greatest abundance so we can know for sure that we are loved. When we associate green with love, it is on a universal level. The key to everything is care which is symbolized in the masonic first degree tracing board as an initiate in green holding a key, which could be interpreted as the opening of the heart chakra.

Second, the movie states that the only way to overcome fear is with will power. This is also erroneous as the opposite of fear is actually love, the only emotion that is more powerful than fear, and has the ability to conquer fear. "There is no fear in love; but perfect love casteth out fear: because fear hath torment. He that feareth is not made perfect in love."[7] Love is the primary energy of existence. If you don't know what love is, then you don't know what God is, because God is love.[8] The thing that was so odd about *The Green Lantern* is that they never mentioned love once throughout the entire movie. Even though there was a lifetime romance between the two main characters, he still could never tell her that he loved her. Together with the other principles this omission was very telling.

When people say to you, "follow your heart," or "love is the answer," is this just flowery hippy speak or could there be something to it? Many believe that conscious awareness originates in the brain alone, however, consciousness actually emerges from the brain and body acting together. Far more than a simple pump, the heart is now recognized by scientists as a highly complex system with its own functional "brain." Fifty percent of heart cells are neural and form their own neural network, the intelligence of the heart. The nervous system within the heart enables it to learn, remember, and make functional decisions independent of the brain's cerebral cortex.

If our thoughts have power in the sub-atomic world, how much more power do emotions have? The heart is an extremely sophisticated organ of perception and center for receiving and processing information. It is electromagnetic, neural and hormonal. Its electric field is sixty times greater in amplitude than the brain and its magnetic field is five thousand times stronger and radiates for several feet out as it interacts with our organs and other structures. Negative emotions produce an erratic, disordered, incoherent pattern in the heart's rhythms. In contrast, positive emotions create a smooth, ordered, coherent pattern. These are measurable by a technique called spectral analysis. Scientists have demonstrated that sustained positive emotions appear to give rise to a distinct mode of functioning called "psychophysiological coherence." This mode is characterized by increased efficiency and harmony in the interactions of the body's systems. Psychologically, it is linked with a reduction in internal mental dialogue, reduced perceptions of stress, increased emotional balance, and enhanced mental clarity, intuitive discernment, and cognitive performance. The heart's field is directly involved in intuitive perception through its coupling to an energetic information field outside the bounds of space and time. Both the heart and brain receive and respond to information about a future event before the event actually happens. Even more surprising is that the heart appears to receive this "intuitive" information even before the brain does.

The Green Lantern is screwed up because Hollywood wants to remove your Slack and influence your desire! Will is another word for desire and here in the 3rd dimension we can't help but have desires. We all want things, but how can we manifest the best possible scenario for our life when we have no idea of the infinite possibilities available? We must entertain the idea of letting someone—or something else help you do the choosing. You do have a free will, but honestly, constantly using your personal will force can be exhausting. In fact, some studies show that having to make too many decisions can leave people tired, mentally drained and more dissatisfied with their decisions. It also leads people to make poorer choices, sometimes at a time when the choice really matters. The brain is like a muscle, it burns calories and can get exhausted. The mere act of thinking about whether you prefer A or B, tires you out so if you have to do something else that takes discipline, you can't do it —you will quit faster. If you have lifted heavy weights in a gym, later trying to lift a 30lb weight is impossible. Albert Einstein used to wear the same suit all the time so he didn't have to make small decisions and could put his brain to better use. His fashion sense greatly improved when his wife took over his choice of clothes.

According to one legend, the Kabbalah is the knowledge given to Adam and Eve to help humanity find its way back to Eden. Having chosen to eat from the Tree of Knowledge, they were forced to leave paradise for this world where they would have to make choices for the rest of their days. In a world of infinite possibilities and parallel universes the pressure to find one's dharma, let alone deal with your karma, can be immense. How can we always know what we want? What if we choose the wrong thing? Life is short, God forbid you make a mistake, right?

"I did not direct my life. I didn't design it. I never made decisions. Things always came up and made them for me. That's what life is." —B. F. Skinner

There is a way to leg'go your ego and "set your will free," meaning that you don't stop having desires but you can gradually get less and less specific with your demands. Pythagoras taught his disciples that when they prayed, they should not ask for things for themselves, because no man knows what is good for him. Jesus prayed not my will by thy will and in Kabbalah the soul triad of the sephira Gebrua-Tiferet-Hesed represents "God's Will" and it is the point where we are willing to hand over the power in our life to the divine. This is not because we have to, but because we finally understand that God knows the wider plan for our life and will direct us toward happiness and spiritual growth.The universe is not a clockwork contraption created by some divine engineer, but now left as an automation to its own devices. It is alive and growing. It is like a giant cosmic activities director who has to take into account all of the individual desires while trying to orchestrate fun for the whole group. Surrendering your specific desires allows for spontaneity and more synchronistic moments. The more options you give over to the universe, the more space it has to arrange something awesome for you.

Enlightenment is a spiritual awareness that transcends personal wants and needs. In Taoism, surrender of the ego/will is the prerequisite to expressing the highest level of our individual free will and creativity. Part of enlightenment is freedom from desire. It is learning to want the thing you have instead of having the things you want. When we are free of the shackels of our infinite desires, this will foster a feeling of "light heartedness" a concept which the Egyptian's regarded as supreme. The Papyrus of Ani, which became *The Egyptian Book of the Dead* depicts the souls' descent into the afterlife. When the deceased enters into the Judgment Hall of Osiris, his heart is placed on a scale and weighed against a feather which represents "truth." The heart and the feather must be in perfect balance and a heavy heart represents a life of sin and is separated from the body and fed to a crocodile like monster.

"Mysticism and spiritualism are arrived at not by willing but by unwilling. The will has to be abnegated before attainment can be possible. In other words attainment is involuntary. The actions preceding attainment are instrumental in banishing the will entirely." —Louis Singer

The philosophy of "Do what thou wilt" at first might seem like the ultimate expression of freedom, however it fails to take into account the law of cause and effect, and also the awareness that we live in a closed eco-system. Our actions always have consequences, for ourselves and also for everything that shares our environment. When a cell in your body does not have access to the proper "information" when it divides, it will be mutated. It no longer recognizes that it is a part of a whole organism and gets busy doing its own thing. In a healthy body these cells would be recognized and neutralized, however, if the environment is toxic enough the mutated cells develop into cancerous tumors. We must face the fact that all humans are part of a larger organism and we are all in this together—for better or worse.

Social communication and interaction is not only based in terms of overt signals expressed through language, gestures and facial expressions. Experiments conducted at the Institute of HeartMath have found remarkable evidence that the heart's electromagnetic field can transmit information between people with a measureable exchange of heart energy between individuals up to five feet apart. A person's brain waves can actually synchronize to another person's heart. This highly influential electromagnetic or "energetic" communication system operates just below our conscious awareness. The nervous system acts as an "antenna," which is tuned to and responds to the electromagnetic fields produced by the hearts of other individuals. So, we are all profoundly effecting one another simply by existing.

Descartes' most famous sentence, "I am thinking, therefore I exist", led people to equate their identity with their mind, instead of their whole organism. As a consequence, most individuals are aware of themselves as isolated ego's existing "inside" their bodies. This fragmentation is extended to society which is split into different nations, races, religions and political groups. The mystic view of the world is organic, all things are interrelated and are but different aspects of the same thing. The tendency to dissect and categorize things as separate is what the Buddists call avidya, or ignorance and is seen as a mental illness. The various schools of Eastern mysticism all emphasize the basic unity of the universe. The highest aim of the Hindu, Buddist or Taoist is to realize this unity and the mutual interrelation of all things and to transcend the idea of an isolated individual self is the key to enlightenment. Their image of Divinity is not that of a ruler who directs the world from above, but of a principle that moves from within everything.

VII. Friendship is Magic!

"Two are better than one; for if they fall, the one will lift up his fellow:but woe to him that is alone when he falleth; for he hath not another to help him."

—Ecclesiastes 4:9-10

What is one of the most closely guarded open secrets of the elite? It is the power of powerful friends. Although, I doubt these ultra-powerful people know the true meaning of friendship, they do recognize the immense potential of connections. The richest people on the planet would have gotten nowhere in life without their powerful friends, family and mentors. The "1%" protect their fellow criminals because they know their fates are tied together and would never turn them over to justice. They are bound by blood oaths and secret ceremonies to be loyal to one another only. Perhaps one lesson that we could take from them is that they take their relationship bonds very seriously. They would never betray someone of their class to help someone they deemed as lowly. According to the Economic Policy Institute, the wealthiest one percent of all Americans households have 288 times the amount of wealth that the average middle class American family does. In the United States today, the wealthiest one percent of all Americans have a greater net worth than the bottom ninety percent combined and they are obsessed with keeping that wealth and power "in the family."

However, Slack Magic is not for them. It is for the underdogs. It is for all those people who "occupied" Wall Street would call the 99%. If there's power in numbers, then "regular" people should be the most powerful force. We are not, however, because we have turned on each other and surrendered our potential over to the elite who use it to enslave us. Since most people do not have the means to live opulently, by mimicking people of a wealthy class (swag) you turn your back on your true friends and keep them as slaves to the system created by the greedy power mongers. We should never be jealous of, or desire to be anything like "the elite." They are the most lost, victimized, confused and unhappy people.

Medical professionals tell us that friendship helps the body's auto immune system resist disease. The Pythagoreans taught that friendship was the truest and most perfect of all relationships. They declared all bonds without friendship were shackles and there was no virtue in their maintenance. They believed that the sympathetic intellect of a stranger was closer than a blood relative whose view point was at variance with his own.

***

There is a parable about how God works through friends called *Dolan & Gooby*:

Dolan was a bright and handsome boy who always strove for perfection and tried his best to be righteous in every way. He studied his religion day and night to make his parents proud. He was always impeccably dressed and groomed but also very uptight. Gooby was a pudgy, good natured soul who never had a bad thought about anybody including himself. He like to stay home and tend to his many animals and plants and eat as much of his mother's cooking as he could. He was not near as smart, sophisticated or studious as Dolan.

One day Dolan came to Gooby with some exciting news he had learned at church. He was lugging around a big Holy Book while Gooby was goofing off in the garden as usual.

"Today the minister told us that if you have enough faith you can make miracles. It only takes the amount of a little mustard seed and you can move a mountain. I go to church all the time and I have more faith than anyone, wouldn't you say?" said Dolan.

"Sure," replied Gooby as he tossed a stick for one of his dogs.

"I am going on a quest to prove my faith. I will travel far up the mountain where I can talk to God and I'm not coming down until I receive a miracle." Dolan declared.

"Can I come and help?" offered Gooby.

"No!" cried Dolan, "You are not as spiritual as me and you might cause me to stumble or lose faith. Just to prove how much I believe in God, I am taking no provisions because I expect my miracle to come quickly!"

"Well, good luck, my friend." Said Gooby, and with that Dolan was off on his mission. He hiked far up the mountain trail for hours and hours until he found a nice spot with a large stone where he kneeled and began to pray. By this time Dolan had become very hungry from his journey and decided that he would ask God to make something to eat appear before him as a miracle. He honestly didn't know if he would have the strength to make it home if God didn't deliver. He prayed and prayed and waited and waited; growing hungrier all the time. He was weak and in tears and it was already dark.

Finally Dolan cried out, "Please, God, if you love me, hear my prayer. I have read all of your teachings and follow them to the letter! I always try to do the right thing and go to church more than anyone! I believe in you! Please, I am so hungry and need you to make some food appear on this rock before me!"

Suddenly, he heard noises coming from behind him. He turned around and saw Gooby with a light and a basket followed by his two hounds who immediately ran up to Dolan and started licking him.

"Dolan! Thank goodness, I finally found you!" said Gooby.

"Gooby! What are you doing here?! You're interrupting my miracle." screamed Dolan.

"You have been gone for such a long time." replied Gooby, as he reached into the basket. "I thought you might be hungry so I've brought you some of my mother's homemade soup, and apples and chocolate and..."

"Gooby, you fool!" cried Dolan, "This is serious. I have asked God to show me a miracle and I told you I'm not leaving until I get it."

"Gee, I'm sorry, Dolan. I didn't mean to spoil it." said Gooby, as he started to leave.

"Get out of here, Gooby." Said Dolan as he turned around and clasped his hands to pray. "I'll die before I lose my faith." And so he did.

The moral of this story is that you must learn to recognize your angels. Just because your miracle didn't come exactly the way you wanted it doesn't make it any less miraculous. Dolan saw Gooby as a buffoon, but who was closer to God? Through Gooby's child-like innocence and caring he was made a vessel for a miracle, essentially an angel, instead of a person making demands on God. It wasn't Dolan's faith that was the problem for the universe did bring him the exact thing he asked for, plus the bonus of friendship, but since Dolan thought he was more spiritual than Gooby, he didn't recognize him as a gift from above. If you recall the story of the war in heaven in the Bible, it says that only 1/3 of the angels were fallen, that means that there are twice as many angels than demons in the world...so where are they? They are there if you know where to look.

In many stories having friends is often what separates the hero from the villain. In fiction, being asocial usually includes a host of other problems: arrogance, selfishness, mental instability, inhumanity, or plain old evil. Humans are social animals. Cooperation along with the invention of language is how we survived and those who were alone often weren't able to reproduce or discuss their innovations with others. Through most of human history collective action was the only practical means of survival. Being extremely selfish, or being shunned, banned or exiled was very often a precursor to slow death by starvation or predators. "Dying alone" is probably the deepest rooted fear that a person could have.

Many orthodoxies will offer you the advice that you should be careful and guarded about who you allow to be your friend. Members of religious sects are encouraged to shun non-members for fear of somehow being tainted by them, but this may be causing harm to other people who may need you. Not everyone will be able to understand you on a profound basis of close communion, but they are still worth knowing. If they are truly toxic you can always limit the intensity of the relationship. Don't be selfish with your friendship and go around cutting people out of your life like weeds. Not every single association you have will be a benefit that you can recognize easily. Some people will need your friendship more than you need theirs. Remember that villains are made from rejection and isolation.

***

The Fool

Let no man deceive himself. If any man among you seemeth to be wise in this world, let him become a fool, that he may be wise.

—I Corinthians 3:18

If Slack Magic had a mascot it would be Forrest Gump. A little boy born to a single mother with a deformed back and low IQ somehow managed to far exceed what anyone thought he could do. Why? Because he had the mind of a child and didn't quite understand the world of Ego. He became a college football star, war hero, international sports celebrity, cultural icon, and multimillionaire. He found the love of his life and had a healthy baby son. Not bad for what the world would call an idiot.

If you are following the Slack Magicians path you may find yourself receiving a lot of ridicule from folks who just don't understand. Ridicule is how you know if you are slacking correctly—or incorrectly, it doesn't matter. You can't screw this up. The Fool is number zero in the Tarot deck. He is the beginning of the magician's journey and represents the soul before its fall into matter. The Fool is immortal and the most powerful of all Tarot Trumps. In royal courts, the jester held a curious role as being the only one who could make a truthful commentary about the folly of the Royals and their sniveling sycophants—the wealthy at court. The jester was safe because his revelations were wrapped in jokes and satire and no one took him seriously anyway. If you want to tell people the truth, you'd better make them laugh or they'll kill you. The jester could move easily between social groups, being accepted by them, but still apart from them. There is a saying in Italian: "To be like the Fool in Tarocchi" which means you are welcome anywhere.

The Fool is untainted by contact with the city and its disbelief and cynicism. He moves freely between the two worlds of imagination and reality and is a conduit to connect them. In the Rider-Waite deck, the Fool is pictured as a youth about to walk off a steep cliff. A little dog jumps at his ankles playfully warning him. This indicates that the Fool is in such close contact with his instinctual side that he does not need to worry about where he is going. If he is innocent enough in his faith he should be able to walk on air (or water). In some versions of the Tarot, the Fool is blindfolded emphasizing his ability to act on insight instead of eyesight, using intuitive wisdom rather than conventional logic. In the Golden Dawn deck, the Fool is pictured as a baby in the wilderness holding a wolf on a leash. The baby's helplessness is what protects him from the elements and even the ferocious wolf cannot harm him for he is so innocent and brings out her protective nature.

***

1. John 10:10, KJV Bible
2. *The Book of the SubGenius,* The Subgenius Foundation
3. Matthew 6:26-29 (Sermon on the Mount)
4. Matthew 6:34 (no thought for the morrow)
5. Mark 6:4-6 (prophet)
6. *The Book of the SubGenius,* The Subgenius Foundation
7. 1 John 4:18 (made perfect in love)
8. 1 John 4:8 (God is love)

Books:
The Secret History of the World, Mark Booth
The Tao of Physics, Fritjof Capra
Pronoia is the Antidote for Paranoia, Rob Brezsny
The Magic of Believing, Claude M. Bristol
TNT: It Rocks the Earth, Claude M. Bristol
Jung and Tarot, An Archetypal Journey, Sallie Nichols
Living the Qabalistic Tarot, Amber Jayanti
Adventures in Understanding, Manly P. Hall
The Subgenius Psychlopaedia of Slack, Rev. Ivan Stang
Articles:
The Heart Has Its Own "Brain" and Consciousness, www.in5d.com

*This is also a saying in Taoism, just replace the word Slack with Tao.

"The world is like a ride in an amusement park, and when you choose to go on it you think it's real because that's how powerful our minds are. The ride goes up and down, around and around, it has thrills and chills, and it's very brightly colored, and it's very loud, and its fun for a while. Many people have been on the ride a long time, and they begin to wonder, "Hey, is this real, or is this just a ride?" And other people have remembered, and they come back to us and say, "Hey, don't worry; don't be afraid, ever, because this is just a ride." And we … kill those people. "Shut him up! I've got a lot invested in this ride, shut him up! Look at my furrows of worry, look at my big bank account, and my family. This has to be real." It's just a ride. But we always kill the good guys who try and tell us that, you ever notice that? And let the demons run amok … But it doesn't matter, because it's just a ride. And we can change it any time we want. It's only a choice. No effort, no work, no job, no savings of money. Just a simple choice, right now, between fear and love. The eyes of fear want you to put bigger locks on your doors, buy guns, close yourself off. The eyes of love instead see all of us as one. Here's what we can do to change the world, right now, to a better ride. Take all that money we spend on weapons and defenses each year and instead spend it feeding and clothing and educating the poor of the world, which it would pay for many times over, not one human being excluded, and we could explore space, together, both inner and outer, forever, in peace." -Bill Hicks

WHO HAS THE

Sigmund Freud

In the late 1800's a dude from Vienna named Sigmund Freud thought up a new theory about human nature that has shaped our culture into what it is today. His ideas about how the mind works have become an accepted part of society and his theories are today's standard for psychiatrists. Freud devised a method he called psychoanalysis by using hypnosis, analyzing dreams and practicing free association, in which patients would lie on a couch and report their spontaneous thoughts. By doing this, he discovered what he said were powerful sexual and aggressive forces, hidden deep within us which were the remnants of our animal past. His hypothesis is that these forces are an unilluminated part of the mind, separate from the conscious mind, which is constantly at work molding our thoughts, feelings and actions. It has been called many things, super-ego, unconscious or the subconscious. It never sleeps and the limits to its power are unknown. It guides us in many ways and when properly employed can perform miracles. The powers that come from the subconscious are intuition, emotion, certainty, inspiration, suggestion, imagination, memory and dynamic energy. It is also a major source of the sorcerer's power when they can tap into it.

This unknown power frightened Freud and he believed that human conflicts were the result of the repression of primitive instincts hidden in the psyche. He taught that if these forces were left uncontrolled it would lead societies into chaos and destruction and he believed that the advent of WWI was evidence of the terrible truth of his findings. Feelings, he said, must be repressed because they were too dangerous.

Goethe's *Faust* was the literary text that Freud most frequently cited and referred to; it was the piece of literature that most powerfully influenced him throughout his life. The central event of the work is a pact between Faust and the Devil. Much of Freud's theory about dream interpretation comes from his occult research and his mythic identification with Satan and Venus. Freud was an extraordinarily controversial figure, even in his day. His followers adored him and his critics found his views to be outlandish and

ON LIFE?

sometimes referred to him as "the most consummate of charlatans." Even today, feelings about him run to either extreme, people tend to love him or hate him.Was Freud a genius with the world's greatest insights into the human psyche or did he just have really good P.R.?

***

Edward Bernays and the Psychology of Shopping

Anyone who has witnessed the footage of frenzied mobs shopping on Black Friday could, like Freud, rapidly begin to lose faith in humanity. But do people tend to act like this on their own like he believed or is there something else guiding them?

Edward Bernays is the father of modern public relations. He was Freud's American nephew and his effects on popular culture were as great as his uncle's.

Bernays was a press agent hired to promote America's participation in WWI based on Woodrow Wilson's decree that the U.S. was fighting against old empires to bring democracy to Europe. He proved so skillful at portraying war efforts in the press that at the end of the war he was asked to attend the Paris peace conference. President Wilson's reception at the Treaty of Versailles astounded Bernays and the other propagandists at how the crowds heralded Wilson as an icon of democracy and liberator of the people. They had made a hero. Bernays wondered if the same type of mass persuasion was possible in peace time.

He turned propaganda, which sounded negative, and called it the Council of Public Relations. He went to New York and set up his council, determined to alter the consciousness of the new industrial society. With millions clustered together in cities, he wanted to control the way these crowds thought and felt. Armed with Freud's book, *A General Introduction to Psychoanalysis*, he used his uncle's theories to form public opinion so that they would think such manufactured opinions were their own. Bernays was hired by William Randolph Hearst to promote his line of women's magazines which included *Harper's Bazaar, ELLE, Marie Claire, Cosmopolitan, Good Housekeeping, Redbook, Sev-*

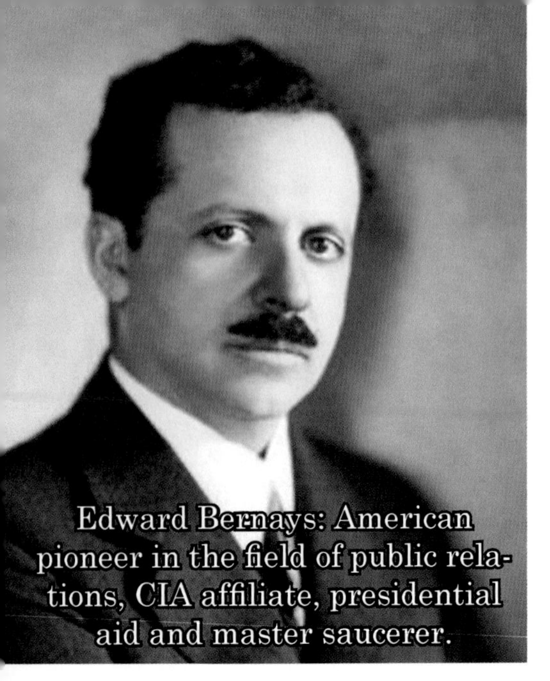
Edward Bernays: American pioneer in the field of public relations, CIA affiliate, presidential aid and master saucerer.

"The conscious and intelligent manipulation of the habits and opinions of the masses is an important element in democratic society. Those who manipulate this unseen mechanism of society constitute an invisible government, which is the true ruling power of our country. We are governed, our minds are molded, our tastes formed, our ideas-suggested, largely by men that we have never heard of...Our invisible governors are in many cases, unaware of the identity of their fellow members in the inner cabinet...It is they who pull the wires, which control the public mind, who harness old social forces and contrive new ways to bind and guide the world."

—Edward Bernays, *Propaganda*, 1928

enteen and many more. Bernays was the first person to show automobile companies how they could sell cars as symbols of male sexuality and prowess. In 1939, New York hosted the World's Fair and Edward Bernays was the central adviser. He insisted that the theme be the link between democracy and capitalism. He wanted people to think that you couldn't have real democracy in anything but a capitalist society. This all went in tandem with the golden age of Hollywood where product placement and movies came together in a perfect storm of American psychological overhaul.

His most dramatic experiment was to persuade women to smoke cigarettes. In 1929 the president of the American tobacco corporation hired Bernays to find a way to break the taboo of women smoking in public. Bernays decided to stage his event at the New York Easter Day parade. He hired a group of rich debutants to hide cigarettes under their clothes and join the parade. At a given signal from him they were to light up the cigarettes dramatically. Bernays informed the press that a group of suffragettes were preparing a protest by lighting up what they called "torches of freedom." The next day it was in newspapers all across the United States and around the world and the sale of cigarettes to woman began to rise. Bernays had made them socially acceptable with a single symbolic ad.

Meanwhile, one of the main objectives at the Tavistock Institute was to achieve the degradation of women. Bernays was Tavistock's top consultant up until the time George Bush became president. In the 1930's the promotion of homosexuality and lesbianism became rampant, not out of any suppressed desires, but as a means of shocking the old establishment of morals, which is a Tavistock strategy. This was also a crucial stage of developing the plan that called for feminine behavior to be reduced to a lower standard of morality than ever thought possible. Radical changes were forced upon women of the time, which seemed impossible to stop, and has quickened at a remarkable pace since hemlines reached the knee. Anyone who has ever seen MTV's show *Jersey Shore* or Bravo's *Real Housewives* can witness how well this psychology has worked. "*Tavistock recognized that Jesus Christ has brought a new place of respect in the order of civilization for womanhood, which prior to his coming had not been present. After Christ's ministry, womanhood gained a respect and a high place in society absent from pre-Christian civilizations...Tavistock sought to change that and the process began immediately after WWI*"[1]

After WWII, the overproduction of mass produced goods transformed the way American consumers thought about products. It was the concern of many corporations that supply would outstrip demand and they feared their merchandise would flood the economy. In the world of advertising, psychology offered limitless potential for manipulation. This was the key to a virtually infinite need for consumption and this would, in turn justify an infinite process of production. "*We must shift America from a needs to a desires culture. People must be trained to desire to want new things even before the old had been entirely consumed. We must shape a new mentality in America. Man's desires must overshadow his needs.*"—Paul Mazer, Lehman Bros.

Bernays taught corporations how to get people to want things they don't need by marketing to their unconscious desires and out of this came a new political idea about how to control the masses. He called his technique of opinion-molding "engineering consent."

In the past, goods like shoes, stockings and even cars were promoted in functional terms for their durability. The aim of the advertisements were simply to show people the products practical virtues and nothing more; but, by the 1960's most Americans already owned televisions, radios, refrigerators, cars and washing machines. There was a prevailing fear in industry that it might level off. People had to be persuaded to buy new models or constantly updated versions of the older ones. This was called the principle of "planned obsolescence" where commodities were produced with a deliberately limited lifespan. Cars, for instance were designed to last approximately three years, after that they would begin to fall apart and the cost of repairs would be less economical than purchasing a new one.

There was also the more sinister principle of "psychological obsolescence" where designs were modified dramatically every few years to make the owners of the old models feel outdated or unfashionable. Nowhere can this be seen more clearly today than in the marketing of Apple products. The opportunity to announce the newness of a product enabled people to flaunt pride in prosperity, while those who could not keep up are encouraged to feel shame. Once people's points of insecurity were diagnosed they were skillfully exploited. By fostering a general anxiety for just about anything, teeth, hair, skin, car, house or status, they were able achieve the systematic creation of dissatisfaction.

While Bernays was becoming rich and powerful in America, Vienna and most of Europe was suffering massive inflation. Freud lost most of his savings and facing bankruptcy and turned to his nephew for help. Bernays agreed to publish his book in America for the first time and at the same time promote the book and see to it that they were successful. Along with this book came emerging studies on the "Group Mind" which they believed operated in the baser animal unconscious irrational level. *"If we understand the mechanism and motives of the group mind, it is now possible to control and regiment the masses according to our will without them knowing it."*—Bernays

Pessimistic and reclusive Freud began to write about group behavior and about how easily the unconscious and aggressive forces in humans could be triggered when they were in crowds. Fearing that he had underestimated their violent tendencies, he began to believe that people were far more dangerous than he had originally thought. He came to the conclusion that man was a ferocious animal. In short, he didn't like people. He wanted to be part of a new elite that could manage the bewildered herd of beasts through psychological techniques. Neither did Bernays think much of the people whose opinions he was engineering. According to his daughter, Ann Bernays:"*...it can be a little hard on the people around you. Especially when you make other people feel stupid. The people who worked for him were stupid, the children were stupid, and if people did things in a way that he wouldn't have done them, they were stupid. It was a word that he used over and over - don't be stupid. And the masses - They were stupid.*"

While Freud and his associates may have done considerable research on behavior, he didn't know everything and he's certainly not the last word on human nature. There have been several scholars who have opposed Freud's theories. One was a German philosopher Herbert Marcuse. He challenged the social world arguing that it was not a world that should be adapted to because society was corrupt, not the human psyche. He disagreed with Freud's ideas and he thought that schizophrenia was induced. Marcuse knew the idea that you needed to control people was wrong. Human beings, he said, did have inner emotional drives but were not inherently violent or irrational. It was in fact a sick society that caused mental illness. He taught that conforming to society and refusing to challenge authority was actually submitting to evil. Willhem Reich was a student of Freud who also had a fundamentally different view. He believed that the unconscious aspect of humans was essentially good and the core of human nature was the underlying libido. He believed that all neurosis was due to lack of orgasms.

After Freud's death, his daughter, Anna, became the acknowledged leader of the world's psychoanalytic movement. She saw her job as to fulfill her father's dream of making his ideas accepted throughout the world. She developed a theory of how to control the inner drives of the man-imals. It was simple—you taught the children to conform to the rules of society. She pioneered the concept that "conformity equals happiness." By the 1950's conformity had become the basis on which a prosperous society was to be established. Corporations began to employ psychological techniques, testing and profiling was used to establish "normality" and ensure conformity. Nowadays "normal" is waking up and getting dressed in clothes you wouldn't normally wear, sitting in traffic, in a car that you don't even own yet, to get to the job with people you don't even like. But you need that job to pay for the clothes and the car and the house that sits empty all day so that you can afford to live in it. Act normal, go to work, watch TV, obey the law, and tell yourself that you are free.

In the past, psychiatrists were far more honest and vocal about the future ramifications of their work. Mad scientists like Dr. Jose Delgado and Dr. Ewen Cameron went public with the idea that no human being has an inherent right to his own personality. The true role of psychiatry, they said, was to reinvent human character, behavior and personality from the ground up. They wanted to have physical control of the mind toward what they called the "Psychocivilized Society."

"TO ACHIEVE WORLD GOVERNMENT, IT IS NECESSARY TO REMOVE FROM THE MINDS OF MEN THEIR INDIVIDUALISM, LOYALTY TO FAMILY TRADITION, NATIONAL PATRIOTISM, AND RELIGIOUS DOGMAS."
—George Brock Chisholm, in a Speech given at the Conference on Education, September 11, 1954.

The issue of mental health is about to become a huge one. Its latest spokesperson is none other than—the representative of the new normal, Lady Gaga. Her fans are almost innumerable. At this time she holds the world's record in downloads and for having the most followers on Twitter - over 32.5 million. That's 10 times than the entire population of Australia. To make sure that all of her little monsters are receiving the best in mental health care, she will be providing psycho-therapy on her upcoming Born This Way Ball concert tour. Gaga announced that the 2013 leg of her tour will feature the BornBrave Bus, where fans can come aboard before each show and receive counseling. Wherever she performs, the BornBrave Bus will follow. The advice and pep talks will come from members of the National Council for Behavioral Health. Gaga and her mother, Cynthia, came up with the idea for their Born This Way Foundation in response to the Sandy Hook Elementary School shootings. *"Now more than ever, our kids need access to support within their communities, including mental health services,"* reads a statement from Gaga's mother.

"The really hopeless victims of mental illness are to be found among those who appear to be most normal. 'Many of them are normal because they are so well adjusted to our mode of existence, because their human voice has been silenced so early in their lives that they do not even struggle or suffer or develop symptoms as the neurotic does.' They are normal not in what may be called the absolute sense of the word; they are normal only in relation to a profoundly abnormal society. Their perfect adjustment to that abnormal society is a measure of their mental sickness. These millions of abnormally normal people, living without fuss in a society to which, if they were fully human beings, they ought not to be adjusted, still cherish 'the illusion of individuality,' but in fact they have been to a great extent deindividualized. Their conformity is developing into something like uniformity. But "uniformity and freedom are incompatible. Uniformity and mental health are incompatible too. . . Man is not made to be an automaton, and if he becomes one, the basis for mental health is destroyed."
-- Aldous Huxley, Brave New World Revisited

"BornBrave Bus Is a place where mental health + depression are taken seriously w/ no judgement, FREE real help available to all. I feel like most kids don't look for help because they feel embarrassed so mom + I wanted to break the stigmas around 'help' and make it fun."—from Lady Gaga's twitter.

Is this really just help for at risk youth from a concerned super star or could it be something more? In light of other recent public shootings, officials are urging the U.N. to address mental health issues on a global scale. The U.N. is setting up a worldwide mental health apparatus to evaluate people's emotional and intellectual stability. It will try to provide itself not only with the authority to evaluate people's mental competence but also the authority to send people to mental institutions and re-education camps if they are not sufficiently docile and open to the appropriate level of "normalcy." Who will be defined as mentally unfit in the future? Those who question mainstream media, the government, 9/11, global warming, chemtrails…just about anything that is outside of the official story.

In the wake of the Sandy Hook massacre, President Obama stated that mental-health services must be made more available, presumably to stave off future killers. Of course, this is ridiculous, since so many killers have acted under the compelling influence of SSRI antidepressants and other brain meds. These drugs are proven to induce violence. His plan would essentially make the American Psychiatric Association and all its doctors into the new psychiatric police state; right alongside local police forces, the FBI, the ATF, DHS, and the US Marshals Service.

***

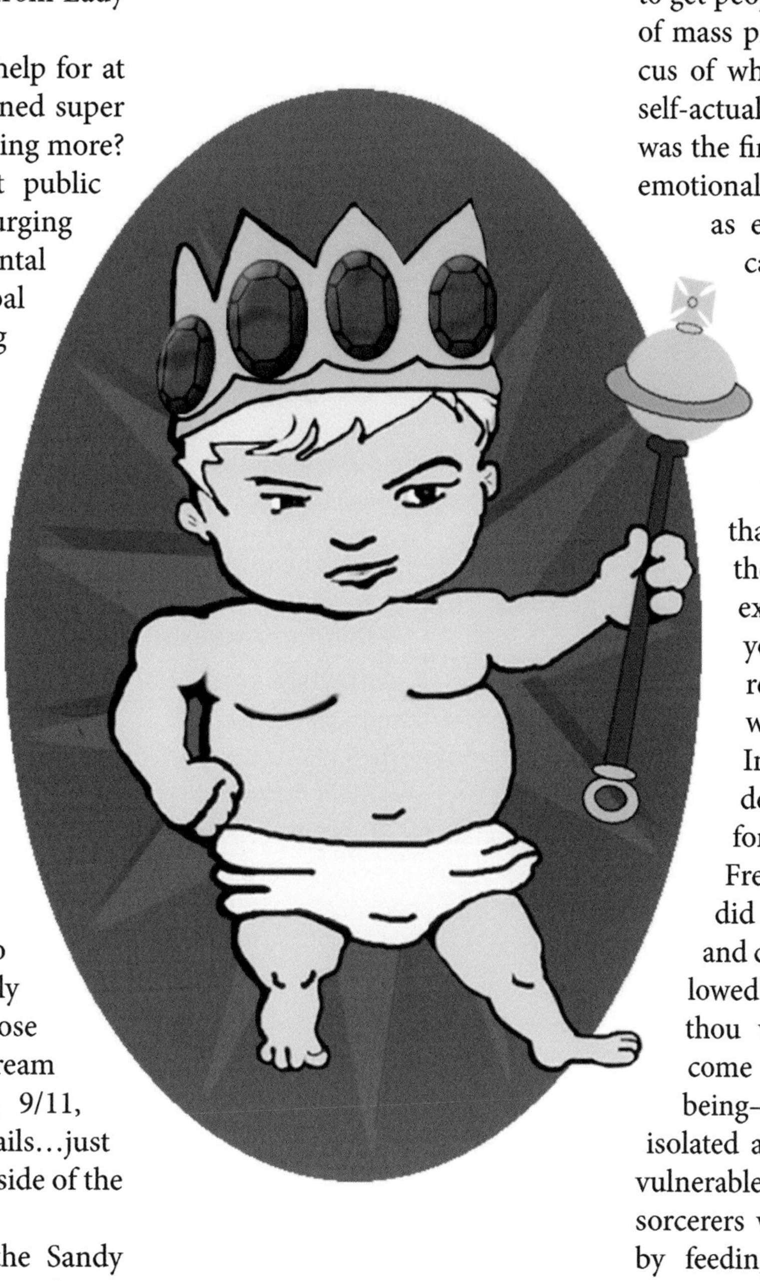

The Consumer is King.

The consumption of mass produced goods, coupled with the Puritan work ethic where God rewarded hard work, meant prosperity could be regarded as an indication of God's favor. Wealth was therefore more than a mere status symbol, it had become a testimonial virtue. The consumer was crowned the King. By the 1980's, Bernays' techniques had worked so well that the American population had been transformed into a veritable consuming machine. Psychoanalysis changed from trying to get people to buy a limited range of mass produced goods to the focus of what psychology called the self-actualizing individual. Bernays was the first person to link people's emotional connection to products as expressions of what they called the "inner self."

Capitalism created the "individual" by marketing products to his so called inner values. The corporations began to convince people that they were unique and then offer to them ways to express it. The notion that you could buy an identity replaced the idea that you were free to create one. Instead of inner animal desires being controlled for the good of society, like Freud taught; the inner self did not need to be repressed and controlled. It should be allowed to express itself. Do what thou wilt. Out of this would come a new type of human being—"the self." But this was an isolated and greedy self, far more vulnerable to manipulation by the sorcerers who would control them by feeding their infinite desires. With the new "self" people's wants seemed to have no limit which was perfect for the corporations. They became increasingly dependent for their identity on business. What you wear became a statement reflecting your inner self and self-expression was reduced to what a person could afford to buy.

The classic image of a devil and an angel on your shoulders comes from Freud's theories. The technical term for this is Psychomachia which means "Battle of the Soul." The devil represents the id, the angel is the superego and the person whose shoulders they stand on is the ego.

The satisfaction of the inner desires of the Self became man's highest priority. Perhaps this is the part of the spirit of Horus, "The Crowned and Conquering Child" that Crowley meant to evoke upon the earth in the twentieth century. This was a spirit of childish selfishness that Bernays and his hidden masters helped create, a culture that Crowley could only dream of. It was a society composed entirely of spoiled brats.

In psychology the Self is identified with the Ego. The Id, Ego, and Super-Ego are the three parts defined in Freud's structural model of the psyche, although these terms are not his own; they are translations. Freud himself wrote of "das Es," "das Ich," and "das Über-Ich"—meaning "the It," "the I," and the "Over-I" or "I above."

The Id is the unorganized part of the personality that contains the basic drives. It acts according to the "pleasure principle," seeking to avoid pain. According to Freud, we are born with our Id. The mind of a newborn child is regarded as completely "id-ridden" in the sense that it is a mass of instinctive impulses and needs immediate satisfaction. The id wants whatever feels good at the time, with no consideration for the reality of the situation or for other people's feelings. When the child is hungry, uncomfortable, in pain, too hot, too cold, or just wants attention, the id speaks up until its needs are met. The id knows no judgments of value, no good and evil, no morality. The "It" doesn't care about reality, about the needs of anyone else, only its own satisfaction. When the id wants something, nothing else is important. Within the first three years, as the child interacts more and more with the world, the second part of the personality begins to develop. Freud called this part the Ego. The Ego recognizes the individual, the self. It is all about me, me, me; I, I, I. It understands that other people have needs and desires, however, it's the ego's job to meet the needs of the id.

By the age of five, the Super Ego should have developed. This is the moral part of us that feels a connection to everything. Many equate the superego with the conscience as it dictates our belief of right and wrong. It would be where the sense of guilt or empathy comes from by living an opulent lifestyle while others have nothing. The super ego would recognize that all is one and there is no such thing as "good for me, bad for you." The ego is constantly swinging back and forth between meeting the needs of the id and grappling with more altruistic nature of the super ego.

By locking us into our lower immature selves—the id and the ego, consumer culture has conquered our society by using our own selfish natures to do so. Instead of being child-like, we are behaving childishly, manifesting the worst possible aspect of childhood—the self-centered brat.

***

"HE ALONE, WHO OWNS THE YOUTH, GAINS THE FUTURE."
–Adolf Hitler

The Monopoly

As far as "choices" go, how much variety do we really get to actualize our inner self when everything that we see is controlled by a small group of people whose values we couldn't even begin to know or understand? When a few people own everything it's called a monopoly. Before it was a board game, the word "monopoly" had negative connotations. Thirty years before Parker Brothers published Monopoly, a man named Charles B. Darrow was introduced to a game by a group of Quakers called The Landlord's Game. It was created as a cautionary tale for children to show how slums will develop if one person was allowed to own all of the property. He copied their board and rules verbatim, then sold it as his own creation. Parker Brothers supported him, putting a copy of the "Story of Monopoly" that cited him as creator in every box.

The most powerful monopoly man on earth today is a cartoon mouse. According to the 2012 Fortune 500 list, The Walt Disney Company is America's largest multimedia conglomerate in history. Disney's assets include movie studios, radio and television stations, magazines, publishing companies, theme parks, sports teams, theaters, tourism and cruise lines. Allied with multimedia giant Apple, Inc., (Apple CEO Steve Jobs is the single largest shareholder in Disney), it is set to become the largest influence in culture creation on the planet.

Understanding Disney's cultural role is not a simple task. Its influence in everyday life is cross-generational, spanning over eighty-five years. Who can forget their first time at Disneyland? This tradition continues from parent to child to grandchild. The Disney philosophy has been protected, venerated and defended over all others as a moral and spiritual authority in the home. In most households, Disney products have a carte blanche seal of approval as representatives of innocence and imagination and for many homes the Disney movie is an integral part of "family time." As an icon of American culture and middle-class family values, it appeals to both parents and children's fantasies while on the other hand working to transform every youth into a lifetime consumer of its products and ideas.

From baby bottles to learning how to read, Disney is there to teach you at every stage in your life. It is the world's most beloved brand name. Parents trust their children to Disney, so much so that the Mouse has become America's most popular babysitter. What is interesting about Disney, with its golden brand image—synonymous with childhood and wholesome entertainment, is that it manages to deflect criticism at every turn. But the same name that produces television programming for kids is also a major distributor of pornography and adult pay-per-views. Also, there is a serious pedophile problem at Disney theme parks that the company seems uninterested in solving, but we'll get to that later.

One frightening thing about Disney is that it markets itself almost exclusively to children. Not since the height of the baby boom, have there been so many children in our midst and for corporate business these kids come to represent the ultimate prize. They are a powerhouse demographic to be scrutinized and advertised to at all costs. The US spends about $263 billion each year on advertising and this is largely aimed at teaching young people to be consumers to a point where some have called it a "hostile takeover of childhood." Kids spend about $40 billion a year and the amount of adult spending that children influence is an astronomical $700 billion a year. Kids and teens have become the epicenter of American consumer culture. Children today are being taught that you are what you own and it doesn't take them long to figure out that you are supposed to buy products for status.

It is technically illegal to advertise to children under the age of eight. At both Federal and state levels, the law requires that advertisers not engage in "deceptive" or "unfair" marketing. In the beginning of the 1980's, children's television advertising was deregulated and the number of commercials aimed at them instantly doubled. Programs themselves became vehicles to sell toys. Ample science and various professionals agree that marketing to children is both deceptive and unfair because they do not have the cognitive capacity to understand that they are being marketed to. Children under three cannot even tell the difference between a commercial and the program that they are watching. They do not comprehend "persuasive intent" which is the linchpin of advertising. Young children do not display the brain activity associated with this kind of conscious awareness until after six years of age. They spend the first years of their lives in the state referred to as the hypnogogic trance. This is the same state that hypnotists induce to implant suggestions directly into the subconscious mind. But in this brave new world of advertising there is no such thing as too young. *"The consumer embryo begins to develop during the first year of existence... children begin their consumer journey in infancy...and they certainly deserve consideration as consumers at that time."* —James U. McNeal, Pioneering Youth Marketer Advertiser.

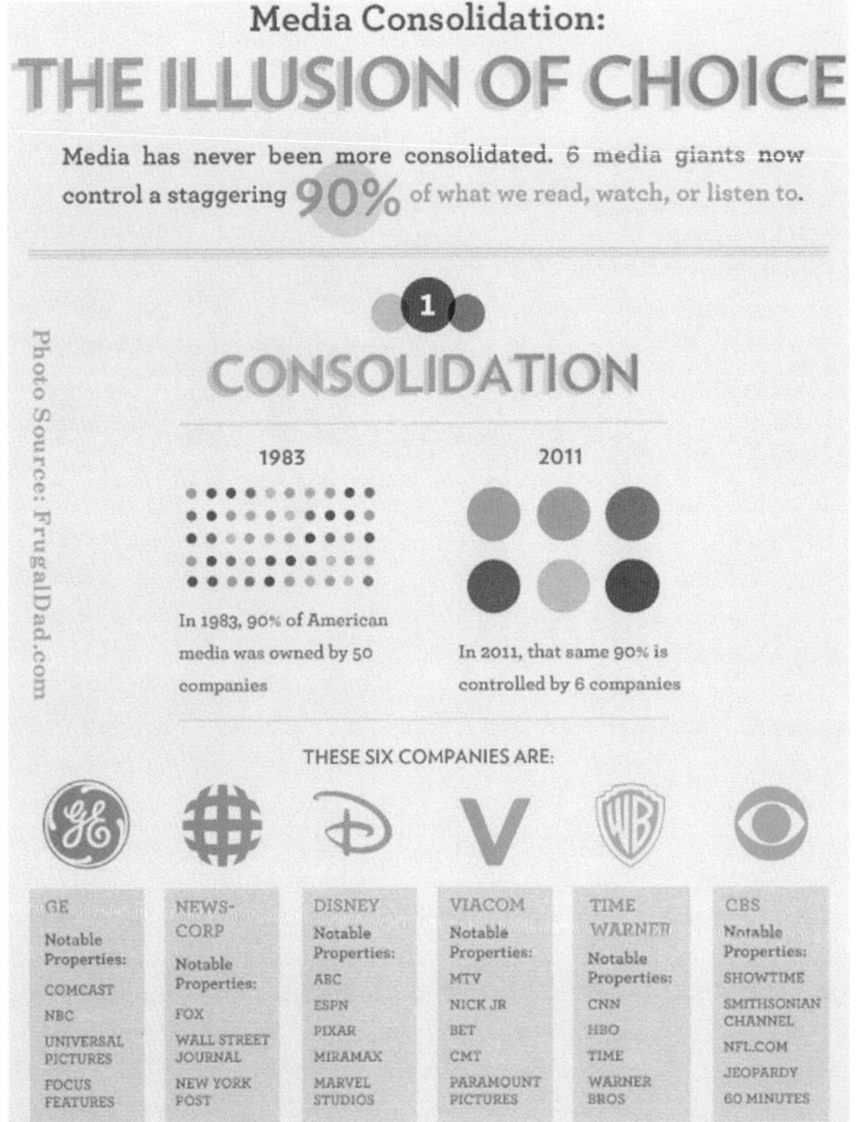

Photo Source: FrugalDad.com

This generation is marketed to like never before. There is a corporate brand logo in front of a child's face every second of every day. This is part of what they call the 360 degree immersive technique where kids are literally inundated with advertising twenty four-seven. The advertisers' number one goal is to make parents absolutely miserable through what they call the nag factor and commercials are designed to maximize the number of times kids will keep asking for things. According to a study from the University of Kansas Medical Center, children's brains are being branded even before they know how to read. The study analyzed children's brains when being shown food logos. The areas of the brain controlling rewards and appetite control "lit up" when shown the logos, similarly to how they would if they were shown actual food. Children can identify McDonald's golden arches even before they know the letter M.

Every child, regardless of how young, is now a potential consumer ripe for being brainwashed into a commercial culture defined by brands. The biggest bucks are in brand loyalty for life. Typical children see about 40,000 ads a year on TV alone, and by the time they enter the fourth grade, they will have memorized 300-400 brands. It is hard to find baby products that are unbranded. The sorcerer's goal is to imprint the brands into the very fabric of the child's existence from birth so that there is no escape. It is disturbing to observe people covering themselves with brand names considering the practice of branding came from the cattle industry where they would burn the ranch owner's logo onto the cow's backside with hot steel.

It is even more disturbing that Disney and other advertisers now work with child psychologists, who study young people in order to better understand children's culture so they can develop marketing methods to be more streamlined and seductive. According to *The New York Times*, Disney is at the forefront of finding ways to capitalize on the $50 billion dollars spent worldwide by young boys between the ages of six and fourteen. As part of the effort, it seeks the advice of educators, anthropologists and even a research consultant with a background in the casino industry, to study all aspects of the culture and intimate lives of young boys to produce "emotional hooks" that lure them into the wonderful world of corporate Disney and turn them into enthusiastic consumers.[2]

Given Disney's desire to expand into boys' culture, the announcement in 2009 that it had purchased Marvel Entertainment Inc. came as no surprise. Marvel's comic book empire owns the rights to about 5,000 superhero characters. *The Wall Street Journal* remarked that by "bringing in macho types such as Iron Man, Thor and Captain America, the Marvel deal would expand Disney's audience, adding properties that appeal to boys from their preteen years into young adulthood." As part of the same effort, in 2012 Disney announced that it had purchased the Star Wars franchise as well. The video game "Epic Mickey," revamps the character of Mickey Mouse in an alleged effort to make him more appealing to today's generation of young men. Mickey will no longer embody a childlike innocence and generosity, but will instead be "cantankerous and cunning" and will exhibit "selfish, destructive behavior."

Mega-corporations, focus on popular culture and constantly expand themselves to reach every available media outlet. Kids have become a captive audience to all forms of media through mobile phones, PDAs, laptop computers and the Internet. The impact of electronic technologies as teaching machines can be seen in some astounding statistics. It is estimated that the average American spends more than six hours a day watching video-based entertainment and, by 2013, the numbers of daily hours spent watching television and videos will match the numbers of hours spent sleeping. The greatest sacrifice associated with surrounding very young children with screen media is a reduction in the time they spend engaging in creative, unstructured play. They're taking away their Slack! Because of this, teachers across the world are reporting that all children's play is beginning to look identical. Children imitate what they see on screen, reenacting rote scripts with licensed products. Play time is conscripted by a commercial world defined by the Disney Company and a few other corporations, and the amount of time spent in this world is frightening.

In 2000, Disney purchased the Baby Einstein Company, a line of products and toys known to mesmerize baby television watchers by displaying vibrant objects while playing a soundtrack of classical music. When I was young, my favorite toy was my Fisher Price 33 RPM record player with read along books. The stories I can remember learning to read by were *Lady and the Tramp, Snow White, Mother Goose* and *The Three Little Pigs*...all by Disney. Now, kids have a hand held toy called Leapfrog whose cartridges are dominated by Disney characters, Star Wars, Spongebob and a few others. Doesn't anyone find it the least bit strange that three different types of teaching media software companies, VTech, MobiGo and Leapfrog, all produce the exact same characters to play with? Today's kids have more money to spend and more electronic toys to play with, but increasingly, they are left all on their own to navigate the virtual worlds created by corporations. Nowhere has it been proven that these types of games make children smarter—in fact most statistics show that too much interface with electronics makes them anti-social and less intelligent. That is because we are not meant to be interacting with our world primarily through virtual reality.

The family unit is the human beings' best defense against dark forces; however, the underlying morals of a corporation such as Disney can escape even the most

vigilant and discerning parent. Your personal family values are being usurped by mega-corporations all toward a lifetime of constant, unthinking consumption where there can be only one kind of value: market value and one kind of success: profit. They are trying to convince children that life is all about buying and it is clear that Disney's goal is to win over the hearts and minds of children to deliver them to the system as just commodities and loyal consumers.

***

> **"When things become precious and people expendable, that is the horror of the true Satanic society. That is when the nightmare begins."**
> **—Anton LaVey**

The Toymakers

Who makes all this stuff you see in the commercials? I'll give you a hint: they're not Santa's elves, but they are short. Turn over pretty much any piece of cartoon merchandise and it will say "MADE IN CHINA" Roughly 75% of all toys come from China. Chances are they were made in a sweat shop by a child. Most factories in China where toys are produced are surrounded by prison-like walls and barbed wire. Living and working conditions are so grim, one Chinese company named Foxconn, a manufacturer of Apple computers, iphones, Sony, Nintendo and HP products, actually had to install safety nets to the sides of their buildings to catch potential suicide jumpers.

In October 2012, a mother from Oregon opened her box of Halloween decorations purchased at Kmart and there was a letter tucked in between two styrofoam headstones. It was a cry for help that had traveled more than 5,000 miles over the Pacific Ocean. The short note was written in Chinese and English. The letter read: *"If you occasionally buy this product, please kindly resend this letter to the World Human Right Organization. Thousands people here who are under the persecution of the Chinese Communist Party Government will thank and remember you forever. People who work here have to work 15 hours a day without Saturday, Sunday break and any holidays. Otherwise, they will suffer torturement, beat and rude remark. Nearly no payment 10 yuan/1 month."* (Ten yuan is equivalent to $1.61.) *"People who work here, suffer punishment 1-3 years averagely, but without Court Sentence (unlaw punishment). Many of them are Falun Gong practitioners, who are totally innocent people only because they have different believe to CCPG. They often suffer more punishment than others."* The letter was not signed.

Chinese children work seven days a week at a factory producing dogs and dolls for Disney, the shift starts at half past six in the morning and doesn't end until midnight. Overtime work can go from 2am until 4am. Most days workers are encouraged just to put their heads down at their stations and to sleep sitting up so they'll be ready to start back to work at 6am. The plastic material that toys are made of can reach 200 degrees Celsius. The environment is so hot they don't call them sweat shops for nothing.

The face of Disney the manufacturer is not a pretty one. Their licensees manufacture in countries few Americans could locate on a map. In Burma, children work 60 hours a week in a factory run by drug lords for 6 cents an hour to produce Mickey Mouse sweatshirts. Those who track child labor sweatshops know that Disney is a prime exploiter and one of the worst offenders. All too often their clothes, toys and trinkets are made by children. The National Labor Committee in New York gives Disney the distinction as being one of the "greediest sweatshop abusers" in the world. At assembly factories owned by Disney suppliers in Haiti, workers toil in tropical heat to meet production quotas for Mickey Mouse and Lion King garments. Minimum wage is about $2.40 a day but most factory laborers rarely make that because they are based on production quotas. Workers must attach 1,600 collars to T-shirts a day, that's about three a minute. The pressure to make the quota is intense and even trips to the restroom may illicit screams and threats from management. At another factory in Haiti, workers produce a clothing line called Classic Apparel (Disney) where a typical pay stub is about a quarter an hour. Working conditions are as horrible as one can imagine, the air is heavy with lint from garments which makes it hard to breathe. Rats are everywhere and drinking water can be found next to the toilet. The people who are making corporate products are living in utter misery.

Did you ever wonder where all that pink princess paraphernalia comes from? The global revenue generated by Disney Princess products increased from $300 million in 2000 to $4 billion in 2009.[3] It does come from girls but they are definitely not given the royal treatment. If the factory that produces your toys are not exploiting underage children; their workforce is probably made up of over 90% women because according to Chinese foremen they are easier to manage. There are young girls operating machines that only a grown man has the strength to operate. At one factory in Vietnam that produces Disney products more than 90% of the 1,800 workers are teenage girls, about the same age as your typical Disney heroine. Their take home pay is .60-.70 cents a day for a nine or ten hour shift. A seven day work week is often mandatory and managers inflict corporal punishment for misbehavior. Girls who remain working at the factory too long face se-

rious health problems. Dozens of workers collapse daily from exhaustion and food deprivation. Toxic fumes like acetone cause headaches, dizziness, nausea, skin damage and affected menstrual cycles. In the plastics department workers often lose half of their right palms and all of their fingers when operating the dying machines. In some cases girls have their hands being eaten away by chemical solvents. They must inhale paint fumes all day without masks and these toys go right into your Happy Meals.

***

Mass Produced Toys as Propaganda

In the past children's consumer culture wasn't as sophisticated as it is today. Kids didn't have money to buy things and there wasn't much for them to buy. The only mass produced toys available were tiny things like wooden guns and dolls and maybe the occasional penny candy. In 1932, the Walt Disney Studio was suffering from a serious lack of cash flow when a big opportunity came along. A merchandiser from New York named George Borgfeldt wanted to give his children Mickey and Minnie mouse dolls for Christmas. He licensed the Mickey image from Disney and from the moment the merchandise became available, it sold out quickly. An international comic strip made Mickey Mouse a familiar face in every part of the world. By 1933 more than eighty major corporations including General Foods, RCA and National Dairy were selling millions of dollars worth of Disney related merchandise. Because of this wild success Walt formed an in house marketing division that eventually became the largest and most successful studio merchandising operation in the world. By 1932, Mickey Mouse Fan Clubs had an enrollment of more than a million members with new clubs opening all the time. The fashionable elite promoted Disney's cartoons and especially merchandise in every way. In 1935, the Queen of England and the Duchess of York selected Mickey Mouse chinaware as gifts for 600 children. Disney rocked the toy merchandise market and soon had a monopoly on children's books as well. When publishing houses first established separate children's sections around 1920 there was an increase in the production of children's books. The 1930's and 40's saw some decline in sales and it was during this time period in 1932 that Western Printing and Lithographing Company, the largest publisher of children's

books in the world, entered into an exclusive contract with Walt Disney Inc. to produce its books. Children's books publishing increased significantly as the baby boom market increased interest in children's reading and federal aid was made available for library materials.

Children's toys and books are not just innocent aids to the imagination. These things serve a purpose in brainwashing and engineering what kind of adults they will turn out to be. Part of the early psychology of marketing toys to children is called gender differentiation where they don't just target kids as a group, they are very soon segregated into boys and girls. Not so long ago babies' clothes and products used to be unisex. It was more affordable to buy for multiple babies where the things could be handed down as more babies came along. In the era before washing machines, kids wore white as a practical matter since the only way of getting clothes spotless was to boil them. Children were allowed to be children and gender issues were not usually addressed until puberty. Now, you can visit the toy section of your local Wal-Mart or Target and you will find something strange. The isles are segregated into boys' toys and girls' toys. What is the underlying message about gender that that these toys are sending to your children? The role models laid out for youth can be reduced into two basic archetypes, G.I. Joe and Barbie.

The girl's aisle will be primarily pink and studded with "bling." For the very young girls it's all about baby dolls and tiny, furry animals--a sorry substitute for letting your nurturing girl keep real plants and animals. If they are not into the stuffed dolls there is a variety of toy cleaning supplies, plastic vacuum cleaners, ironing boards and brooms and dustpans…all in pink of course. There are also a range of fake beauty products, salon chairs and make up tables. The next group of toys focuses primarily on the princess. Tiaras, jewelry and tawdry costumes dominate. Any type of art and craft is about appearance, its either hair, make up, nails or plastic jewelry. Almost every doll in this group is a little demented. Brands like the hyper sexualized Bratz dolls and Novi Stars look like a type of alien-human hybrid. In some stores mega-brands like Disney Princess and

Barbie have a giant pop out marquee over the isle so that you'll be sure to know who's in control.

It is obvious that in this context "pink" means that what you look like determines your value. Young girls are taught only to be sexy and alluring or useful in chores and preparing food. Girls who haven't gone through puberty but still want to act slutty can now call themselves a "tween" meaning in between child and teen. Due to the marketing strategy of "age compression" the bottom end of tween can go as low as six years old. When the Barbie doll was introduced her target audience was nine to twelve year olds; today its three to seven. One of the most common criticisms of Barbie is that she promotes an unrealistic idea of the body image for a young girl. In 1963, the outfit "Barbie Baby-Sits" came with a fake book entitled, "How to Lose Weight" which didn't open and on the back simply read: "Don't eat!" The same book was included in another ensemble called "Slumber Party" along with a pink bathroom scale permanently set at 110 lbs. At 5'9" tall and weighing 110 lbs, Barbie would have a body mass index of 16.24 and fit the weight criteria for women with anorexia. She would lack the minimum 17 to 22 percent body fat required for a girl to even menstruate.

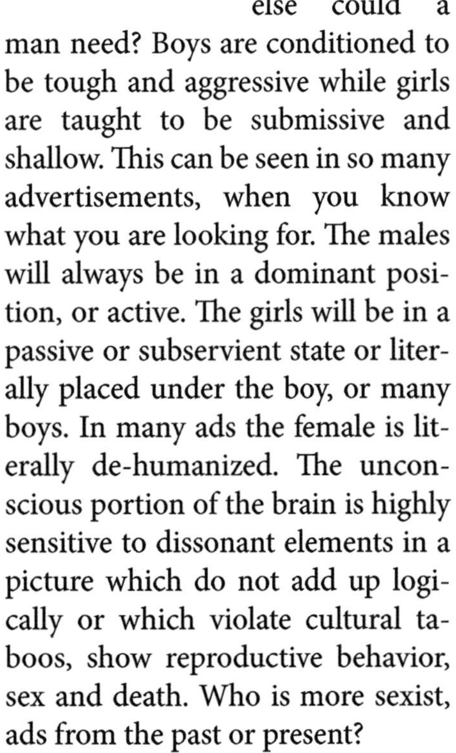

In the corporate toy world there is only one game for girls to play and that is the game of seduction. The inventor of the Barbie doll was Ruth Handler, the president of the toy manufacturer Mattel. She took the idea from a German porn doll—a gag gift for men called the Bild Lilli Doll that she saw in a tobacco shop. Lilli was based on a comic strip character in an early German smutty tabloid called Bild. She was a sassy and provocative cartoon who hinted at taking money from rich old men for sexual favors. This was the model that Mattel took back to Los Angeles, re-named Barbie and sold her as the all-American girl.

The boys' aisle is primarily blue and all toys are themed with manliness, aggression, automobiles, machinery, warfare and domination. Superhero's, cars and sports...what else could a man need? Boys are conditioned to be tough and aggressive while girls are taught to be submissive and shallow. This can be seen in so many advertisements, when you know what you are looking for. The males will always be in a dominant position, or active. The girls will be in a passive or subservient state or literally placed under the boy, or many boys. In many ads the female is literally de-humanized. The unconscious portion of the brain is highly sensitive to dissonant elements in a picture which do not add up logically or which violate cultural taboos, show reproductive behavior, sex and death. Who is more sexist, ads from the past or present?

IT JUST
TASTES
BETTER
Look good in all you do
IT'LL BLOW
YOUR MIND AWAY
CLOSE
attraction.

Boys' toys focus primarily on the use of battle images, power and violence as entertainment. These are also dominated by a few mega-brand names like Star Wars and Marvel. Boys are inundated with the idea that they are "Masters of the Universe" through violence. Young boys used to be able to build things from their imagination out of Legos or Erector Sets. Now you can only buy Legos systems which feature the toys mostly built already and based on the same themes and characters as the rest of the toys. There is only one game for boys to play—the game of war. While toy company Mattel could barely keep up with demand for its Barbie dolls in the early 1960's, its competitor, Hasbro, realized the market had no counterpart for boys. The answer was G.I. Joe, and his name was a shorthand symbol for the typical serviceman, or "Government-Issue Joe." In 1963, Hasbro began development on a military-themed line of dolls that, like Barbie, could be accessorized with different outfits and equipment and the original strategy called for a different figure for each branch of the military.

In the toy department, the sorcerers use an occult technique called the "flashing colors" in which they use opposite colors of the spec-

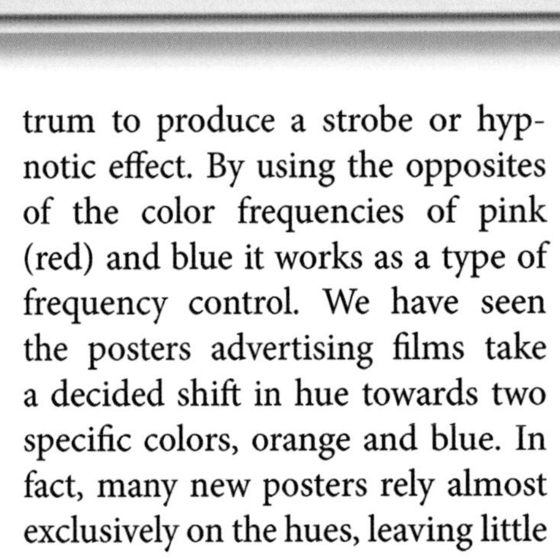

trum to produce a strobe or hypnotic effect. By using the opposites of the color frequencies of pink (red) and blue it works as a type of frequency control. We have seen the posters advertising films take a decided shift in hue towards two specific colors, orange and blue. In fact, many new posters rely almost exclusively on the hues, leaving little but details to the other colors. The dynamic color duo has a large visual impact, as they also reside on opposite sides of the color wheel. These are also considered flashing colors. They keep the brain in duality, constantly swinging back and forth between the left/right and masculine/feminine hemispheres and never allowing it to be in the balance of green. You can see this evidence in the color choices for political parties, national flags, sports teams and police cars. They want to control the way the two sides of the brain communicate with each other, so they secretly talk to the right brain through symbolism and subliminal message, while the person is only conscious of their left brain activity which is the physical view of the world. In masonry, the black and white checkerboard floor of the house represents dual-

ity or base consciousness and not understanding your spiritual nature. In this state you are ignorant of both good and evil, just as in your "id" phase. You can't go any lower than the floor and the object of masonry is to bring your mind off the floor and climb the ladder into higher consciousness which is accomplished by balancing the left and right hemispheres of the brain.

Labeling us, differentiating us, psychoanalyzing us and separating us is a strategy of the sorcerers. In the sixties everyone was united against the war in Vietnam. People of every rank, file and persuasion; professors and students, veterans and hippies, blacks and whites, all came together. They had a singular motivation, they were a unified front against the war and they we actually making progress. For the social engineers this created a problem and their answer was more segregation. Groups like the Black Panthers and various women's rights and gay rights groups were established to divide the people and get them fighting amongst each other for their own rights so that the effort against the war slowly died out. Any way they can find to separate us and make us feel apart from each other means we are more vulnerable to them. By placing us into categories like male/female, gay/straight, white/black they deceive us with the concept of duality.

***

The Military Industrial Complex and the Economy

In the avant-garde, esoteric movie, *The Holy Mountain*, you are shown in an artistic way how toys are manufactured to impose a certain, carefully planned agenda. In this scene in the movie the narrator begins: *"My name is Sel and my planet is Saturn."* A clown rides through the streets on an elephant followed by an angel and a group of tiny Santas handing out treats to all the boys and girls. When the parade arrives at the toy factory the clown is revealed to be a stern businesswoman. *"We manufacture war toys,"* she says. *"We have an electronic computer programmed with the politics of the government. The government is our client. We feed the computer data on coming wars and revolutions. It tells us what kind of toys to produce, to condition children from birth...for fifteen years in advance we condition the children to hate the future enemy...these children will go off to war to kill with pleasure."*

The heavy production of war themed toys and games began just before WWII. Hundreds and thousands of toys of a military nature, like the board game, *Sink the Invader*, were quietly introduced by manufacturers and publishers to promote political agendas and instill fear. Produced well before US entry into the war, games like *Black Out-Today's Game of Thrills* and *The Game of Intrigue* quite accurately predicted all the major combatants that made up the allies and the axis powers. One toymaker named Keystone called its line of dollhouses "the homes worth defending. Little girls keep house while the little boys defend their families…with military equipment illustrated."[4] During the war, manufacturers like Milton Bradley produced games like *Fighting Marines, Bataan* and *Battle of the Tanks*, games they said were "as timely as tomorrow's headline." Toys and games of a military theme were just as popular with the children of our "enemies" over in Europe as they were here. Their approach was actually quite similar, only the targets and planes were different. Ger-

man children had a huge range of war games to choose from in the thirties and through the war years. Some were even tied to Hitler Youth activities including *Tanks Forward, Bombs Over England* and *The New Game of Our U-Boat Service.*

Today's economy is not driven by any conscious or unconscious desires of the masses, nor the quest for self-expression. Now, warfare is defined as the ultimate capitalist enterprise and the United States of America's economy is a war economy. Starting or fostering wars is a "great" business proposition and the 1940's marked the start of the era of systematic wars for profit. The extraordinary efforts of citizens during that time turned the United States into a giant global arms factory. It was even credited as the main factor in ending the Great Depression. The boys go off to war to subdue other countries so that the girls can afford to buy things from the slaves that those wars have created. The heart of today's economy is driven by the consumer princess and the bloodthirsty warrior.

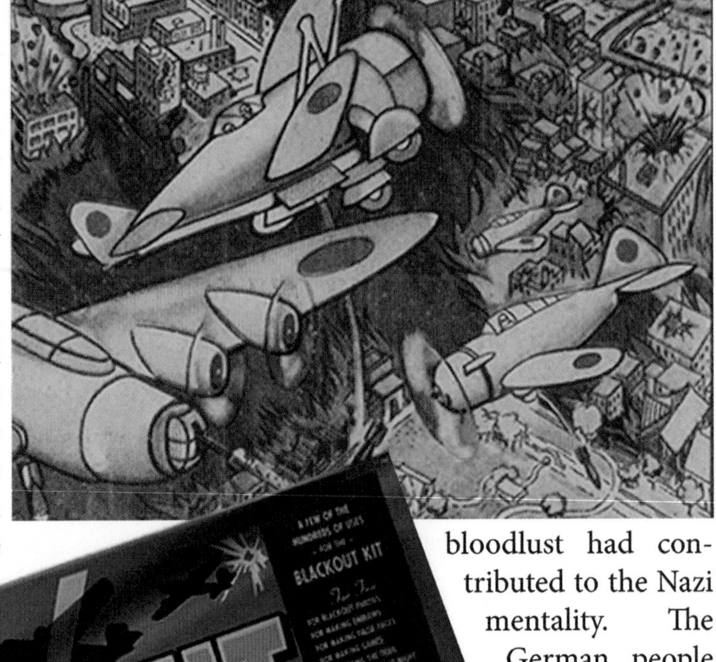

When the war ended in 1945 reports began to come out about the concentration camps, and the horrors and atrocities that people had suffered at the hands of the Nazi's. Officials were brought to Nuremburg and tried for war crimes. Allied commanders banned the publication of Grimm brothers' stories in Germany, claiming their bloodlust had contributed to the Nazi mentality. The German people were discriminated against and demoralized by the rest of the world for allowing such things to happen. Because of its consumerism and overseas aggression America is set to be the next target of degradation globally. You may begin to see more and more anti-American propaganda and the systematic vilification of the war mongering United States.

In 1938 Gum Inc. began including a graphic "Horrors of War" card in their penny gum packets. The series of 288 cards covered scenes from various wars.

***

1. *The Tavistock Institute of Human Relations*, Dr. John Coleman
2. "Disney Expert Uses Science to Draw Boy Viewers," *New York Times* (April 14, 2009)
3. Disney Consumer Products Corporate Information, 2009
4. *Games and Toys During the WWII Years*, Jack Matthews

Books:

Disney, The Mouse Betrayed, Peter & Rochelle Schweizer
The Elixir and the Stone, Michael Baigent & Richard Leigh
Toys Go To War, Jack Matthews
Walt Disney, Hollywood's Dark Prince, Marc Eliot

Movies:

The Century of the Self, Adam Curtis
Consuming Kids, Adriana Barbaro & Jeremy Earp
Santa's Workshop-Inside China's Slave Labor Toy Factories, Lotta Ekelund & Kristina Bjurling

You Tube:

Mark Passio, Free Your Mind Conference (2011)

WeirdStuff!

Mega Corporations:

How many times can Wal-Mart "accidentally" decide to build their stores on sacred Indian sites? There have been numerous cases involving destruction of Native American burial grounds and other culturally significant sites by Wal-Mart. In the mid-'90s, developer JDN was involved in the relocation of numerous native graves while building a store in Canton, Georgia. The store set up a permanent display of unearthed Indian artifacts next to its layaway counter. When an Indian burial ground was discovered during construction of a Wal-Mart Supercenter in the northern California community of Anderson, the company proceeded with the project anyway, opening the store in 2007. To make up for the site's desecration, the store erected a bronze statue of a native Wintu feather dancer that was vandalized before the dedication ceremony. In 2004, Wal-Mart opened a store in Mexico within view of the 2,000-year-old pyramids of Teotihuacan, despite months of protests by local residents as well as prominent Mexican artists and intellectuals. About five years ago, while building a Sam's Club and Wal-Mart Supercenter in Hawaii, workers unearthed 64 native Hawaiian graves. For at least three years afterward, the bones remained locked in a trailer, awaiting reburial. There are many other cases where Wal-Mart would have disturbed sacred sites but were dissuaded by protest.

"AND SHALL WE JUST CARELESSLY ALLOW CHILDREN TO HEAR ANY CASUAL TALE WHICH MAY BE DEVISED BY CASUAL PERSONS, AND TO RECIEVE INTO THEIR MINDS IDEAS FOR THE MOST PART THE VERY OPPOSITE OF THOSE WHICH WE SHOULD WISH THEM TO HAVE WHEN THEY ARE GROWN UP? WE CANNOT!"

—PLATO, 340 B.C.

"Modern psychology has a word that is probably used more than any other word in psychology; it is the word 'maladjusted.' It is the ringing cry of modern child psychology; maladjusted. Of course we all want to live the well adjusted life in order to avoid neurotic and schizophrenic personalities—but, as I move toward my conclusion, I would like to say to you today, in a very honest manner, that there are some things in our society and some things in our world for which I am proud to be maladjusted—and I call upon all men of good-will to be maladjusted to these things until the good societies realize. I must honestly say to you that I never intend to adjust myself to racial segregation and discrimination. I never intend to adjust myself to religious bigotry. I never intend to adjust myself to economic conditions that will take necessities from the many to give luxuries to the few and leave millions of God's children smothering in an airtight cage of poverty in the midst of an affluent society."

—Martin Luther King Jr., 1967

Times Square, New York City

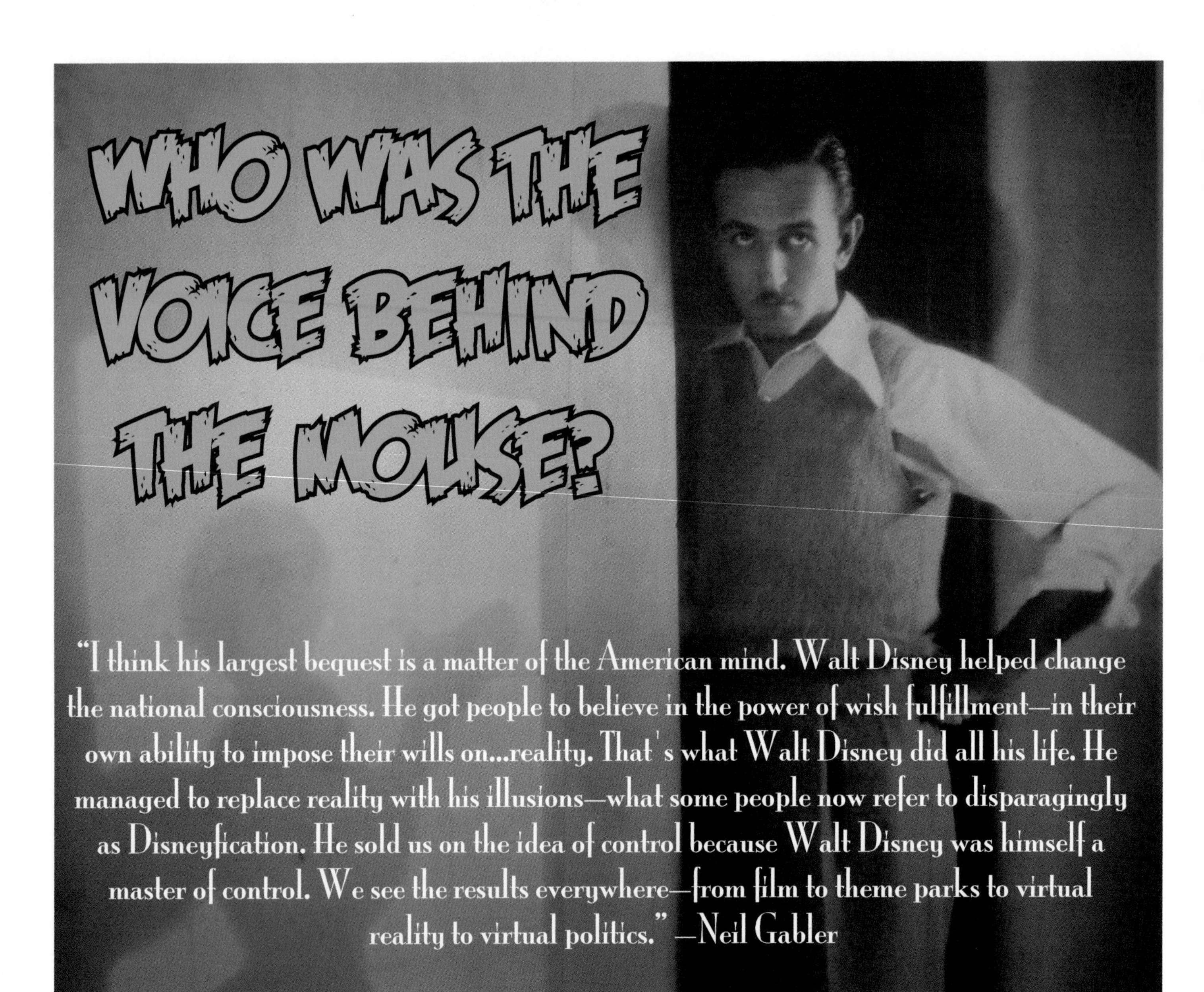

Accolades

Walt Disney is probably one of the most beloved names on the planet. His status as an international icon and his influence on popular culture cannot be underestimated. Few people have been awarded more accolades and honors. He has personally won 22 Academy Awards out of 59 nominations and holds the record for both. Additionally, he has also earned four honorary Oscars, his last one being granted posthumously. Disney, along with members of his staff, have received 48 Academy Awards and 7 Emmys and more than 950 honors and citations from almost every nation in the world.

His personal awards include honorary degrees from Harvard, Yale, the University of Southern California and UCLA, France's Legion of Honor and Officer d'Academie decorations; Thailand's Order of the Crown; Brazil's Order of the Southern Cross; Mexico's Order of the Aztec Eagle; and the Showman of the World Award from the National Association of Theatre Owners. In 1964, he was awarded the Presidential Medal of Freedom, which is the highest honor that a civilian can be awarded. Though it may be given for singular acts of momentous import, it is generally conferred only for a lifetime of service. Disney is heralded as the exemplary model of character and American enterprise. Was he the ultimate example of a human being or the ultimate example of the ability of the sorcerers to create an idol? As we are about to see, behind the curtain, Walt was a deeply troubled individual.

***

Early Life

The official story is that Walter Elias Disney was born in Chicago, Illinois in 1901, a fourth son to Elias and Flora Disney. The baby was named after the preacher of the St. Paul Christian Church, Walter Parr. In 1903, Elias began preaching out against the moral corruption of the big city and moved the family to a farm in Marceline, Missouri. Walt's

father was a very strict fundamentalist who considered himself morally righteous, but he also had a dark side. He loved bars, loose women, whiskey and gambling; and the debts he incurred may have been the reason for the family's sudden relocation.

In Missouri, little Walt and his brother, Roy, were forced to earn their keep at the family apple farm. Elias would use corporal punishment to increase productivity and woodshed beatings were administered daily. This trauma caused the boys to cling to each other to secretly wonder and hope that Elias was not their real father. The Disney family's evening dinner often included long diatribes from Elias against the capitalist economy and the exploitation of America's working class by what he thought was a conspiracy of wealthy Jews in control of the world's investment banks. Despite his father's harsh treatment and hard work on the farm, Walt saw his time in Missouri as the happiest in his life. He loved the town so much that he incorporated it into the Disneyland theme park. Before entering the Magic Kingdom each guest must pass through the idealized Main Street of Marceline.

In 1909 the family moved to Kansas City where Walt and Roy were forced to work their father's

Above: Baby Walt, 10 months old
Below: Walt in France, circa 1919

paper route delivering two daily editions, seven days a week, for no pay. Walt could often be found taking catnaps in the ally for some much needed rest since the route would have them waking up at 3:00 am. For the rest of his life he would have a re-occurring nightmare that he had missed a customer along his route and had to deliver it before his dad found out. When Walt could sneak in some playtime, his favorite game was to play "Jimmy Dale" a junior secret agent. Before Roy ran away from home, he taught Walt how to stand up to their father so that he would be alright without him. Walt confronted Elias when he was just ten years old and his father never tried to beat him physically again.

In 1917, Roy enlisted in the Navy to fight in WWI and Walt made up his mind that he would enlist too. When the local recruiter asked to see his birth certificate, Walt wrote to the Hall of Records in Chicago and they answered that there was no record of it. He tried contacting the Department of Vital Statistics and their response only added to the mystery. There was record of a "Walter Disney" born to Elis and Flora Disney in 1891, which was impossible as he was obviously not twenty-six years old. When he questioned his parents about it, they reacted strangely and gave him vague answers and an empty promise to look further into the matter. He no longer felt he could trust them from that time on. He feared that he had uncovered a terrible secret that he might be adopted or illegitimate.

Walt managed to get into the war by getting his mother to sign a permission slip to join the Red Cross. His father was against this but his mother knew that he was determined. He was still a year too young so when his mother made out an affidavit saying that he was born in 1901, when she turned her back Walt picked up the pen and changed the "1" into a "0." In November 1918, Walt sailed to France aboard the Vauban as part of the Red Cross Ambulance Corps. During his service overseas, he was a chauffeur to officers and military officials in France and through the Rhine country of occupied Germany. For money he would take battle relics and dress them up, coating the insides of helmets with grease, hair and blood and put holes in them to make them into expensive souvenirs. This shows that Walt could be deceptive if he saw an advantage in it.

***

Disney: Babylon's Last Hope

During the onset of the great depression, many Americans believed that the countries financial hardships were the result of its moral decline. A large part of the blame was focused on Hollywood which they called "Babylon" and "Sin City." Hollywood has always been associated with ancient Babylon. The columns and décor of the Kodak Center come from the set of a 1916 movie, *Intolerance*, by D.W. Griffith, who dared to re-create the colossal court of Belshazzar the king of Babylon from the book of Daniel.

After the stock market crash there was an enormous bitterness from Americans towards who they felt were responsible for the nation's collapse—the Jewish financiers on Wall St. The movie industry was also well known to be run by Jews and many people blamed them for the moral degradation that Hollywood had introduced. To defend itself, the leaders of the film industry needed a wholesome role model whose films could be seen as fun for the whole family and they found their best hope in Disney. Rabbi to the stars, Edgar Magnin, was the spiritual leader of the major moviemakers who were part of the Los Angeles B'nai B'rith. He encouraged those in the Jewish mafia and others who were B'nai B'rith movie producers that Hollywood needed to protect itself by putting Walt Disney in the limelight as a Christian "white knight with family values." Many of the major filmmakers were so corrupt that they were out of touch with moral issues, but they thought that Walt knew black from white. Walt was named 'Man of the Year' in 1955 by the B'nai B'rith chapter of Beverly Hills.

In 1930, the movie industry made a production code, which stated that it must make a special effort to create movies appropriate for children. Hollywood directly praised Disney in that code as an exemplary model of what the industry wanted to do. Almost overnight, movie studios that had been turning out violent, sexually suggestive, albeit profitable films, all jumped on the bandwagon and were now eager to show Walt's clean, wholesome and politically correct cartoons. Hollywood mogul, Carl Laemmle, who had essentially stolen Disney's cartoon character, Oswald the Lucky Rabbit, was now interested in the first talking character called Mickey Mouse in the cartoon *Steamboat Willie*. Walt was the facade Hollywood needed to hide behind to make Americans think that they had morals.

While Hollywood was immersed in scandals from the start, Walt Disney Studios had strict standards. In the 30's Disney had a dress code that required men in ties and women in sober colored skirts.

If a man looked at a woman in the wrong way, he risked being instantly fired. Walt was the perfect example of the strictest legalism. Even during the 50's if an employee were caught saying anything considered a cussword such as "hell" they were instantly fired no matter who they were. Walt would not allow his employees to have any facial hair even though he himself had a moustache. He never allowed employees to have alcohol at the studios, but was known to drink heavy amounts of liquor in his private office for decades.

***

Success

With the power of the B'nai B'rith and the Anti-Defamation League behind him, Walt began sailing to fame. In 1937, he and his family took a European vacation. Wherever the group traveled, Disney's name appeared in giant letters on movie marquis. The most famous international figures of film, literature, religion, science and politics lined up to meet with him. In England, Disney dined with the royal family and met privately with science fiction writer H.G. Wells who was the first to outline and help make plans for a "New

World Order." When in Rome, Disney was granted an audience with the Pope and Mussolini. In Paris, the League of Nations awarded him with a special medal, which he accepted using the voice of Mickey Mouse. In 1938, Disney received an Honorary Master of Fine Arts from Yale for having "created a new language of art." By the early 1960's, the Disney empire was a major success, and Walt Disney Productions had established itself as the world's leading producer of family entertainment. He was the Head of Pageantry for the 1960 Winter Olympics.

In 1940, Walt began his foray into political activism. Nurtured by his staff attorney Gunther Lessing, they began attending American Nazi meetings and rallies. One of Walt's motives for doing so may have been to regain favor with the Nazi-occupied countries where American films were banned. Arthur Babbitt, Walt's co-worker and union activist recalls: *"In the immediate years before we entered the war, there was a small but fiercely loyal, I suppose legal, following of the Nazi party. You could buy a copy of Mein Kampf on any newsstand in Hollywood. Nobody asked me to go to meetings but I did out of curiosity...On more than one occasion I observed Walt Disney and Gunther Lessing there along with a lot of other prominent Nazi affiliated Hollywood personalities. Disney was going to meetings all the time. I was invited to the homes of several prominent actors and musicians, all of whom were actively working for the American Nazi party."*[1] When Nazi film maker, Leni Reifenstahl, visited Hollywood in 1938 to promote her documentary, *Triumph of the Will*, Walt greeted her publicly. Walt admired Hitler for his orderliness and totalitarianism. Hitler, however, hated Mickey Mouse and called him the most miserable ideal ever revealed and unsuccessfully tried to have it banned from his Reich.

***

Rebellion!

Life at the Disney studios was not a fairy tale. Walt's large number of employees never received any credit or recognition for their years of creativity and hard work, which was essentially stolen. Credit was given to Walt by the elite establishment to build his image. Employees at Disney did not have titles; it was faceless egalitarianism with an all-powerful dictator at the top. It was said that he could bring his artists to tears or anger in a matter of seconds. The studio was racially elitist, anti-semetic and sexist too. The only full-time African-American employee during Walt's lifetime at Disney was a black shoeshine man. At the studio in Burbank, Disney built a private club for his animators with a coffee shop, gymnasium, theater and sun decks. Since only men were allowed in the animating department he called it a "womanless paradise." In a press release describing the club Disney declares: *"The women may have taken over the bars and the barber shops, but they still can't crash the profession of animation. The only skirted artists in the studio are the girls who trace the animator's drawings onto celluloid and paint them.*"[2] Disney thought of his segregated studio as the perfect creative environment. Employees were required to punch in and out on the time clock whenever they had to go to the restroom, get a drink of water or sharpen a pencil. In spite of his public distaste for communism, his magic empire was run like a socialist dictatorship.

Walt considered himself not just an employer at his studio but also a type of father to his "boys" as he often referred to his artists. When the artists demanded union representation, Disney took it as an act of family betrayal and refused to negotiate with them. Studio employees went on strike in May of 1941 with over 1,000 picketers including 580 Disney employees appearing in the first hour.

With the strike already in its second month, Walt was having a nervous breakdown. He could not believe that his "family" had turned against him. Fearing his brother's rapidly deteriorating condition, Roy appealed directly to J. Edgar Hoover for help. They arranged an ambassador of "goodwill" trip for Walt to South America and to help persuade him to take the trip, the government paid $100,000 to make films during the tour. They departed in August on the much-publicized journey. The footage he took on that trip would become the movie *The Three Caballeros*, which features Donald as a lecherous and horny duck chasing Spanish women. In Walt's absence, Roy worked with U.S. Department of Conciliation to help settle the strike that officially ended in September 1941. The strike soured Walt's attitude towards unions, so in 1944 together with other Hollywood personalities, he helped form the anti-communist Motion Picture Alliance for the Preservation of American Ideals. The group served as a body of supporters within the film industry that were willing to testify publicly against possible communists in Hollywood.

***

Walt's Birth Scandal

Barack Obama and Adolph Hitler are not the only ones with a high profile birth certificate scandal. Walt Disney's true origins are about as obscure as the architect of the pyramids and, trust me, researching this topic is bound to make you want to stab a fork in your eye. Barcelonan historian Carlos Almendros spent ten years studying the family origins of Disney without a concrete conclusion. Many people, from F.B.I. agents to Franciscan Monks, have attempted to piece together his lineage but no one can come up with a solid answer. Birth certificates are found either in error or falsified. I read every scrap of information I could about Walt's origins and came up more confused than I was when I began and nowhere closer to knowing anything. The mysteries surrounding Disney's birth are here to stay. Finding out his true parentage isn't just the bane of my existence but apparently it was Walt's as well. The possibility that he was adopted or born out of wedlock haunted him almost his whole life and was a shadowy part of his character. So far all we have is a chronology of events:

In 1890, Walt's father, Elias, left his wife and two children to seek his fortune in the second wave of the California gold rush. He arrived home only weeks before the still unexplained listing of a birth of a "Walter Disney" on January 8, 1891, according to the Illinois Department of Vital Statistics. Around this time he hired a maid who remained in the family employ for thirty-five years. When Elias died, Walt hired her as his personal housekeeper. She was said to be from a remote village of Mojacar, Spain.

There is a story told by the villagers of Mojacar of a beautiful washerwoman named Isabelle Zamora Ascensio. She had an illegitimate baby with a doctor named Jose Guirao. Shortly after, the doctor died and Isabelle decided to take a boat to America. She ended up on the west coast at a Franciscan monastery. This was in 1890 and would have put her in California at the same time as Walt's father.

When Walt became an official informant for the FBI in 1940, two agents were sent on a mission to Mojacar. Their stated objective was to obtain a baptismal certificate for an illegitimate baby named Jose Guirao, born around 1890, to a lady named Senora Isabelle Zamora. This date is 11 years off of Walt's birth date, so what the heck?

Shortly after returning from his ambassador trip to South America, Hoover contacted Walt about the secret mission to Spain. The Bureau had traced the origins of a woman who they believed could be his real mother. This news devastated Walt and he locked himself up in his office and sobbed through the night.

One unproven theory is that Elias and Isabella met in California and he brought her back to Chicago where he supported her. In 1893, they had a son and Elias convinces his wife to accept the baby as theirs rather than have the families' reputation ruined. This would have been Walt's older bother, Roy who looks nothing like his two older siblings.

In 1901, Elias brings home another baby who they named Walter. The two illegitimate children do not look like the older sons of Elias, and they never have much to do with them, but cling to each other as brothers. When the local minister found out, Elias suddenly uprooted his family and moved to the Midwest. Elias kept Zamora as his housekeeper so that she has an excuse to move in with them without creating suspicion and do most of the care and raising of the two boys. This is just one of many convoluted stories you will find in trying to research his origins but one thing is for sure is that nothing adds up.

Stories about his Spanish birth have become so established that eyewitnesses claim to have seen a plaque in the town of Mojacca (another spelling of Mojacar?) announcing it as the birthplace of Walt Disney. In this version, a village maiden named Consuela Suarez had a baby with a local boy who died before they could get married. With the help of a local priest, the baby was adopted by an American couple who took him to the United States and Consuela followed as their nanny. Only when she came home later on did she reveal to townsfolk that her son was the famous Walt Disney.

Writing these few paragraphs took two weeks of my life and I refuse to dedicate any more time to the subject. I really hate this story and I will leave it here for some braver and more dedicated researchers—knock yourself out.

***

Walt Disney and the FBI

One thing we do know for sure, according to documents that have come to light under the Freedom of Information Act, is that from 1940 until his death in 1966, Walt Disney served as a secret informer for the Los Angeles office of the Federal Bureau of Investigation. The five films, *Snow White, Pinocchio, Bambi, Dumbo*, and *Fantasia* are considered Disney's golden era. These were the films that Walt personally had a hand in creating and have the common theme of a lost child's quest to find their real parents. If Walt Disney was an illegitimate child with mysterious origins, that would give the government something to blackmail him with, or maybe they took advantage of Walt's neurosis about family values and made the whole thing up.

A communication about Walt's family history between Disney and Hoover appears in a July 1936 memorandum, one of the many attempts they had made as part of an ongoing campaign to recruit him. In it Hoover writes, *"I am indeed pleased that we can be of service to you in affording you a means of absolute identity throughout your lifetime."* The meaning of "absolute identity" is unclear, but the document signifies the beginning of a long-term relationship between the two men.

The government was aware of Disney before he was officially introduced in 1936. During his first months in the FBI in 1918, J. Edgar Hoover was busily involved with the prosecution of draft dodgers in WWI. In keeping with the logic of the Bureau, he would also get to know the names of those volunteers like Disney who were so eager to serve they would do anything to get into the military. It crossed his desk that Walt Disney had committed the crime of forging the document to join the Red Cross. Years later, when Disney became famous, the FBI ran a preliminary background check on him. It uncovered the story of when Walt tried to find his birth certificate to join the army. J. Edgar Hoover skillfully used this information to exploit Disney's great conundrum and insure his loyalty to the FBI.

In November 1940, the deal was officially struck. Hoover offered Disney the unlimited services of the FBI to find the truth of his parentage. In exchange, Walt agreed to assist in Hoover's crusade against the spread of communism in Hollywood by becoming an official informant. As a bureau contact, Disney reported on the activities of Hollywood actors, writers, producers, directors, technicians and union activists suspected of political subversion. Walt perceived his FBI commission not only as his patriotic duty but a high moral obligation. He became as obsessively devoted to spying as he had once been to making cartoons.

In return, Disney sought cooperation from the bureau for filming. In 1956, they requested the right to use the bureau's offices in Washington for the Mickey Mouse Club show. Disney officials promised that the Mouseketeers would be seen having fun with agents on their shooting range and that they would be the type of adults which the children would look up to. The FBI found this satisfactory, but insisted that some changes should be made in the script.

Because of the information Disney provided to the bureau, he was made a "full Special Agent in Charge Contact" in 1954. An "S.A.C. Contact" was usually a trusted informer who could provide transportation and equipment as well as public relations services to the bureau. Disney was not the only important informer in Hollywood; while president of the Screen Actors Guild in 1947, Ronald Reagan was designated "Source T-10" by the F.B.I., meaning he was a confidential source with the code name "T-10."

The F.B.I. and Disney found an opportunity for mutual benefit in Disneyland, which opened in 1955. A document in his file reads: *"Mr. Disney has recently established a business association with the American Broadcasting Company-Paramount Theaters Inc. for the production of a series of television shows, which for the most part are scheduled to be filmed at Disneyland, a multi-million-dollar amusement park being established under Mr. Disney's direction in the vicinity of Anaheim, Calif. Mr. Disney has volunteered representatives of this office complete access to the facilities of Disneyland for use in connection with official matters and for recreational purposes."*[3]

***

WeirdStuff!

Bambi

Today's Satanic, Darwinian environmental movement, heavily backed by Disney has its roots in a book called *Bambi*, written by English pornographer, Felix Salten. In Walt's original vision, Bambi was to receive a Christ-like manger birth, with the animals hailing him as a "prince." Most of Disney's nature films focus heavily on the predator-prey relationship, "the law of the jungle" which is also the basic law of Satanism as defined by Anton LaVey. Many scenes involve the stalking, killing and consuming side of nature while the peaceful, balanced symbiotic relationships are ignored. This is meant to convince us that "survival of the fittest" is the philosophy of nature and man is nothing more than the top of the food chain and he is a destructive element to the environment. The extension of this logic is the basis for ideas of population reduction and eugenics. The story of *Bambi* appealed to Walt because he always said he liked animals better than people. In the book, tame animals view humans as gods, while free animals see humans as demons that they simply refer to as "Him." By the end of the book the animals view all humans as simply being on the same level as animals, a vicious creature fit to be killed.

Walt & DeMolay

If you google "Disney Freemason" you will most likely find yourself dwarf-deep in masonic conspiracy territory. There is no evidence to say that he was a Freemason, although, his brother, Roy Disney, was a member. Walt was, however, heavily involved in the order of DeMolay which is a fraternal organization created for boys who had lost their fathers during WWI. DeMolay begins as many Disney films do, with the death of a parent. When a young man named Louis Lower lost his father, a Fellowcraft Mason, it spurred the Senior Warden of Ivanhoe Freemasonic Lodge to call his masonic brother, Frank Land, to ask for help. Land asked Lower if he would you like to form a club and meet at the masonic temple. Louis thought the idea had possibilities and showed up the next week with eight other boys.

They sought a name for the club and after many Biblical and fraternal names were discarded, one young man suggested that the name be something connected with Masonry. At the time, Frank was serving as the head of one of the Masonic Groups as the Commander for the DeMolai Council of Kadosh. He told them the story about the last leader of the Knights Templar whose name was Jacques DeMolay or as they say in history books, James of Molay. There were nine original Poor Knights of Christ otherwise known as the Knights Templar. The mythic Knights were sanctioned by the Roman Catholic Church in 1128 to guard the road between Jerusalem and Acre, and were also legendary for their participation in the Crusades. Since there were also nine boys gathered there to form the club, the order was founded under the name of the martyred Templar, Jacques DeMolay.

March 24, 1919 was the day in history that launched the Order of DeMolay. During the next few years, however, the date of March 18, the day that had witnessed the death of Jacques DeMolay, came to be more frequently used. Although none of the youth groups are "masonic organizations" as such, DeMolay is considered to be part of the general family of Masonic and associated organizations, along with other youth groups such as Job's Daughters and Rainbow Girls. A young man does not need to have family connection to Masonry in order to join DeMolay.

DeMolay was founded in Kansas City and Walt Disney joined in 1920, at age 19, and became the 107th member of the original Mother Chapter of DeMolay. In 1931, Walt received the DeMolay Legion of Honor. He wasn't just a member; he was also a "hometown boy." In Walt's address at the De Molay Conference he emotionally declared: *"I feel a great sense of obligation and gratitude toward the Order of DeMo-*

lay for the important part it played in my life. Its precepts have been invaluable in making decisions, facing dilemmas and crises. DeMolay stands for all that is good for the family and for our country. I feel privileged to have enjoyed membership..."

While Walt's Freemasonic connections are obscure, many like to refer to the super expensive private Club 33 of Disneyland to say that he was given an honorary membership to the Supreme Mother Council of Freemasonry which is the 33rd or highest degree of the Scottish Rite, but this cannot be proven. There are other clues to suggest that Freemasons do indeed have their hands in Walt Disney's World. As you rumble down the Big Thunder Mountain rollercoaster, you pass a box labeled "H. Abiff's Working Tools." Any Freemason would recognize this as the tools of the first Master Mason, Hiram Abiff.

***

Odd Behavior

It seems that Walt was under tremendous amounts of pressure for his entire life. Not only from his parents, the government and the public but also from himself. He genuinely wanted to be the upstanding Christian example like his father preached but this burden was also what caused him to crack. Behind fronts of strict observances of "morals" you will often find massive amounts of guilt and a dirty mind. Adolf Hitler would obsessively wash his hands many times a day which is a sign of a guilty conscience. So did Walt, several times an hour, every hour.

Walt had black hair and a mustache, he used his own facial features to clue artists on how to draw Mickey Mouse's features. He was usually the voice behind Mickey but his unsupportive mother told him she didn't like Mickey's voice and that he sounded like a sissy. The next time Mickey would appear he was mostly silent in *Fantasia.* Supposedly the idea for *The Sorcerer's Apprentice* came from a dream Walt had of having "complete control of the Earth and the elements."

He liked specially rolled brown cigarettes which he smoked up to 70 a day. He picked up his smoking habit in the army and loved expensive Scotch Whiskey. He played lots of Golf with Bob Hope at his Ranch in Palm Springs. Between his ranch, the studio and his private quarters above the fire station on Main St. Disneyland, Walt was hardly ever at home at his estate in Holmby Hills. He would go for weeks on end without seeing his family. Often the main topic at the studio was Walt's bizarre behavior. He would never be available until late afternoon when he emerged from the studios subterranean underground where he was supposedly "chatting with the maintenance engineers" all day.

In 1945, he was suffering from a kind of nervous breakdown. He retired as president of the studio and appointed Roy as the new one. He began to spend all his time sequestered in his private inner office which some employees jokingly called Walt's "chamber of horrors." He would play with trains to pass the time and supervise by intercom, the building of a miniature steam locomotive for his house in Holmby Hills. He painstakingly saw to it that every detail of the train was perfect. He stopped going to work, missed meetings and meals and refused to go to bed so he could keep riding his "choochoo." The only thing that brought him out of his funk was a legal battle with his former co-worker, Arthur Babbit.

People who knew Walt personally knew he had an obsession with buttocks. He told butt jokes to his staff quite frequently and most of his jokes had to be edited from cartoon scripts. Many Disney cartoons feature characters' butts provocatively twitching. One that

got by the editors was a Christmas special where a little boy is unable to button the drop seat of his pajamas. The little boy's problem in maintaining his modesty is the running gag of the cartoon and in the end, Santa gives him a chamber pot. Another example of his butt fetish was in the movie *Fantasia* when two mating centaurs bring their backsides together to form a single beating heart. Apparently Walt was not only obsessed with the anus, but also what came out of it. One co-worker recalls that he could talk about turds for thirty minutes straight.

For an artist, Walt was pretty unromantic. He treated his marriage like a business partnership. Walt and Lillian spent their wedding night on a train from Idaho to Los Angeles. He suddenly developed a toothache and began to pace up and down for almost an hour. He visited the club car where he had his shoes shined dozens of times over and over all night. When they arrived in Los Angeles they boarded a steamer for Seattle and it wasn't until they reached Washington that Walt was able to consummate the marriage. The next day he cut the honeymoon short stating that he had to get back to work at the studio right away. This came as no surprise once he explained his motivation for the marriage in the first place: *"I realized that I'd need a new roommate, so I proposed to Lilly."* He was also quoted as saying that girls bored him and that he loves Mickey Mouse more than any woman he ever met.

For someone who was supposed to be providing the ultimate in family entertainment he didn't like kids very much. According to Kenneth Anger, he used to "open a small, rounded door in the wall—a fairy tale door that creaked—and take his guests down a winding staircase into a dungeon filled with racks and Iron Maidens scaled to the size of a five year old. 'Now this is how I really feel about the little bastards' he'd say, and puff on his cigar."[4]

Walt had two daughters, Diane Marie and Sharon Mae. He was very distant towards both of them. He was a man with a lot of money but took no joy in spoiling them. His daughter, Diane, recalls that he would not allow her any money for horses, which she loved, clothes or anything else. He was also famous for his ten-cent tips at restaurants. During the military occupation of his studio he decided that he would start going to church and spending more time with his kids.

Sharon Mae was adopted and arrived at the Disney home December 1936. The newspapers around the country announced that Lillian had given birth to Sharon, and the Disney family kept up this lie for years. The reason given for Sharon's adoption was that Diane needed a playmate. In June of 1948, when Sharon was twelve, Walt took her to Alaska with him for about two months. For most of this trip they were alone together. A father, who had ignored her for years, was now totally obsessed with her. He bathed Sharon every night, combed her hair, washed her underwear, and carefully dressed her each night from head to toe before taking her to nice restaurants.

Walt hated the idea of death, he avoided funerals and if he had to attend one it would always put him in a deep depression. When he died in 1966, no details were made public and all reporters were able to discover was that "secret rites" had been conducted at Forest Lawn Cemetary. His employees at the studio were encouraged to act as if he were still alive by quoting him in the present tense. i.e. "Walt says..."

Disney is the epitome of the sorcerer's ability to create images. His golden name was methodically engineered to be so. He had a personal image builder, Joe Reddy, who worked full time to build Walt's image. Today, every employee of Disney, from a top manager to a food service vendor is required to attend an employee orientation experience called "Traditions" the first day on the job. The course is designed to immerse each employee into the Disney vision and mission. Its very purpose is to build and continue a desired organizational culture where they "learn to enjoy thinking the Disney way."

***

1. *Walt Disney, Hollywood's Dark Prince,* Marc Eliot
2. ibid
3. ibid
4. *High Times Reader,* Annie Nocenti & Ruth Baldwin

Books:

Disney's World, Leonard Mosley
Walt Disney an American Original, Bob Thomas
Deeper Insights into the Illuminati Formula, Fritz Springmeier
Walt Disney: The Triumph of the American Imagination, Neal Gabler

"No studio devoted more of its time or resources to wartime activity than Walt Disney's."
–Leonard Maltin

On December 7, 1941, Japanese planes attacked Pearl Harbor. Within twenty four hours war had been declared and approved by Congress and the United States officially entered WWII. The next day, Walt Disney arrived to work at his studio in Burbank only to be stopped at a check point and made to confirm his identity. The entire studio had been commandeered by the military as a primary defense station to guard the nearby Lockheed plant against a possible air strike. All film equipment was replaced by anti-aircraft weaponry and the parking lot was filled to capacity with crates of ammunition and Jeeps. During this military occupation the Disney studio became a virtual war factory with well over 90% of its production in the service of government training, education and propaganda films. Donald, Pluto and Goofy all get drafted in cartoons and even Minnie Mouse is encouraged to save her leftover kitchen grease to help make ammunition. Some of these films were top secret and concerned the secret psychological tactics of the Americans. One film was called *Army Psycho Therapy,* about stress, the adrenal glands, the basics of fear and how to instill fear.

Disney was outraged when he learned that his was the only studio to be turned into a makeshift military base. He always felt victimized by the army and would openly complain about it until, in 1942, he won the prestigious Irving Thalburg award for his high quality propaganda cartoons. When the studio occupation ended, Walt chose to stick with the military theme in his project, *Victory Through Air Power,* which ended with a triumphant obliteration of Tokyo. The cartoon reduces war to machines fighting machines and leaves out the consequence of human suffering and death. One critic of the time called it a "gay dream of holocaust." Winston Churchill liked it so much that he requested a private screening for himself and Franklin Roosevelt to help convince the president to go ahead with a long range bombing program.

***

Chicken Little

In the classic 1943 version of *Chicken Little,* we can clearly see how the sorcerers view people and how they use us against each other. In this story we are introduced to a coop of chickens that mirror human society. There is Cocky Locky, head man, chicken inspector, supervisor of egg production and a good guy to know. Henny Penny, who enjoys knitting, bridge, going to the hair salon and most of all, gossip. Turkey Lurkey and the smart set who spend all day discussing what is wrong with the world. The Jitterbirds who are a pretty feather brained crowd that just want to dance and have fun. Ducky Lucky and the other good time ducks who spend their time as barflies; and then there is Chicken Little, the youngest, most naïve chicken of the town, but generally a good egg.

Finally, there is Foxy Loxy the sly, hungry fox. He ponders the best way to catch a chicken and is put off by the tall sturdy fence and farmer's shotgun. He decides, why should he jump into the coop and risk his life to catch one chicken when he can use psychology to get all of them to go where he wants them to go? The animators wanted to title the fox's book after Hitler's book, but instead just labeled it "Psychology." Foxy Loxy quotes

from his book **"If you tell 'em a lie, don't tell a little one, tell a big one."** This concept of the big lie is straight from *Mein Kampf* where it states: *"All this was inspired by the principle--which is quite true in itself--that in the big lie there is always a certain force of credibility; because the broad masses of a nation are always more easily corrupted in the deeper strata of their emotional nature than consciously or voluntarily; and thus in the primitive simplicity of their minds, they more readily fall victim to the big lie than the small lie, since they themselves often tell small lies in little matters but would be ashamed to resort to large-scale falsehoods. It would never come into their heads to fabricate colossal untruths, and they would not believe that others could have the impudence to distort the truth so infamously."*

In the film, Foxy Loxy steals a piece of wood with a five pointed star painted on it from a sign advertising astrology. He throws it over the fence and it hits Chicken Little in the head. The fox whispers to him through a hole in the fence: **"This is the voice of doom. The sky is falling."** Chicken Little rushes to warn all of the other chickens and shows them his proof, the star and the bump on his head. The chickens are frightened until Cocky Locky appears as the voice of reason and identifies the star as a hunk of wood. The fox is temporarily foiled but he has other mind control techniques up his sleeve. Again, he quotes from his book: **"Undermine the faith of the masses in their leaders."** The fox infiltrates the different social groups spreading rumors through the fence. He provokes the chickens to fight amongst themselves and they demote Cocky Locky as king of the roost.

"By the use of flattery, insignificant people can be made to look upon themselves as born leaders." The fox convinces Chicken Little that it is his turn now that Cocky Locky has fallen out of favor and he should be the one to step up and lead the chickens. He screams that he is their new leader and begins to debate with Cocky Locky about the validity of his claims that the sky is falling in front of the whole town.

The fox then hits Cocky Locky in the head with another pentagram. All the chickens witness the event and run to Chicken Little for guidance. The fox councils him to rush everyone to the caves, breaking their secure fence in the process, down a path set up by the fox. Be warned this tale does not have a happy ending, unless you're a fox. The moral of the story as narrated by Foxy Loxy is: **"Don't believe everything you read."**

The significance and poignancy of this cartoon is as apparent today as it was seventy years ago, maybe even more so. If controlling the masses was so streamlined at that time, imagine how much more sophisticated it has become. Many in the modern day "Patriot" movement are nothing more than Chicken Littles who, guided by misdirection, present the so called evils of the world, which are designed to engineer society into a particular polarity. They miss the true dangers that are not comprehended because they choose not to look over the fence.

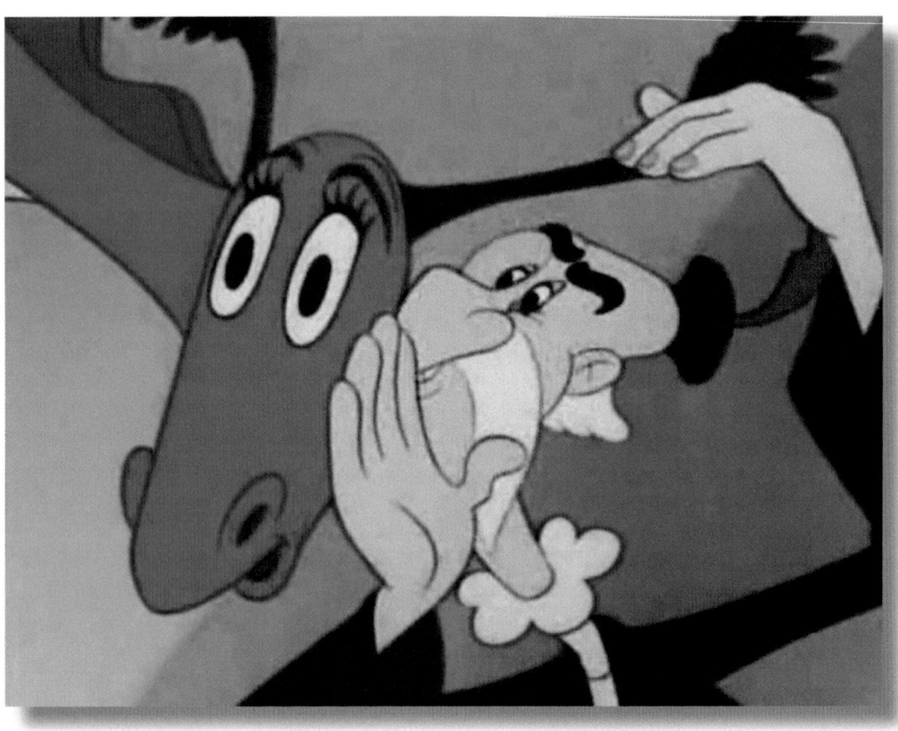

***

League of Nations

It has been evidenced that events such as Pearl Harbor and 9/11 were false flag operations which are covert missions designed to deceive the public in such a way that they appear as though they are being carried out by other entities to gain support from American citizens to go to war. In the book, *Pearl Harbor: The Mother of all Conspiracies,* author Mark E. Wiley asserts that the US was warned by the governments of Britain, Netherlands, Australia, Peru, Korea and the Soviet Union that a surprise attack on Pearl Harbor was coming. All important secret Japanese codes about the air strike were broken and deciphered before the event. Roosevelt, Marshall and others knew the attack was coming, allowed it to happen and covered up their knowledge. This is because of the promise FDR had made to the American people, solemnly given and repeated, not to send their sons into foreign war unless attacked. Since all previous attempts to provoke Hitler to declare war on the US had failed, there needed to be an attack on American soil to create an emotional response and foment America's participation in the war.

This had been planned long before by the League of Nations, which is an inter-governmental organization founded as a result of the Treaty of Versailles following WWI. The League of Nations would become the modern day United Nations. Other organizations such as the Bilderberg Group, G20, The Council on Foreign Relations, the Trilateral Commission and the Bohemian Club consist of the international elite in the areas of politics, banking, business, the military and media. Each conference is held under intense security and secrecy.

In 1941, Disney released a cartoon called *The Reluctant Dragon* that gives us a glimpse of what these secret meetings are all about. The film is about a young boy, a shepherd's son, who considers himself an authority on knights and dragons. One day his father races down the hill, surrounded by his flock of sheep. The sheep represent the population and how the elite view them. The shepherd alerts his son that he has just seen a giant scaly monster. The boy identifies it from his book as a dragon and the father, once again races off to warn the townspeople. Does this sound familiar to *Chicken Little*?

The boy goes off to investigate the dragon for himself and discovers something surprising, the dragon is a shy, effeminate poet who knows nothing of terrorizing country sides or devouring damsels. Meanwhile, the villagers have summoned the knight, Sir Giles, a famous dragon slayer. The boy, determined to warn the knight that the dragon is not dangerous, sneaks in on him while he is bathing. He discovers that the mighty Sir Giles is actually a white haired old man with a monocle who is also a poet.

The ancient Greeks were among the first cultures to make

a connection between poetry and prophesy. They believed that when the poet became inspired or "possessed" he was actually in contact with divine beings who revealed visions of past and future events. Throughout western occultism, wizards, Druids and shamans are expected to be poets as well as prophets. In Celtic druidism the poet or bard was a living and walking library. Because of the absence of writing, his memory held the history, legends, songs, customs, and legal codes--the entire heritage of his tribe or people. Anyone who laid his hand against a poet was considered an outlaw and accursed. The bard of ancient Ireland was authorized to appear on the battlefield and, by a simple command, impose a truce between warring factions.

When the boy introduces the knight to the dragon they hit it off and recite verses to one another. The boy reminds them that the townspeople are expecting a fight so they conspire to act out the battle for the reaction of the crowd. When the dragon inquires about the moral implications of such a deception, Sir Giles reminds him that it's all in the boy's book and that they are simply following the script. The battle is played out the next day and Sir Giles successfully "slays" the dragon for all to see. In the real world of politics, the very elite from all over the world who attend these secret meetings do not oppose each other. They get together and plan wars for us to fight and villains for us to slay and we just follow the script.

The ending of *The Reluctant Dragon* is even more peculiar when the dragon does not stay hidden; but is said to be "completely reformed" by the knight whereupon the satisfied villagers welcome him into society. What could this dragon be, first feared, then "conquered" and finally "resurrected" as an integral part of society?

***

Operation Paperclip

After the war ended in 1945, victorious American and Russian intelligence teams began a treasure hunt throughout occupied Germany for military and scientific discoveries. They were looking for things like new rocket and aircraft designs, medicines, and electronics. They were also hunting down the doctors and scientists whose work had nearly won the war for Germany. They rounded up all the Nazi scientists they could and brought them to America. The government had originally intended only to debrief them and send them back to Germany but when they realized the extent of the scientists' knowledge and expertise, the War Department decided it would be a waste to send them back home. There was only one problem, it was illegal. The law explicitly prohibited Nazi officials from immigrating to America, and as many as three-quarters of the men in question had been ardent Nazis. Convinced that German scientists could help America's postwar efforts, President Truman agreed in September 1946 to authorize Project Paperclip, the Office of Strategic Services (OSS) program to bring selected Germans to work on America's behalf during the Cold War. This later opened up many umbrella projects stemming from Nazi mad scientist research such as MK-ULTRA. These longtime members of the Nazi party and the Gestapo had conducted experiments on humans at concentration camps, used slave labor, and committed other heinous war crimes. These men were given key positions in science, military and education.

By 1955, more than 760 German scientists had been granted citizenship in the U.S. and given prominent positions in the American scientific community under Project Paperclip. These men brought with them V-2 rocket plans, UFO designs, microwave technology and mind control experiments. Wernher von Braun, Paperclip's most famous beneficiary, was an SS officer who helped develop the V-2 rockets that devastated England, and later went to work for NASA, rising to the post of deputy assistant director of planning. Von Braun worked on guided missiles for the U.S. Army and was later director of NASA's Marshall Space Flight Center. He became somewhat of a celebrity in the 1950's and early 1960's, as one of Walt Disney's experts on the World of Tomorrow. In 1970, he became NASA's associate administrator.

The ideals of the Nazis also found a home with scientist and member of the Ordo Templi Orientis, Jack Parsons of Jet Propulsions Laboratory who was co-founder of The California Institute of Technol-

Walt Disney & Wernher Magnus Maximilian Freiherr von Braun

ogy. Von Braun would acknowledge Parsons as the father of America's space program. The Californian O.T.O. was saved from extinction by Parsons in 1939. He was a fervent admirer of Crowley and enthusiastic practitioner of sexual magic and a Thelemite. He saw no contradiction between his scientific and magical pursuits, and before each rocket test launch, he would invoke the Greek god Pan. Working with the formula of Thelemic magick, he supposedly established contact with extraterrestrial beings of the order of Aiwass. During this period of sex-magical operations, Parsons was engaged in nuclear research and paved the way for the present-day passion for things strange and occult, for drugs, UFOs and communicating with other worldly intelligences capable of transforming life on this planet, a phenomenon which Crowley spent a lifetime trying to accomplish.

***

"The powers of financial capitalism had another far-reaching aim, nothing less than to create a world system of financial control in private hands able to dominate the political system of each country and the economy of the world as a whole. This system was to be controlled in a feudalist fashion by the central banks of the world acting in concert, by secret agreements arrived at in frequent private meetings and conferences. The apex of the system was to be the Bank for International Settlements in Basle, Switzerland, a private bank owned and controlled by the world's central banks which were themselves private corporations." —Carroll Quigley, *Tragedy and Hope: A History of the World in Our Time*

Taxes

Walt Disney has stated that he always saw Donald Duck as the common man, yet, he portrays Donald as one who is irrational, ill-tempered, lecherous and impulsive, of low intelligence and one who is easily manipulated. In the 1942 cartoon entitled, *The New Spirit,* Donald is implored by a voice on the radio to help stamp tyranny from the earth by paying his income taxes. The radio tells him that more money is needed for guns, ships and democracy, imparting to him the motto "Taxes to beat the axis." When Donald rushes his payment to Washington DC we discover exactly where the tax revenues went...to factories working day and night to produce *"guns, machine guns, anti-tank guns, long range guns, guns, Guns all kinds of GUNS!"*—the narrator of the cartoon cries with morbid enthusiasm. *The Spirit of 1943* also features Donald being duped into paying income tax once again—by Scrooge McDuck none the less.

Why would the government need to use Donald Duck to remind people to pay their taxes? Perhaps because in 1942 Americans were just getting used to the idea. The income tax was instituted in 1862 but until the 1940's only those who worked for or were involved with the federal government paid annual income tax. Few people know that prior to 1913 federal income tax was considered unconstitutional.

Following an orchestrated stock market crash in 1907, a meeting was held in 1910 at a J.P. Morgan estate on Jekyll Island off the coast of Georgia. It was there that a central banking bill called the Federal Reserve Act was written. A group of elite bankers of the Rothschild-Rockefeller-Morgan-Harriman families met in secret to discuss a bill they wished to pass to establish a bank they had always wanted—the Federal Reserve. This legislation was written by bankers under such strict secrecy that the authors could only address each other by their first names. In 1913, Woodrow Wilson signed the legislation and the law was put to a vote by congress two days before Christmas when most of the congressmen were away on vacation. To complete the trap they introduced a Federal Income Tax Bill, but to do this they needed an Amendment to the Constitution that required at least thirty-six states to vote for it. Only two states agreed but they simply lied and announced that it had received the required majority and the bill was passed. The enforcement of money paid to federal income tax is illegal to this day. The IRS is also a privately owned company. All money collected as income tax only goes to pay the interest on money "borrowed" from the Federal Reserve.

The Federal Reserve is a private corporation owned by international bankers. It is under no regulations by the U.S. government. It loans currency to the government at interest and up to thirty-five percent of the average Americans' wages goes to pay the interest on the money lent by the Federal Reserve Bank. Federal Income Tax is a direct unapportioned or "excise" tax and according to the constitution all direct taxes must be apportioned to be legal. There is no law or statute in existence that requires you to pay this tax, but if Donald Duck is convinced, then apparently no further evidence is needed.

Today the U.S. tax code is over three million words long and is updated and republished every year. What a waste of trees. Seventy-five years ago, the instructions for the

1040 Form were two pages long, today, they are 189 pages long. According to The Tax Foundation, the average American has to work until April 17th just to pay federal, state, and local taxes. When the U.S. government first implemented a personal income tax back in 1913, the vast majority of the population paid a rate of just 1%, and the highest marginal tax rate was only 7 %.

When it dawned on President Wilson what he had done, he regretted his actions terribly and stated in 1919 that, *"I am a most unhappy man. I have unwittingly ruined my country. A great industrial nation is now controlled by its system of credit. We are no longer a government of free opinion. No longer a government by conviction and vote of the majority; but a government by the opinion and duress of a small group of dominant men."*

From 1921 to 1929 the Federal Reserve increased the currency supply by sixty-two percent, this coupled with the practice of the margin loan, or fractional reserve lending, led to the economic boom of the roaring twenties. In 1929, all loans were called in almost simultaneously crashing the market and signaling the beginning of The Great Depression. Congressman Charles Lindbergh stated in 1921 that *"Under the Federal Reserve Act, panics are scientifically created. The present panic is the first scientifically created one worked out as we figure a mathematical equation."*

Most of the tax debate today is focused on income taxes. People will say, if you don't pay taxes how will things like roads, schools and hospitals get built? As we have seen, not one penny of income tax goes to pay anything but interest on money "lent" to us by the Federal Reserve. Income tax money goes straight into the pockets of wealthy internationals. For things like street lights, roads, schools, law enforcement and hospitals, Americans pay dozens of other taxes every single year and here is a crazy list of them:

Building Permit Taxes
Capital Gains Taxes
Cigarette Taxes
Court Fines (indirect taxes)
Dog License Taxes
Federal Unemployment Taxes
Fishing License Taxes
Food License Taxes
Gasoline Taxes
Gift Taxes
Hunting License Taxes
Inheritance Taxes
Inventory Taxes
IRS Interest Charges (tax on top of tax)
IRS Penalties (tax on top of tax)
Liquor Taxes
Luxury Taxes
Marriage License Taxes
Medicare Taxes
Property Taxes
Recreational Vehicle Taxes
Toll Booth Taxes
Sales Taxes
Self-Employment Taxes
School Taxes
Septic Permit Taxes
Service Charge Taxes
Social Security Taxes
State Unemployment Taxes (SUTA)
Telephone Federal Excise Taxes
Telephone Minimum Usage Surcharge Taxes
Telephone State and Local Taxes
Tire Taxes
Toll Bridge Taxes
Toll Tunnel Taxes
Traffic Fines (indirect taxation)
Utility Taxes
Vehicle License Registration Taxes
Vehicle Sales Taxes
Workers Compensation Taxes

This boggling list of taxes is even more interesting considering the impetus for many colonial Americans to join the Revolutionary War came from the imposing of ridiculous taxes, such as a "fresh air tax," by the king of England. George III's Currency Act, forced the colonists to conduct their business by only using printed bank notes borrowed from the Bank of England at interest. After the revolution, the new United States adopted a radically different economic system in which the government issued its own value-based money, so that private banks were not siphoning off the wealth of the people through interest-bearing bank notes.

"The refusal of King George III to allow the colonies to operate an honest money system, which freed the ordinary man from the clutches of the money manipulators, was probably the prime cause of the revolution."

—Benjamin Franklin

The Real Economy

If you listen to any political debate you will hear the same word repeated over and over…"we must boost the economy, it's not good for the economy, we're in a bad economy…how can we save the economy?!...heading towards a global economy…we need jobs for the economy…" We know that war is horrible, but we tolerate it because it's good for the economy. It is this giant invisible entity that greatly effects our lives, yet we know so little about it. Politicians would have us believe that if we are innovative enough and work hard enough that we can somehow save this dying system. It is the system, however and not us, that is the problem. In September, 2011, a protest movement began on in Zuccotti Park, located in New York City's Wall Street financial district. The protesters' slogan was "We are the 99%" which referred to the issue of income inequality which has reached disparaging levels. The Occupy Movement spread to just about every major city and countless small towns. Their primary issue was with the wealthy insurance companies and investment bankers who had crippled the economy and whom they felt deserved no bailouts—and rightly so, because bankers suck and always have.

The Rothschild family international banking dynasty is the most successful business family in history. The story of how they took over the financial system of Europe is worth repeating as it is a perfect example of how the economies are allowed to collapse and how fortunes are made. In 1815, French Emperor Napoleon's army stood against the Duke of Wellington and the British at the Battle of Waterloo. The victor would decide the fate of the continent. If Napoleon

won, France would be the undisputed master on the European front. If he lost, England would hold the balance of power in Europe and would be in a position to greatly expand its sphere of influence.

Meanwhile, the Stock Exchange in London was at fever pitch as traders awaited news of the outcome of this battle. The Rothschild's spy network was well known and extensive. A Rothschild representative from the battlefield jumped on board a specially chartered boat and headed out into the channel in a hurried dash for the English coast. In his possession was a top secret report on the progress of the crucial battle. The moment he read the report, Nathan Rothschild sped to the trading floor. He leaned against 'his' pillar, emotionless, expressionless and instructed his agents to sell, sell, sell. Word began to sweep through the stock exchange: "Rothschild knows." "Wellington has lost at Waterloo." The selling turned into a panic as people rushed to unload their 'worthless' stocks. Emotionless as ever, still leaning against his pillar, he began to give subtle signals that only his highly trained agents could detect. On the cue from their boss, dozens of agents made their way to the order desks around the Exchange and bought every stock in sight for "pennies on the dollar." A short time later the official news arrived that Wellington had actually won the battle and within seconds the values skyrocketed. As the word spread, the value of consuls rose even higher. Nathan Rothschild had bought control of the British economy overnight and the family's already vast fortune was multiplied twenty times over.

The First Bank of the United States was founded in 1791, largely through the efforts of the Rothschild's chief US supporter, Alexander Hamilton. By the end of its twenty year charter the bank had almost ruined the nation's economy, while enriching the bankers. Congress refused to renew the charter and signaled their intention to go back to a state issued value based currency on which the people paid no interest. This resulted in a threat from Nathan Rothschild against the US Government, "Either the application for renewal of the charter is granted, or the United States will find itself involved in a most disastrous war." Congress still refused to renew the charter, and Rothschild decide to teach those Americans a lesson. Financed by the Bank of England, Britain then launched the war of 1812 to recolonize the United States and force them back into the slavery of the Bank of England and the plan actually worked. Even though the War of 1812 was technically won by the United States, Congress was forced to grant a new charter for yet another private bank issuing the public currency as loans at interest, the Second Bank of the United States. Once again, private bankers were in control of the nation's money supply and cared not who made the laws.

Nathan Mayer Rothschild 1777-1836

Today we live in a neo-feudalist system in which the super-rich and mega-corporations pull all the strings. When talking about the ultra-wealthy, it's not just about people that have a few million dollars. The ultra-wealthy have enough money sitting in offshore banks to buy all of the goods and services produced in the United States during the course of an entire year and still be able to pay off the entire U.S. national debt. Not only that, the Oxfam organization has reported that the world's 100 richest people earned a stunning total of $240 billion in 2012 alone – enough money to end extreme poverty worldwide four times over. That amount of money is so large that it is almost incomprehensible to the average person.

The tax code is absolutely riddled with loopholes that big corporations and the ultra-wealthy use to minimize their tax burdens as much as possible. The biggest welfare recipients of all are the mega-corporations. What they are able to get away with is absolutely amazing.

It turns out that instead of paying in taxes to the federal government, they are actually getting money back. These are combined figures for the tax years 2008, 2009 and 2010 for some corporations:

Honeywell
Profits: $4.9 billion
Taxes: -$34 million
Verizon
Profits: $32.5 billion
Taxes: -$951 million
General Electric
Profits: $7.7 billion
Taxes: -$4.7 billion

Under this neo-feudalist system, all the rest of us are debt slaves, including our own governments. The elite use a sprawling network of secret societies like Skull and Bones, think tanks such as The Tavistock Institute, charitable organizations like The World Wildlife Fund and non-governmental organizations like the Rockefeller Foundation to advance their own agendas. They control how we view the world through their ownership of the media and their dominance over the education system. Over the years, the Rockefeller Foundation and other elitist organizations have poured massive amounts of money into Ivy League schools which are considered to be the standard against which all other colleges and universities are measured, and the last four U.S. presidents were educated at Ivy League schools.

They "elite" fund the campaigns of most of our politicians and they have an enormous amount of influence over international organizations like the United Nations, the IMF, the World Bank and the Word Trade Organization. The international bankers created the central banks of the world, including the Federal Reserve, and they use those central banks to get the governments of the world ensnared in endless cycles of debt from which there is no escape. Government debt is a just way to "legitimately" take money from all of us, transfer it to the government, and then transfer it into the pockets of the ultra-wealthy. Most Americans have never even heard of the Bank for International Settlements, but it is at the very heart of the global financial system.

Have you ever wondered why things never seem to change in Washington D.C. no matter who we vote for? It is because both parties are owned by the establishment. It would be nice to think that your votes matter for something but in the real world, the politician that raises more money wins more than 80% of the time. Researchers that have looked into the ownership of the big Wall Street banks that dominate the Fed, find the same names keep popping up over and over: the Rockefellers, the Rothschilds, the Warburgs, and the royal families of Europe.

There is nothing more lucrative to the large international banking interests than war. It is important to remember that prior to the creation of the Federal Reserve, there was no such thing as a world war. Financially, wars are created to

Bank for International Settlements,
Basel, Switzerland
http://theeconomiccollapseblog.com

force private central banks onto nations and our back-breaking labor only goes to enrich the already super wealthy.

In 1941, Disney released a cartoon called *The Seven Wise Dwarves.* In it, the Dwarves sing a happy tune: "*We dig dig dig dig, dig dig dig in our mine the whole day through... To dig dig dig dig, dig dig dig is what we like to do... We dig up diamonds by the score, 1,000 rubies, sometimes more, but we don't know what we dig 'em for. We dig dig dig-a-dig dig.*" Indeed. Not even the seven wise dwarves can understand why we have to work so hard, and who are we working for? Once the dwarves bags are full of jewels they march along to the beat of "Hi-ho, hi-ho" another day of work happily completed, "It's off to buy we go." What is the reward for all of their diligent labor? Are they allowed to enjoy any dwarf women, dwarf food or dwarf entertainment? Or maybe the Dwarves use it to put food on their tiny families' tables? No. They trade their rocks in for paper, war bonds to be exact. Is there anything in this exchange that would be very useful to the natural needs of a dwarf or a human for that matter? In the end, they march home singing "Hi-ho, Hi-ho, we'll win the war with five for four" as war bonds transform into shells used to shoot down Nazi airplanes. "Keep your money fighting, buy more and more."

In the 1943 cartoon, *Der Fuhrer's Face,* Donald wakes up in dystopia, a Nazi land where his home is plastered with swastikas. His cuckoo clock chimes "seig heil" while posters of dictators hang on the wall. In this symbolic inundation, it is as if artists were predicting the cartoon merchandising craze. During his meager breakfast in the cartoon Donald is handed a copy of *Mein Kampf* and ordered to "improve his mind." He is told he is free but still has to work like a slave at the ammunitions factory. In the end, he wakes up from this nightmare only to find that the red and black swastikas have been replaced by red, white and blue stars and Hitler is now the Statue of Liberty. He has simply traded one dangerous philosophy for another one. This environment represents the inescapable ideology first used by the Nazi's and then later by the Disney corporation themselves. In Donald's Nazi nightmare, when Donald looks out the window he sees that the trees and shrubs and fences have been sculpted into swastikas. Ironically, later on, the bushes and shrubs at Disneyland would be carefully trimmed to look like Disney characters.

Books:

The Creature from Jekyll Island, G. Edward Griffin

Movies:

Zeitgeist, Peter Joseph

Walt Disney Treasures: On the Front Lines, Walt Disney Studios

Article:

All Wars are Bankers Wars, Michael Rivero

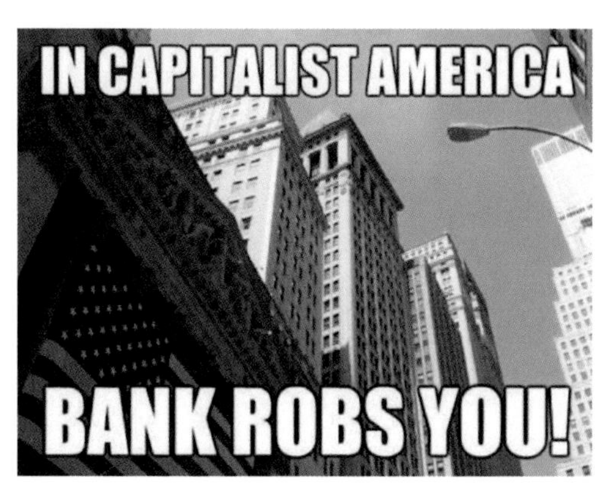

WeirdStuff!

On Jan. 7th, 1942, a month after the Pearl Harbor attack, the owner of Sun Rubber Company, T.W. Smith Jr., presented the sketches of the Mickey Mouse gas mask to Major General William N. Porter, the Chief of Chemical Warfare Service. The mask was made for children, and was given the look of the famous Mickey Mouse to reduce the fear of actually wearing a gas mask. Walt Disney himself was very fond of the idea and gladly approved the production of the cute—but creepy gas mask. —*Weird Hollywood*

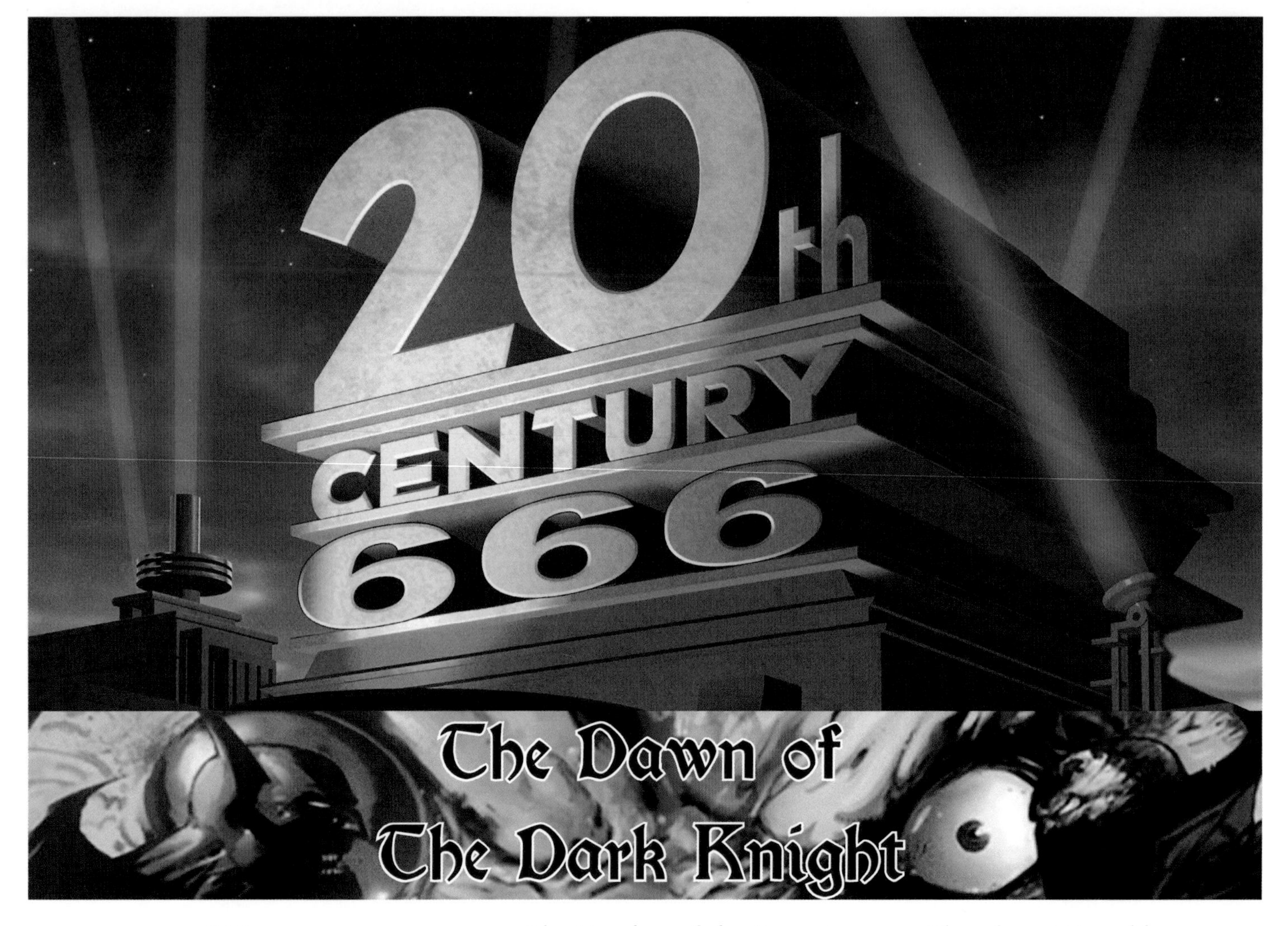

666:
The Number of the Beast

Everything that defines the cultural and social revolutions of the 20th century, namely sex, drugs and rock and roll can be traced back to Aleister Crowley whose number was 666. To honor this notion, he took on the name Master Therion derived from the Greek for "Number of the Beast," Arithmos tou Thēriou.

For many people, just saying the number sends shivers up their spines, as it conjures up ominous images of secret occult ceremonies and the cataclysmic final days of Bible prophecy. Some have refused to accept phone numbers, license plates, and credit cards containing "666." There is even a very long word made up for the sole purpose of describing this superstitious phobia — "hexakosioihexekontahexaphobia."

The Number of the Beast is described in Revelation 13:15–18 and the actual number is only mentioned once, in verse 18: *Here is wisdom. Let him that hath understanding count the number of the beast: for it is the number of a man; and his number is Six hundred threescore and six.* Scholars who lived in biblical times calculated that Nero was the Beast because his name equaled 666. Now, the number of the beast is believed to be embedded in barcodes. Two lines together on a barcode equal 6. There are two lines on the outsides and two lines in the middle making 666.

The Bible calls 666 the number of man and the number of the beast. The carbon atom is the basic building block for all life on earth. The isotope of carbon contains six protons, six neutrons and six electrons. Therefore, 666 could represent man in base consciousness or a man with the mind of a beast.

In 2007, Procter & Gamble (P&G) won a $19 million dollar lawsuit against distributors of Amway over rumors that their corporate logo, featuring a bearded man looking over a field of 13 stars, was Satanic. The Amway reps, James and Linda Newton, circulated allegations that P&G's moon and stars trademark was a satanic symbol and claimed on national TV that the company provided financial support for the Church of Satan. This slur has been around since the early 80's. The Procter & Gamble Co. has redesigned its traditional moon-and-stars symbol and removed the supposed 666 from the beard. The court forbade the Newtons from circulating false information about

P&G products and required them to issue a retraction labeling the rumors as completely false. Plagued by such allegations, P&G has decided to step up prosecutions of individuals responsible for spreading them.

While P&G may have won their lawsuit, there are plenty more examples of 666 appearing in the corporate world. For starters, the large hadron collider known as CERN, has the particle accelerator encapsulated in 666 as their logo. It is very close to the intentional 666 of Lucis Publishing Co. formerly known as Lucifer Publishing. There used to be a US Route 666 but it was renamed Route 491 in 2003. It runs through the four corners area of New Mexico, Colorado, Arizona and Utah, an area famous for paranormal phenomena. Over time, the route became known as the "Devil's Highway" where accidents and curses became legend. We see 666 around us every day but most representations are not so obvious. It is said that there are many 6's in Walt Disney's signature. Can you spot them?

***

The Beasts

There is an urban legend about a three-story super computer in Belgium called "the beast." Its function is to database all human life, but perhaps that is actually Disney World's job. George W. Bush and the Obama family ride around in a limo known as "the beast." There's a Beast in the X-Men and in World of Warcraft. It's even an American crime drama series starring Patrick Swayze.

In the Bible, the first of two symbolic beasts comes out of the sea. The description of the beast is found primarily in Revelation chapters thirteen and seventeen and chapter thirteen gives the fullest description of him. The beast comes out of the sea, from the abyss, where the Dragon at the shoreline greets him. His name is not given anywhere in the book, however, the numerical value of his name is 666. This number is associated with a particular man. He is described by John as having the appearance of a leopard, the mouth of a lion and feet like bear paws. The beast has seven heads with blasphemous names written on them and ten horns, each having a crown. One of the heads of the beast appears to have a fatal wound but the wound is healed causing people to believe in him and follow him.

Fundamentalists equate the first beast with the Antichrist which has two meanings: that which is against Christ and that which counterfeits or takes the place of Christ. This future world leader is called by other names in Bible prophecy. He is called the little horn (Dan. 7: 8) king of fierce countenance (Dan 8:23) the prince that shall come (Dan 9:26) man of sin, son of perdition (2 Thes 2:3) and the beast (Rev. 13: 1-4) The Antichrist will not earn or inherit the right to wear his crown. It will be a gift from the power brokers of the world.

The Bible says that during his rise to power, he will present himself as a man of peace, but his sweet sounding words will not match his acts of war. Many will think they have met the Messiah, but he will really be the Antichrist. John said, *"And I saw, and behold a white horse: and he that sat on him had a bow; and a crown was given unto him: and he went forth conquering, and to conquer"* (Revelation 6:2). The bow was a weapon of war and a symbol of military power in John's day. The

La Bête de la Mer, a medieval tapestry of the False Prophet, the Dragon, and the Beast of the Sea

Antichrist will appear with a bow in his hand, but he will have no arrows. He will have weapons of war, but will act like he is unarmed. Daniel said, "by peace shall destroy many" (Daniel 8:25).

The second beast comes out of the earth and his appearance is not described, other than having two horns like a lamb, and speaking like a dragon. Christians call him the false prophet. His purpose is to promote the authority of the first beast with the ability of performing great wonders, even making it rain fire. He commands the people of the Earth to make an image of the beast from the sea and to worship him. It is declared that anyone who does not would be killed, even beheaded. The false prophet also ensures that everyone under this power bears the mark of the beast on either the right hand or forehead.

The Bible says the Antichrist/Beast will "ascend out of the bottomless pit" (Rev. 17:8). This is the gruesome subterranean abode holding the very worst demonic spirits. The scriptures indicate that the demons are aware of a future time when they will be bound and cast into the abyss for one thousand years and it will be a place of torment even for them. The term "bottomless," is a transliteration of the Greek "abussos" or abyss, and refers to a place of confinement of supernatural beings. In Kabbalistic magic, the Abyss is a hidden node on the Tree of Life. These nodes are called Sephirah, there are ten visible, and one hidden, called Da'ath which separates the lower sephirah from the higher. From the Hermetic Order of the Golden Dawn's view of Genesis, Da'ath represents the fall of man from a unified consciousness into a duality between ego and divine nature. The Abyss is guarded by the demon, Choronzon who manifests during the third ceremonial method of crossing this gulf. Choronzon is the Existential Self at the last gasp. *"Beyond Choronzon we are no longer our Self. The 'personality' on the brink of the Abyss will do anything, say anything and find any excuse to avoid taking this disintegrating step into 'non-being'."*[1]

Talpa, the producers of *The Voice*, use the Tree of Life as their corporate logo with one dramatic change; Heaven is in the Abyss. Within the abyss exist the shades of the dead who are known as the Qliphoth, (pronounced Klee-phot) and they represent the dark side of the tree of life. The Qliphoth are separation and negative representations of divinity such as the fallen angels Samael, Beelzbub, or Lillith. Robert Anton Wilson calls them "souls of those who died insane." They may contain a formula of magical power but to understand the qliphothic powers fully can result in the destruction of the psyche, and therefore lead to actual madness. Com-

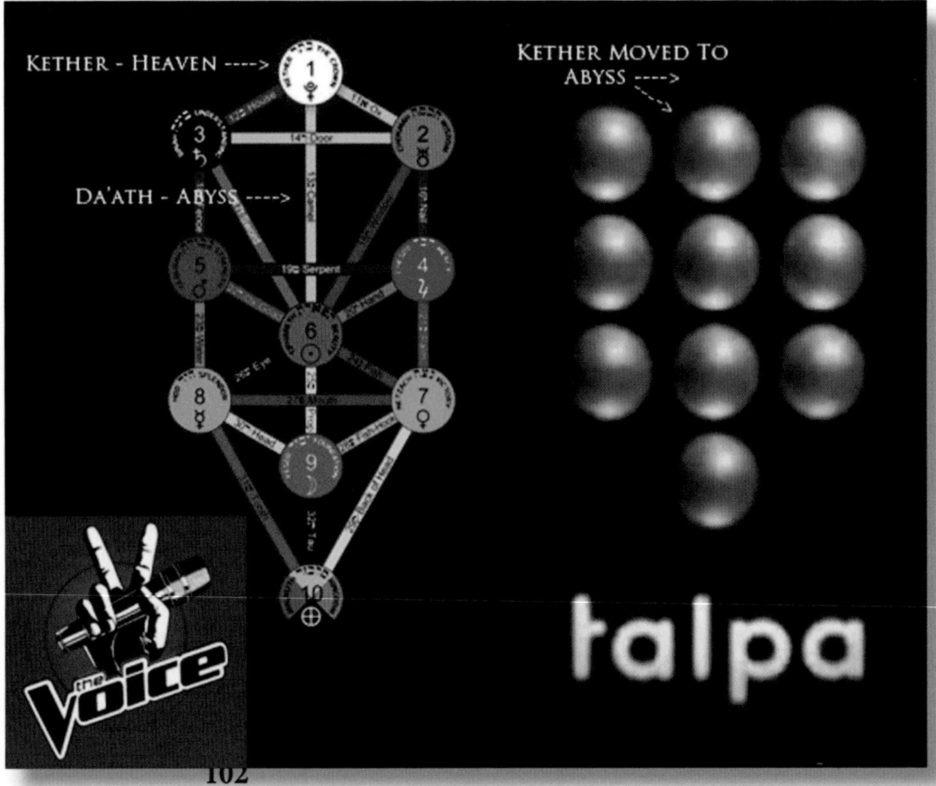

munication with these beings of the nether realm is attained through Goetic evocation which is the basest form of magic, catering to the magician's most carnal desires. *"On a scale of spiritual practices one might find Goetia sandwiched somewhere between 'Pacts with the Devil' and addiction to the Ouija board. This attitude is understandable. After all, Goetia is the intentional conjuration of spiritual beings who are, by definition, Fallen Angels, Evil Spirits and Demons!...If he is unskilled or loses control even for an instant, he runs the risk of being obsessed, possessed or even destroyed. This sounds uncomfortably like Black Magick."*[2]

The Qlippoth on the Tree of Life
"Shells" Shades of the dead whose names appear in the Book of Thoth and the Book of the Law. RAW calls them the "souls of those who died insane."
Complete understanding could result in the destruction of the ego and therefore lead to actual madness.
Dealing with the Qlippoth is the psychic equivalent of working with toxic waste.

Excrement

Entities of the Black Tarot

Kether	Thaumiel	The Two Contending Forces
Chokmah	Ghogiel	The Hinderers
Binah	Satariel	The Concealers
Chesed	Agshekeloh	The Breakers in Pieces
Geburah	Golohab	The Burners
Tiphareth	Tagiriron	The Disputers
Netzach	Gharab Tzerek	The Ravens of Death
Hod	Samael	The Liar or Poison of God
Yesod	Gamaliel	The Obscene Ones
Malkuth	Lillith	Queen of Night and Demons

***

Nine

The Hebrew characters are not only letters; they are also numbers and hieroglyphs. The literal Kabbalah is a set of techniques that meditatively explore the relationships between the letters of ancient alphabets, such as Hebrew, Greek and Latin, and their numerical equivalents. One of these techniques is known as Gematria, a system of recognizing a correspondence between the ten sephirah, and the twenty two letters of Hebrew. In gematria, letters of a word are converted into their numerical equivalents.

The number 6 is also the letter V and looks like a nail and means nail or hook as a connecting hook used when the mishkan (tabernacle) was assembled. Vav is considered the connecting force of God, the divine "hook" that binds together heaven and earth. 666 in Hebrew actually looks just like the Monster Drink logo whose slogan is "Unleash the Beast!" In gematria numbers can be reduced to a single digit. For example, 666 would become 9 because 6+6+6=18, 1+8=9. According to Anton LaVey, nine is the most Satanic number because it is the most selfish number, always multiplying back to itself: 9x3=27 2+7=9. This works with any multiple of nine. *"Despite others attempts to identify a certain number with Satan, it will be known that nine is his number. Nine is the number of the Ego, for it always returns to itself. No matter what is done through the most complex multiplication of nine by any other number, in the final equation nine alone will stand forth."*[3]

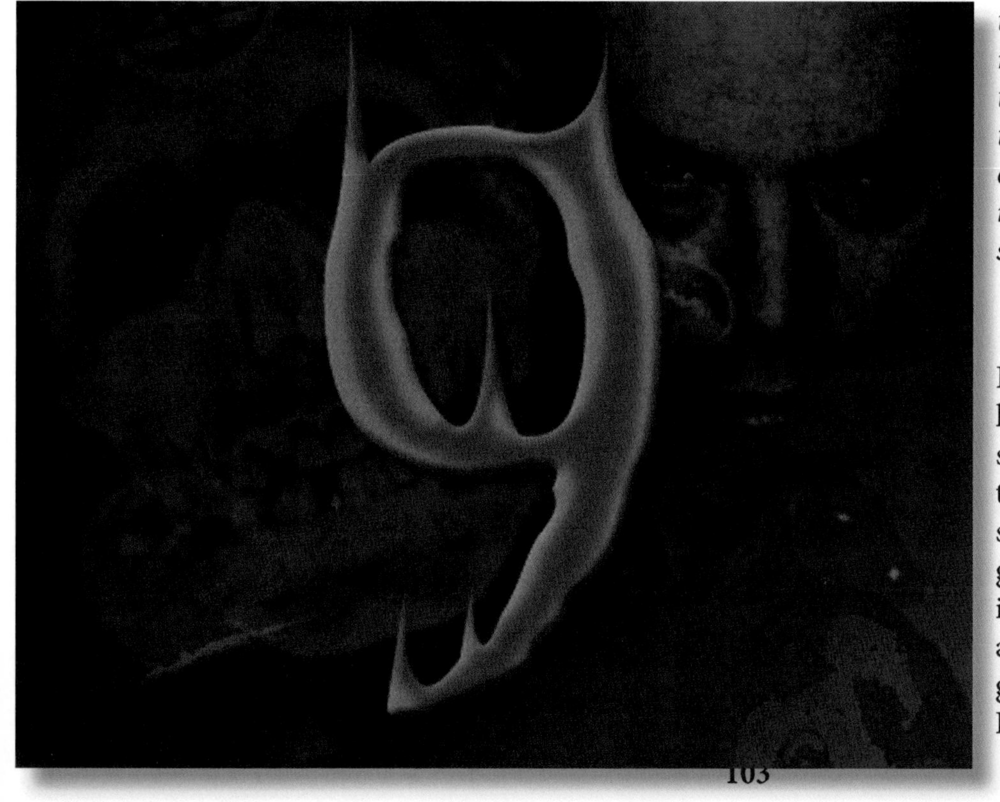

***

11/K

In 1893, at the age of eighteen, Crowley determined to put "Magick" on a sound scientific basis. He explained that he adopted the old English spelling of magick in order to distinguish it from all its counterfeits. "K" is the eleventh letter of several major alphabets. How many corporate logos use the letter "K"? K-mart, Circle K and Kum & Go come to mind.

By this spelling Crowley intended to indicate the peculiar nature of his teachings, which has a special affinity with the number eleven. Because the number ten was regarded by Kabbalists as the stable number of the system of Divine Emanations, or sephirah, the number eleven was considered accursed as it was outside the system. There is an ancient doctrine that all manifestation is in ten aspects or phases. The Kabbalist *Book of Formation* says, *"ten ineffable numerations, ten and not nine, ten and not eleven."* Master Therion (Crowley) therefore adopted eleven as his "Magickal" formula. Eleven stands for all the higher numbers above ten which is why it is the number of sorcery and the number of the battle with demonic elements. In *The Book of the Law,* the goddess Nuit of the Ennead or "The Nine" exclaims: "My number is 11, as all their numbers who are of us." (AL 1:60)

"Thinking about it logically you would expect that nowadays nine and eleven would be the 'unlucky' or 'evil' numbers because they are on either side of our present number of perfection ten. Since 11 is the general number for magic and since 11 is also the number of Daath on the tree of life, the 'non-existent' sephirah and the gateway to the other side."[4]

Western numerology got very confused when we switched from a base 12 counting system to our present base 10 or decimal system. We count in English nine, ten, eleven, twelve, thirteen fourteen and so on, showing that the cycle used to start over again after 12. German and other northern European languages also have separate names for eleven and twelve that do not match the counting system. That is because we used to count from 1 to 12 instead of 1 to 10. Historically, units of time in many civilizations are duodecimal because you can equally divide 12 more times than 10. The Egyptians invented the twenty four hour day and twelve months in a year. The reason that thirteen was considered unlucky was because it was one more than the number of perfection, 12. For this same reason 11 and 13 were considered unlucky because they were on either side of perfection. Any way you slice it, eleven seems to be a sinister number.

The number 11 can also be seen as two 1's, representing duality. The Pythagoreans worshiped the "1" god, which they called the Monad. The Duad, their name for the number 2, was seen as evil because it was the symbol of polarity. It was called "audacity" because it was the first to separate itself from the divine One. This may have been the origin of depicting the devil with two horns. *"The devil, diable, or dual one was the double or twin (cf. doppelganger) of the earliest phases of mythology... the double has long been associated with ideas of misfortune, disaster and death ...Superstitions connected with twins, doubles and simulacra, date from remote antiquity"*[5] Therefore, 9/11 is a compounded number of Satanic value. Going from 9 to 11 on the Tree of Life without the balance of the unity of 10 (Heaven), symbolizes selfish agendas to destroy the lives of many along with the world's sense of security. 9/11 is a Luciferian Symbol of man becoming God.

***

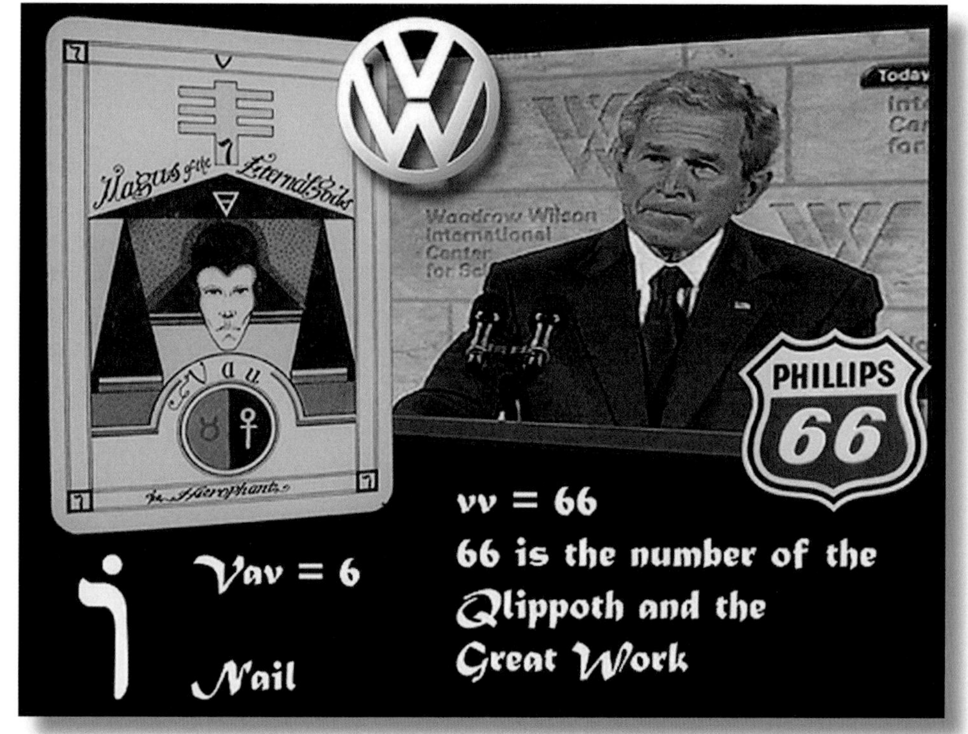

66

In *Star Wars: Revenge of the Sith*, the Emperor Palpatine executes Order 66 or Operation: Knight Fall. These were orders that clone troopers were trained to obey without hesitation. It was the formal beginning of the great Jedi purge and Order 66 signified the rise of the great galactic empire. In Kabbalistic magic, the Qliphoth, or Fallen Angels, are represented by the number 66 or VV. In English, 66 is FX, OX or FF.

Kabbalistic signs and ciphers are being used around us at all times. Hitler's war machine, the Volkswagen, expressed this same meaning with their corporate logo of two V's, and took it a step further. When the two V's are interlaced they form another V making 666. You will also notice that gas station, Phillip's 66's crest has 6 points. It is the same for Highway 66 which was the first military road to the west to gather the gold. If one is privy to this information and couples this with global politics, predictions for world events are possible. This is the path to World War III. First you must defeat the people's hearts, then you can defeat them in war. With knowledge of the codes it became easy to predict who would be forced into office in 2001, the "W."

The letter "W" in Kabbalism is emblematic of the dark side of magick. It actually means excrement. Dealing with the Qlippoth is the psychic equivalent of working with toxic waste and it became our President. The event of forcing "W" into office was the next step in the long-term agenda of the New World Order. People were supposed to know of the voter fraud and link it to Jeb Bush. Now, the people blame the Bush family and lost sight of the true sorcerers creating their reality and they have been properly incensed about losing control of "their" government.

V for Vendetta's contrivance to facilitate vengeful violence from a virtuous vantage verifies the villainy of the Wachowski Brothers. Encoded within Village Roadshow's logo is 66; 6 V's making one, once again, the sign of the fallen ones. Take this a step further and one finds that Village Roadshow's partner, Warner Bros, uses a crest with WB. B is the letter assigned the Magician in the Tarot. In magic, this would transliterate to magicians of the fallen ones. Madonna's use of the VV and OX symbols at the 2012 Super Bowl immediately comes into question. Celebrities too often say that they sold their souls to Satan. Could this be true and can we find the Mark of the Beast?

***

The Mark of the Beast

And he causeth all, both small and great, rich and poor, free and bond, to receive a mark in their right hand, or in their foreheads:
And that no man might buy or sell, save he that had the mark, or the name of the beast, or the number of his name. Revelation 13:16-17

The mark is believed to be a combination of letters and symbols that will be physically and permanently placed on your forehead or right hand. It is an outward, physical symbol, showing that the wearer has chosen to worship the beast and receive him as God. Some believe that the mark is an implanted microchip or RFID. When you are required by law to get the mark of the beast and when you can't buy or sell without it how will you live?

When Crowley died, the leadership succession of the O.T.O. became a controversial and legal issue. Rival groups formed and Kenneth Grant became the head of one of them, called the Typhonian O.T.O. Grant identifies the mark of the beast as the fusion of O and X (the Phallus and the Kteis). "*The Heart of the Sigil of Nodens is identical with the Mark of the Beast… the fusion of O and X which produces the lightning flash.*"[6] Nodens is the "Lightning War God" and the "only named Elder God" of the Great Deep or Abyss in the occult realms of H. P. Lovecraft and is a legend known amongst mystery school initiates concerning the secret abode of Isis.

OXOX is not all hugs and kisses. OX is the Mark of the Beast! Could this explain the X-Men symbol on The Beast or the logo of Russell Brand's *Brand X* on the channel FX!?

So subtle are the satanic gestures that a friction match could easily go unnoticed. Few people know that a friction match is also called a Lucifer. Check your dictionary if you don't believe me. You will also find that Venus is Lucifer, but that is a subject for another time. Phoenix Pictures uses a friction match burning into a phoenix as their corporate logo. Their productions include such films as *Apt Pupil*, a Stephen King story about Nazi worship, and *The 6th Day* with cloning advocate Arnold Schwarzenegger illustrating the dangers of human cloning. Their movie, *Holes*, was produced in conjunction with Walt Disney Pictures and features Sigourney Weaver dominating a child labor camp.

***

FOX

In English the letters that represent 666 are F, O, and X. F being the 6th letter, O the 15th (1+5=6) and X the 24th (2+4=6). You find FOX used everywhere as if the fox were a global icon. We have Firefox, Lucius Fox, 20th Century Fox, Carfox, Fox Broadcasting, Fox Group, and Fox Head clothing to name a few. Britney Spears scrawled 666 on her forehead while attempting suicide in the Promises Addiction Treatment Center screaming she was the Antichrist. She went on to judge *The X Factor* on FOX which has 3 X's as their symbol which, of course, equals 666.

The Fox Film Corporation began their career with princess programming in 1914. Their first film, *The Thief*, is about a woman in love with a man who believes that a

woman's clothes are more important than the woman herself. She puts herself into debt to impress him with a new wardrobe, she carries on with a spending spree and steals from her rich friends to finally be financially rescued by an entirely different man before the man she's conning can find out. This situation has become normal.

Fox then released *Sirens from Hell* followed by *A Fool There Was* about a predatory female vampire starring Theda Barra. In 1908, she appeared in Broadway's *The Devil* and was then cast as the vampire in *A Fool There Was*. This role gave us the word "Vamp" describing a woman who saps the last sexual energies from middle-aged respectable men leaving no more than slaves crawling at her feet. In some of Theda's publicity photos all that remains of her devoured victims are their skeletons before her feet, reminiscent of Kali's blood lust.

20th Century Fox released the film *From Hell* in 2001. The film is based on Alan Moore's graphic novel and seemed to be an advertisement to become a ritual killer for the Freemasons. I was studying the Masonic connections to corporate logos at that time and was surprised as the brazen Masonic compass and square that appeared on the silver

screen. *From Hell* is based on an old conspiracy theory that Jack the Ripper was never punished because of his affiliation with Freemasonry and the Royal Family. In the end, the Masonic agent is lobotomized to conceal the truth. I expected to see "Ripper" or something similar in the news headlines. It wasn't a year later when the word Sniper was on every newsstand.

***

Dumbed Down by the FOX

Fox Film Corporation produces many morally degraded shows such as, *Married with Children*, *That '70s Show*, and *The Simpsons*. Now, I'm not saying they are Satanic but what is Satan but the Adversary? They have destroyed the concept of a nuclear family. *Married with Children* was FOX's first attack on the family morals developing the cast of characters for our "Modern Family" including the ignorant father, the selfish wife, the illicit daughter and the insubordinate son.

We all love Homer Simpson because he is fat, lazy, greedy, stupid and selfish, "just like one of us." More likely translated as: what they want us to be; a rabid consumer, self-absorbed, alcoholic, obsessed with sports, addicted to TV and inept at parenting. Marge dreams of a better life but cannot haul her way out of the rut. Again, she's just like me or you. Bart is the obvious fool, he perpetuates that it's alright to be stupid, as long as you are cool and funny. Don't respect anybody, especially not your parents or your teachers. Lisa is by far the most interesting character. She is intelligent and spiritual. No one appreciates her wisdom and she is bullied constantly. In the episode where she is accepted by the cooler kids, she has to become just like them.

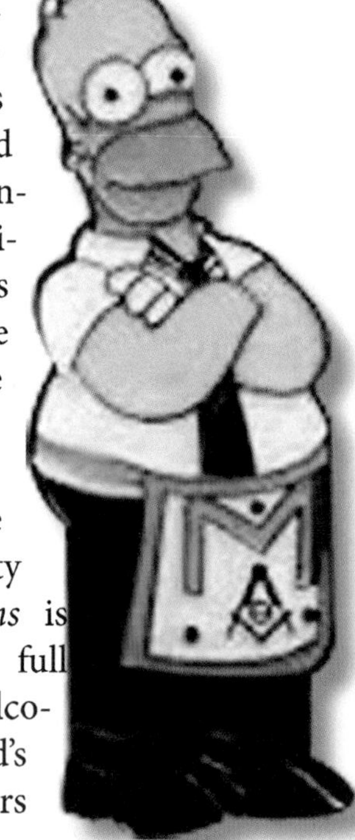

The general society of *The Simpsons* is dysfunctional, full of depressed, alcoholic men; Kid's TV Presenters who are sexual degenerates; stupid, illiterate teachers who hate children; the list goes on and on. Conspiracy theorists have found a bounty inside of Springfield to blog about from Homer's Masonic ritual to 9/11 being displayed in a New York ad in the cartoon prior to 2001. Harry Shearer, the voices of Mr. Burns, Smithers, and Ned Flanders, visited Bohemian Grove and made a satire film about it called *The Teddy Bears' Picnic*, sparking more fears that Bohemian Grove is where the elite go to "cremate their care" and perform rituals, such as burning effigies under a 30ft stone owl.

The communist idol Vladimir Lenin thought that the degradation of the family was the best way to breed people who would be loyal to the government. *"Lenin had said: 'The best revolutionary is a youth devoid of morals.' His word being law in Communist organizations, all members work secretly to make young capitalistic exploitation. The child is encouraged to educate the parents in regard to modern and progressive ideas. They are warned that, for their own good, they must refuse to be dominated or disciplined by their parents. The purpose of this subversive campaign is to destroy the sanctity, and unity, of the home which is the foundation upon which our civilization is founded."*[7]

Television programming works hand in hand with the educational system's "deliberate dumbing down" of our culture. Benjamin Bloom, the psychologist that developed the classification of educational objectives, has stated that the purpose of education is to change the thoughts, actions, and feelings of students. Good teaching, he said, is challenging the student's fixed beliefs and to bring about attitude and value changes through their emotions. Bloom believed he could change a Christian to an atheist in one hour. *hands. They try to change me but they realize they can't. If you gonna be my man understand, I can't be tamed, I can't be blamed, I'm wired a different way. It's set in my DNA. Don't change me. I can't be tamed."*

1991 New York State Teacher of the Year, John Taylor Gatto speculated about his role in education: *"Was it possible, I had been hired not to enlarge children's power, but to diminish it? That seemed crazy, on the face of it, but slowly, I began to realize that the bells and confinement, the crazy sequences, the age-segregation, the lack of privacy, the constant surveillance, and all the rest of the national curriculum of schooling were designed exactly as if someone had set out to prevent children from learning how to think, and act, to coax them into addiction and dependent behavior."*[8]

***

people of both sexes anti-social and immoral. Children up to teen-age are taught to rebel against the discipline of the home. Parents are represented to their children as old-fashioned. Parental authority is scoffed at. The subverters argue that parents have lied to their children since they were old enough to listen, regarding Santa Claus and where babies come from. The subversives claim parents are the victims of reactionary teachings and

Using psychodrama, the teachers can instill cultural beliefs such as "The Elite vs. The Poor." Hannah Montana programming can be seen to do the same as she represents "The Best of Both Worlds" being the high status Hannah Montana but also, the lowly Miley Stewart. It must be mentioned that in her "coming out" video as Miley Cyrus, she is shown in a cage as a black angel singing, *"I go through guys like money flyin' out the*

"I fully believe the animated picture will emerge as one of the greatest mediums, not only of entertainment but also of education."
—Walt Disney

Disney/Nazi Propaganda

Fox Head clothing designs sports gear and apparel with a fox that is often shown burning or with lightning bolts and skulls. Have you ever seen a Nazi uniform? The Nazis were fascist and according to *Walt Disney: On the Frontlines,* Walt's techniques taught the Reich Minister of Propaganda in Nazi Germany a thing or two. *"Walt and his staff knew how to present serious material in a palatable form. A perfect example is Education for Death which bears the subtitle, The Making of a Nazi. Hitler's propaganda minister Joseph Goebbels admired the quality of Walt Disney's animation and was inspired to use the same medium to generate some propaganda of his own."*[9]

As one of Adolf Hitler's closest associates and most devout followers, Joseph Goebbels was appointed chancellor and Minister of Enlightenment and Propaganda. He held this post until 1945. Goebbels was a notorious womanizer and his wife wanted to divorce him after one liaison too many. Hitler refused to give his permission for the divorce as he had spent much time cultivating the importance of family values to the German public much like Walt Disney was doing in America for the Motion Picture Alliance for the Preservation of American Ideals. *"The essence of propaganda consists in winning people over to an idea so sincerely, so vitally, that in the end they succumb to it utterly and can never again escape from it."*--Geobbels

Hitler and Goebbels knew the power of controlling what people thought. They realized early on that by combining staged events with a charged narration, audiences could be swayed beyond reason through their emotions. By producing pro-Nazi documentaries and hosting enormous rallies they turned the German people into beings who, Goebbels stated would, "obey a law they did not even know but which they could recite in their dreams." Color film, at this time, was not considered a viable source of political programming but, Goebbels had seen the success of Donald Duck's campaign to get Americans to pay their taxes and he recognized the future.

Nazis, such as Wernher von Braun, would later join the Disney forces but some were not so lucky. As the war ended, Goebbels stayed with Hitler in his bunker, friends to the end. In his diary, he blamed the defeat of Germany, not on Hitler, but on the German people. On May 1, 1945, he gave poison to his six children and then shot his wife and then himself. In Nazi fascism, the State controlled the corporations. In America, the opposite is true.

***

"Three slain in Batman-inspired porn theater shoot out. Details to follow..."

Fantasy?

In the 1986 comic book, *The Dark Knight Returns*, a lone gunman with reddish orange hair strolls into a crowded theater and starts shooting, killing 3 people. His motive stemmed from his hatred for heavy metal music and pornography. Author, Frank Miller had changed the landscape of superhero comic books forever. Before *The Dark Knight Returns*, dark, gritty protagonists fighting in an ultra-violent world were the exception, not the rule. This new Batman took on a seriousness not shown in the campy 60's televi-

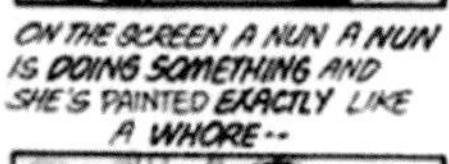

sion series and the drama of the D.C. Universe was intensifying.

Superman, the epitome of American values, has sold his soul to the government, and the world seems to cry out for a hero who will do something. In Miller's stark world, doing "something" means taking the law into your own hands and fighting back, something Batman is eager to do. As a companion piece to *The Dark Knight Returns*, Batman joins forces with the character Spawn, while searching for a villain that has been kidnapping and decapitating the homeless for use in robots. Spawn/Batman is a 1994 one-shot comic book written by Frank Miller with art by Todd McFarlane and published jointly by DC Comics and Image Comics. Spawn spends his time agitated by the demon Violator and his villains include pedophiles and rapists. Spawn's noted abilities include shapeshifting, necroplasmic energy blasts and resurrection.

Comic books have been labeled as a major source of societal troubles since the 1950's. Psychiatrist, Frederick Wertham's book, *Seduction of the Innocent,* was based on his thesis that comic books are a danger to children. His criticism of comics inspired a U.S. Congressional inquiry into the industry and lead to the beginning of the Comics Code Authority, which banned overly violent and horrific comics, leaving only code-approved "safe" super hero books available to the general public for almost 50 years. Wertham's book also inspired parents to confiscate their children's comic book collections, and even lead to mass comic book burnings in some communities. What are children learning from these comic book examples? Could they cause adverse behavior in young adults? It seems so, but there is something much more sinister going on.

Did you know that in the 1966 television series of Batman, Bruce Wayne's great grandfather was a founding member of Skull and Bones? "Tapped for it!? Sir, he founded Skull and Bones!" said Aunt Harriet Cooper in episode 33. *The Dark Knight Rises* 2012 movie is not to be confused with the 1986 comic, *The Dark Knight Returns. The Dark Knight Rises* is based on a Batman series known as Knightfall which came out in the late 90's and set the stage to have a Fallen Angel take over as the Batman. In 1993, Bruce Wayne had his back broken by Bane in Knightfall #11 and the suit needed a new Batman. The mantle was given to a bloodthirsty, vengeful character named, Azrael. Beyond being Gargamel's cat on the Smurfs, Azrael is known as the Angel of Death in the Book of Enoch. It is written that he will be the last to die, recording and erasing constantly the names of men at birth and death in a large book. Of the Fallen Angels that took wives in Genesis, Azrael is said to have taught mankind the art of war and fashion. The comic book character Azrael sees visions of his dead father, who had programmed him at birth to be a deadly weapon. When Batman began using lethal force to apprehend villains, the new vigilante's tactics of ripping out criminal's spines disturbed many readers. Soon Bruce Wayne had to return to duel Azrael for rights to the Bat. To rehabilitate his skills, Bruce asks the famed as-

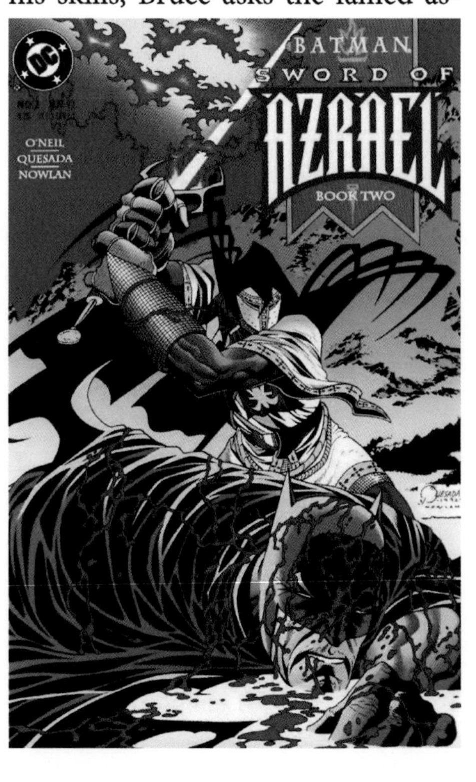

sassin Lady Shiva to retrain him. She continued to pit him against martial artists only declaring him worthy when he pretended to break his vow never to kill.

Superman or Kal-El is very similar to the Nephilim or the Sons of God in Genesis. Kal-El is Hebrew, which makes sense since Siegel and Shuster, the creators of Superman, were Jewish. It can be interpreted to mean either "all of God" or "the voice of God," depending on what vowels you use. Greek and Norse mythology have been invoked to show that Superman resembles a god who comes to earth and walks among men in mortal guise. Superman screenwriter, David Newman, sees more exalted implications in the legend: *"It begins with a father who lives up in heaven, who says, 'I will send my only son to save earth.' The son takes on the guise of a man but is not a man. The religious overtones are so clear."*

From 1992 to 1993 we witnessed the death and resurrection of Superman that ended with The Reign of Supermen. Of the dignitaries to visit Superman's funeral in Metropolis were Bill and Hillary

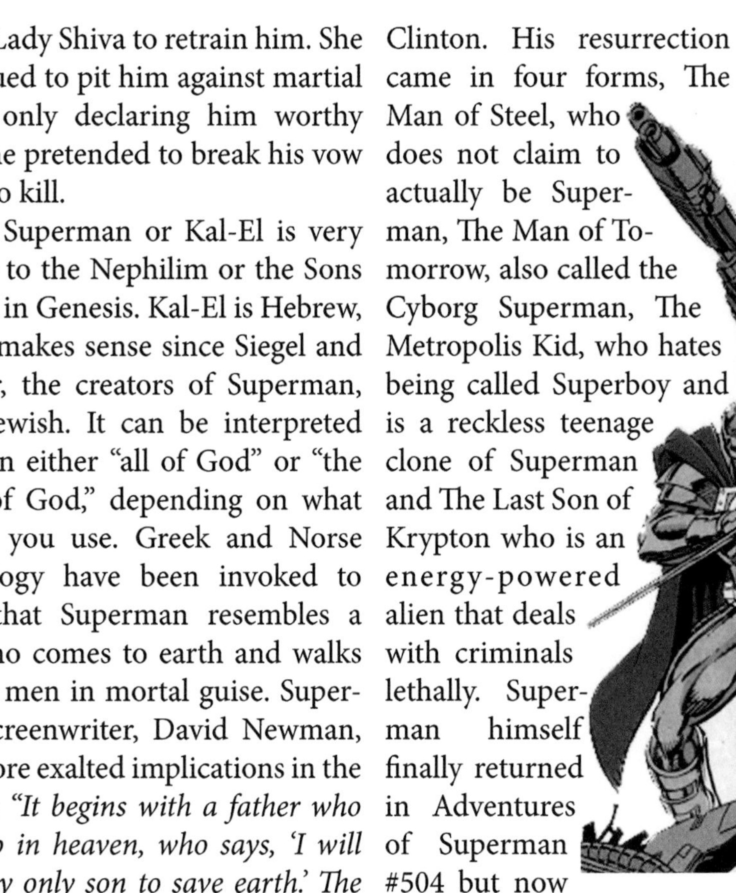

Clinton. His resurrection came in four forms, The Man of Steel, who does not claim to actually be Superman, The Man of Tomorrow, also called the Cyborg Superman, The Metropolis Kid, who hates being called Superboy and is a reckless teenage clone of Superman and The Last Son of Krypton who is an energy-powered alien that deals with criminals lethally. Superman himself finally returned in Adventures of Superman #504 but now dressed in black without the cape and sporting guns on his hips. He is the military's Superman now. Kal-El had lost his appeal with the war gaming generation and most of their attention went to the new super hero, Spawn or Hell Spawn; a Superman for the vengeful Age of Horus.

Reality?

On July 20, 2012, James Holmes dyed his hair red, dressed all in black wearing a ballistic helmet, a tactical ballistic vest, ballistic leggings, a throat protector, a groin protector, a gas mask and tactical gloves, armed with an AR-15 assault rifle, a Remington 870 shotgun, and two Glock handguns, and headed into the midnight showing of the new Batman movie, *The Dark Knight Rises.*

The theater was crowded with people and it is reported that Holmes tossed tear gas canisters and then opened fire on the unsuspecting audience. Most of them thought that it was all part of the show. They had just seen gangsters pop out of the movie screen and open fire on them in the preview for the movie, *Gangster Squad*. When Holmes was finished, 12 people lay dead and 59 others were wounded. Police Commissioner Ray Kelly said: "It clearly looks like a deranged individual. He had his hair painted red. He said he was 'The Joker', obviously the enemy of Batman."

Conflicting reports state that Holmes was a "Lone Nut Killer." The problem is that an eyewitness describes a man with a goatee in the front row of the theater that received a call on his cell phone and opened the theater emergency door. Moments later, Holmes dressed similar to the character Bane, came in the back door and reportedly opened fire with an AR-15 assault weapon. He is said to have fired hundreds of rounds meaning he would have had to stand there and change clips around six to ten times.

After the massacre, Holmes calmly told detectives he had taken 100mg of the prescription painkill-

er Vicodin, and identified himself as "The Joker." The same drug was found in the system of actor Heath Ledger when he died of an accidental overdose of prescription drugs in 2008. Ledger played The Joker in the previous Batman film *The Dark Knight*. There are many odd and ritualistic facts surrounding the death of Heath Ledger after he played the disturbed character, a role that reportedly took a toll on his health.

In a not-very-publicized article from the Denver Westword, prisoner Steve Unruh, interviewed at the jail, claims that Holmes told him that he was programmed to kill by an "evil therapist." He added that Holmes said, "he felt like he was in a video game" during the shooting and that "he wasn't on his meds" and "nobody would help him." "They're going to try to discredit my story," Unruh said. "But I was able to have a four-hour talk with him. I talked him out of suicide. When he got out to his car, he wasn't programmed no more," Unruh says. "It sounded kind of crazy. He was trying to run it by me, basically."

James Holmes was pursuing a neuroscience doctoral program at the University of Colorado's Anschutz Medical Campus. Drew Griffin of the Special Investigations Unit claims that he "was hardly the loner everybody's describing. He was one of the smartest kids in the class." University spokeswoman Jacque Montgomery said Holmes enrolled a year ago and was in the process of withdrawing at the time of the shootings. He was an honor student and a member of the Golden Key Honour Society along with Ronald Reagan and Bill Clinton. He was also reportedly addicted to the videogame Guitar Hero.

Holmes had been working on a theory of the "subjective experience" which is what takes place inside the mind as opposed to the external world. Video footage of Holmes was taken at Miramar College in San Diego showing him explaining that "temporal illusions" are "an illusion that allows you to change the past." He also worked with Mars Candy and DARPA to develop a "magic" chocolate bar to keep troops going under fatigue. In 2006, Holmes worked as a researcher at the Salk Institute for Biological studies, which specializes in diseases, neuroscience and behavior. Wolf Blitzer of CNN said, "He may have been relatively normal, at least until he arrived in Colorado…It seems to be centered around this elite neuroscience he was involved with."

At the theater massacre scene, two gas masks were found and reports from eyewitnesses said that gas canisters came from two different directions. Holmes did not seem to be working alone. The first report of suspects was of two men fleeing the theatre, both wearing backpacks. There were reports of three people dragging an unknown individual into a non-descript vehicle and speeding off.

Holmes immediately warned the arresting officers of the explosive booby-traps he had set up in his apartment. This is as strange as the fact that he was waiting at his car to be arrested. He left techno music blaring in his apartment, much like the shooter of the 1986 Batman

comic. His neighbors had stopped by to try and silence the noise and fortunately walked away. Aurora Police Chief Dan Oates said Holmes' apartment was booby-trapped with a 'sophisticated' maze of flammable devices. It could take hours or days for authorities to disarm it. Oates said the apartment appears to be filled with "trip wires, jars full of ammunition, jars full of liquid and things that look like mortar rounds. I personally have never seen anything like what the pictures show us is in there."

On the same day, just 15 miles away, the tragedy that played out in the Aurora movie theater was ironically paralleled as a classroom learning experience at the Rocky Vista University College in the town of Parker. One of the scenarios being used to train the students was how to respond if a shooter fires at people in a movie theater and uses explosives. "The irony is amazing, just amazing," said Rocky Vista Dean, Dr. Bruce Dubin.

It was said that this was the worst mass shooting in the U.S. since the Nov. 5, 2009, attack at Fort Hood, Texas, where an Army psychiatrist was charged with killing 13 soldiers and civilians and wounding more than two dozen others. It was also one the deadliest since the Columbine High School massacre on April 20, 1999, when two students opened fire in the Denver suburb of Littleton, killing 12 classmates and a teacher and wounding 26 others before killing themselves. Columbine High School is about 12 miles from the theater in Aurora. Leonardo DiCaprio acted out the events of Columbine in a film called The *Basketball Diaries* four years before it happened. In the years following the infamous school shooting incident at Columbine, law enforcement agencies and local school districts across America developed plans and protocols to safeguard against and respond to similar acts of school violence.

***

Putting Sandy Hook on the Map

Sandy Hook is marked as a possible terrorist target on the *Dark Knight Rises*' promotional map of Gotham City. Warner Brothers curiously sent out promo kits containing a map vividly depicting super-villain Bane's strike zones and "Sandy Hook" is listed as "Strike Zone #1." In the movie, Sandy Hook is the place Bane begins his crusade to take control of Gotham City by destroying Gotham stadium. In reality, it seems Sandy Hook is the staging ground for ending the right to bear arms.

On December 14, 2012, Adam Lanza allegedly shot his mother to death at the home they shared, then drove to Sandy Hook Elementary School in her car wearing a black outfit with a mask and a bulletproof vest carrying several hundred rounds of ammunition, a Bushmaster AR-15 rifle and two or possibly four handguns. He is said to have forced his way in by shooting through a steel-reinforced door and opened fire on the nurse and principal approaching him and then killed 20 children and four other adults be-

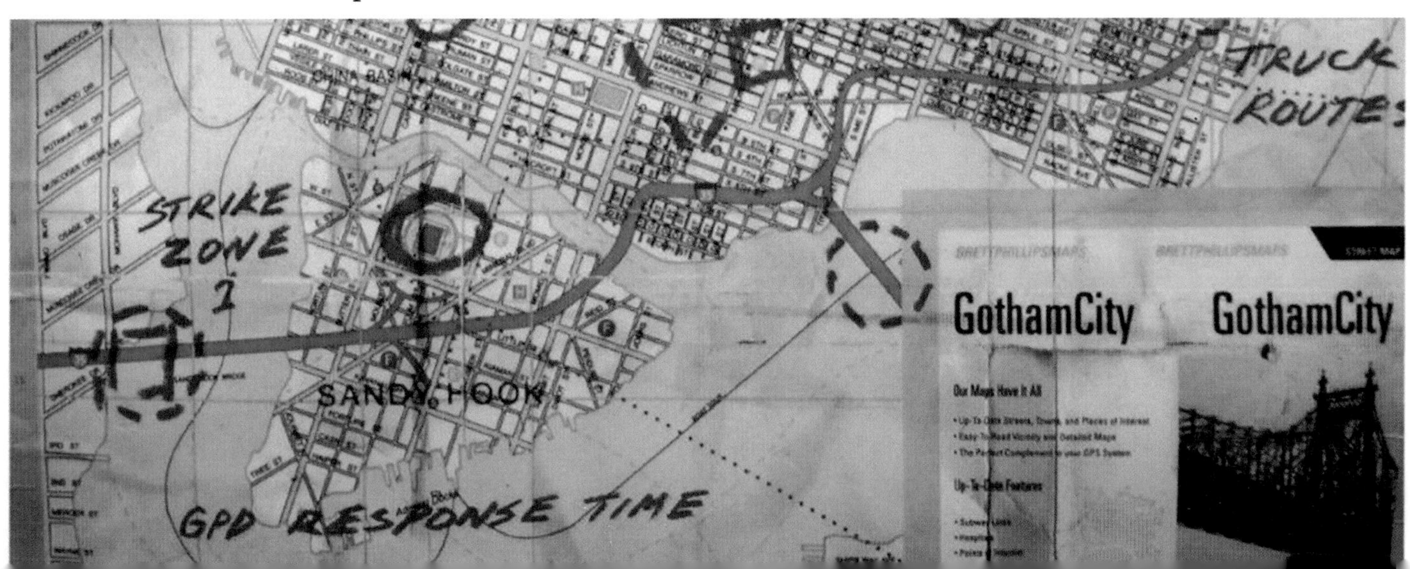

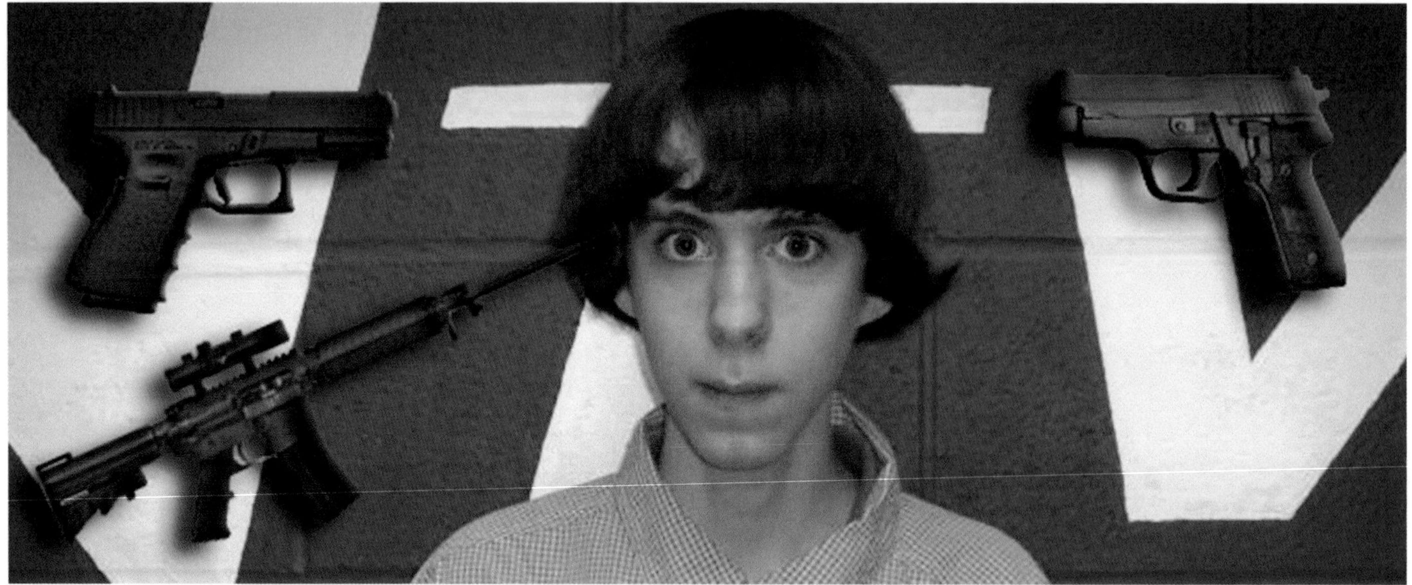

fore taking his own life. Authorities said that Lanza used a high-power rifle to kill but it seems he took his own life with a pistol. Police were reportedly on the scene "instantaneously," according to Connecticut State Police Commander, Lt. Vance. Perhaps, this is because nineteen miles from Sandy Hook Elementary School, at the exact time of the shooting, FEMA was conducting a drill: L-366 Planning for the Needs of Children in Disasters. Never waste a crisis…

President Obama stated that, "We're going to have to come together and take meaningful action to prevent more tragedies like this, regardless of the politics" which gladdened proponents of stricter gun laws. Appearing on The O'Reilly Factor, Fox News correspondent, Geraldo Rivera, voiced his own solution: "I want an armed cop at every school."

Unimaginable is a word that was used to describe the massacre at Sandy Hook countless times, but imagine is exactly what the horrified audience was left to do. With so many inaccuracies and story changes being reported, it was up to the public to determine what actually happened the day of the "parents' worst nightmare." Sandy Hook Principal, Dawn Hochsprung, told the *Newtown Bee* that "a masked man entered the school with a rifle and started shooting." Interesting testimony given that Dawn Hochsprung was reported to be the first victim.

It seems impossible that a young man described as having Asperger's Syndrome and weighing 120 lbs. could carry all of this expensive equipment much less be able to take down a reinforced door with safety glass. The children interviewed said it sounded like someone was kicking a door or that a janitor had dropped something. Some have suggested that the event never occurred. Professor James Tracy of Florida Atlantic University, claims trained "crisis actors" may have been employed by President Obama's administration to get public opinion behind gun control laws. After the event, President Obama signed 23 executive orders designed to address the problem of gun violence in America.

Much like Holmes, Lanza is said to have been carrying a Glock, a Sig Sauer, and a Bushmaster AR-15 or .223 semi-automatic rifle which were reported to be his mother's. Nancy Lanza has since been painted as a "survivalist" who loved firearms, taught her sons how to shoot and was stockpiling because she was worried about economic collapse. The only weapon missing from Holmes' list is the Remington 870 shotgun. A shotgun was later found in the suspect vehicle's trunk at Sandy Hook. The suspect vehicle seemed to be owned by Christopher Rodia, a man with a penchant for stealing copper wire

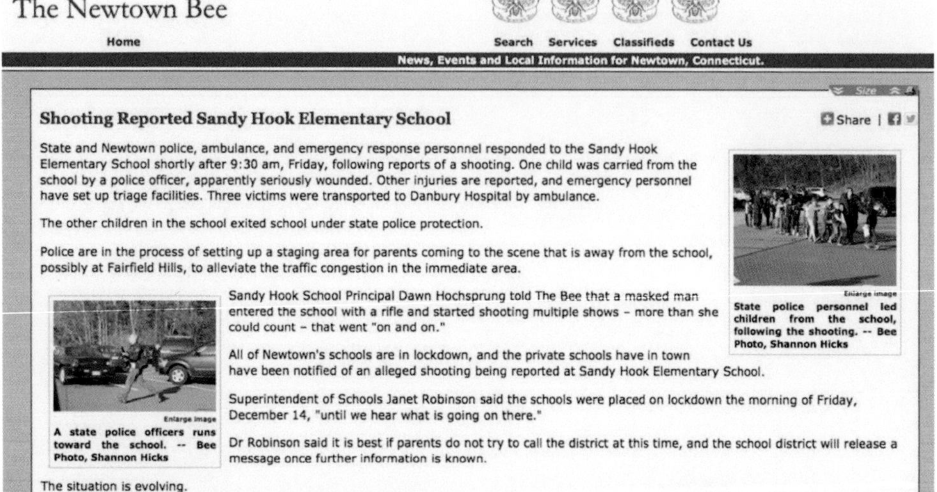

The Newtown Bee

Home Search Services Classifieds Contact Us

News, Events and Local Information for Newtown, Connecticut.

Shooting Reported Sandy Hook Elementary School

Share

State and Newtown police, ambulance, and emergency response personnel responded to the Sandy Hook Elementary School shortly after 9:30 am, Friday, following reports of a shooting. One child was carried from the school by a police officer, apparently seriously wounded. Other injuries are reported, and emergency personnel have set up triage facilities. Three victims were transported to Danbury Hospital by ambulance.

The other children in the school exited school under state police protection.

Police are in the process of setting up a staging area for parents coming to the scene that is away from the school, possibly at Fairfield Hills, to alleviate the traffic congestion in the immediate area.

Enlarge image

State police personnel led children from the school, following the shooting. -- Bee Photo, Shannon Hicks

Sandy Hook School Principal Dawn Hochsprung told The Bee that a masked man entered the school with a rifle and started shooting multiple shows – more than she could count – that went "on and on."

All of Newtown's schools are in lockdown, and the private schools have in town have been notified of an alleged shooting being reported at Sandy Hook Elementary School.

Enlarge image

A state police officers runs toward the school. -- Bee Photo, Shannon Hicks

Superintendent of Schools Janet Robinson said the schools were placed on lockdown the morning of Friday, December 14, "until we hear what is going on there."

Dr Robinson said it is best if parents do not try to call the district at this time, and the school district will release a message once further information is known.

The situation is evolving.

and dealing drugs and not Adam Lanza. Rodia was not at the scene, but his car was.

Authorities said Adam had no criminal history, and it was not clear whether he had a job. A law enforcement official who spoke on condition of anonymity because he was not authorized to discuss the matter publicly said Lanza was believed to have suffered from a personality disorder. They found no note or manifesto from Lanza of the sort they have come to expect after rampages such as the Virginia Tech shooting in 2007 that left 33 people dead. Lanza's computer hard drives were found destroyed.

Besides anonymous 'law enforcement officials' telling the media that Adam Lanza was a former pupil at the school, they also said his mother was currently a teacher there, that she was found among the dead and that her son had specifically sought out her classroom first. But when it emerged that teaching staff at the school had never heard of a Nancy Lanza, it was suggested that she was a substitute teacher whose name therefore might not appear on staff lists. It is now known that Nancy had no connection with the school. Adam was homeschooled and at age 16 he enrolled at Western Connecticut State University.

When the news stories began, Ryan Lanza was reported as the shooter. For six hours the news provided statements that they had found Ryan's identification. It is openly admitted that there is no physical evidence that Adam Lanza even existed after 2009. No drivers' license, no banking statements, nothing. His brother, living in New Jersey, said he had not seen Adam in three years.

It was reported that Adam had arrived at his former elementary school to have an altercation with the staff the day before the shooting. Investigators said they believe Adam Lanza attended Sandy Hook many years ago, but they had no explanation for why he went on a rampage. Serious Internet researchers have found a SSDI or Social Security Death Index from New Hampshire for Adam Lanza dated December 13th, the day before the shooting! Nancy Lanza's Social Security Death Index was found as well, dated for the day of the shooting, December 14th, but also registered to New Hampshire. According to Headline News, Nancy Lanza had left Adam home alone with an arsenal of weapons in the $1.4 million mansion while she went on mini-breaks to Bretton Woods in New Hampshire. Adam Lanza did not appear in his mother's obituary.

Nancy Lanza: Social Security Death Index (SSDI) Death Record

Name:	Nancy Lanza
State of Issue:	New Hampshire
Date of Birth:	Tuesday September 06, 1960
Date of Death:	Friday December 14, 2012
Est. Age at Death:	52 years, 3 months, 8 days
Confirmation:	Proven

Continue Discovering Your Family's Past

Use these links to continue exploring the **Lanza** family history:

- **Lanza** family Recent Obituaries (1977–Today)

Adam P. Lanza: Social Security Death Index (SSDI) Death Record

Name:	Adam P. Lanza
State of Issue:	New Hampshire
Date of Birth:	Wednesday April 22, 1992
Date of Death:	Thursday December 13, 2012
Est. Age at Death:	20 years, 7 months, 21 days
Confirmation:	Proven

Continue Discovering Your Family's Past

Use these links to continue exploring the **Lanza** family history:

- **Lanza** family Recent Obituaries (1977–Today)
- **Lanza** family Historical Obituaries (1704–1999)
- **Lanza** family in Newspaper Archives (1690–2010)
- Search all of GenealogyBank for the **Lanza** family

The scene outside Sandy Hook Elementary School can only be imagined. Yes, imagine a stage set with a doughnut cart and all the actors milling about. From the news helicopter footage not one child is seen leaving the elementary school. Families were told that the bodies of their children would have to remain in the school overnight. The parents were told, "it's over, just go home." Later reports stated that the bodies were "spirited away" in the night. The ambulances were sequestered away at the fire station and the road to the school was completely blocked by random vehicles. No parents were shown their child; they were only shown pictures taken by the coroner's team. There were no scenes like Columbine of children running out in fear. From the vantage of the helicopter, the scene looked like an over enthusiastic bake sale...without parents or children.

When the news of the incident first broke, there were so many news helicopters flying above the school that they were lucky they didn't have to deal with an aircraft accident as well. An "off-duty tactical squad police officer from another town" is shown running into the woods behind the school. As he was dragged past the families of the victims he claimed, "I didn't do it!" This fleeing suspect, wearing camouflage gear, a bulletproof vest and armed with four guns, has since disappeared from media coverage.

Robbie Parker interviewed after tragedy.

Emilie Parker Photoshopped in family portrait.

Perhaps most astonishing is that this suspect arrested in the woods was named in an Associated Press report as 24-year-old Ryan Lanza. This was despite the fact that Ryan had already been named as the deceased suspect inside the school, lying next to two handguns. Law enforcement officials were placing both Lanza brothers at the scene of the shooting. Only when Ryan began posting, "Hi, I'm alive, I didn't do it, and I live and work down here in New Jersey!" on Facebook, did the story change to a "Lone Nut Killer" scenario.

"I looked down toward the end of my lawn and I saw six children. I thought that was so peculiar because they were sitting in kind of a semi-circle, and they looked okay. Then I saw a man talking very loudly and harshly to them saying, 'It's gonna be okay! It's gonna be okay!' and I thought he was talking in a very loud manner and I thought it's part of a skit or a play and the kids are just pretending."
—Gene Rosen

What the heck is a crisis actor?

Characters like Gene Rosen began to pop up seemingly straight from the actor's guild. Rosen can be seen rehearsing his lines and gave many incredible accounts of disappearing bus drivers and stuffed animals. His story makes no sense. Either an incompetent school bus driver dropped a load of traumatized children at his door without a word of why and left them to enter this stranger's home to sit and play with a pile of stuffed animals and his dog for an half hour; or an angry man left them at his doorstep depending on which news report you watched. Rosen later stated that the bus driver came into his home with the children while they phoned parents and attempted to understand what had happened to these children.

The father of victim Emilie Parker, Robbie Parker, drew much fervor for what seemed to be crisis acting. As he approached the news camera, he seemed to get into character coming from a smiling friendly approach to hyperventilating to appear disturbed before he talked about the loss of his daughter. Actors use this technique often. Internet aficionados quickly discerned

Is this Emilie with the President after the shooting?

that the Parker family portraits had Emilie Photoshopped into them and were certainly amazed when Emilie seemed to be shown with Barack Obama after the shooting. Was that Emilie's little sister in the same dress? The questions have not ended.

The Internet shows that funding websites for the tragedy began three days before the incident. Many of the people interviewed appear to be crisis actors. Grieving parents can be seen laughing and joking before getting into character for the news. It is as if Newtown, Connecticut is a make believe town! Suzanne Collins, author of *The Hunger Games* lives there, The Church of Satan has a P.O. Box there, and the Prop Master that put Sandy Hook on the map in Batman *The Dark Knight Rises* lived and died there. Scott Getzinger, the property master that provided the props died in a head-on collision with another vehicle in Newtown, Connecticut four months before *The Dark Knight Rises* opened. State police initially characterized his injuries as non-life threatening.

In *The Dark Knight Rises*, Bane uses an algorithm to track the Gotham elite's spending, leading him to Bruce Wayne and he uses this information to start a class war. The father of Aurora Colorado movie theater shooter, Dr. Robert Holmes, is the lead scientist for the credit score company FICO and worked with DARPA to develop "Cortronic Neural Networks" that enables machines to translate aural and visual stimuli and simulate human thinking. He is the creator of one of the most sophisticated computer algorithms ever developed, a predictive system of credit and banking fraud models and reports say he was scheduled to testify in the largest banking scandal in U.S. history, the LIBOR Scandal.

Sixteen international banks have been implicated in the manipulation of trillions of dollars rigging contracts with The London Interbank Offered Rate or LIBOR which is the average interest rate at which banks can borrow from each other. Peter Lanza, father of Adam Lanza, is a VP and Tax Director at GE Financial and worked with FICO. Although there is no evidence to suggest that he was scheduled to testify for the Securities and Exchange Commission, it is significant that top GE Capital executives have been arrested as part of the LIBOR investigation.

The 1997 movie, *Wag the Dog*, reveals a hidden truth behind tragedies and the media. The movie is based on a book called *American Hero*. Author, Larry Beinhart, found the presentation and pageantry of the Gulf War highly suspicious and had serious doubts about the validity of the media coverage of the war. Just as *Wag the Dog* was released, which featured the President involved in a scandal with an underage girl, reports began to break about President Clinton's affair with Monica Lewinsky. The main premise of the movie was about creating a war in the press. This notion is not as unusual as one might think, nor is the idea that they would hire Hollywood to do it. Publisher William Randolf Hearst virtually created the Spanish American War for public consumption. "You supply the photographs, I'll supply the war," he told reporters when he headlined the rumor of the Spanish sabotaging American ships in Havana harbor.

The line between news and propaganda has always been a thin one. During WWI the US government hired D.W. Griffith to "document" the war. He was the only filmmaker allowed on the front lines and staged several battle sequences to bring back to America as "news reels" to help the war effort. During WWII, Frank Capra headed a team of Hollywood directors for the government to produce a propaganda series called "Why We Fight."

In *Wag the Dog*, the newsmakers rely on a disenchanted public. They know if they can just entertain people, they can distract them from actual events. They know that the public will never explore the realities because they rely on a press focused on ratings and shock value. Although the evidence is still coming in for the Sandy Hook shooting, legislators of gun control and the President have not wasted any time passing executive orders calling for gun confiscation.

***

The Age of the Dark Hero

Could a seemingly innocent thing such as a comic book have a massive geo-political impact and could it also be part of a highly detailed agenda? According to the practice of Sigil Magic, it absolutely could. The term sigil refers to occult signs which represent various angels and demons which the magician might summon. The magical training books called grimoires often listed pages of such sigils. A particularly well-known list is in *The Lesser Key of Solomon*, in which the sigils of the seventy-two princes of the hierarchy of hell are given for the magician's use.

The concept was modernly

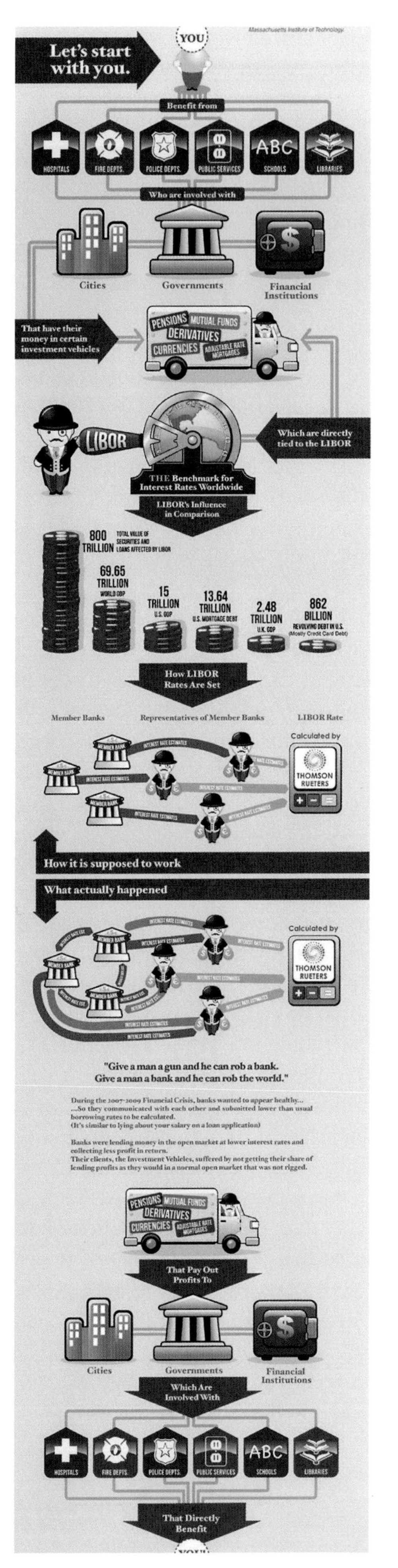

popularized by Austin O. Spare, who published a method by which the words of a statement of intent are reduced into an abstract design; the sigil is then charged with the will of the creator. This technique, now known as sigilization, has become a core element of chaos magic. Sigils are used for spells as well as for the creation of thought-forms. With traditional sigils, creators made use of lore passed down from generations or from books. Today, a corporate logo is an example of a magical sigil; a symbol whose meaning is only fully known by the creator. The word logo comes from the Greek 'logos' meaning 'word', which is also synonymous with God in the book of John and this expression is the keynote and theme of the entire gospel. Today, corporate logos have become omnipresent, replacing the feeling of being surrounded by God into being inundated with occult symbols, and the intent behind them, we know nothing about.

Magician, Grant Morrison wrote his comic book series, *The Invisibles*, as an attempt to explain an alien abduction experience he had in Kathmandu in 1994. The series is what he calls a "hypersigil" which is an extended work of art with magical meaning and charged with willpower; created using the process of sigilization. He found that through his writing he could make things happen in reality. He based the main character on himself and he discovered that if he put his hero through trials, he would experience those same trials in his own reality. Characters that he made up seemed to manifest in real personalities coming into his life.

***

"It is time for their world to be destroyed. It is time for a new age, the Age of Horus. It is time for a new standard, a new canvas, and a new artist. We must forget this wasted generation and amputate it before the mind rots away with it. Paint it, record it, write it down before they kill you with their slow poisonous stupidity. Make yourself heard. This Internet is your middle finger to the universe, don't let them break it."

--Marilyn Manson

Vengeful Justice

The Age of Horus is the New Aeon proclaimed by Aleister Crowley beginning in 1904 when *The Book of the Law* was transcribed and ending in 3904. Its principle definition comes from the belief in the rulership of three gods, Isis, Osiris and Horus, whose influences determine the fate of the world. *"This 'God,' Horus, has a technical title: Heru-Ra-Ha, a combination of twin gods, Ra-Hoor-Khuit and Hoor-Paar-Kraat. The meaning of this doctrine must be studied in 'Magick.' (He is symbolized as a Hawk-Headed God enthroned.)"*[10] Within Crowley's Thelemite religion, each of these aeons is believed to be characterized by their own specific magical formula, the use of which is very important and Horus is a god of war.

"Everywhere his (Horus) *government is taking root. Observe for yourselves the decay of the sense of sin, the growth of innocence and irresponsibility, the strange modifications of the reproductive instinct with a tendency to become bi-sexual or epicene, the childlike confidence in progress combined with nightmare fear of catastrophe, against which we are yet half unwilling to take precautions. Consider the popularity of the cinema, the wireless, the football pools and guessing competitions, all devices for soothing fractious infants, no seed of purpose in them. Consider sport, the babyish enthusiasms and rages which it excites, whole nations disturbed by disputes between boys. Consider war, the atrocities which occur daily and leave us unmoved and hardly worried. We are children."*[11]

Horus is the spirit of vengeful justice. Clive Barker was one of the first to produce a role reversal from monster to hero. In his book,

Cabal, a group of monsters known as "Nightbreed" are hiding in a place called Midian from the evil humans who only wish to do them harm. It is a tale of a man set up as a serial killer by an evil psychiatrist who seeks sanctuary with the monsters and the hero believes that he is one. The monsters know better, but they had a prophecy. Their god Baphomet was to bring judgment and after his resurrection, the human visitor would bring the destruction of their world. The judgment came in the form of human police officers rampaging Midian to burn it and its inhabitants to the ground. The Nightbreed took the remaining pieces of Baphomet and searched for a new home.

"Be yourself, be unique, be a monster!" is now a slogan for a girl's doll toy line known as Monster High. Fans of Lady Gaga call themselves "little monsters" and the monsters keep coming. The character, Hell Spawn, who is sent back to earth by Beezlebub to replenish Hell's army, changed the comic book world forever. Todd MaFarlane's break with Marvel lead the new independent comic, Image, to be rated by Wizard Magazine as No.1 in the list of events that rocked the comic industry. McFarlane had broken the bounds of the comic masters such as DC and Marvel and brought many of the best artists with him.

"HE ARRIVES, SILENT ASTRIDE HIS MASSIVE STEED, A DARK HERO WITH GRIM PURPOSE, A MAN OF WONDERS IN AN AGE OF MIRACLES."
-- Medieval Spawn Toy

The tale of Spawn is one of love lost and seeking longevity through pledging allegiance to the Dark One. Malebolgia, a name derived from Dante's *Inferno*, is Spawn's former master and one of the major Lords of Hell. He is one of Hell's many rulers, a being from the "Eighth Circle of Hell" who has been around for approximately 70,000 years, forming an army in his war against Heaven and God.

Blood-soaked scenes splatter the covers and pages of Spawn. Todd Toys pronounced themselves appropriate for ages 4 and up! The character, Hell Spawn, was created out of a CIA assassin that made a deal with the Devil to see his wife one more time. His human character, Al Simmons, was murdered by his own forces in Operation Knightstrike. Now known as Spawn, Al's first few adventures are anti-hero in nature: he takes down street gangs and organized crime and he kills a child molester/murderer. Spawn then takes over the alleys that comprise "Rat City" and befriends the homeless within it, becoming their champion. Alan Moore, an avid follower of Crowley's beliefs, authored Spawn's *Blood Feud* comics, opening with a demon feeding on the "frightened cattle race" otherwise known as a family. Spawn wakes up in a blood-splattered mess of bodies. He learns that his symbiotic suit feeds on his pain and anguish and Spawn is hunted as a monster much like *The Dark Knight.*

Alan Moore brought the anti-hero into the 21st Century with *Watchmen* and *V for Vendetta* which extolls the merit of being "freed of the obsession of the doom of the Ego in Death" as Evie is tortured by the hero, V. An internet group known as Anonymous uses Alan Moore's character, V, as their icon never knowing Moore's comic stems from Aleister Crowley's magickal beliefs wrapped up in Adam Weishaupt's Illuminati's philosophy.

The character V is based on Guy Fawkes who was the original "Fall Guy" that took the blame for the Gunpowder Plot; an attempt to blow up King and Parliament to restore a Catholic monarch to the throne on the 5th of November. Each of the condemned would be drawn backwards to his death by a horse, their genitals would be cut off and burnt before their eyes, and their bowels and hearts removed. They would then be decapitated, and the dismembered parts of their bodies displayed so that they might become "prey for the fowls of the air" which is part of the blood oath that every Mason must take to be raised in the lodge. Fawkes was the last to stand on the scaffold. Although weakened by torture, Fawkes managed to jump from the gallows, breaking his neck in the fall and thus avoiding the agony of the latter part of his execution. His lifeless body was nevertheless quartered and, as was the custom, his body parts were then distributed to "the four corners of the kingdom," to be displayed as a warning to other would-be traitors.

Let this be a warning to those that would take these stories at face value and march into the streets shouting, "Kill all the fanatics!" Much is being done to manipulate your values and guide the course of history in favor of the sorcerers. Both scripts are written for the villain as well as the hero. Public reaction is calculated and maneuvered to facilitate a global dictatorship and you might never know that you are being used as "The Fall Guy." The hacker group known as Anonymous have become infamous for their computer savvy, using the Internet to cause chaos in online polls and contests. Their targets range from the Federal Reserve website to Westboro Baptist Church to the Twitter account of Burger King and they may be used to end the Internet.

Many of the inflammatory reports by the alternative media surrounding Sandy Hook caused serious distress and death threats to people like Robbie Parker, Chris Rodia, and Gene Rosen, and may cause a backlash on independent media. "Misinformation is being posted on social media sites," Connecticut State Police Lt. J. Paul Vance said at a news conference. "These issues are crimes. They will be investigated, statewide and federally, and prosecution will take place when people perpetrating this information are identified." The hacking power Anonymous seems to wield could be used as the ultimate threat to push the "Kill Switch" on the Internet. Could they have known this when they selected Alan Moore's Guy Fawkes mask as their symbol?

***

1. Grant Morrison, *Book of Lies: The Disinformation Guide to Magick*, Richard Metzger
2. *Aleister Crowley's Illustrated Goetia: Sexual Evocation*, Lon Milo DuQuette
3. *The Satanic Rituals*, Anton LaVey
4. *The Magicians Dictionary*, E.E. Rehmus
5. *The Magical Revival*, Kenneth Grant
6. *Aleister Crowley and the Hidden God*, Kenneth Grant
7. *Pawns in the Game*, William Guy Carr
8. *Dumbing Us Down: The Hidden Curriculum of Compulsory Schooling*, John Taylor Gatto
9. Leonard Maltin, *Walt Disney: On the Frontlines*
10. The introduction to *The Book of the Law*, Aleister Crowley
11. Ibid.

"How will human culture change in the next millennium as a result of conscious evolution? Will we feel it proper to cater to our earth so that beauty supplants blind ambition? Will our technological advancements be turned to providing free time for the inhabitants of earth? Can everyone participate in a giving and receiving interaction that perpetuates an exchange of information that would become everyone's new work, our new economic orientation? We should pay the people who have touched our hearts. Our gifts should go to the people who have brought us spiritual truth. When people come into our lives at just the right moment to give us the answers we need, we should give them money. This is how we start to supplement our incomes and ease ourselves out of the current limiting system. As more people engage in this spiritual economy we will begin a real shift into a culture that provides the beauty and potential to lift mankind's economic orientation. As we discover the energy dynamics of the universe, principles come forth to support that giving creates receiving. This knowledge will create a critical mass that will push this evolution, which will be a dramatic movement of individuals from one occupation to another. Creating the power for others through giving will open those souls to fulfill their potential and direct the course of reality to heights of intuition that raises everyone's abilities, accelerating the pace of our evolution to that divine place we all hold in our hearts. The world is being directed to change. It is our time to be that change. No longer should we concern ourselves with what we don't want. It's time to turn our attention toward what is beautiful and vital."

—Freeman, *The Sync Book 2*

WeirdStuff!

Energy Drinks:

There is an eerie message displayed on the can of the drink Lost 5-0 by Monster. It reads: *"For centuries cults and governments have used juice to subdue and conform the masses. Now after extensive R&D ...Lost Enterprises has harnessed the hypnotic power of juice. THE TRUTH HURTS!"* Beside the message, next to the barcode, can be found the classic Eye in the Pyramid of the Illuminati. One energy drink named 666 comes in two flavors, Lucifer's Lemonade and Virgin Sacrifice Cherry and their motto is "Get Some Evil in Ya!!"

The number of people seeking emergency treatment after consuming energy drinks has doubled nationwide during the past four years, the same period in which the drink industry has surged in popularity in convenience stores, bars and on college campuses. From 2007 to 2011, the government estimates the number of hospital visits involving the neon-labeled beverages shot up from about 10,000 to more than 20,000. Most of the cases involved teens or young adults. In 2011, *Beverage Digest* found that sales volume for energy drinks rose by almost 17 percent, with the top three companies – Monster, Red Bull and Rockstar – each logging double-digit gains. The drinks are often marketed at sporting events that are popular among younger people such as surfing and skateboarding.

Dr. Masaru Emoto seems to believe that what we think and more importantly what we feel have a tremendous effect on water; to prove it he came up with the water crystal experiment. Dr. Emoto froze individual water crystals placing different intents and emotions on them. What he found was when he used words like love, truth, wisdom and thank you, the water crystals were formed into beautiful geometric patterns. When he used phrases like "you disgust me" and "anger" the crystals that formed were distorted and ugly. If thoughts can do that to water, and we realize that the earth and our bodies are made up of over 75% water...what effects do drinking a can of Venom, Demon or Monster have on you?

Weird Stuff ~ Operation: Culture Creation, Part 2

Stuff only gets Weirder from here! Project Crazy Bitch, the Secret Signs of Freemasonry, Kabbalah and the elusive Shekinah or Holy Spirit will shine forth from the pages of the next issue of Weird Stuff ~ Operation: Culture Creation.

How does Scientology fit into this picture? What is the truth behind Trauma-Based Mind Control and Monarch Slaves? Is the New Atlantis on the rise? Who will design it? Is humanity truly evil or have we been Programmed for War? Weird Stuff will be nine issues in three volumes that will cover the vast subjects of Illuminati Conspiracy, Occult Rituals, Technocracy, and Governmental and Religious Shenanigans.

WeirdStuffMagazine.com

The Art of Disney

Printed in Poland
by Amazon Fulfillment
Poland Sp. z o.o., Wrocław